The Pluralistic
Vision

THE PRESBYTERIAN PRESENCE:
THE TWENTIETH-CENTURY EXPERIENCE

Series Editors

Milton J Coalter

John M. Mulder

Louis B. Weeks

The Pluralistic Vision: Presbyterians and Mainstream Protestant Education and Leadership

Edited by
Milton J Coalter
John M. Mulder
Louis B. Weeks

Essays by
John M. Mulder and Lee A. Wyatt,
Steve Hancock, Bradley J. Longfield and
George M. Marsden, Ronald C. White, Jr.,
John B. Trotti and Richard A. Ray,
Craig Dykstra and J. Bradley Wigger,
David C. Hester, Richard W. Reifsnyder,
Lois A. Boyd and R. Douglas Brackenridge,
Keith M. Wulff and John P. Marcum, and
Barbara Brown Zikmund

Westminster/John Knox Press
Louisville, Kentucky

Book design by Gene Harris

First edition

Published by Westminster/John Knox Press
Louisville, Kentucky

This book is printed on acid-free paper that meets the American National Standards Institute Z39.48 standard. ∞

PRINTED IN THE UNITED STATES OF AMERICA
9 8 7 6 5 4 3 2 1

Library of Congress Cataloging-in-Publication Data

The Pluralistic vision : Presbyterians and mainstream Protestant
    education and leadership / edited by Milton J. Coalter, John M.
    Mulder, Louis B. Weeks ; essays by John M. Mulder . . . [et al.]. —
    1st ed.
            p.   cm. — (The Presbyterian presence)
    Includes bibliographical references and index.
    ISBN 0-664-25243-5
    1. Presbyterian Church—United States—History—20th century.
2. Presbyterian Church (U.S.A.)—History.   3. Presbyterian Church—
Education—United States—History—20th century.   4. Christian
leadership—Presbyterian Church—History—20th century.
5. Religious education—United States—History—20th century.
6. Religious pluralism—Christianity—History—20th century.
I. Coalter, Milton J.   II. Mulder, John M., 1946– .   III. Weeks,
Louis, 1941– .   IV. Series.
BX8937.P58   1992
285′.1—dc20   91-32252

For Robert Wood Lynn

Contents

Series Foreword

This series, "The Presbyterian Presence: The Twentieth-Century Experience," is the product of a significant research project analyzing American Presbyterianism in this century. Funded by the Lilly Endowment and based at Louisville Presbyterian Theological Seminary, the project is part of a broader research effort that analyzes the history of mainstream Protestantism. By analyzing American Presbyterianism as a case study, we hope not only to chronicle its fate in the twentieth century but also to illumine larger patterns of religious change in mainstream Protestantism and in American religious and cultural life.

This case study of American Presbyterianism and the broader research on mainstream Protestantism arise out of an epochal change in American religion that has occurred during the twentieth century. Mainstream American Protestantism refers to those churches that emerged from the American Revolution as the dominant Protestant bodies and were highly influential in shaping American religion and culture during the nineteenth century. It includes the Presbyterians, Episcopalians, Methodists, Congregationalists (now the United Church of Christ), Disciples, and American or northern Baptists.

In this century, these churches have been displaced—religiously and culturally—to a significant degree. All have suffered severe membership losses since the 1960s. All have experienced significant theological tensions and shifts in emphasis. All are characterized by problems in their organization as institutions. And yet they remain influential voices in the spectrum of American religion and retain an enduring vitality in the face of a massive reconfiguration of American religious life.

The result is a complex phenomenon that is not easily described. Some would say the term "mainstream" or "mainline" is itself suspect and embodies ethnocentric and elitist assumptions. What characterized American religious history, they argue, was its diversity and its pluralism. Some groups may have believed they were religiously or culturally dominant, but the historical reality is much more pluralistic. Others would maintain that if there was a "mainstream," it no longer exists. Still others would propose that the mainstream itself has changed. The denominations of the evangelical awakening of the nineteenth century have been replaced by the evangelical churches of the late twentieth century—Southern Baptist, charismatic, Pentecostal.

Some propose that the term "mainline" or "mainstream" should be dropped in favor of talking about "liberal" Protestantism, but such a change presents additional problems. Like "evangelical," the term "liberal" is an extremely vague word to describe a set of Christian beliefs, values, and behavior. Furthermore, virtually all the "mainstream" churches contain large numbers of people who would describe themselves as either evangelical or liberal, thus making it very difficult to generalize about them as a denomination.

Despite the debates about terminology and the categories for analyzing American Protestantism, there is general agreement that American culture and American Protestantism of the late twentieth century are very different from what they were in the late nineteenth century. What has changed is the religious and cultural impact of American

Protestantism. A study of American Presbyterianism is a good lens for examining that change, for in spite of their relatively small numbers, Presbyterians are, or were, quintessential mainstreamers, exerting a great deal of influence because of their economic, social, educational, and cultural advantages.

When did the change occur? In a pioneering article written more than fifty years ago, Arthur M. Schlesinger, Sr., pointed to the period from 1875 to 1900 as "a critical period" in American religion. In particular, American Protestants confronted the external challenges of immigration, industrialization, and urbanization and the internal challenges posed by Darwinism, biblical criticism, history of religions, and the new social sciences.[1] Robert T. Handy has maintained that the 1920s witnessed a "religious depression." The result was a "second disestablishment" of American Protestantism. When the churches lost legal establishment in the U.S. Constitution, they attempted to "Christianize" American culture.[2] But by the 1920s, it was clear that both legal and cultural establishment had been rejected. Sydney Ahlstrom points to the 1960s as the time when American religion and culture took a "radical turn" and the "Puritan culture" of the United States was shattered.[3] Wade Clark Roof and William McKinney build on Ahlstrom's argument, proposing that the 1960s and 1970s represent a "third disestablishment," in which mainstream churches lost their religious dominance.[4]

These diverse interpretations underscore the fact that the crises of mainstream Protestantism did not appear suddenly and that the developments within one tradition—American Presbyterianism—are mirrored in other denominations as well. While some of our studies reach back into the late nineteenth century, most of our studies focus on the period after the fundamentalist controversy within Presbyterianism during the 1920s and 1930s. For a variety of reasons, that became a watershed for Presbyterians and ushered in the twentieth century.

The value of this substantial Presbyterian case study can be seen from at least two perspectives. First, this research is designed to write a chapter in the history of American religion and culture. It is the story of the attempt of one tradition—its people and its institutions—to respond to the crosscurrents of the twentieth century. Second, it is an attempt to illumine the problems and predicaments of American Presbyterianism so that its members and leaders might better understand the past as a resource for its future direction.

The series title was carefully chosen. Presence is more than passive existence, and it connotes the landmark that we hope these groups of studies provide for comparing the equally important pilgrimages of other mainline Protestant denominations through the past century. Missiologists have characterized the Christian responsibility as one of "profound presence" in the world, patterned on the presence of God in providence, in the incarnation, and in the work of the Holy Spirit. In the words of missionary and theologian John V. Taylor, Christians "stand" in the world in the name of Christ to be "really and totally present . . . in the present."[5]

Has the Presbyterian presence declined into mere existence? Have the commitments of Presbyterians degenerated into lifeless obligations? What forces have informed, transformed, or deformed our distinctive presence within the Christian community and the society? And can changes in our life together invigorate our continued yearnings to represent Christ in the world today? These are the questions posed in the series.

More than sixty researchers, plus students at Louisville Seminary and generous colleagues in seminaries, colleges, and universities throughout the United States, have cooperated in the research on American Presbyterianism. Many are historians, but others are sociologists, economists, musicians, theologians, pastors, and lay people. What has excited us as a research team was the opportunity of working on a fascinating historical problem with critical implications for the Presbyterian Church and mainstream Protestantism. Animating our work and conversations was the hope that this research might make a difference, that it might help one church and a broader Christian tradition understand the problems more clearly so that its witness might be more faithful. It is with this hope that we issue this series, "The Presbyterian Presence: The Twentieth-Century Experience."

Milton J Coalter
John M. Mulder
Louis B. Weeks

Acknowledgments

As the publication of the results of research continues, our debts of gratitude also increase. In addition to those who have made all the efforts possible—secretaries and other colleagues at Louisville Seminary, collaborators in research, supportive friends from the Lilly Endowment, and capable editors at Westminster/John Knox Press—we have grown to depend more than ever upon a network of scholars, leaders, and members of the Presbyterian Church (U.S.A.) who are in dialogue with us about the meaning of our findings. Members of the clergy and laity in other communions are also helping us enormously, and they too deserve words of thanks.

We keep recognizing the superlative work of our secretaries: Beverly Hourigan, Kem Longino, Jean Newman, and Elna Amaral. Their cheerful and competent management of appointments, correspondence, and offices permits us the freedom to concentrate frequently on the study. A host of other administrators and staff members also make our work possible. We appreciate their help.

We commissioned the researchers trusting they could exercise both care and critical distance in the investigation of their subjects. We are deeply grateful to them for their thoroughness, and we delight in bringing their efforts into print. Those whose essays are published in this volume had some of the more challenging assignments, and yet they did not despair. Instead, they have brought insights for us in our ongoing work. We are grateful.

Faculty colleagues at Louisville Seminary may be more ready for us to complete our project than we are to do so. Surely many of them grow weary of our injecting this or that finding into every discussion of curriculum, course design, evaluation, strategic planning, or whatever. We depend on their patience and forbearance, as well as on their good advice and wisdom, in the portions of the project they oversee. By now scores of students have also helped us in a host of ways, and we acknowledge our indebtedness to them.

Both financial support and intellectual challenge have come steadily from the officers and members of the staff of the Lilly Endowment. Robert W. Lynn, formerly Senior Vice President for Religion, initially invited us to embark on the project. We depended on his encouragement and his insights every step of the way. This volume is dedicated to him.

Craig Dykstra, who now serves in the capacity of Vice President for Religion, finished his own research on this project in the midst of his undertaking that responsibility. The disciplined energy and commitment of both Bob Lynn and Craig Dykstra have served as good examples for us. We also appreciate the continuing encouragement from Fred L. Hofheinz, Jacqui L. Burton, Jeanne Knoerli, S.P., James P. Wind, James Hudnut-Beumler, Edward Queen, Lois Lewis, and other friends there. Dorothy Bass, James Lewis, and Diane Freemyer, our colleagues in the Louisville Institute, keep finding ways to help us too.

Members of our particular families continue to provide us sustenance and joy. We say "Thanks" and try to convey much deeper gratitude to spouses and children, parents and other relatives who pay a price for our attention to this project.

Last, but very important, is mention of the growing network of Presbyterians and others who share their wisdom and engage us in new learning about "The Presbyterian Presence." We acknowledge our dependence on them, and we are grateful for their guidance and wisdom.

Milton J Coalter
John M. Mulder
Louis B. Weeks

Contributors

Lois A. Boyd is the Assistant to the Vice-President for Academic Affairs, Trinity University. She attended the University of Texas and Trinity University. She is the co-author with R. Douglas Brackenridge of *Presbyterian Women in America: Two Centuries of a Quest for Status* and *Presbyterians and Pensions, 1717–1988.*

R. Douglas Brackenridge is Professor of Religion, Trinity University, and the author of *Eugene Carson Blake: Prophet with Portfolio,* coauthor with Lois Boyd of *Presbyterian Women in America: Two Centuries of a Quest for Status* and *Presbyterians and Pensions, 1717–1988.* He graduated from Muskingum College, Pittsburgh Seminary, and the University of Glasgow.

Craig Dykstra is Vice-President for Religion, the Lilly Endowment, Inc. His B.A. is from the University of Michigan, and his M.Div. and Ph.D. are from Princeton Seminary. He has served on the faculties of Louisville Seminary and Princeton Seminary. His books include *Vision and Character: A Christian Educator's Alternative to Kohlberg,* and *Faith Development and Fowler,* edited with Sharon Parks.

Steve Hancock is Dean of Students at Louisville Presbyterian Seminary, and he serves as an adjunct professor with responsibilities in the areas of homiletics and spiritual development. A graduate of DePauw University and Louisville Seminary, he also served previously as pastor of the First Presbyterian Church, Dale, Indiana.

David C. Hester is Professor of Christian Education at Louisville Presbyterian Seminary. A graduate of the University of Utah, Bangor Theological Seminary, and Duke University, he taught religion and Bible for almost a decade at Berea College in Kentucky. He is the author of numerous scholarly articles and of curriculum materials in the Presbyterian and Reformed Educational Ministries.

Bradley J. Longfield is Visiting Assistant Professor of American Religion at Duke University. He studied at Wesleyan University and Duke University. He recently published *The Presbyterian Controversy: Fundamentalists, Modernists, and Moderates.*

John P. Marcum is Associate for Survey Research, Office of Research Services, Presbyterian Church (U.S.A.), and Administrator of the Presbyterian Panel. A graduate of Georgetown College in Kentucky and the University of Texas at Austin, where he received a Ph.D. in sociology. He writes frequently both on areas of general interest for the church and on specialized areas of demography and sociology.

George M. Marsden is Professor of the History of Christianity in America at the Duke Divinity School, Duke University. He graduated from Calvin College, Calvin Seminary, and Yale University. His publications include *Fundamentalism and American Culture* and *Reforming Fundamentalism: Fuller Seminary and the New Evangelicalism.*

John M. Mulder is President and Professor of Historical Theology at Louisville Seminary. He studied at Hope College, Princeton Seminary, and Princeton University, where he received a Ph.D. His publications include *Woodrow Wilson: The Years of Preparation* and *The Presbyterian Symbol.* He codirected the study of the Presbyterian Church, and he coedits *The Presbyterian Presence.*

Richard A. Ray is pastor of the First Presbyterian Church, Bristol, Tennessee. His degrees are from Davidson College and Union Seminary in Virginia. He previously served as Editor in Chief of John Knox Press.

Richard W. Reifsnyder is pastor of the First Presbyterian Church, Oyster Bay, Long Island. He attended Duke University and Yale Divinity School, and received a Ph.D. from Princeton Theological Seminary. He also contributed "Managing the Mission: Church Restructuring in the Twentieth Century," appearing in *The Organizational Revolution: Presbyterians and American Denominationalism.*

John B. Trotti is Professor of Bibliography and Librarian for Union Theological Seminary in Virginia. His degrees are from Davidson College, Union Seminary, Yale Divinity School, and the University of North Carolina. He served as a pastor before being called to Union Seminary. He has collaborated on several published bibliographies.

Ronald C. White, Jr., a John Randolph and Dora Haynes Huntington Fellow at the Huntington Library in San Marino, California, has published *Liberty and Justice for All: Racial Reform and the Social Gospel,* and, with Garth Rosell and Louis Weeks, *American Christianity: A Case Approach.*

J. Bradley Wigger is a Ph.D. candidate at Princeton Seminary in the area of Christian education. He studied previously at Southeast Missouri State University and Louisville Seminary.

Keith M. Wulff is Research Coordinator, Office of Research Services, Presbyterian Church (U.S.A.). He studied at the University of Wisconsin at Madison, Wartburg Theological Seminary, and the University of Texas at Austin, where he received a Ph.D. in sociology. He publishes frequently in denominational periodicals. At present, he is studying the sermons preached on "The Protestant Hour" radio program.

Lee A. Wyatt is associate pastor of the Harvey Browne Presbyterian church in Louisville, Kentucky. He graduated from Belhaven College, Columbia Seminary, and Louisville Seminary. His articles have appeared in *Perspectives on Science and Faith* and the *Asbury Theological Journal.*

Barbara Brown Zikmund is President and Professor of Church History at Hartford Seminary. She studied at Beloit College, Chicago Theological Seminary, and Duke University. Her publications include *Discovering the Church,* and she was editor of *Hidden Histories in the U.C.C.* and on the editorial board for the *Journal of Ecumenical Studies.*

Introduction

The Presbyterian Church in the United States of America was born in pluralism. Scots sought subscription to the Westminster Standards while British Puritan connectionalists feared confessional statements might supersede direct scriptural authority. According to Leonard Trinterud, a new, American tradition was forged as the competing priorities gave way to common purpose.[1] In addition, French Huguenots, Dutch Calvinists of several stripes, German Reformed, Welsh, and other traditions blended from the first decades of settlement in North America. African American, Hispanic, Native American, and Asian Presbyterians added their own accents to the church's witness by the close of the nineteenth century.[2] On the one hand, pluralism is nothing new to Presbyterians in the United States.

On the other hand, nineteenth-century Presbyterians shared a rather homogeneous theology and a wide-ranging system of institutions for nurture and evangelism which now seem quite foreign. They may have remained quite pluralistic in ethnicity and in social situation, but they sought confluence in belief and doctrine. When serious differences arose in theology or in ethics, Presbyterians tended to exclude the minority perspective. The Cumberland Presbyterian Church, perhaps even a major portion of the "Christian" movement in the early nineteenth century, began as Presbyterians eschewed a pluralistic vision.[3] In several respects, the Old School/New School division, and the split of both according to region, proves how Presbyterians in mid-nineteenth century prized unity in theology and mission. Even the discountenancing of "Higher Life" Presbyterians and the exclusion of fundamentalists and dispensationalists from a share in leadership more recently buttress the argument. A common sense of meaning and purpose was worth fighting for.[4]

In the past several decades, changes in American culture and changes in the worldviews of both members and officers in the Presbyterian Church have brought myriad pressures to bear upon any common sense of identity and purpose. The word "pluralism" has come to receive in many quarters a positive, rather than a negative valence. The word has come to signify the variegated perspectives and values and the differences in theology and cultural location among Presbyterians. At the denominational level, and frequently in other church arenas, people are chosen for membership on committees and other bodies because of their differences rather than their common loyalties.

The word "pluralism" also carries an even more positive meaning. It assumes that commonality transcends differences. In pluralism, the whole is more than the sum of its distinctive and distinguishable parts. Pluralism implies coherence and common purpose among the members of the whole, while at the same time maintaining and supporting the variegations among groups of participants.

The essays in this volume point to the fact that seldom have the Presbyterian churches achieved a synthesis and common vision that is more than the sum of its parts. Presbyterians and others can at least glimpse what such a constructive pluralism might entail.

By way of illustration, consider the mandate of the Articles of Agreement of the Plan for Reunion of the Presbyterian Church (U.S.A.). The Moderator was to "appoint a committee representing diversities of points of view and of groups within the reunited Church to prepare a Brief Statement of Reformed Faith."[5] The significance of differences prevailed over other considerations, at least explicitly, in the agreement. The evidence of a pluralistic vision is in the Brief Statement of Faith itself, a document accepted by the church and now helping to form the theological affirmations of Presbyterians.

Or consider the composition of the Presbyterian Hunger Program Committee, just one of the dozens of permanent working groups at Assembly level in the PC(USA). Among its members, fewer than twenty in all, are men and women from Africa, Latin America, and the Caribbean, African Americans, Hispanics, and Native Americans, ministers, elders, and members chosen for their diversity. Yet they meet and together allocate the gifts of Presbyterians collected for alleviating hunger.

These committees are strikingly different in composition from those of previous generations of Presbyterians, and the story of the changes in various aspects of church life forms one theme of this book. Another theme is the straining for a common vision today, as diversity and complex cultural forces work their ambiguity on the Presbyterians.

John M. Mulder and Lee Wyatt, in the first essay, examine the teaching of theology in Presbyterian seminaries during the twentieth century. Following the catalogs of Presbyterian seminaries, they outline the changing character of the theological curricula and the theological faculties.

In the late nineteenth and early twentieth centuries, according to Mulder and Wyatt, the "Princeton theology," or Old School Calvinism, reigned in the seminaries. It offered a sense of permanence and claimed close kinship with the Bible itself. It also helped foster the fundamentalism that emerged in the early decades of the twentieth century.

Neo-orthodoxy, continental and domestic, offered something of a theological oasis for Presbyterian seminaries after the traumas of the fundamentalist-modernist controversies. Mulder and Wyatt point to the temporary and partial nature of this respite, even though it and the related movement of biblical theology seemed quite securely in control of Presbyterian seminaries in the 1940s and 1950s.

Scholastic Calvinism continued to be represented in several schools, but the demands of neo-orthodoxy for historical theology and for biblical theology brought into curricula the work of a wide variety of Christian scholars, both Catholic and Protestant. The ecumenical movement also affected instruction before the revolution of the 1960s.

Mulder and Wyatt trace both the dissolution of the informal neo-orthodox, biblical theology establishment and the movement to permit student autonomy during that decade. To assess the 1960s, they quote James I. McCord as saying that theology was "a shambles." But they also give a more tempered reading, understanding "the developments in Presbyterian seminaries as a flawed but creative attempt to move the church beyond neo-orthodoxy into a deeper and more sustained dialogue with the cross-currents of the modern world."

Mulder and Wyatt find that theological pluralism has characterized the theological curricula of seminaries since that revolution. The contributions of feminist, African American, and other liberationist perspectives, together with process theologians and a host of others have enriched the curricula. But the greater pluralism came at the price of an integrated vision of theology and a distinctive Reformed identity. No common theological vision incorporating and transcending these pluralistic perspectives is yet discernible.

Mulder and Wyatt suggest that a preoccupation with social ethics has frequently offered a cohesion other portions of the theological enterprise could not. They also say the pluralism has remained very much partial in nature, not offering inclusion or even recognition of the "third force" in Christendom—the charismatic, Pentecostal movements so important in the West but even more so in the third world. They point directly to the need for cohesion and theological integration on the part of seminaries and their curricula.

In a quite different vein, Steve Hancock also studies the

seminaries and asks about spiritual formation and attention to the nurture of piety. He polled graduates of four seminaries over a period of forty years concerning their seminary experiences. The great majority through all the years considered seminary years a "time of significant spiritual growth." At the same time, most seminary graduates wish their schools had done much more to help them grow spiritually.

But there were noticeable changes. Prayer groups, extremely important for some in the 1940s, had almost disappeared in significance during the late 1960s. Graduates of 1988 again found prayer groups important in their formation. Service opportunities and involvement in justice issues played a more significant role in the piety of those from 1968 than in development of seminarians either before or after.

Chapel services, important through the years, have more recently been supplemented by retreats and workshops on spirituality. This institutionalization of spiritual development is a discernible trend in seminaries. Another is the increasing familiarity of seminarians with models of Catholic spirituality. Given the limited data from women who have graduated from Presbyterian seminaries, Hancock could find no major differences in what they considered significant for their own spiritual development.

Hancock explores some of the similarities and differences between Catholic and Protestant, especially Reformed, understandings of ministry, piety, and worship. He also hints at the differing backgrounds and cultures of seminarians in the different decades, implying that more explicit formation efforts are necessary in a more pluralistic environment today. Again, the seminaries, as other agencies and institutions of the Presbyterian Church, have not offered a common vision of what comprises spiritual formation or what is requisite for leadership in the church.

Presbyterian seminarians possess varying backgrounds today, much more than they did a generation ago. For example, fewer by far come from Presbyterian colleges, and the nature of Presbyterian colleges has changed enor-

mously. That transformation receives attention from Bradley Longfield and George Marsden.

Longfield and Marsden claim that concerted denominational oversight of Presbyterian colleges began in the
1880s, at the time the church established tighter controls in
finance, mission, and other parts of its life. Higher education had been extremely important for Presbyterians before
the late nineteenth century, and many colleges had been
founded under Presbyterian auspices. Some had already
become secular institutions. During the 1880s, however,
the PCUSA determined that its schools needed regular
oversight—both for the good of the church and in order to
resist the secularization that threatened Christian higher
education.

The denomination specified that members of faculties
should be professing Christians and members of some
evangelical church. Its colleges should maintain the teaching of the Bible, regular chapel exercises, and a "positive
Christian perspective" in the teaching of all subjects. These
institutions were expected to give primary attention to
the development of Christian character. In most cases, the
presidents of these church-related colleges were Presbyterian ministers.

Southern Presbyterian colleges received similar oversight
beginning in the 1910s. Simultaneously, PCUSA schools began to struggle with the fundamentalist-modernist controversy. The remainder of the twentieth century, according to
Marsden and Longfield, has been a history of the loosening
of the ties between Presbyterians and their church-related
colleges.

By 1940, a form of liberal theology dominated most
PCUSA denominational colleges. By 1947, the southern
church dropped its requirement that teaching conform to
the Westminster Standards. By the 1950s many church
thinkers questioned the possibility of maintaining distinctively Christian colleges. Mandatory chapel, where it still
took place, became a flash point in schools. Abolition of
required chapel and other mandatory assemblies took place
almost universally by the early 1970s.

At a deeper level, the church did little to stem the secularization of its schools during the revolution that took place in the 1960s. By the end of the decade, the United Presbyterian Church in the U.S.A. (UPCUSA) had, generally, largely abandoned its denominational oversight of colleges. In many places faculties no longer were required to be Christian, though in other schools such a requirement continued until the early 1970s.

Longfield and Marsden point to the attempt currently on the part of some colleges to renew their denominational ties. The two researchers conclude, however, that in order for real renewal of ties to occur a theology calling the church to stand against the world would have to prevail among Presbyterians. Presbyterians, including the editors of this volume, might differ with their conclusion. But the achieving of a common vision for church-related colleges after the divorce of the earlier decades has only become a matter for denominational discussion in very recent years.

If the twentieth century has seen a decline in the substance of denominational affiliation in Presbyterian colleges, it has witnessed both the rise and the decline of campus ministries. Ronald White begins with a look at some of the antecedents for and ingredients in Presbyterian (and other) campus ministry—the piety of presidents and faculty members in nineteenth-century colleges; the office of chaplain in many schools; the work of nearby congregations; the student-led movements that originated in the late 1800s.

In 1905, the PCUSA Assembly called for the appointment of "special ministers" for the burgeoning universities that had emerged across the country. In 1911, the Department of University Work was established. Gradually, all such "educational" enterprises were gathered under the responsibility of the Board of Christian Education. Campus ministers during the early decades of the twentieth century had the primary task of evangelizing college students, especially those who came from Presbyterian backgrounds.

Gradually campus ministry was perceived in more expansive terms, and the work of the campus pastor for the whole of the university came to be emphasized. Westminster Houses, begun in the 1920s, were extremely important in centering this ministry.

White declares that the PCUS followed a similar path somewhat later, but in the South the work of particular congregations stands out as a vital ingredient in the mix of campus ministry from its inception.

In its heyday of the early 1950s, Presbyterian campus ministry included more than five hundred efforts at colleges and universities throughout the country. This was the very time when a growing estrangement of the campus ministries from the churches can be seen. Liberal theology and liberal politics were connected for most campus ministers. Evangelism, previously one of the major goals of Presbyterian campus ministry, gradually shifted to para-church organizations.

The 1960s and 1970s increased the lines of demarcation between campus ministries and local Presbyterian churches, at least in general terms. Congregations as well as campus ministries became more ecumenical and more concerned with social ethics, but in the process campus ministries frequently seemed to lose a discernible Presbyterian identity.

If Presbyterian colleges and Presbyterian campus ministers in the early decades of the twentieth century formed part of a denominational "ecology" to support and sustain a particular culture, so did denominational publications. John Trotti has examined the roots of Presbyterian publication and particularly the efforts of the Westminster and John Knox presses.

The Board of Publication for the PCUSA, active from the beginning of the Old School Assembly and continuing after reunion, began in 1897 to use the name Westminster Press. Through the first decades of the twentieth century, that press produced primarily Sunday school materials. It received Assembly criticism for neglecting to print more serious scholarship for ministers. In the early 1940s, this pattern changed, and soon excellent works began to appear—*The Westminster Dictionary of the Bible* (1945), *The Westminster Historical Atlas to the Bible* (1945), Nelia

White's *No Trumpet Before Him* (1948), and a host of others by prominent scholars.

After 1958, the small Geneva Press of the United Presbyterian Church of North America, which had not aspired to mainstream publication efforts, became a part of Westminster Press. During the 1960s, Westminster published a number of controversial books, including J. A. T. Robinson's *Honest to God* (1963) and Joseph Fletcher's *Situation Ethics* (1966).

Though executives at the press considered their work still responsive to Presbyterian needs, the controversial books provoked another call for limits to pluralism and some concerted effort to regain a Reformed identity.

Presbyterians in the PCUS started John Knox Press in 1938. Actually, it was separated from previous publication efforts of the denomination's "editorial department" of former Christian education committees. In the late 1940s, John Knox also began to offer more substantial theological and biblical works. In 1983, with the merger of the UPCUSA and the PCUS, negotiations eventually produced a consolidated publishing house, Westminster/John Knox Press.

Trade, scholarly, and other monographs from Westminster and John Knox presses represent one side of the Presbyterian denominations' attempt to provide educational resources. Another is the Christian education curricula of the denominations. Craig Dykstra and Bradley Wigger explore these materials by examining their form. They argue that the form of the curricula had significant implications for the content and methods of teaching.

They recall that the first Sunday schools—for the poor, for those learning to read, and for nurture of the children of the faithful—were very popular in nineteenth-century America. For those efforts, the Presbyterians and the voluntary societies produced libraries rather than curricula. Instruction depended primarily on the spiritual character of the teacher, rather than on any technology of instruction. Sunday school teachers taught their faith more than lessons about the faith of others.

With the appearance of the Uniform Lessons and their

offspring, the International Lesson System, curriculum eventually appeared. Presbyterians used the interdenominational materials and eventually developed the *Presbyterian at Work/Westminster Teacher*. Teachers were now supposed to share the lesson, which still centered on a portion of scripture. But over time the role of the teachers' own faith became less important than the content of a particular curriculum.

Christian Faith and Life and the Covenant Life Curriculum, the major curricular efforts at mid-century of the PCUSA and the PCUS respectively, generally followed this pattern. They demanded greater knowledge and teaching skills on the part of teachers because of the complexity of their perspectives. Dykstra and Wigger speculate that during this time of emphasis on curriculum, other materials gradually replaced the Bible as the center of church school instruction.

The newer efforts, *Christian Education: Shared Approaches* and now the Presbyterian and Reformed Educational Ministry, according to Dykstra and Wigger, continue the emphasis on lessons. The accompanying guides focus on instructions for teachers more than on the faith of the teachers.

Dykstra and Wigger call for a new vision of educational strategy in the light of the current situation: the lack of a total ecology of support for Christian education. The family devotions, Sabbatarianism, church-related higher education, and many other elements that supported learnings from church school now play much less a part in the Christian formation of Presbyterians than they did in previous generations. And they call for careful consideration of a common vision in the form as well as the content of Christian education.

Presbyterians have consistently voiced their allegiance to the authority of scripture, even as educational methods may have undermined it. Thus David Hester has focused on the use of the Bible in the church by looking at the Christian education curricula of the denominations during the twentieth century.

Hester traces the intentions of Presbyterian educators as well as assessing their offerings in successive denominational curricula. From the Uniform Lessons, he follows explicit designs through the Westminster Graded Lessons, Westminster Departmental Graded Materials, *Christian Faith and Life,* Covenant Life Curriculum, and the *Christian Education: Shared Approaches,* to the Presbyterian and Reformed Educational Ministry. He points to the inherent tensions involved in commitments to the authority of scripture, to historical-critical approaches to the Bible, and to prevailing methods of education in each generation.

Hester, like several other scholars, points to the costs of increasing Presbyterian reliance on "experts." Experts, who can discern linguistic and historical-critical insights concerning the Bible, become both the writers and the models for teaching for the complex enterprise. As a result, volunteer teachers in church schools have been expected to uncover layers of complex interpretation and to learn much more about the disciplines related to modern study than did their counterparts in previous generations. Teaching people how to teach also becomes a more complex task, yet more necessary as well. Again, a common vision transcending the differences is not apparent.

Increasing demands arising from complex cultural contexts also is a theme for Richard Reifsnyder, whose essays study Presbyterian leadership in the twentieth century. He has followed the biographies of more than one hundred administrators in national agencies, looking first at the PCUS, then at those in the two streams forming the UPCUSA, and finally at the PC(USA).

In the PCUSA and the UPCNA, Reifsnyder found common histories. Those chosen for administrative leadership between 1920 and the beginning of the merged UPCUSA in 1958 were overwhelmingly white, male, and ministers. Most had grown up in the denomination, studied at their denomination's colleges, and served pastorates before entering administration. Most had strong personalities. Women did exert leadership in church administration, directing women's programs and assisting in supervision of foreign missions. During the first half of the century, the church was already moving toward endorsing administrative service as a specialized career pattern, and that pattern has become even more pronounced in subsequent decades. "Women and racial/ethnic minority persons [to follow the parlance of the church] held virtually no top positions until the 1973 reorganization."

In the UPCUSA a previous pattern persisted—fewer administrators became Moderators of the denomination, and none were elected after 1968. Nevertheless, strong personalities generally continued to exercise control in this stream of Presbyterianism until the reorganization of 1973.

The UPCUSA then seemed to move away from strong leaders in reaction to the authoritative and hierarchical patterns of leadership that had previously prevailed.

After the 1960s, church structures increasingly reflected the desire of Presbyterians to democratize power and to broaden the patterns of leadership. As the church became more inclusive, it also fostered fewer ways for leadership to exercise initiative. Reifsnyder has claimed that "suspicion" increasingly characterized the attitudes of Presbyterians toward their leadership.

In the PCUS, Reifsnyder had found a similar movement to call on career administrators, though less pronounced than in the UPCUSA. Although the number of years administrators spent in the pastorate declined in the southern church, that reduction was less dramatic or steep than the one in the UPCUSA.

Few women or minorities among membership held top responsibilities in the PCUS. Although the PCUS followed the UPCUSA trend toward greater anonymity for denominational executives, that change did not seem to Reifsnyder as pronounced as in the other stream.

Of course, the new PC(USA) has existed for only a few years, yet patterns seem to be emerging similar to those established in the predecessor bodies—preference for management skills prevailed as those involved assessed their priorities in selecting executives for the denomination. The convoluted governmental arrangements in the new church compound the issues. The challenge remains to build on an inclusive style something of a common vision for the church.

No aspect of the changing Presbyterian Church is more apparent than the emergence of women in positions of responsibility throughout the entire denomination. Lois Boyd and Douglas Brackenridge have examined one portion of this movement—the ordination of women as ministers in the church. Many still consider ordination of women a novelty; and with both Catholic and Southern Baptist perspectives predominating in various portions of the country, such a reaction should not be surprising.

Boyd and Brackenridge point to some of the blind spots and breakthroughs in the history of the ordination of women in the various streams of Presbyterianism. Today, they find, women still are not serving as heads of staff in many larger churches, or as deans and presidents of any seminaries of the PC(USA). In addition, women ministers are generally finding it more difficult to relocate than are men.

The researchers call for full acceptance of women at all levels of the church's life, especially at the congregational level. They claim that the legislative attempts to provide fairness will have to be supplemented by other ways of helping change the climate among Presbyterians.

Jack Marcum and Keith Wulff examine some hypotheses concerning the current Presbyterian leadership situation. Ministers, for example, who are taken to be more liberal than laity, consider personal evangelism more important than does the membership of the Presbyterian Church. Though they find some support for a "new class" emerging in the church, Wulff and Marcum also find considerable diversity in the views of those with comparable educational backgrounds.

Wulff and Marcum conclude that compatibility within congregations, and between pastors and their congregations, will be important with such diversity in the larger church. Thus they advocate development of congregational cultures and subcultures. In similar fashion, Barbara Brown Zikmund, in the final essay of the volume, advo-

cates developing Presbyterian subcultures of many kinds.

Zikmund explores the nature of pluralism itself, in contemporary Protestantism generally and in the PC(USA) in particular. She looks at some of the theological and biblical underpinnings of the value. According to Zikmund, diverse immigrant populations, theological splits within denominations, growing racial ethnic diversity, fluctuations in American demography, decreasing culturalization of leaders, and the power of struggle and advocacy groups all contribute to the attractiveness, if not the necessity, of pluralism in the PC(USA) today.

Zikmund sees a minimization of pluralism and the ideal of integration as less winsome, by way of response, than the development of what she terms "post-Enlightenment communities of faith." Presbyterians must become in effect bilingual, she argues, maintaining the rationalism and cognition of the dominant American culture, but at the same time developing a special vocabulary and resources to enable transcending the individualism and quest for merely personal fulfillment which are societal goals. Presbyterians and other mainstream Protestants should not reduce the rich texture of the faith, but rather they should nurture and draw upon the faith in its fullness to enter into dialogue with other living religions and with the secular world as well.

All these essays together point to the complexity of the contemporary situation. Presbyterians, as other Christians who have typically sought to live "in" the world, but not "of" it cannot withdraw from society as might other portions of the Christian family. Nor can Presbyterians easily forget the admonition of Paul, in Galatians 3:28, that all are one in Christ, that "there is neither Jew nor Greek, there is neither slave nor free, there is neither male nor female."

But how can the Pauline, biblical vision be inculcated in an American denomination? How can the "body of Christ" function with harmony and mutual upbuilding? These and similar questions may be distinct ones in this day, but attempts of Christians to remain faithful and to nurture one another have been perennial, indeed.

1

The Predicament of Pluralism: The Study of Theology in Presbyterian Seminaries Since the 1920s

John M. Mulder and Lee A. Wyatt

At the turn of the twentieth century, the melancholic Henry Adams declared, "My country in 1900 is something totally different from my own country of 1860. I am wholly a stranger in it. Neither I, nor anyone else, understands it. The turning of a nebula into a star may somewhat resemble the change. All I can see is that it is one of compression, concentration, and consequent development of terrific energy represented not by souls, but by coal and iron and steam." The intellectual change, he noted, was even more dramatic than the social and economic changes that had transformed American society. "In essentials like religion, ethics, philosophy; in history, literature, art; in the concepts of all science, except perhaps mathematics, the American boy of 1854 stood nearer the year 1 than to the year 1900."[1]

Such was Adams's description at the end of an era defined by Arthur M. Schlesinger, Sr., as "a critical period in American religion." Spanning the years from 1875 to 1900, this epoch brought particular strains to American Protestantism. It was, in fact, the somewhat delayed confrontation of American Protestantism with both the social and the intellectual challenges of modernity. Urbanization, industrialization, and immigration transformed the character of American society, while biblical criticism, Darwinism, and the new social sciences raised troubling questions for religious belief. The "princes of the Victorian pulpit" did indeed have large followings; a Protestant ethos infused the culture as a whole. But beneath the surface was what Paul Carter described as "the spiritual crisis of the Gilded Age."[2]

In the midst of the maelstrom stood Presbyterian denominational seminaries—seemingly impervious to the forces that would shake the churches and American culture during the twentieth century. Lefferts A. Loetscher saw the Presbyterian Church of the early twentieth century as "a decidedly conservative force in theological education." "In accordance with the Church's longstanding traditions," he wrote, "Presbyterian seminaries continued to favor systematic theology and its foundations in Biblical studies over against the newer disciplines. . . . This emphasis by Presbyterian seminaries on the historically 'given' aspect of Christianity was of course a bulwark against theological innovation in general."[3]

Change and innovation in theological education were scarcely desirable in a church in which Union Seminary in Virginia proclaimed in 1926: "The interpretation of Scripture teachings promulgated by the Westminster divines is believed to be the most perfect creedal statement drawn from the Scriptures to date."[4]

The fortress of Presbyterian theological education was constructed on the foundation of Old School Calvinism. This tradition was given its clearest and most persuasive expression in the work of Charles Hodge, professor of theology at Princeton Seminary from 1820 to 1878, and it became known as the Princeton theology. Hodge taught more seminarians than any other American in the nineteenth century and was known for his oft-quoted aphorism that "a new idea never originated" at Princeton Seminary while he was there.[5] What Hodge's remark underscored was his basic belief that all Presbyterian theology must remain faithful to biblical faith as codified in the Westminster Standards.

Such confessional commitment, a hallmark of nineteenth-century Old School Presbyterianism, had its southern proponents in James Henley Thornwell and Robert Lewis Dabney, who also helped formulate the characteristic southern Presbyterian doctrine of "the spirituality of the church."[6]

While Old School Calvinism was challenged by its New School counterpart, by the late nineteenth century New School theology had lost much of its institutional bases. The Princeton theology had succeeded in dominating nearly every theological seminary of the Presbyterian churches, although McCormick moved to a more moderate theological stance in the early twentieth century. By the 1930s Lane had closed, and Union in New York no longer was affiliated with the Presbyterian Church in the U.S.A. By the late thirties Auburn had moved to Union in New York.[7] However, New School theology persisted to some degree and contributed to theological changes in American Presbyterianism.

The following analysis of the study of theology in Presbyterian denominational seminaries is based largely on the seminaries' catalogs.[8] As such, it focuses on internal developments within the Presbyterian theological institutions. However, there were other factors affecting these seminaries and Protestant theological education, and these developments played a critical role in the transformation of theological study and theology itself.

First, the American university, symbolized by the founding of the Johns Hopkins University in 1876, emerged during the late nineteenth century as a powerful new institution of higher education.[9] Although nineteenth-century Presbyterian seminaries had some faculty members who had graduate training at European universities, the more common pattern was the well-read and self-taught minister with an honorary doctorate. Throughout the twentieth century seminaries gradually replaced these faculty with professors with Ph.D.'s from both European and American universities. Such faculty members carried with them the ideals of the modern university, which were sometimes in tension, if not opposition, to the values of the church.

Second, following World War II many colleges and universities, including state institutions, created departments of religion and recruited faculty members to staff them. In the succeeding decades, these college-based religion professors far outnumbered the faculty of theological seminaries, and their work dominated the study of religion itself. Consequently, not only has the sociological setting of the study of religion changed but also the field itself. Theology has become more broadly defined, dependent on dialogue with other disciplines, and less related to the church. Furthermore, the social sciences in particular have made a deep impression on the theological curriculum, especially in the practical disciplines. Coupled with the expansion of the churches' expectations of ministers, the social sciences have contributed to the vast expansion of the practical area of the curriculum of theological seminaries. Even more important, the social sciences, the history of religions, and historical criticism have raised implicitly and explicitly the degree to which theologians could make claims to transcendent truth.[10]

Third, during the 1930s Protestant theological schools moved to establish national norms for theological education. The American Association of Theological Schools was formed in 1936 and began accrediting schools in 1938.[11] Two Presbyterians, Edward Roberts of Princeton and Lewis Sherrill of Louisville, and one Lutheran, Luther Weigle of Yale, were the pioneers of the standardization of theological education through AATS. The rise of accreditation reduced the anarchy of theological curricula and improved the quality of theological seminaries. At the same time, national educational standards introduced another authority for theological institutions, creating the potential for tension and conflict with the denominations that supported and sponsored them. These standards also made theological institutions more susceptible and responsive to national trends in theological education.

These and other developments contributed to the demise of the theological and confessional uniformity in Presbyterian theological education. The change did not come suddenly, but in the half century following the fundamentalist controversy of the 1920s and 1930s, Presbyterian theological seminaries moved away from a homogenous theological perspective and single-minded adherence to the Westminster Standards to a more inclusive and pluralistic understanding of Christian theology and Christian faith.

It is a story of people and institutions seized by a vision of reform of church and society. It is also a saga of significant change with ambiguous results. The magnitude of this intellectual transformation of Presbyterian theology and the churches' institutions makes this a major watershed in the history of American Presbyterianism, bringing with it both intriguing promises as well as disturbing perils.

The 1920s and 1930s: The Demise of the Princeton Theology

The Princeton theology drew on three traditions—the scholastic orthodoxy of Francis Turretin, Scottish common-sense philosophy, and Baconian science with its inductive approach to knowledge. It was codified in Hodge's three-volume *Systematic Theology* (1871–1873), and Hodge's trilogy was the touchstone for Presbyterian theology as it entered the twentieth century. Most of the seminaries used his *Systematic Theology* as a primary text, and those which did not used slightly more readable tomes—all heavily dependent on Hodge's methodology (for example, works by Dabney, Augustus H. Strong, and W. G. T. Shedd).[12] The pervasiveness of Hodge's thought did more than provide the content of the regnant Presbyterian theology of the early twentieth century. It also forged an imposing and powerful theological ethos for the church and set the stage for the battles of the 1920s and 1930s.

When the fundamentalist controversy arose in the twenties, it was at first glance a dispute within the Presbyterian Church in the U.S.A. (PCUSA) and a fight over ordination standards. However, it also affected both the United Presbyterian Church of North America (UPCNA) and the Presbyterian Church in the U.S. (PCUS). In the annals of theological education in the PCUSA, the fundamentalist controversy became a titanic struggle for control over the home of Presbyterian orthodoxy—Princeton. It was, in short, a virtual war over the theological identity and future of American Presbyterianism. Nearly every seminary felt the traumatic effects of the controversy. When the dust settled and when J. Gresham Machen and his followers had left Princeton to found Westminster Seminary and later the Orthodox Presbyterian Church, Presbyterians both North and South and their theological seminaries faced a turning point in their theological history.[13] The Princeton theology still held sway in both the faculties and the curriculum of most of the seminaries, but the door had been opened to a greater degree of doctrinal diversity.

Into the breach came Karl Barth, whose commentary on Romans had already exploded like "a bombshell on the playground of the theologians."[14] The 1930s also witnessed the Presbyterian seminaries' beginning to adjust to the standardization of the theological curriculum through accreditation, the implications of biblical criticism, the earlier revision of the Westminster Confession in 1903, and the turmoil of the Great Depression. By the end of the decade the shape of the curriculum, its content, and the faculties of Presbyterian seminaries were gradually moving in new directions.

The seminaries entered the 1930s with no particular shape or organizational schemes by which the departments were structured. The areas of study were simply listed in no particular order. Depending on the seminary, nine to twelve "departments" comprised the curriculum. During the thirties, McCormick, Louisville, Princeton, Columbia, and Union revised their curricula into the classic "fourfold pattern"[15] or some variation of it—grouping departments into biblical, historical, doctrinal, and practical areas. The explicit rationale for this revision was a greater degree of simplicity and unity in the shape and progression of the seminary course.[16] Within the next decade the remainder of the seminaries also adopted this pattern.

Early in the twentieth century seminaries experienced

pressure to add more electives to the curriculum, and during the thirties Presbyterian seminaries responded in various ways.[17] Austin, for example, maintained a fully "prescribed" curriculum with no electives throughout the 1930s. Louisville, in contrast, developed in 1932 a curriculum equally divided between required and elective courses, and Johnson C. Smith allowed students to choose two thirds of their courses. On average, approximately 20 percent of the curriculum was elective in the remainder of the schools.

New faculty appointments have had a tremendous effect on the character of theology in the Presbyterian seminaries, and this was particularly the case during the 1930s. Many of the new faculty brought a "neo-orthodox" perspective to American Presbyterianism. Some were Europeans driven to the United States by the rise of Hitler, and others were Americans who had studied in Europe and brought the "theology of crisis" to Presbyterian schools. The change was especially dramatic at Princeton, where only two members of the faculty in 1929 continued beyond 1937.[18] Elmer Homrighausen, Otto Piper, Emil Brunner, and Josef Hromádka all came to the Princeton faculty during the latter half of the thirties; Hugh T. Kerr (Louisville and later Princeton), Donald MacKenzie (Western), Lewis Sweet (McCormick), and Aaron J. Ungersma (San Francisco) brought Barth and other neo-orthodox voices into the curriculum at their schools. But there were dissenting voices: at Columbia, W. C. Robinson criticized neo-orthodoxy from a more conservative and polemical posture.

Courses dealing with Barth's thought and influence appeared early in the decade at San Francisco (1931–1932) and McCormick (1932–1933), and by the end of the decade nearly all the schools offered regular surveys of Barth's thought. Special lectures at Presbyterian seminaries also featured neo-orthodox theologians—Emil Brunner at Princeton (1938–1939), Don Riddle (1937) and Wilhelm Pauck (1938) at Dubuque, E. Birch Hoyle (1934–1935) at Western, and Hendrik Kraemer at Western and McCormick (1937–1938).[19] Barth's protest against apologetics as an independent theological discipline can also be traced at several Presbyterian seminaries where the course was either dropped (Dubuque, 1937) or changed into "theological prolegomena" (Union, 1935–1936) or some version of the philosophy of religion (San Francisco, 1938–1939).

In short, Old School Calvinism, its defenders, and its explication in the classic textbooks that had dominated the curriculum were gradually replaced with works by Barth and, especially, the more readable Brunner, as well as others, by faculty members who propounded the new theology, and by a curriculum that supported the neo-orthodox vision of Christian doctrine.

The triumph of Barthian theology, or the broader "neo-orthodox" movement, was halting and partial. In biblical studies, historical criticism established itself in most of the Presbyterian seminaries during the thirties. Yet it does not appear to have had much effect on biblical theology courses or disturbed the relationship between biblical theology and systematic theology. In most New Testament courses, historical and literary traditions were identified in the biblical text, but they were assumed to be complementary. This assumption posed a theological unity for the New Testament that subsequent study found problematic. For example, at Columbia, Dubuque, and Johnson C. Smith biblical theology courses were offered by the systematic theology department, and at Pittsburgh/Xenia in 1937–1938 the course "Biblical Theology: The Theology of Jesus" was offered by the systematics department; it was apparently taught as Jesus' own "systematic theology."[20]

Neo-orthodoxy seemed to offer an option to not only the perceived bankruptcy of liberalism but also the rigidity of the Old Princeton theology and its fundamentalist defenders. The sense of theological creativity and excitement were caught by Princeton's Elmer Homrighausen, who characteristically expressed the spirit of the times in a panegyric. "I unqualifiedly granted God his lordship! No longer did I *seek* the truth—it had now become a matter of *accepting* God, who was not abstract or remote, but close at hand. He had come to man—and to me. And I let him be God!"

Homrighausen continued: "I began to live as though the Word of God were true. That Word was Jesus Christ the God-man. He became the foundation of my thinking, of my emotional life and of my action. My life had a sure foundation in God. . . . I believed, but I could not prove. The inner law, the intellect, and the sentiments were not obliterated. They now had a master."[21] Homrighausen may have been more effusive than most, but for both faculty and students it seemed a day of theological renewal.

Amidst the excitement, there were strains. Gradually the historical consciousness of modernity made its way into American Presbyterian theology of the thirties through the use of historical-critical methodology and the awareness of the culturally conditioned character of creeds and confessions. Theologians denounced denominations as "a scandal" in Christianity because they denied the unity and integrity of the body of Christ; the ecumenical impulse in American Protestantism was nurtured and strengthened. The rise of totalitarianism in Europe and the erosion of confidence in American capitalism raised the question of whether "a Christian America" was possible and desirable.[22]

Two developments in Presbyterian seminaries of the thirties, perhaps only straws in the wind, seemed to indicate their desire to ensure some unity amidst such rapid intellectual and cultural upheaval. First, during the mid-thirties, most of the seminaries renewed their emphasis on English Bible courses. Columbia and Union introduced required Bible content exams for all graduates (Austin and Louisville already had them), and at San Francisco and Dubuque, English Bible course offerings grew more comprehensive and aimed at exposing students to the full content of scripture. The emphasis on English Bible eventually declined as faculty stressed the study of the Greek and Hebrew texts, but in its day English Bible instruction was a source of stimulation and excitement for students.

Second, there was an increasing trend toward emphasizing the credo ("I believe") over the creed. As Presbyterian seminaries gradually moved away from trying to produce defenders of Old School Calvinism, the responsibility for forging theological identity subtly shifted away from the seminaries or even the church to the individual. In the words of the Dubuque Seminary catalog in 1937, the goal of theological study was "to help students to think their way through to an adequate Christian philosophy, a comprehensive synthesis of beliefs, rather than to place the emphasis on a purely dogmatic theology."[23] The change seemed minor at the time, but this emphasis on the individual contributed eventually to the flowering of pluralism in Presbyterian theology and the denominations' seminaries.

The 1940s: The Rise of Neo-Orthodoxy

If the 1930s saw a gradual and sometimes painful and incomplete transition from a unified theological ethos at Presbyterian seminaries, based on the Princeton theology, the 1940s saw the consolidation of the movement of "neo-orthodoxy" in Presbyterian seminaries. Sometimes called a "theology of crisis," its tenor was appropriate to the United States as it entered another world war and confronted the terror of totalitarianism.

John Mackay's lead editorial in the first issue of *Theology Today* in 1944 captured the contemporary mood: "When the earth quivers beneath the flail of total war, when battles mount in fury around the globe, when the most momentous year in modern history is running its course, why should a new journal be issued?" he asked. Although the world was at war, Mackay also recognized the intensity of religious conflict in twentieth-century America which made it difficult to articulate a unified Christian vision. In words that would become even more true in subsequent decades, Mackay inquired, "Why . . . should they only appear to possess conviction and authority who belong to an extremist fringe on the religious right or left? Why does not the center become articulate, and move forward with clear eye and passionate heart?" The answer, he said, was "because those at the center have in these last times largely ceased to understand the faith to which they are heirs, and have come to wear as a conventional badge what they should unfurl as a crusading banner."[24]

Mackay's editorial exuded the theological ethos of Presbyterian seminaries in the 1940s—the sense of theological excitement and challenge, the perception of Western civilization and Christianity in crisis, the urgency to return to the Bible and to Reformation themes, the desire to create a middle ground between liberalism and fundamentalism, and the need for theology and the church to be "relevant" to the modern mind. True to the heritage of mainstream Protestantism as a mediating force between extremes, Mackay clearly envisioned a journal that would eschew both "a fantastic apocalypticism . . . that despairs of this world" and "a utopian humanism that deifies it."[25]

Though Mackay's own theology defied precise categories, a broadly defined "neo-orthodox" perspective increasingly permeated the faculty and curriculum of Presbyterian seminaries of the 1940s.[26] With its emphasis on the centrality of Jesus Christ as God's self-revelation, to which the Bible is a historically conditioned witness, neo-orthodoxy was able to affirm the authority and uniqueness of scripture without rejecting modern scholarship and its findings *in toto.* This sense of intellectual freedom can be found, for example, in the description of McCormick's Department of Philosophy of Religion and Ethics in 1942, which read in part: "The accepted conclusions of modern science and scholarship as to matters of fact are presupposed."[27]

In the backwash of the fundamentalist-modernist controversy, neo-orthodoxy in its various expressions became a welcome mainstream Protestant option. It held that the Bible was authoritative without being inerrant; that theology, confessions, and doctrine were important, but human, constructs of a finally ineffable divine mystery; and that culture, though structurally flawed by sin, was potentially gracious and redeemable through the witness of the church to Jesus Christ.

New faculty appointments at the seminaries encouraged the growth of neo-orthodoxy and the movement of Presbyterian theology out of its Old School Calvinist enclave. Jo-

seph Haroutunian (McCormick), James I. McCord
(Austin), Felix Gear (Columbia), Paul Lehmann and
George Hendry (Princeton), Arthur Cochrane (Dubuque),
and Kenneth Foreman (Louisville) in theology; C. Ellis
Nelson (Austin) in religious education; and Floyd Filson
(McCormick), John Bright (Union), and John Wick Bow-
man (San Francisco) in biblical theology were among those
actively leading the seminaries into new lines of thought.

The theological reorientation of the seminaries in the
1940s was achieved without the bitter acrimony that characterized the height of the fundamentalist controversy in
the twenties and early thirties. The case of Kenneth Foreman at Louisville is a good illustration. In 1930, as a member of the faculty at Davidson College, Foreman published
an article questioning the Hodge-Warfield understanding of
the plenary and verbal inspiration of scripture. He became
so suspect that at least one church put one of its students on
its prayer list when it learned that the student was studying
with Foreman. In contrast, when he was named to the faculty at Louisville in 1947, Foreman's appointment brought
no outcry from the church; by this time he was considered
to be a respected, progressive leader of the denomination.[28]

Special lecturers at Presbyterian seminaries also reinforced the new theological trends in the 1940s. The broadly
neo-orthodox approach was exemplified in people like Elmer Homrighausen, Josef Hromádka, Otto Piper, Hugh T.
Kerr, John A. Mackay, Wilhelm Pauck, and Reinhold Niebuhr, all of whom gave special lectures at Presbyterian seminaries during the period. In 1949 H. Richard Niebuhr
delivered the lectures at Austin Seminary that were published in 1951 as the widely influential volume *Christ and
Culture.*[29]

Though steadily losing ground, scholastic Calvinism was
not without a voice during the decade. At Columbia Seminary, W. C. Robinson introduced into the curriculum in
1945–1946 a course on the thought and influence of B. B.
Warfield, to which he himself was sympathetic. At Pitts-
burgh/Xenia a new course in 1941–1942, "Modern Trends
in Theology," stated as its aim "to evaluate contemporary

opinion and maintain orthodox evangelical bearing." Addison Leitch, who came to the Pittsburgh/Xenia faculty in the mid-forties in philosophy of religion and religious education, moved to the systematics chair in 1948 and resisted the inroads of neo-orthodoxy as did his colleague John Gerstner. Likewise, Andrew Rule at Louisville and John E. Huizinga at Princeton were representatives of Calvinist scholastic orthodoxy.[30]

The seminaries experimented episodically with varying the number of required and elective courses and developed accelerated programs for those entering military service in World War II, but beneath these changes in the curriculum were two major crosscurrents with profound implications for theology in Presbyterian seminaries.

The first was the ecumenical movement, described by Archbishop William Temple as "the great new fact of our era."[31] Animated by the 1937 Life and Work Conference in Oxford, the ecumenical movement of the 1940s was driven in large measure by theological concerns that spanned the Protestant traditions and even began to take modest cognizance of Roman Catholic thought. For example, throughout the 1940s Johnson C. Smith offered a course comparing American Protestantism and Catholicism, and in 1949–1950 Union's John N. Thomas introduced a course on Roman Catholic and Protestant doctrines of the church. Presbyterians were also leaders in ecumenical theological discussions of the 1950s; they included Arnold B. Come, Theodore A. Gill, Robert C. Johnson, Hugh T. Kerr, John A. Mackay, James I. McCord, W. C. Robinson, Holmes Rolston, Henry P. Van Dusen, and Albert C. Winn.

The second trend was the increasing awareness of the importance of historical theology as a necessary complement to the task of contemporary systematic theology. At Union, E. T. Thompson's courses in historical theology were eventually listed in the systematics department in 1947–1948. At Austin, James I. McCord described his approach to systematic theology: "In all classes primary sources will be read and analyzed, and the historical approach to theological systems will be stressed." Students were increasingly

required to read Luther and Calvin, rather than eighteenth-
or nineteenth-century interpreters of the Reformers, and
courses on the history of nineteenth-century theology began to be offered. At Johnson C. Smith, courses on contemporary theology and the history of the Black church appear
for the first time in the 1940s, but the Black church course
was later dropped in the 1950s. In fact, the curriculum of
Johnson C. Smith as late as the 1960s is notable for its lack
of explicit attention to issues unique to the Black church (at
least as far as the catalogs are concerned) and its parallels to
the curriculum in other Presbyterian seminaries.[32] At every
school the consciousness of history and the importance of
historical theology were gradually becoming a major force
in shaping theological methodology and the understanding
of doctrine itself.

The ascendance of neo-orthodoxy in southern Presbyterian seminaries must be understood as not only the displacement of Old School Calvinism but also the assault
on its doctrine of "the spirituality of the church." As the
twentieth-century South grappled with the legacy of racism and segregation, southern Presbyterians saw in neo-
orthodoxy a doctrine of the church that would not only
allow but compel it to address social and political
problems. The issues of race and ecclesiology are inextrica-
bly tied to transformation of southern Presbyterian theology and the rejection of Old School Calvinism.[33]

The most significant feature of Presbyterian seminaries
in the 1940s was their emancipation from the Princeton
theology and Old School Calvinism and the adoption of
neo-orthodox perspectives. Within the seminaries few saw
the victory as total or complete, and the theological atmosphere continued to be charged by the echo of the fundamentalist controversy. But the fundamentalists themselves
knew that Presbyterians had made a break with the Hodge-
Warfield tradition. Two events of the 1940s marked both
the retreat of the fundamentalists from Presbyterian circles
and the beginning of a fundamentalist-evangelical resur-
gence: the formation of the National Association of
Evangelicals in 1943 and the founding of Fuller Theologi-

cal Seminary in 1947 as the perpetuator of the old Princeton theology and as a coalition of conservatives and
evangelicals.[34]

The growing institutional strength of the fundamentalists
and their progeny, the "neo-evangelicals," and the scars
from theological combat during the 1920s and 1930s
heightened the resistance of Presbyterian seminary faculties to theological conservatism and evangelicalism and encouraged a tendency in Presbyterian seminaries to be even
more receptive to other theological alternatives. The battles of the recent past thus set the stage for the future quest
for the identity of Presbyterian theology and the church
itself.

The 1950s: Rumblings of Change

The 1950s are sometimes viewed as the "placid decade,"
described by Sydney Ahlstrom as "a halcyon time when
peace and peacefulness prevailed." It saw a revival, fueled
by the suburbanization of America and the postwar baby
boom. Membership in the PCUSA steadily grew from 2.4
million in 1950 to 2.8 million in 1958; the merger with the
UPCNA in 1958 brought total membership in the United
Presbyterian Church in the U.S.A. (UPCUSA) to
3,159,562; in the PCUS similar growth raised membership
from 702,266 to 873,065 during the same period. With
seminary enrollments rising, the number of active PCUSA
ministers grew from 9,384 in 1950 to 10,424 in 1958; comparable growth for the PCUS was from 2,717 to 3,564.
President Dwight D. Eisenhower's oft-quoted aphorism
seemed to epitomize this era of religiosity and "piety along
the Potomac": "Our government makes no sense unless it
is founded on a deeply felt religious faith—and I don't care
what it is."[35]

In fact, the fifties were a paradox of both "peril and
promise" for American mainstream Protestantism, as Robert Wuthnow has suggested. The rhetoric of growth and
prosperity was tempered by apprehension spawned by the
horror of the Holocaust and the threat of atomic war, com-

munism, and nationalism in developing countries. American Protestantism, which had been so intimately linked to the American political experiment, seemed to find itself increasingly discomfited by its own success and disturbed by its forbidding future. Voices within both American Presbyterianism and other denominations raised perplexing questions about the integrity of the church's witness.[36]

The result was an internal critique of American Christianity and especially American Protestantism, which had been building since the 1930s in the work of Reinhold Niebuhr, H. Richard Niebuhr, and others and became increasingly evident in the curricula of the Presbyterian seminaries during the 1950s. One conspicuous example of this critique is the emergence of ethics, and particularly social ethics, as established parts of the curriculum, with faculty specializing in the field. No longer considered a subdiscipline of theology, ethics emerged as a subject of inquiry in its own right and found an institutional base.[37]

The influence of the Niebuhrs, especially Reinhold Niebuhr, can be seen in the broadening of the ethical agenda of the church and its seminaries. San Francisco established an entire section of the curriculum to Christian social ethics, which treated a panoply of concerns, including property, problems in world diplomacy, marriage, family, urbanization, industrialization, and labor. The "issues" approach was common, and communism was the one most frequently addressed. For example, distinct courses on communism were offered at Princeton, Union, Dubuque, McCormick, and San Francisco. Other approaches included Johnson C. Smith's survey of "current problems"—"the family; racial, economic, and labor problems; public opinion and the church"—and courses that applied biblical material to contemporary problems, such as those taught at Columbia on the social teachings of the Old and New Testaments. An interesting barometer of the times appeared in a symposium from the Louisville faculty, *The Church Against the Isms*.[38]

The emergence of social ethics and theological ethics fed a criticism of American Protestantism that it was imbued with middle-class values of the culture and resistant to social and political change. Other schools of thought brought biblical and theological perspectives to a critique of the church's life and witness. Foremost among these was the biblical theology movement, which allied itself with neo-orthodoxy in emphasizing scripture as the source of theological reflection. The study of history also exercised a decisive influence in two directions. It encouraged a fresh reading of the sources of the Reformed tradition in Augustine, Luther, and Calvin. Historical study also broadened the awareness of the culture in which the church witnessed, of other branches of Christianity (the growth of ecumenism), and the theological significance of the world of philosophy and movements for social and political change.

McCormick Seminary of the 1950s is a striking microcosm for measuring the influence of neo-orthodoxy and the biblical theology movement in Presbyterian theological education. The faculty included Floyd V. Filson, George Ernest Wright, Frank M. Cross, and Clinton D. Morrison in biblical studies. In church history and theology the neo-orthodox perspective was offered by Leonard J. Trinterud, Joseph Haroutunian, and Edward A. Dowey. Haroutunian's year-long, required course in systematic theology stressed that "Reformed theology will receive primary emphasis, and will be considered in the light of Scripture and the modern situation."[39]

Another indication of the power and even the persistence of neo-orthodoxy and the biblical theology movement was the *Christian Faith and Life* curriculum and the Covenant Life Curriculum. Although not published until the 1960s, two books in the Covenant Life Curriculum have become best sellers for both congregational and seminary use: A. B. Rhodes's *The Mighty Acts of God* (1964) and Shirley C. Guthrie's *Christian Doctrine* (1968).

Throughout the 1950s, neo-orthodoxy consolidated its position as the prevailing theological outlook at the Presbyterian seminaries. Arthur Cochrane at Dubuque described the aim of the systematics curriculum in unambiguously Barthian terms: "It is critical inquiry about the agreement

of the Church's witness with God's Word." His required
sequence of courses followed the outline of Barth's *Church
Dogmatics*. At Columbia, the shift to neo-orthodoxy was
dramatically evident in the apologetics course. Described
in the 1955–1956 catalog as "the history of and the present
need for Apologetics in the current revolt against historic
Christianity," apologetics only one year later was seen as a
process whereby "the Christian begins intellectually where
God has graciously placed him, that is, in Jesus Christ."[40] A
more sudden about-face within the same tradition could
scarcely be imagined.

The biblical theology movement made its presence felt in
various ways. Important biblical ideas or concepts became
the structure for courses exploring the theology of the Bible
and the biblical worldview. Courses on "covenant,"
"grace," "law," "promise," and "redemption" are examples of additions to the curriculum at Dubuque, Louisville,
and Princeton by the 1950s. Heightened attention was also
paid to the Old Testament, which was formerly treated as
the historical description of the rise and development of
Israelite religion, rites, and institutions. Under the influence of biblical theology, the Old Testament was increasingly studied for its theological richness, its relationship
with the New Testament, and its relevance for the modern
world.[41] The vitality of the biblical theology movement was
underscored by a flood of lecturers and visiting professors
setting forth its emphases: Floyd Filson, George Ernest
Wright, Donald Miller, James Muilenburg, A. M. Hunter,
H. H. Rowley, John Wick Bowman, Markus Barth, W. F.
Albright, T. W. Manson, and William Manson.

The biblical theology movement was heavily informed
by an awareness of history as both a methodology and a
subject of theological reflection, and history exerted a profound influence on the study of theology itself during the
1950s. Historical theology assumed increasing importance
in the teaching of Edward A. Dowey (McCormick and later
Princeton), John Leith (Union), E. A. Smith (Western),
Shirley C. Guthrie, Jr. (Columbia), Martin Schmidt (Columbia and San Francisco), James I. McCord (Austin), W.

C. Robinson and Paul Fuhrmann (Columbia), and Kenneth Foreman (Louisville). Furthermore, courses on a theology of history appeared in the curricula, probing the meaning of history in the light of the devastation wrought by the Holocaust, the atom bomb, and modern warfare.[42]

The theological curricula of the seminaries also demonstrate an increasing concern to engage contemporary philosophical thought. The most prevalent influence came from existentialism, particularly Kierkegaard, as well as twentieth-century existentialists such as Buber, Heidegger, and Sartre. Paul Tillich, who gave the Sprunt Lectures at Union in 1953, was also the subject of courses or was read at nearly all the seminaries during the 1950s. Even process theology, rooted in the philosophy of Alfred North Whitehead, moved beyond its home base at the University of Chicago and into theology courses at Presbyterian seminaries.[43]

Burgeoning interest in the ecumenical movement left its imprint at the denomination's seminaries. All of them offered a basic course in ecumenics or the ecumenical movement. The course description at Johnson C. Smith was typical. The course was "designed to give the history of various efforts to reach Church unity throughout the centuries; special emphasis centered on ecumenical movements since the beginning of the nineteenth century, culminating in the realization of various types of Christian cooperation, association, federation, and organic church unions."[44]

Among the most significant changes in the theological curricula during the 1950s was the explosion of courses in the practical disciplines, particularly in pastoral care. Courses in pastoral care had often been taught by faculty in Christian education, but as the pastoral counseling movement developed greater strength, the two fields became distinct. Four figures dominated the pastoral counseling crusade in Protestant theological education—Methodists Carroll A. Wise and Paul Johnson, Southern Baptist Wayne Oates, and Presbyterian Seward Hiltner. The writings of Carl Rogers permeated the seminaries' courses in pastoral care and counseling. The movement coincided with the fascination with psychology during the 1950s and the interest in therapy, which only escalated later. E. Brooks Holifield has noted, "In 1939 few theological schools had even bothered to offer counseling courses that would introduce students to the latest psychological theories. By the 1950s almost all of them did, over 80 percent offered additional courses in psychology, and 80 percent could list at least one psychologist on their faculty." One index of the strength of the movement was the establishment of centers for clinical pastoral education. By the end of the fifties, there were 117 such centers affiliated with more than forty theological schools.[45]

The explosion of interest in pastoral counseling was significant for several reasons. It was part of a broader development in theological education in which seminaries attempted to respond to the increasing demands from churches for various skills, ranging from counseling to administration to specialized ministries—youth, the aging, urban and rural congregations, for example. Courses and faculty to teach them multiplied so extensively that the number of faculty in the practical fields sometimes rivaled those in the biblical, theological, and historical fields. A related change was the expansion and improvement of supervised field education. The structural result was the gradual erosion of the domination of the curriculum by theological and biblical studies and the escalating influence of practical disciplines and skills.

Furthermore, driving the early pastoral counseling movement was an aggressive antimoralism and a suspicion of theological categories, including those of neo-orthodoxy. Although this emphasis undoubtedly liberated both pastors and lay people and helped them gain new appreciation of mental and emotional illness, the attack on moralism and theology had deleterious effects as well. It undermined the idea of a distinctive religious point of view and the contributions of theology itself. By the end of the 1950s the study of theology was no longer the primary core of Presbyterian theological education and found itself in both intellectual and curricular competition with other disciplines and differing visions of ministry.[46]

Although there were intellectual movements sparking theological, cultural, and political criticism of the church and American society, it is worth emphasizing that the study of theology in Presbyterian seminaries in the 1950s remained remarkably uniform. Dominated by neo-orthodoxy and the biblical theology movement, it was overwhelmingly indebted to Western theology written by white males from the Protestant tradition, mainly Lutheran and Reformed. Even as late as 1965 Claude Welch's survey of theology unapologetically covered only Protestants; similarly, Sydney Ahlstrom's 1967 anthology, *Theology in America,* contained no Roman Catholic or Jewish representatives.[47] Although there was some justification for this approach, the theological debate of the fifties was lively and spirited, but circumscribed. Slowly emerging were the forces that fed the revolution in theology of the 1960s.

The 1960s: "The Radical Turn in Theology and Ethics"

According to Sydney Ahlstrom, the sixties was the era of "the radical turn in theology and ethics." It represented the end of "a Great Puritan Epoch" in Anglo-American history, spanning more than four centuries. Writing at the end of the sixties, Ahlstrom argued that the decade "was a time . . . when the old grounds of national confidence, patriotic idealism, moral traditionalism, and even of historic Judaeo-Christian theism, were awash. Presuppositions that had held firm for centuries—even millennia—were being widely questioned. . . . The nation was confronting revolutionary circumstances whose effects were, in the nature of the case, irreversible."[48]

Ahlstrom believed that neo-orthodoxy left an ambiguous legacy, particularly among mainstream Protestant churches. Its chief contribution lay in a revitalized and reshaped social gospel. Neo-orthodoxy, wrote Ahlstrom, gave people "a more realistic awareness of institutional power, social structures, and human depravity"; helped make people "more biblical in their standpoint and less utopian in their advocacy"; and built bridges to both modernists and conservatives. However, he believed it also put down "a very thin sheet of dogmatic asphalt over the problems created by modern critical thought."[49]

The neo-orthodox movement was accompanied by searching criticism of American religion as heavily acculturated and decisively shaped by middle-class values and mores. Among the widely read diagnoses of the fifties and sixties were Will Herberg's *Protestant, Catholic, Jew,* Peter Berger's *The Noise of Solemn Assemblies,* Gibson Winter's *The Suburban Captivity of the Churches,* and Martin Marty's *The New Shape of American Religion.*[50] But neo-orthodoxy's critique of society and the church emerged from denominations and thinkers who still operated with a sense of theological confidence and cultural recognition.[51]

The sixties witnessed a shaking of the neo-orthodox consensus and a recognition of the displacement of mainstream Protestant churches as definitive shapers of American culture. The transformation of theology arose in part out of the awareness of a social crisis in American society—racism and civil rights, Vietnam, the environment, and feminism. However, it was also fed by a growing sense that the nature and task of theology itself had changed.

The most revolutionary development, measured against the larger framework of the history of Christianity, was the emergence of Roman Catholic theology after Vatican II and the collapse of Protestant-Catholic polemics. Protestants and Catholics, who had defined themselves polemically and intramurally for more than four hundred years, now recognized the challenge of formulating a Christian identity. The shift, which was remarkably sudden and extraordinarily irenic, symbolized the predicaments of pluralism that would escalate during the next decades.

Hugh T. Kerr's *Theology Today* editorial of 1964, "Time for a Critical Theology," was an early and insightful analysis of the new theological climate, spawned by religious and social upheaval. Marking the twentieth anniversary of the journal, Kerr declared that "if anything can teach the Christian church in these days what it means to think and act self-critically, it will be the racial revolution." Further-more, Kerr declared, "one of the massive ironies of religious history is being dramatized before our eyes: the Roman Catholic Church is rapidly emerging in the eyes of the world as the symbol of progressive ecclesiastical and theological *reform!"* The response, Kerr suggested, should be twofold: "First, the times call for an interpretation of the *function* of theology as a critical discipline; and second, the *perspective* of theology must be open enough to take in a multiplicity or pluralism of possibilities." Theology would be "not so much a structure or content as . . . a way of thinking," and since "we have begun to accept the pluralism of denominations, even of faiths, and perhaps someday of religions," Kerr said, "why should it be so difficult to accept the plurality of theological expression at many levels?"[52]

Kerr's hailing of a new departure in theology captured the critical, if not iconoclastic, mood of the sixties. Institutions, systems of thought, values, and traditions were subject to penetrating scrutiny. Todd Gitlin, a participant in "the movement" of radical politics, recollected that "especially at the start, beneath the Sixties' dramatic displays of iron certainty, invisible from the outside, there were questions, endless questions, running debates that took their point from the divine premise that everything was possible and therefore it was important to think, because ideas have consequences. Unraveling, rethinking, refusing to take for granted, thinking without limits—that calling was some of what I loved most in the spirit of the Sixties."[53]

In biblical studies the contemporary mood grew more favorable to the thought of Rudolf Bultmann. Although his form criticism had been studied in Presbyterian seminaries during the 1950s, Bultmann's critique achieved a significant base by the sixties, and the "salvation-history" hermeneutic of the biblical theology movement underwent severe scrutiny. By the end of the decade, Columbia, Pittsburgh, McCormick, San Francisco, and Princeton each had at least one course dealing with Bultmann, and he was widely read at other seminaries.[54]

The influence of Roman Catholic scholarship also made inroads at Presbyterian seminaries. It appeared first in the biblical fields during the 1950s, following Pius XII's landmark encyclical *Divino Afflante Spiritu* of 1943, which sanctioned the use of modern biblical criticism. Catholic biblical scholars began to participate in scholarly organizations once dominated by Protestants, and Catholic commentaries began to be widely used in Protestant circles. The work of Raymond Brown and Roland Murphy, as well as the publication of the *Jerome Biblical Commentary,* were harbingers of this new era in biblical scholarship. Pope John XXIII's call for *aggiornamento* and the Second Vatican Council, with its Protestant observers, further opened the doors for Protestant-Catholic dialogue. By the mid-1960s, the works of Karl Rahner, Hans Küng, Gregory Baum, and Pierre Teilhard de Chardin began to appear in the theological curricula of Presbyterian seminaries.[55]

Several interpreters identify the sixties as the period of disestablishment of mainstream Protestantism in American culture and the unraveling of a cultural consensus about social and religious values.[56] Although the implications of this dislocation were only partially perceived at the time, a widespread sense of a religious and cultural crisis in Western society permeated the ethos of Presbyterian seminaries of the 1960s. Rather than the church setting the agenda for the world, theologians argued that the world and its desperate needs provided the priorities for theological reflection and the church's mission. Many theologians urged the church to recognize the value and promise of secularization. No other work so thoroughly captured the spirit of the sixties as Harvey Cox's *The Secular City,* which heralded the promise of secularity and technology. Cox and others argued that secularity would liberate people from false securities and provide the freedom for what Dietrich Bonhoeffer had eliptically described as "the nonreligious interpretation of biblical concepts.[57]

Bonhoeffer's works were read in Presbyterian seminaries during the 1950s, but his appeal to radical Christian ethics and his critique of religion found an especially hospitable reception in the 1960s. Other critics of Christianity—Feuerbach, Marx, Nietzsche, Freud, and others—were read and expounded, less with an eye toward apologetic rebuttal than with a desire to hear and engage them in dialogue. The "death of God" theologians also had ephemeral notice in Presbyterian theological seminaries.[58] More significant was the rise of theological perspectives that placed justice at the center of Christian truth and discipleship. For the sixties, this point of view was argued most forcefully by Black religious leaders and theologians—notable examples being Martin Luther King, Jr., James H. Cone, and J. Deotis Roberts.[59] The idea of revolution, in theology and politics, became a common construct for understanding the church's response to a world in crisis and the church's displacement at America's cultural core.

The ethical debates of the 1960s over Vietnam, civil rights, the environment, sexual mores, and women's rights occurred both within the church and in the society. The Presbyterian response was multifaceted, and it is symbolized in Presbyterian seminaries by the expansion of course offerings in ethics and church and society and by the appointment of additional faculty members in those fields. At Johnson C. Smith, for example, the curriculum was reorganized in 1964, with a separate department for "The Church and the World."[60]

A striking indication of the prominence of ethics in Presbyterian theology during the 1960s is the Confession of 1967. The committee that drafted it was drawn heavily from Presbyterian seminaries, and the confession itself relied on the concept of reconciliation as its unifying theme. In contrast to other possible concepts such as "redemption" or "salvation," reconciliation offered the possibility of emphasizing a social dimension to Christian faith. Arnold B. Come observed, "The most original and distinctive contribution of C-67 [is that] it brings a social ethic within the scope of God's reconciling work in Christ."[61]

A similar impulse can be seen in "A Declaration of Faith," a confession that was never adopted by the PCUS but was eventually used widely for liturgical purposes in both denominations. Symbolically, "A Declaration of Faith" marked the demise of the doctrine of "the spirituality of the church" in the PCUS. Just as Presbyterians had broken with scholastic Calvinism in the 1930s, so also in the 1960s they attempted to forge an understanding of Christian social responsibility that would deal with the traumas of American culture.

The fragmentation of American culture and the increasing pluralism of Presbyterian theology can also be traced in the structure of the curricula of the seminaries themselves. Responding to student pressure and the self-critical atmosphere of the decade, the seminaries conceded the need to open up the curriculum and provide greater freedom to students in selecting courses. Five of the seminaries (Princeton, San Francisco, McCormick, Pittsburgh, and Louisville) virtually abandoned all required courses.[62]

The structureless curriculum of the 1960s was a radical and extreme response to the social crises and theological ferment of the decade. In a sense, it was a capitulation to the anti-institutionalism and iconoclasm of the era, which questioned not only the traditional forms of theology but the actual content of Christian faith. If theologians were unable to describe the nature of Christian theology, then there was no unifying core to a theological curriculum. In a bleak assessment at the end of the 1960s, Princeton President James I. McCord concluded that theology was "a shambles."[63]

Another less pessimistic assessment of theology in the 1960s would recognize the developments in Presbyterian seminaries as a flawed but creative attempt to move the church beyond neo-orthodoxy into a deeper and more sustained dialogue with the crosscurrents of the modern world. Whatever verdict might be reached, the fact remains that the Presbyterian seminaries entered the 1970s amidst theological and pedagogical ferment.

The 1970s and 1980s: The Quest for Unity

The prevailing theme of Presbyterian theological education during the 1970s and 1980s has been the quest for some kind of unity amidst the pluralism of theology, other disciplines, the church, and society itself. The forging of a new theological foundation was illusory for two reasons. First, as Ahlstrom has noted, "in the seventies, for reasons that are not easily diagnosed, creative theology virtually passed from the scene, though one can surmise that this dearth can be attributed to the swirling social events that agitated the nation as a whole. That lack of theological concern—whatever its cause—can only be regarded as a tragedy."[64]

Second, the pluralism hailed in the 1960s as a liberating force assumed both an institutional and intellectual life of its own, resisting attempts to forge a Reformed theological or ecclesiastical identity.[65] Presbyterian seminary campuses were no longer bastions of scholastic Calvinism or even neo-orthodoxy, but forums for diversity. A majority of faculty and students continued to be Presbyterian, but theological education became an ecumenical and increasingly cross-cultural exploration of the nature of Christian faith and witness.[66]

The Presbyterian seminaries responded to the waning trauma of the 1960s by quickly abandoning the idea of a totally elective curriculum. By the end of the decade every seminary that experimented with the plan had abandoned it. The only exception was McCormick, but even there fully twenty-one of the twenty-seven courses needed for graduation were strongly "recommended."[67] The prevailing emphasis fell on trying to integrate "experience" with "reflection," although there remained uncertainty about what constituted experience and what the goal of reflection might be. The ambiguity is reflected in a description of Dubuque's curriculum, introduced in the late seventies. "The aim of these courses," the catalog stated, "is to help the student make connections between what he/she is learning and what he/she already knows and to apply new knowledge to a wide variety of situations in human life. The student learns to examine the phenomena of human life from a theological perspective, and to compare this perspective with the results of examining human life from other perspectives."[68]

The sixties left a legacy, and in no other area was the change more dramatic than in the presence of women on Presbyterian seminary campuses and the rise of feminist theology. The Association of Theological Schools began keeping statistics on the enrollment of women in the early 1970s when they started attending seminaries in growing numbers. By 1975 there were already 313 women enrolled in ordination-degree programs in Presbyterian seminaries. By 1980, the number had grown to 419, and by 1985 there were 600 women students. During that period women comprised roughly half of the ordination-degree enrollment (M.Div. or B.D.), and nearly 90 percent attended the northern Presbyterian seminaries. Without the influx of women, Presbyterian seminary enrollments would not have grown during the 1970s and 1980s.[69] Their presence transformed seminary communities.

New courses reflected the presence of women students and the growing number of women faculty who were appointed to Presbyterian seminary faculties during the 1970s and 1980s. The emphasis shifted away from courses designed to raise consciousness about women's issues to exploration of theoretical and theological feminist concerns. These courses ranged from "Biblical Exegesis: From Adam's Rib to the Bride of Christ" (McCormick, 1978–1979) to "Women in American Religious History" (Columbia, 1973–1974) to "Human Sexuality, Marriage, and the Family in Theological Perspective" (Austin, 1975–1976). By the 1980s, feminist theology continued to draw heavily from liberation theology, but also increasingly proposed a reconstruction of Christian doctrine freed from patriarchal assumptions.[70]

The impact of ethics on the curriculum of the seminaries, which began in the fifties and escalated in the sixties, became more extensive in the 1970s and 1980s. African American theologians continued to find a hearing in courses in the Presbyterian seminaries, and they were joined by not only feminists but also liberation theologians from Asia, Latin America, and Africa and their North American interpreters. Reinhold Niebuhr's early criticism of capitalism and his far-reaching ethical concerns spawned a more sustained analysis of economic institutions, the environment, the impact of science and technology, and especially war and peace.[71]

A preoccupation with ethics became one way of dealing with the "structureless" and pluralistic approach to theology launched in the 1960s. A concern for methodology became another, and Presbyterian seminaries in the seventies and eighties were marked by a variety of methodological approaches to theological reflection. For example, the social sciences were treated in John Burkhart's "Social Theory and Theological Method" at McCormick in 1975–1976. In the 1980s sociological theory exerted a profound influence in biblical studies through such biblical critics as Norman Gottwald in Old Testament and Gerd Theissen and Wayne Meeks in New Testament.[72] The work of Claude Lévi-Strauss, Hans-Georg Gadamer, and Paul Ricoeur provided other methods of interpreting texts, and interest in novels, the structure of narrative, and communication theories shaped course offerings in both the theological and biblical fields.[73]

A significant change at Presbyterian seminaries during the 1970s and 1980s was an emphasis on the spiritual development of students and the use of "spiritual disciplines" in ministry. Although hardly ignored in earlier Presbyterian theological education, such concerns were usually handled informally outside the curriculum or among students themselves. The new accent in the seminaries was partly due to a reaction to the ethos of the sixties, which had elevated activism at the expense of piety, and the ecumenical influence from Roman Catholic seminaries with their long tradition of spiritual formation. Courses and programs in spiritual development were often met with considerable initial opposition from faculty members, but by the end of the 1980s they were well established within the seminaries. Students of the era indicate that both traditional forms of spiritual discipline, as well as involvement in social justice, significantly shaped their spiritual growth.[74]

Throughout the 1970s and 1980s, pluralistic understandings of both the content and methodology of theology gained a significant place in Presbyterian theological education. The emergence of pluralism was a product of external influences that affected the seminaries—the self-consciousness and assertiveness of minority groups and women who had not played major roles in theological education, the awareness of the global character of Christianity, especially outside the West, the increasing fragmentation of theology even in the West, and the extraordinary expansion of ecumenical theological reflection. But pluralism became as well a consciously accepted policy for the Presbyterian seminaries, as they sought to be open to differing understandings of Christianity that recognized but also transcended race, sex, class, national boundaries, and a variety of confessional traditions.

The Predicament of Pluralism

In his 1954 survey of the fundamentalist-modernist controversy, *The Broadening Church,* Lefferts A. Loetscher offered a perceptive and prophetic conclusion about the implications of that strife for the future of American Presbyterianism. "In sweeping away by a stroke of interpretation much of the previously exercised power of the General Assembly to define and thus to preserve the Church's doctrine, the commission established a principle which has much broader implications than the Church has yet had occasion to draw from it," Loetscher wrote. "If the Church now has no means of authoritatively defining its faith short of the amending process—which could hardly function in the midst of sharp controversy—ecclesiastical power is seriously hindered for the future from preventing more radical theological innovations than those discussed in the 'five points.' " Noting the "increasing odium against heresy prosecution," Loetscher believed that the Presbyterian Church was now depending on "its group mind" rather than any form of authoritative doctrine or ecclesiology.[75]

It was precisely this "group mind" of American Presbyterianism that was fragmented in the post–World War II decades, presenting the denomination with a genuine predicament regarding the pluralism within its own ranks.[76] Today there are few voices within the Presbyterian Church (U.S.A.) who would urge a return to the theological scholasticism and doctrinal rigidity of the Princeton theology and subscription to the Westminster Standards alone. Presbyterians had to break with their arid fundamentalist past and engage the modern world. Similarly, Presbyterians needed to recognize their broader confessional tradition and their links with the faith of the church catholic, symbolized in the *Book of Confessions.*

Also few would dispute the intellectual excitement and spiritual vitality that pluralism has brought to American Presbyterianism and its theological seminaries by the introduction of new voices—Roman Catholic, women's, African Americans', and third-world theologians'. Furthermore, the multiplicity of theological methodologies and the conscious borrowing of methodologies and insights from other disciplines have enriched and broadened the character of theology as an academic discipline.

It should be noted, however, that the Presbyterian embrace of pluralism is itself a partial hug. In its seminaries and throughout the denomination, the Presbyterian Church has demonstrated a distinct reluctance to deal with the powerful "third force" in Christendom—the Pentecostal and charismatic movements transforming Christianity in the third world. Furthermore, perhaps because they were attempting to escape their past, Presbyterians and their theological seminaries have been distrustful, if not hostile, to the contemporary evangelicals in their midst and their own legacy of evangelicalism from the nineteenth and early twentieth centuries. In the process, the denomination has often missed the creative developments taking place in evangelical circles.[77] Pluralism is desirable, it seems, only if it embraces more options from the left, not the right.

Even if pluralism in its creative and truncated form has helped Presbyterians respond to their cultural displacement from the mainstream of American religious life, it also has real and inherent limitations. The mediating func-

tion that mainstream Protestant churches often provided
has been impossible to achieve amid the proliferation of
theological methodologies and the polarization of theological perspectives. The so-called "middle ground" has
eroded. Harvard Divinity School Dean Ronald F.
Thiemann concluded in 1987, "Theology has been in a
state of disarray since the passing of the theological giants
of the so-called neo-orthodox movement." The result has
been both the increasing fragmentation of the theological
curriculum and a cleavage between theology and the
church. In 1986 John B. Cobb issued a categorical and only
partially correct lament: "Theological faculties have, on the
whole, moved from the center to the periphery of the
thought-life of the church."[78]

The malaise of theology has had effects on both the seminaries and the church itself. One of the central findings
about membership decline in the Presbyterian Church and
other mainstream Protestant churches is that they do not
lose their members primarily to more conservative
churches. In fact, conservative churches have been and
continue to be one of the main sources of new members for
Presbyterians and other mainstream Protestant denominations. Instead, researchers have found that these Protestant
groups lose their members to the nonaffiliated and the un-
churched. As Roof and McKinney have put it, the competition for these churches "is not the conservatives [they
have] *spurned* but the secularists [they have] *spawned.*"[79]

At least part of the reason for this disaffiliation seems to
lie in the erosion or blurring of the identity of American
Presbyterianism and other mainstream Protestant traditions. The problem of identity was sufficiently acute in the
Presbyterian Church (U.S.A.) in the 1980s that the denomination developed a new Christian education curriculum
explicitly focused on the Reformed tradition, a reversal of
its earlier endorsement of an ecumenical approach during
the 1960s and 1970s. A sign of the partial recovery of the
church's theological vision and clarity may be "A Brief
Statement of Faith," approved by the 1990 PC(USA) General Assembly. However, theological pluralism persists

from within and without the Presbyterian Church and inhibits the denomination's speaking clearly and persuasively about its distinctive identity within the Christian tradition.

The Presbyterian seminaries have played an important role in encouraging the rise of pluralism—with ample reason and considerable justification. Yet the unintended consequence of the enrichment of theological discourse within these educational institutions has been the impoverishment of a distinct theological vision, informed by the Presbyterian and Reformed traditions. A blurred and inchoate identity has been imparted to the church's leadership and to its members, some of whom find it insufficiently compelling to warrant their faith and obedience.

Roof and McKinney believe that for Presbyterians and other mainstream Protestants, a critical step will be to recognize that they no longer dominate either the cultural or religious center of American life. But they also need "to recapture some sense of particularity as a community of memory and not merely as a custodian of generalized cultural values." This will require among other things, they maintain, "a countering of the secular drift that has had a disproportionate impact on [their] constituency." These churches "need their own particular language of faith to communicate with the 'cultured despisers' of the modern world, in a manner that lays claim upon the self and community."[80]

Thus, in addition to the demographic factors that have affected the decline in membership in the Presbyterian Church (U.S.A.), a fundamental factor has been and continues to be theological, and Presbyterian seminaries have been crucial in stimulating a significant theological reorientation of the denomination. The theological pluralism represented in the seminaries—their faculties, students, curricula—is now part of the church itself. But pluralism itself is not strong enough to bind people to one another or to the God whom they worship. The predicament of pluralism finally asks the question implicitly posed by Loetscher: How broad can a broadening church be?

The challenge before the Presbyterian Church and its theological seminaries is the forging of a vision of what it means to be Christian in a pluralistic world and the assertion of its distinctive identity as a Reformed communion. Presbyterians and other mainstream Protestant denominations no longer enjoy the cultural support that has sustained them in American society for nearly two centuries. Instead, they are being thrown back on their own resources of faith and tradition, and the question of their identity as Christians looms before them. The resources for answering that question are now richer than ever before, and the challenge is more complex and intriguing. The struggle is for the soul of American Presbyterianism, and how Presbyterians respond will be a key to the future vitality and integrity of their tradition.[81]

2

Nurseries of Piety? Spiritual Formation at Four Presbyterian Seminaries

Steve Hancock

Faith is essential to a minister's life and work. There are many reasons for this, but an important one is that church members want ministers who are persons of deep and abiding faith. Search committees looking for new pastors to serve their congregations will certainly check out candidates' skills in preaching, teaching, counseling, and the like. They will try to ascertain if candidates have at least a working-level knowledge of the Bible, theology, church history, and so on. But underneath these concerns is the more foundational matter of faith: Do the candidates have a sure trust and confidence in the God known in Jesus Christ? Does their way of life and witness in the world flow out of that trust and confidence? This is crucial because church members recognize that ministry is more than possessing biblical and theological knowledge and skillfully performing the functions of ministry. The "more" has to do, one way or another, with faith, with trust and confidence in God and the promises of God.[1]

When American Presbyterians decided to start seminaries in the early nineteenth century, they recognized the importance of faith among the clergy. They also assumed the seminary would play a role in nurturing the faith of the students preparing for the ministry. The report to the General Assembly of 1810 (which authorized the founding of theological seminaries for Presbyterians in the United States) contained the following:

> Filling the church with a learned and able ministry without a corresponding portion of real piety would be a curse to the world, and an offense to God and the people [of God], so the General Assembly think it their duty to state that, in establishing a seminary for training up ministers . . . it will be their endeavor to make it . . . *a nursery of vital piety, as well as of sound theological learning,* and to train up persons for the ministry who shall be lovers as well as defenders of the truth as it is in Jesus. [Emphasis added.][2]

This dual focus on sound learning *and* vital piety is consistently echoed in Presbyterian seminary catalogs of the twentieth century. In 1948, the catalog of San Francisco Theological Seminary stated that the aim of the seminary "is to prepare young men and women to meet the high responsibilities of the church of Christ. Professors and students alike lay continual emphasis on the devotional life. Vision and consecration, as well as high standards of learning, mark the atmosphere of the seminary."[3] Twenty years later, the Louisville Presbyterian Theological Seminary catalog said much the same thing: "The seminary understands that, without lessening in any way its demand for academic and professional excellence, it must also be in its own place the household of faith and the body of Christ on earth. Therefore, its purpose is not finally achieved until it welds students and faculty into a genuinely Christian community which . . . aids all its members to grow in grace."[4]

Columbia Theological Seminary signaled this concern in its 1978 catalog: "In each dimension of its life, the seminary seeks to facilitate the personal growth of students, and thereby deepen their love for Christ, to encourage them in spiritual maturity, and to inspire them with a zeal for service."[5] Princeton Theological Seminary expressed the ideal in its 1988 catalog: "The seminary seeks to strengthen and deepen the spiritual life of students, and through classroom and other academic activities to confront them in critical discussions about the Bible and Christian doctrine with probing questions about faith and life in today's world."[6] The wording varies from seminary to seminary and changes over the years, but these catalog statements clearly show that Presbyterian seminaries understand themselves to be more than graduate schools teaching theology or vocational schools teaching skills; they define themselves to be in the business of preparing students spiritually, as well as intellectually and practically, for the responsibilities the students will face as ordained ministers.

Despite this commitment, Presbyterian and Protestant seminaries in general have not been clear how to go about this important part of their work of "training up" persons for the ministry. Roman Catholic seminaries, on the other hand, have had much greater clarity about their task. At most Roman Catholic seminaries in this country there is a full-time "spiritual formation team," which has responsibility for assisting students with the personal integration of pastoral, academic, and spiritual dimensions of preparation for the priesthood. Each student is accountable to a "spiritual director." The purpose of this director-directee relationship is to provide students with a structure for continuing attention to corporate and individual faith appropriation and integration. Participation in this aspect of the seminary program is not optional for students; it is required, and students are accountable in this area as they are in their academic work and field education.

Presbyterian seminaries have not adopted this approach, for several reasons. One has to do with the very different theological underpinnings of the Roman Catholic understanding of the priesthood and the Reformed/Calvinist understanding of the ministry. Roman Catholics assume that the functions of the priesthood rest on a much deeper, ontological state of *being* a priest. The theology of priesthood is based on the reality of the "state of being" a priest, a "state of being" different from that of those not ordained to the priesthood.[7] This contrasts directly with the Reformed/Calvinist notion of ordination to the *function* of ministry in

the church, not ordination to a special "state of being."
Thus, preparation for the priesthood in the Roman Catholic Church was designed to "shape" or "form" a different
kind (not just different in degree) of clerical reality than
that of the Reformed/Calvinist tradition. This produced a
seminary program which, prior to Vatican II, was more focused on spiritual and moral development than on academic learning. The seminary was primarily a place for
moral and spiritual formation, and only secondarily was it
an academic institution. Since Vatican II there have been
significant changes, and Roman Catholic seminaries have
developed strong academic and field education programs.
But even now, these programs are set within the context of
issues related to formation.[8]

A second reason why Presbyterian seminaries have not
adopted the Roman Catholic approach to spiritual formation involves the difference between the two traditions in
the development of "piety" or "faithfulness." Roman
Catholics assumed that it was within the structured, en-
closed environment of the seminary that candidates for the
priesthood could be subjected to a rigorous spiritual regi-
men that would bring about the spiritual and moral state
desired of the clergy. According to Reformed/Calvinist assumptions, on the other hand, spiritual formation takes
place through growing up and participating in the life of
the church. People (lay and clergy) come to faith and grow
in life in Christ by participating in the ongoing life of the
believing community. While Presbyterian seminaries
have acknowledged the role they play in nurturing the
faith life of students, they have not understood themselves to be the primary place where spiritual formation
of the clergy takes place. Spiritual formation is the task of
the larger Christian community, and the seminary is not
seen as a substitute for participation in the life of the
church. Related to this is the Reformed/Calvinist notion
that individuals' private spiritual lives derive from their
corporate experience within the community of faith.[9] To
Calvin's way of thinking, the church precedes the individual, and it is in the context of the worshiping community,

more than in the private prayer closet, that Christian growth takes place.[10]

A third reason why Presbyterian seminaries have not adopted the Roman Catholic approach to spiritual formation has to do with the ambiguity in the Reformed/Calvinist tradition regarding the relationship between intentional spiritual disciplines or practices and spiritual growth and development. On the one hand, it is affirmed that certain practices and disciplines are important in nurturing one's spirituality. Yet there is a reluctance to draw any *causal* relationship between the disciplines and spiritual growth, because such an understanding might seem to limit the freedom of a sovereign God or to manipulate the movement of the Holy Spirit, which, like the wind, "blows where it wills."[11] Shirley Guthrie puts it this way:

> There is nothing we can do to force the Spirit of God to come to us and give us faith, hope and love. We cannot manipulate [the Spirit] to work according to our schedule and desires. . . . [The Spirit] is free to work when, where and how [the Spirit] chooses. [The Spirit] takes initiative and not we. But that does not mean that we can do anything we please or nothing at all, excusing our lack of faith, our hopelessness or our unloving attitudes by complaining that the Spirit has not chosen to come to us. We have been told who [the Spirit] is, and where and how [the Spirit] is promised. Although we cannot control [the Spirit's] coming and going, we can at least place ourselves in the kind of situation in which we know [the Spirit] accomplishes [the Spirit's] work.[12]

There has been a significant amount of literature in recent years focusing on spiritual formation among seminarians. Since 1972, the Association of Theological Schools has devoted substantial sections of three issues and one full supplement of its journal, *Theological Education,* to this matter.[13] The *Christian Century* focused on it in its 1985 issue on theological education.[14] The Alban Institute published a book in 1986 by Forster Freeman entitled *Readiness for Ministry Through Spiritual Direction.*[15] The World Council of Churches circulated a report called *Spiritual Formation in Theological Education* in 1987.[16] Much of this literature is critical of seminaries and suggests that the schools have failed in their responsibility to prepare students spiritually for the work of ministry. The emphasis falls on the need for seminaries to do more to help students grow in their spiritual lives.[17]

This present study was designed to find out what role, if any, Presbyterian seminaries have actually played in the spiritual development of candidates for ministry during recent decades. Having rejected the Roman Catholic approach, how have Presbyterian seminaries pursued the task of preparing students spiritually for the work of ministry? What are graduates' perceptions of what happened in their lives and on their campuses during seminary years in the area of spiritual development? What was helpful and what was not? What changes in the "spiritual climate" have taken place on seminary campuses over the last forty years?

It became clear early in our study that much confusion surrounds the issue of "spirituality." For some, the term appears nebulous and ill-defined. For others, it covers up loose thinking and seems to encourage people to escape into a subjective and private world, thereby avoiding engagement with the harsh realities of injustice in the world. We are defining spirituality as "having to do with one's relationship with God and with the way that relationship is conceived and expressed."[18] Spiritual formation is understood as "involving all the . . . provisions we may have for nourishing our faith life as members of the body of Christ."[19] Such provisions may be intentional means of attentiveness to grace, such as corporate worship, personal prayer, and journal-keeping, or the unintentional formative events in our lives, such as an encounter with a friend or relationship with a mentor. Thus, a variety of factors can contribute to a person's "spiritual formation."

It also became clear that the current discussion of issues related to spiritual formation in theological education is hampered by lack of empirical data, and that such data were necessary to carry out the purposes of this study. We designed and mailed a questionnaire to selected classes of M.Div. or B.D. graduates of four Presbyterian Church

(U.S.A.) seminaries: San Francisco, Louisville, Princeton, and Columbia.[20] The questionnaires were mailed to graduates in the classes of 1948, 1958, 1968, 1978, and 1988. Questionnaires were sent out to 1,002 individuals, and 510 were returned and analyzed. The purpose of the questionnaire was to ascertain the graduates' perceptions of what happened on their campus in the area of spiritual development.[21] Second, the catalogs of the four seminaries published in the above-mentioned years were examined. The purpose of this research was to discover how the seminaries understood their responsibility for students' spiritual development. Did the seminaries perceive part of their task to be to foster spiritual development among students, and if so, how did they go about it? Our hypothesis was that it would prove quite interesting to compare the stated intentions of the various seminaries in the area of spiritual development with the graduates' perceptions of what actually took place.[22]

Findings

1. Most graduates remember seminary years as a time of significant spiritual growth, but most wish their seminary had been more intentional in helping them grow spiritually.

In light of the above-mentioned literature, which is generally critical of seminaries, we were quite surprised that there was overwhelming agreement among respondents that "my seminary years were a time of significant spiritual growth for me." Eighty-three percent either "tend to agree," "agree," or "strongly agree" with the statement. In the words of some respondents:

> The professors and fellow students . . . helped me to develop the spiritual life already begun in my home, church, military service and college years. I thank God for my seminary. It truly was "the nearest thing to heaven we would ever experience on earth." What a foundation for being Christ's minister in this generally unheavenly world.

Seminary had a significant impact on my spiritual life by opening me to new experiences, avenues, and techniques for connecting with God.

My time in seminary was the most important period of my life.

I was an activist in the '60's initiating a biracial ministerial group in Mississippi. Resources of inspiration and persistence that kept me going were directly related to key individuals in my seminary career. The spirituality formed has served me well through over thirty years of pastoral ministry.

Women agree with the statement "My seminary years were a time of significant spiritual growth for me" a bit more than men (86% to 82%), but by and large the percentage of respondents agreeing is consistent, regardless of the year of graduation, age at graduation, family situation while in seminary, or whether or not the student lived on campus.

One sometimes hears comments that suggest there is an inherent contradiction between academic pursuit and spiritual growth. While not discounting the fact that part of the seminary experience is critical examination of and reflection on one's faith (and the potentially threatening nature of such examination and reflection), the vast majority of respondents rejected the notion that the academic focus of seminary life "got in the way" of their spiritual growth. Eighty-two percent of the respondents either "strongly disagree," "disagree," or "tend to disagree" with the statement "The rational, intellectual study of theology while in seminary impeded my spiritual growth." We did not ask how many would agree with Karl Barth that the study of theology is itself a "spiritual discipline," but a number of respondents spoke of the positive role academic study played in their spiritual growth. In the words of one respondent: "Seminary's model of spirituality consisted of great classes that gave me new visions of what the Christian faith and discipleship are meant to entail."

It is not unusual to hear students complain about the hectic pace and compulsive busyness of seminary life. The 1986 study entitled "A Profile of Contemporary Seminarians"[23] by Larsen and Shopshire found "not enough time to do all the things asked of me" to be the number-one cause of stress among today's seminary students. And in the words of one seminary president, "The most precious commodity on our campus is students' time." In this context, we expected graduates to cite "busyness" as a detriment to the development of regular devotional practices while in seminary. To our surprise, this did not turn out to be so for the majority of respondents. Two thirds (67.7%) either "strongly disagree," "disagree," or "tend to disagree" with the statement "I was too busy in seminary to develop a devotional life or regularly engage in prayer and other spiritual disciplines."

It is very clear, however, that while most respondents perceive themselves to have grown spiritually while in seminary, most would have liked more help from the seminary in this area. Seventy-four percent either "tend to agree," "agree," or "strongly agree" with the statement "I wish my seminary had been more intentional in helping me cultivate patterns for my spiritual growth." Men and women answer about the same on this question, and, again, year of graduation, family situation, and housing situation (on or off campus) while in seminary does not make much difference in the responses.

The issue of the seminary's lack of intentionality in helping students grow spiritually is the area where seminaries were most criticized by respondents. Some indicated they felt their seminary offered no help at all:

> This is the one area of my Christian life development in which I feel that my seminary let me down. The emphasis was almost entirely on intellectual development and on acquiring practical skills for ministry. The assumption seems to have been that if we hadn't already developed an adequate interior spiritual life, we would somehow manage it on our own. The seminary seems to have felt no responsibility in this area.

> My seminary was woefully disinterested in spirituality. . . . Seminary was a school for the mind. No heart. No soul. I learned no model of spirituality in seminary. Isn't that sad?

Others seemed to feel that while their seminary offered limited help in the area of spirituality, they would have preferred a "more intentional and balanced approach" that was not so much "left to the individual":

> [My] era was the civil rights/Vietnam period when corporate worship and personal devotional life were secondary to social justice issues. It would have been helpful to us to have had a more intentional and more balanced approach to spiritual formation.

> The state of a person's spirituality was left to the individual. After having entered parish ministry, I feel this is the one area in which I entered the "workforce" unprepared.

The sense that "a person's spirituality was left up to the individual" was a note sounded again and again in the responses.

2. *Most of the efforts seminaries have made to help students in the area of spiritual development have been outside the formal, required curriculum. Opportunities for attention to spirituality have been available on seminary campuses, but it has been left up to students whether they would participate.*

Seminaries have offered a variety of activities over the years intended to nurture the faith life of students. These have included retreats, workshops, special emphasis weeks, opportunity for spiritual direction, prayer groups, chapel services, courses, opportunities for service, and involvement in activities promoting peace and social justice. Figure 2.1 shows what graduates remember their seminary offering to promote spiritual growth among students. The numbers in each column represent the percent of respondents in a particular graduating class who remember the activity being offered.

Retreats were remembered by a majority of graduates at three of the four seminaries in 1948 and 1958, at none of the seminaries in 1968, at two of the seminaries in 1978, and at all of the seminaries in 1988. In 1948 and 1958, at

Fig. 2.1. What Graduates Remember Their Seminary Offering to Promote Spiritual Growth

Year of Graduation	Retreats	Workshops	Special Weeks	Spiritual Direction	Prayer Groups	Required Chapel	Optional Chapel	Elective Courses	Req'd Courses	Service	Work for Justice
1948	52.2%	20.5%	65.1%	28.9%	65.2%	34.1%	80.5%	65.2%	9.8%	90.0%	42.5%
1958	63.4	32.3	69.3	38.4	58.9	28.0	80.2	75.7	16.3	87.4	49.0
1968	26.9	37.5	48.1	32.1	49.4	19.3	87.1	68.7	7.4	90.4	85.5
1978	52.2	43.8	39.4	27.7	64.9	.9	99.1	65.2	5.3	89.4	86.5
1988	72.4	63.8	34.0	43.0	75.2	.7	98.6	83.7	2.9	95.9	93.2

least one seminary began the year with an all-seminary retreat, and the intention was to "set the tone" for the coming year. A description of the retreat sounds similar to a
Fellowship of Christian Athletes campout:

> At the first meeting of the classes, the previews of courses
> indicate that some hard work is in store, but that in a give and
> take comradeship professors and students are about to take
> off on some high adventures together. In conversation, the
> retreat is often mentioned. Then the first Monday comes.
> Faculty members turn up at seminary in khaki trousers, open
> shirts and sweaters, and with a roll of blankets under arm—
> from which a casting rod may stick out. Food and athletic
> equipment have already been packed in the truck. Presently
> the whole student body and faculty are off to some spot in the
> hills . . . for retreat. On arrival, bunks are spotted for the
> night and after a little exploration the welcome word comes
> from the mess hall that "soup's on." After lunch a senior
> leads devotions. Then follow group games—touch football,
> baseball, volleyball, horseshoes. After dinner, a professor in-
> troduces some vital theme of mature Christian living. The
> discussion which follows is spontaneous, frank, and search-
> ing. New students make the comforting discovery that se-
> niors haven't learned all the answers, that faculty members
> can say, "I don't know," that unity and mutual respect can
> prevail despite varieties of experience and conviction. Next
> day at noon, against a background of vigorous play, intense
> thinking, miscellaneous wisecracks, intimate sharing, and
> high aspirations, retreat comes to its climax in a communion
> service. The luncheon dishes are quietly cleared, the portable
> organ begins to sound forth the strains of gospel hymns, one
> faculty member makes a soul searching talk, reads the memo-
> rable words of institution, and consecrates the elements with
> prayer, and other faculty members distribute them. In silent
> prayer, high resolves are made in the light of a fresh vision of
> the cross. Not all voices are clear as they join in "Blest be the
> tie that binds," but when the benediction is pronounced there
> is a welcome new reality in the words "the peace of God
> which passeth understanding," and a new seminary year has
> begun on the high plain of retreat.[24]

As Figure 2.1 indicates, workshops offered by the seminaries dealing with personal prayer and other matters re-

lated to spirituality have significantly increased over the years. Participation in these workshops by students was optional, and the workshops were not part of the formal seminary curriculum. One interesting note is that while spiritual development workshops have increased over the years, special weeks emphasizing spiritual growth (sometimes derisively referred to by students as "be kind to God week") have decreased in similar proportion.

More 1988 graduates report the opportunity for one-to-one spiritual direction was available to them than did graduates of earlier years. Spiritual direction is a term borrowed from the Roman Catholic tradition, and can be defined as "direction offered in the prayer life of the individual Christian. It is an art which includes helping to discern the movements of the Holy Spirit in our life, assisting in the difficult task of obedience to these movements, and offering support in the crucial life decisions that our faithfulness requires."[25] We did not ask who on the various campuses was offering spiritual direction (faculty members, chaplain, pastor of nearby church, for example). We were simply trying to determine if the opportunity was available to students.

Prayer and faith-sharing groups seem to have been widely offered in 1948, less so in 1958 and even less in 1968, and then increased again in 1978 and 1988. The majority of 1988 graduates at each of the seminaries remember the availability of such groups on their campus. No doubt there were also a number of student-initiated and -led prayer groups through the years.

Only one of the four seminaries involved in our study had a required course on the spiritual life. The course was entitled "The Pastoral Office," and was "a study of the minister's personal conduct, spiritual life and professional habits."[26] It was required at least through 1958, but was dropped as a requirement sometime before 1968.

All the seminaries studied have regularly offered limited numbers of elective courses in the area of prayer and spirituality. Some of these courses, such as one entitled "The Devotional Use of the Bible," were taught in the Bible department. That course focused on the "utilization of the resources of the Bible for individual spiritual enrichment."[27] Others were offered in the theology department. In "The Christian Pattern of Life," attention was given to Bunyan's *Pilgrim's Progress,* and to the "discipline of body, soul and spirit integrated as a whole."[28] A course entitled "Prayer" gave a "historical and theological consideration" to the topic.[29]

In recent years, such courses seemed to take less of a theological and historical approach and were more experiential in nature. A course entitled "Developing Faith for Ministry" was described this way: "In this course you will participate in experiences designed to help you get in touch with the deep spiritual needs of your faith. A variety of retreat forms and uses of spiritual disciplines . . . will be explored. . . . Your own spiritual growth will be an objective to which you will contract to be opened."[30] A 1986–1987 catalog described "Spiritual Formation in Preparation for Ministry" as a course which "provides a setting for spiritual growth. It offers instruction in prayer, provides structured group experience and mutual support, and aims to strengthen ministerial formation."[31]

As Figure 2.1 indicates, a consistently high percentage of respondents remembers "opportunities for service to others" available during seminary years. The percentage of graduates who remember "opportunities to participate in activities designed to promote social justice and peace" dramatically increases over the years, from 42.5% in 1948 to 93.2% in 1988.

3. *Chapel services have been the most consistent and primary means by which Presbyterian seminaries have sought to assist students in their spiritual growth and development. Graduates remember chapel as being helpful, along with the rendering of service to others, courses on prayer and the Christian life, and prayer and faith-sharing groups.*

Responses to the questionnaire indicate that only one of the seminaries required chapel attendance in 1948; chapel attendance at the other three seminaries was not required. Services range from as seldom as twice a week to as often as daily on the seminary campuses. The frequency of the celebration of the Lord's Supper also varies. Faculty and students typically share in the planning and leadership of chapel services. It is clear from the catalogs that the seminaries understand these corporate services of worship to be a primary means of grace which help students and faculty grow spiritually.[32]

In our questionnaire we asked graduates what events, programs, or courses were helpful in nurturing their spiritual growth while in seminary. The composite results are listed in Figure 2.2. The numbers in each column represent the percent of respondents who marked each program as "most helpful," "second most helpful," or "third most helpful" in nurturing their spiritual growth. Chapel services were rated most helpful, showing up in the "top three" on 74.2% of the responses. Judged second most helpful were "opportunities for service to others," which was in the "top three" of 47.8% of the responses. Next were "courses on prayer, the Christian life, classics of Christian devotion, etc.," at 46%, and then "prayer and faith-sharing groups," at 36.7%.

Fig. 2.2. What Graduates Found Helpful in Nurturing Their Spiritual Growth While in Seminary

Program	Most Helpful	Second Most Helpful	Third Most Helpful
Retreats	3.2%	8.2%	7.8%
Workshops	2.5	3.3	1.8
Special Weeks	3.2	8.2	9.1
Spiritual Direction	6.6	6.1	7.3
Prayer Group	14.8	10.8	11.1
Chapel	35.5	22.5	16.2
Courses	15.0	13.8	17.2
Service	11.4	17.4	19.0
Social Justice	8.0	9.6	10.4

Figure 2.3 cross-tabulates year of graduation with the event or program the respondent found most helpful to his or her spiritual growth. In Figure 2.3, the numbers in the columns represent the percent of graduates in that particular year who found the activity most helpful to their spiritual growth. While chapel services were ranked number one each of the five years, the percentage ranking them first dropped steadily (except in 1968) from 45.2% in 1948 to 29.2% in 1988. Prayer groups and courses dropped from 14.3% each in 1948 to 6.8% each in 1968, then went back up in 1988 to 21.5% for prayer groups and 17.7% for courses. On the other hand, service opportunities and involvement in justice issues rose from 4.8% and 2.4% respectively in 1948 to 16.2% and 13.5% in 1968, then dropped back to 9.2% and 10% in 1988.

4. *Concern for spiritual growth of students has become "institutionalized" to a greater degree in recent years, while students in recent years seemed less satisfied with the way their school approached and provided opportunities for spiritual development.*

In our questionnaire we asked graduates who, if anyone, on the seminary campus had "responsibility for planning events, programs, etc., designed to foster students' spiritual growth." The options for response were "faculty member or administrator," "committee made up of faculty and students," "no one," or "don't know." The responses can be seen in Figure 2.4. As the table indicates, over half of the 1988 respondents said either a faculty member, administrator, or committee had responsibility for planning events and programs designed to foster students' spiritual growth. This is a significantly higher percentage than in earlier years.

Yet while seminaries seem to be taking more responsibility at the institutional level for nurturing the faith life of students, this has not made much impact on the students themselves. We noted above that "lack of intentionality" in helping students grow spiritually is the area where seminaries were most criticized by respondents, and this is as true

Fig. 2.3. What Graduates Found Most Helpful to Their Spiritual Growth
Cross-tabulated by Year of Graduation

Year of Graduation	Retreat	Workshop	Special Week	Spiritual Direction	Prayer Group	Chapel	Course	Service	Work for Justice
1948	7.1%	0%	2.4%	9.5%	14.3%	45.2%	14.3%	4.8%	2.4%
1958	3.0	1.0	10.1	5.1	11.1	39.4	19.2	10.1	1.0
1968	2.7	2.7	2.7	8.1	6.8	40.5	6.8	16.2	13.5
1978	4.3	3.2	1.1	5.4	14.0	32.3	14.0	15.1	10.8
1988	1.5	3.8	0	6.9	21.5	29.2	17.7	9.2	10.0

Fig. 2.4. Who Had Responsibility for Fostering Spiritual Development?

Year of Graduation	Faculty or Administrator	Committee	No One	Don't Know
1948	6.4%	19.1%	19.1%	55.3%
1958	9.3	26.9	13.9	50.0
1968	3.5	18.6	19.8	51.8
1978	5.3	38.9	14.2	41.6
1988	17.8	38.4	17.1	26.7

for 1988 graduates as for graduates of earlier years. While the schools seem to be doing more in terms of planning events and programs designed to foster the spiritual life of students, fewer and fewer students in recent years understood "the fostering of spiritual growth" to be one of their seminary's primary purposes, as Figure 2.5 indicates.

Fig. 2.5. Response to the Statement: "My seminary did not understand the fostering of spiritual growth to be one of its primary purposes."

Year of Graduation	Strongly Disagree, Disagree, Tend to Disagree	Tend to Agree, Agree, Strongly Agree
1948	66.7%	33.3%
1958	67.3	32.7
1968	52.5	47.5
1978	45.0	55.0
1988	40.3	59.7

Many of the 1978 and 1988 graduates who did not perceive the fostering of spiritual growth to be one of their seminary's purposes were critical of the school because of this. One respondent who felt this way wrote:

> The seminary I attended struggled between an identity as a graduate school with an emphasis on academic achievement

or a place for persons called to ministry to prepare for service in the church and world. In my opinion there was an overemphasis on intellectual pursuits resulting in a competitive and emotionally barren environment. There seemed to be little spirituality practiced or shared by the faculty and staff. Students were totally on their own when it came to developing a spiritual life.

5. *Spiritual growth and development of seminary students often seems to come as an "indirect result" or "by-product" of other activities. Such activities include participation in field education, rendering acts of service to those in need, engaging in activities promoting peace and social justice, and relationships with professors and other students.*

Seminarians do not participate in field education, serve others, promote peace and justice, or form relationships with professors and other students for the purpose of their own spiritual growth. Yet these aspects of theological education were consistently cited by graduates as being helpful to their spiritual growth while in seminary. Personal relationships with other students and members of the faculty were particularly important. Eighty-two percent of the respondents "strongly agree," "agree," or "tend to agree" with the statement "Personal relationships with other students had a significant and positive impact on my spiritual development while in seminary." In the words of one respondent:

> What made seminary important spiritually to me were the friendships I developed there with peers. This was an exceedingly important and fruitful time in my own personal growth, and I quickly identified it as having a spiritual basis. I found acceptance and understanding among classmates I had never found before.

And another:

> There was a great emphasis made on getting people together in faith sharing/support groups. As a single parent I was running as fast as I could to keep up. Still I found support and nurture and conversation with others in the housing unit I lived in.

Three fourths of the respondents (74.8%) agree with the above statement when the words "particular professors" are substituted for "other students." A number of respondents were appreciative of faculty members:

> One professor brought it all together for me. She opened the door of Jesus Christ on a feeling level and my spiritual growth was off and running. My spiritual journey has been enriching and fulfilling ever since.

> It was helpful to have such accessible professors who also shared their deep love of God's word.

> Most of my professors were models. Their deep spiritual life was most evident and was shared with the students through chapel services, small groups, personal calls to dorm rooms and everyday life.

Spiritual development is not typically stated as a goal of seminary field education programs, but for most respondents it did seem to be a by-product. Seventy-seven percent "tend to agree," "agree," or "strongly agree" with the statement "My participation in field education had a significant and positive impact on my spiritual development while in seminary." By the same token, students do not usually perform acts of service for those in need for the purpose of their own spiritual growth, but it does seem to be an indirect result for many. Eighty-one percent "tend to agree," "agree," or "strongly agree" with the statement "My rendering of specific acts of service to others had a significant and positive impact on my spiritual development while in seminary." The same holds true for worship. The purpose of worship, as Calvin frequently reminded, is to glorify God. Yet, as noted above, respondents rated chapel services as the "most helpful" activity in terms of nurturing their spiritual growth and development while in seminary.

6. *The 1960s was a "watershed" period on seminary campuses as social service and political action gained acceptance as legitimate forms and expressions of spirituality.*

The social activism of the 1960s had a significant effect on patterns of spirituality of seminary students. As Figure

2.3 indicates, 1968 graduates were more likely to cite "service opportunities" and "involvement in justice issues" as "most helpful" to their spiritual growth than graduates of previous or subsequent decades. They were also less likely to cite such activities as retreats or prayer groups as being particularly helpful. Along the same lines, 1968 graduates found congregational worship less significant, as Figure 2.6 indicates. While the majority of respondents are on the "agree" side each of the five years, the percentage drops substantially from 1948 to 1968, and then rises by 1988 to slightly above the 1948 level. This may say more about the relationship between seminary students and the institutional church than it does about spiritual development per se, but it is clear that worship participation in local congregations was less significant for seminarians in the 1960s than it was in the two previous or subsequent decades.

Fig. 2.6. Response to the Statement: "My participation in the worship and life of a local congregation had a significant and positive impact on my spiritual development while in seminary."

Year of Graduation	Strongly Disagree, Disagree, Tend to Disagree	Tend to Agree, Agree, Strongly Agree
1948	26.7%	73.3%
1958	33.9	66.1
1968	43.5	56.5
1978	36.2	63.8
1988	24.2	75.8

Another signal of the change in the "spiritual climate" on seminary campuses is the attitude toward prayer. Figure 2.7 cross-tabulates year of graduation with response to the statement "A predominantly negative ethos toward prayer and personal devotional life was present at my seminary." While the majority of respondents are on the disagree side every year, significantly more graduates felt there was a negative ethos toward prayer and personal devotion in 1968 than had in earlier years.

Fig. 2.7. Response to the Statement: "A predominantly negative ethos toward prayer and personal devotional life was present at my seminary."

Year of Graduation	Strongly Disagree, Disagree, Tend to Disagree	Tend to Agree, Agree, Strongly Agree
1948	91.5%	8.5%
1958	91.5	8.5
1968	74.4	25.6
1978	77.8	22.2
1988	77.2	22.8

Interesting responses were generated by the statement having to do with the relationship of one's participation in activities promoting social justice and peace to spiritual development. Overall, graduates were evenly split between the agree and disagree side in responses to the statement "My participation in activities designed to further the causes of social justice and peace had a significant and positive impact on my spiritual development while in seminary." A clear pattern develops, however, when responses to this statement are cross-tabulated with year of graduation.

Fig. 2.8. Response to the Statement: "My participation in activities designed to further the causes of social justice and peace had a significant and positive impact on my spiritual development while in seminary."

Year of Graduation	Strongly Disagree, Disagree, Tend to Disagree	Tend to Agree, Agree, Strongly Agree
1948	72.5%	27.5%
1958	65.7	34.3
1968	45.2	54.8
1978	48.0	52.0
1988	37.4	62.6

The percent on the agree side is double in 1968 what it was in 1948 (54.8% to 27.5%) and rises to over 62.6% in 1988. This would seem to indicate a growing awareness over the years of the link between justice and spirituality. Students increasingly saw that these are not contradictory, but complementary, aspects of the Christian life. As one respondent put it:

> I would characterize spirituality as "shalom"—shalom in the sense of wholeness and integrity. That is to say, spirituality is to be experienced and lived in every arena of one's life, rather than in some isolated notion of a "devotional life." The devout life was not sneered at or ignored [at my seminary]. Rather, it was presented and seen as one of several arenas in which one's spirituality was to be explored and nurtured. Of equal importance were the academic endeavors of working for justice, the personal endeavors of Christian fellowship with others and the opposite joy of "aloneness" and meditation. In each of these areas and more, spirituality was a front and center issue. One did not study theology or do exegesis simply for credit, but because God spoke to and through these disciplines. One did not get involved in social justice issues because of political leanings, but because of one's relationship to a God who demanded justice. One did not make friendships simply for human needs, but out of the sense that "where two or three are gathered, God is in the midst . . . ." Spirituality was equated with Christian lifestyle. All that one did had to do with one's relationship to God.

7. *Women and men seem to be more similar than different in terms of spiritual development while in seminary.*

While only 17% of the responses to our questionnaire were from women, we did separate the data on the basis of gender to see what similarities and differences there might be in the spiritual development of men and women seminarians. As Figure 2.9 indicates, the responses of men and women were remarkably similar, with one exception, on the question of what was helpful to their spiritual growth while in seminary. Chapel was rated highest by both men and women (albeit higher by men at 76.6% than by women at 63.1%). "Courses on prayer, the Christian life, classics of

Fig. 2.9. Program Most Helpful, Second Most Helpful, and Third Most Helpful to Spiritual Growth

		Retreat	Workshop	Special Week	Spiritual Direction	Prayer Group	Chapel	Course	Service	Justice
M	(1)	3.7%	2.0%	3.7%	5.9%	12.9%	37.4%	14.9%	12.1%	7.6%
A	(2)	8.7	3.5	9.3	6.1	9.9	22.7	14.0	17.4	8.4
L	(3)	7.6	1.3	10.1	7.0	11.4	16.5	16.5	19.9	9.8
E										
TOTAL		20.0	6.8	23.1	19.0	34.2	76.6	45.4	49.4	25.8
F	(1)	1.3%	5.1%	1.3%	10.1%	20.3%	26.6%	16.5%	8.9%	10.1%
E										
M	(2)	5.1	2.6	3.8	5.1	15.4	21.8	12.8	17.9	15.4
A										
L	(3)	9.3	4.0	5.3	8.0	10.7	14.7	20.0	14.7	13.3
E										
TOTAL		15.7	11.7	10.4	23.2	46.4	63.1	49.3	41.5	38.8

Christian devotion, etc." were ranked second by women at 49.3%, while second-ranked for men were "opportunities for service to others," at 49.4%. Third-ranked for women were prayer groups, at 46.4%, while men ranked courses third, at 45.4%. Men and women responded pretty much the same on the helpfulness of spiritual directors, prayer groups, and retreats. Women seemed to find workshops and "activities promoting social justice and peace" more helpful than did men. This difference was also reflected in responses to the statement "My participation in activities designed to further the causes of social justice and peace had a significant and positive impact on my spiritual development while in seminary." Seventy-three percent of the women respondents were on the agree side; only 42% of the men were on the agree side.

8. *There is a close relationship between the devotional practices a person used while in seminary and what she or he engages in now.*

Figure 2.10 shows the percentage of graduates who engaged in a specific devotional practice while in seminary who use it now. With the exception of fasting (for which many lose a taste) and journal-keeping, it is clear that the seminary experience is formative for ministers' spiritual

Fig. 2.10. What percent of graduates who engaged in a devotional practice while in seminary engage in it now?

	Then and Now
Corporate Worship	97.1%
Personal Prayer	97.4
Meditation	93.7
Contemplative Prayer	90.5
Fasting	54.4
Journal-keeping	63.3
Scripture and Other Spiritual Reading	97.1
Service to Others	96.7
Activities Promoting Peace and Social Justice	87.8

practices. While this does not imply that a person cannot develop new ways of conceiving of and expressing her or his spirituality after seminary graduation, the continuity after graduation of devotional practices used while in seminary points toward the importance of developing healthy patterns of spirituality while in seminary. These patterns will serve one well as a foundation for ministry. Responses indicate that those who find ways to meet their spiritual needs while in seminary will continue to do so long after seminary graduation.

Conclusions and Questions

The Reformed/Calvinist assumption that spiritual formation takes place as part of the process of a person's participation in the ongoing life of the church has undergirded the way Presbyterian seminaries have gone about spiritual formation during the last half century. While seminaries have acknowledged their role in nurturing the faith life of students preparing for ministry, they have not understood themselves as the primary place where spiritual formation of the clergy takes place. This is the task of the larger Christian community. Although spirituality is valued and assumed on seminary campuses, concern for spiritual development has not been built into the formal seminary curriculum. Opportunities for students to focus on spiritual development through such activities as chapel services, prayer and faith-sharing groups, retreats, workshops, and a few elective courses have been available. Although most graduates acknowledge that these activities were helpful, most would have preferred a more intentional approach to spiritual development at their seminary. Most graduates do remember seminary years as a time of significant spiritual growth, and cite such "unintentional influences" as relationships with professors and other students, participation in field education, rendering of service to others, and working for peace and justice as particularly important in the growth process.

Is such an approach viable for the present and future? There was a time when students who came to seminary came from homes where traditional forms of piety were a part of everyday life. Life was characterized by regular Bible-reading, family prayers, weekly Sunday school attendance, and Sunday participation in worship. Seminary students were more likely to have been "reared in the faith," and many attended church-related colleges.

Today's seminarians are much more diverse, not only in age, but also in church and educational background, life experiences, and patterns of prayer and devotion. Since World War II, students increasingly have come from homes where traditional forms of piety have not been practiced, and frequently they have had limited nurture in the life of the church. What happens when many of the students have *not* been subject to a long process of community formation through participation in the life of the church? Ought seminaries structure their curriculum (that is, the content of courses and the allocation of time) to address seriously the matter of spiritual formation? If the answer to this question is yes, then it leads to a host of other questions, such as:

What does it mean to teach spirituality?

Can this be done in the classroom?

How can courses in spirituality avoid sliding from the academically acceptable into something that is personally "meaningful" but intellectually indefensible?

Is it appropriate to have quite different expectations of students in such offerings?

If spirituality is not taught in the classroom, then where and how can it be included in the seminarian's experience?[33]

One of the interesting discoveries we made in our research is that there has been an escalating demand in recent years that Presbyterian seminaries take more initiatives in nurturing the faith and piety of students, and that seminaries (to varying degrees) have responded. Yet the striking irony is that the more spiritual nurture has been institutionalized, the more students have judged their theological educations inadequate in terms of spiritual formation. This irony may say something about the way in which the seminaries have institutionalized the programs, or it may point to the counterproductive effect of institutionalizing something like spiritual development. But, at a deeper level, it may reveal the inherent and unequal conflict between education (understood in the classic Enlightenment tradition of critical inquiry) and the nurturing of faith and piety in Presbyterian settings. In other words, the more mainstream Protestant churches and their seminaries attempted to abide by the canons and norms of the academy with its commitment to academic standards and scientific (especially social scientific) methodologies, the more they have relativized the very faith they assumed students would bring to seminary. Since seminaries are attempting to do something more, the problem does not disappear. Instead, the conflict and stress between the ideals become even more acute for students *because* it is highlighted and institutionalized.[34]

One of the most hopeful developments in theological education over the past twenty-five years has been the increased ecumenical dialogue between Protestant and Roman Catholic seminaries. Roman Catholics have strengthened their academic and field education programs during this period, in part due to models they have observed and lessons they have learned from Protestant schools. In a similar way, it is clear that Protestants have much to learn from Roman Catholic seminaries in the area of spiritual formation. Roman Catholics have more experience at it, and while Protestants will not share in the theological rationale and assumptions that gave rise to Roman Catholic spiritual formation, Protestants can benefit from critical dialogue with those who have been at it for such a long time.

For the present, we are left with the humble recognition that the spiritual growth and development that graduates of Presbyterian seminaries report taking place during seminary years is less the result of planned activity and intention on the part of the students and seminaries than it is the gift of God. As such, the history of spiritual formation at Presbyterian seminaries is yet another chapter in the larger story of God's grace.

3

Presbyterian Colleges in Twentieth-Century America

Bradley J. Longfield and
George M. Marsden

In nineteenth-century America Presbyterians were among the leaders in the nation's higher education. By 1860 they had founded over one quarter of the country's 180 church-related colleges and played a leading role in a number of other private and state-supported institutions.[1] Emphasis on higher education often seemed a hallmark of Presbyterianism.[2]

Yet by 1990 the presidents of the sixty-nine Presbyterian schools forming the Association of Presbyterian Colleges and Universities were warning that "the Presbyterian Church could be close to the point where its involvement in higher education might be lost forever." This was not the first such warning, and the presidents were determined, as their predecessors had been, that the church should "reclaim its mission in higher education."[3] Nonetheless, even a most sympathetic observer had to concede "the erosion of Christian identity of mainstream Protestant colleges," while another asked more pointedly whether such colleges were "church-related or Christian."[4]

Two points have to be emphasized in assessing what happened from the heyday of Presbyterian higher education in the nineteenth century to the late twentieth century, when the Presbyterian Church (U.S.A.) seems to show little interest in its colleges, most of which in turn seldom display substantive Christian identity.

First, there was no lost golden age. In the nineteenth century American colleges, whether church-related or not, were small, usually elitist, racist, and sexist, with mediocre standards and strict regulation of students' lives. They included strong Christian components, but many of these were formal, like required daily chapel and required church attendance on Sunday. Such coerced religious attendance had mixed effects on students, as did attempts to regulate their personal lives. Furthermore, though higher education included many Christian components and often was conducted by professing Christians, including clergymen presidents and many clergy on faculties, the actual curriculum was secular in many respects. Most of it was a study of pagan Greek and Latin classics, supplemented largely by smatterings of science, mathematics, and some other practical or humane disciplines. Formal Christianity was taught largely through chapel addresses, Sunday sermons, and Bible study, and in a capstone course in moral philosophy offered by the clergyman-president to the seniors. Even such courses have been seen as mixed blessings, and the price of having substantial theological traditions was often that of having substantial theological controversies.[5]

On the other hand, the recognition that there was no golden age should not obscure the many positive Christian achievements of the early colleges. While it is easy to point out their faults, they did care for the spiritual and intellectual welfare of their students and trained them to serve the larger society.

The second preliminary point to emphasize is that the twentieth-century erosion of Christian identity was almost always an unintended consequence of other adjustments in Presbyterian higher education that seemed either forced by circumstance or justifiable improvements. Sometimes the very steps that seemingly brought schools for a time to an optimal balance between their religious and educational goals would eventually undermine their distinctly Christian emphases. For instance, if Presbyterians were to maintain their leadership in higher education, it seemed obvious that they had to adjust to the best educational standards of the time. As education became more specialized and professionalized, Presbyterian colleges had to keep pace. So they dropped many of the clergy faculty in favor of academically trained laity. Clergy presidents and the courses they taught also largely disappeared in the interest of higher professional, academic standards. Eventually, however, this same trend of conforming to the demands of the dominant academic profession led to the point where faculty hiring had lost almost all reference to religious commitment.

Other changes, especially those taking place during the first two thirds of the twentieth century, were often initially motivated by efforts to improve the quality of Christianity on campus. The most obvious example is the shift from required to voluntary chapel. Also, reflecting mainline Protestant trends of the era, Christian emphases in the curriculum shifted from theology to ethics and from Presbyterian or Christian particularism to inclusivism. In the short run, from the point of view of the dominant theology of the time, these changes were seen as steps toward enhancing the quality of Christianity on campuses. In the long run, when other pressures arose, they undermined the reasons for emphasizing Christian identity at all.

Broader social circumstance often virtually forced some of the changes. Presbyterians, showing a strong instinct at the beginning of the twentieth century to preserve the Christian identity of their institutions, typically maintained smaller liberal arts colleges, rather than universities, where pressures to secularize were much stronger. After mid-century, however, with the vast increase in government support for education, small private colleges struggled to meet the competition. Denominational loyalties and church support for the colleges were also eroding, so colleges had to be more responsive to the market.[6] Among other things, this meant they had to become more sensitive to changing national mores. Changing student expectations already had forced loosening of campus regulations, but after mid-century, and especially with the cultural revolution of the 1960s, such forces seemed almost irresistible for market-driven schools. Similar forces demanded conformity to more secular intellectual and academic trends and standards.

Perhaps the clearest example of the dilemmas of maintaining Christian identity at colleges came in dealing with the question of cultural pluralism. In the era after World War II, mainline Protestant churches helped to take the lead in combating racial and religious prejudice in public life. Given this commitment, Protestant colleges, which were in some ways public as much as private institutions, could hardly retain a distinct Christian identity without seeming to engage in uncivil discrimination on the basis of religion.

The story that follows of the erosion of distinctly Christian emphases and practices at Presbyterian colleges, then, is the story of Christian educators who have had to face serious dilemmas, who made short-term choices, many of which seemed either admirable or inevitable, and who often could neither foresee nor control the long-term consequences of their decisions. Such analysis suggests that if indeed the trends are to be reversed, there will have to be critical rethinking of some of the fundamental assumptions that have carried Presbyterian-related colleges this far.

Though Presbyterians had founded 49 colleges prior to the Civil War, the Presbyterian Church U.S.A. did not establish an ongoing policy of support for its schools until 1883.[7] In that year the General Assembly put the case for Presbyterian higher education:

> Through her doctrines and her form of government the Presbyterian Church is committed to education by something more than the historic past of Protestant Christendom. She "educates by necessity as an instinctive law of self-preservation." Her doctrines are such that they require intelligence for their grasp and retention. They demand and stimulate mental activity. The symmetry and severity of their logical structure make it impossible that they should be widely received or held long in a condition of permanent ignorance.[8]

Self-preservation, however, was not the only reason for the Presbyterians to educate the nation's young. More broadly, the church had a calling to "save the nation from mere godless learning."[9] If Christians did not control higher education, then secular learning would win the day and secularism win America. Christian education, for the sake of the church and the nation, was the task of the church-related college.

In proclaiming the need for Presbyterian higher education, the General Assembly was echoing the purposes determined by the founders of numerous Christian colleges earlier in the century. For example, at the founding of the University of Wooster (now the College of Wooster), related to the Presbyterian Church U.S.A., in 1866, the trustees declared:

> We enter upon the work of establishing the University of Wooster with the single purpose of glorifying God in promoting sanctified education, and thus furthering the interests of the church and its extension over the whole earth.

They continued:

> We will in every way possible strive to imbue all our operations with the spirit of Christianity and bring religious influence and instruction to bear earnestly upon all who may be connected with the institution.[10]

Colleges related to the Presbyterian Church in the U.S. and the United Presbyterian Church were every bit as dedicated to providing distinctively Christian education and promoting the mission of the church.

The means by which these schools accomplished their missions were varied. Key among these means was the selection of evangelical presidents and faculty. Though developing universities in America such as Johns Hopkins, Yale, Harvard, and Stanford had abandoned the tradition of clergy presidents by the early twentieth century, most Presbyterian schools still selected ministers as their leaders. Just as important to the religious tenor of the campus was the selection of Christian faculty. While schools in the

North were generally satisfied with faculty if they held to
the broad tenets of evangelical Christianity, southern Presbyterian colleges, more closely connected with the doctrinally oriented Old School Presbyterian heritage, required
not only that their faculty be Christian but also that their
teaching conform to the standards of the Westminster Confession.[11]

The faculty were encouraged in their faith by boards of
trustees that were predominantly, if not entirely, composed
of Christians. Though colleges had various official ties to
the church, the boards of trustees were frequently elected
by a judicatory of the church. Among the colleges of the
Presbyterian Church in the U.S.A. synods elected or ratified the election of trustees at such schools as Maryville,
Wooster, and Westminster (Missouri).[12] Likewise, at
United Presbyterian schools—such as Muskingum, Illinois
College, Monmouth, and Westminster (Pennsylvania)—
and at many southern Presbyterian colleges—such as
Belhaven College and Presbyterian College (South Carolina)—the governing boards were largely elected or approved by synods or presbyteries.[13]

By the early twentieth century the curriculum at most of
these schools, though influenced by the rise of electives and
increasing stress on vocationalism, still required a strong
dose of religion. The 1910 bulletin of Davidson College an-
nounced that the Bible was taught "over three years of the
curriculum," and went on to declare that "All divergence
from this supreme authority [the Bible] leads to agnosti-
cism and skepticism, if not to an absolute denial of all
moral distinctions."[14] While prior to the turn of the century
most schools required Bible study, this instruction was frequently not included in the formal curriculum. After 1900,
however, many colleges, encouraged by the denominations,
made concerted efforts to create chairs and departments of
Bible.[15] Maryville, for example, established a Bible training
department in 1907, Westminster (Missouri) hired a professor of Bible and philosophy in 1909, and Hastings College endowed a Bible chair in 1918.[16] Under a plan adopted
by the United Presbyterian Church, all their colleges ac-

quired professors of Bible by 1919.[17] While the approach to biblical instruction varied from school to school, the claim of Muskingum College that "we assume the infallibility and inspired nature of the Bible" was probably typical of all Presbyterian schools until World War I.[18]

Though concerned to maintain a Christian witness through the curriculum, Presbyterian colleges in the early part of the century were no less diligent in their oversight of extracurricular activities. Social regulations included the prohibition of alcohol, tobacco, card playing, dancing, and profanity. Moreover, relations between the sexes were strictly controlled. At Grove City College in Pennsylvania, for instance, men and women were segregated during morning devotions, and at Trinity University in Texas the catalog expressly declared, "Students of the opposite sex are strictly forbidden all communication with each other of any kind."[19] Enforcing these regulations was, of course, a major responsibility of the faculty.

Chief among the events that cultivated the Christian faith of the students was daily chapel. At the turn of the century virtually all Presbyterian schools required their students to attend chapel during the week and worship on the Sabbath. Thus at Trinity University and Maryville College students were expected to attend morning chapel, Sunday school, and Sunday worship as regularly as they attended their daily classes.[20]

Presidents and faculty worried not simply about the outward appearance of student piety but also about the spiritual health of their charges. At Tusculum College, President Gray privately classified the students as "Not Christians," "Christians, but not Church Members," and "Members of Church but not Christians," and in 1913 reported to the board of trustees that "During the special meetings [revivals] held in February there were 44 conversions, and for the most part they were genuine."[21] Likewise, the 1910 catalog of Wooster boasted that "More than ninety per cent of the students are Christians. Gracious revivals have been experienced, and the religious life is constantly stimulated by earnest work on the part of the Christian Associations."[22]

In the wake of World War I, the orthodox doctrine, Victorian mores, and traditional piety that had governed most Presbyterian colleges North and South came under attack. In the Presbyterian Church in the U.S.A. modernists like Henry Sloane Coffin took the lead in questioning traditional church positions on biblical interpretation, doctrine, and confessional subscription. The General Assembly of the church, which had repeatedly affirmed that acceptance of biblical inerrancy, the virgin birth of Christ, his substitutionary atonement, bodily resurrection, and miracle-working power were essential for ordination, decided in 1927 that it had no authority to make such doctrinal pronouncements. This decision signaled, among other things, a growing tolerance in the church and its colleges for liberal theology and an increasing acceptance of the assumptions of historical criticism.[23]

In addition to these changes, the church, having restructured its administrative boards, rewrote its requirements for church-related schools and determined that its colleges should maintain:

> 1. The professors and instructors [as] professing Christians and members of some evangelical church.
> 2. Teaching of the Bible organized into the regular curriculum with a professor ranking as a faculty member.
> 3. Regular services of public worship in which student attendance and faculty participation are expected.
> 4. Positive Christian point of view in the teaching of all subjects laid down in the curriculum.
> 5. The development and culture of Christian character as the supreme end of all academic influences.[24]

Notably, here, as had always been the case, the church refused to set up any specific doctrinal requirements for faculty at its schools, choosing instead to rely on the broad consensus of evangelical Protestantism to keep its schools Christian. But that consensus, as the fundamentalist-modernist controversy demonstrated, had been unraveling for years. For the church to require that all faculty be members of an evangelical church was becoming less and less a guarantee of religious orthodoxy or faculty homogeneity.

The effect of the growing split between conservatives and liberals on college life was shown perhaps nowhere more clearly than at Muskingum College, a United Presbyterian (UPCNA) school. Despite the efforts of the trustees of Muskingum to "reaffirm the position of Muskingum College in the matters of the fundamentals of the faith," controversy erupted in the late 1920s. One angered conservative wrote the president of the college, "It is bad enough to have a modernist in the chair of Biology but it is much more serious to have one in the Bible chair."[25] This was apparently a reference to G. Reid Johnson, a theological liberal who held a Ph.D. from Edinburgh and joined the faculty of Muskingum in 1922. Because of severe differences between Johnson and his conservative colleague Hugh Kelsey, President J. Knox Montgomery divided the Bible department into the Department of the English Bible and the Department of Religion in 1927.[26]

That these theological tensions were manifested not just in the Department of the Bible but throughout the faculty is suggested by the fact that a committee to draw up a confession of faith for faculty subscription was never able to complete its task. Indeed, in 1927, President Montgomery conceded that despite his efforts to maintain an orthodox faculty, it was not easy "to gather together some sixty men and women of scholarship, initiative, and ability whose ideas accord altogether with those we seek to realize at Muskingum."[27]

While Presbyterian colleges in the North were drifting gradually to the left by the 1920s, southern Presbyterians maintained a stricter orthodoxy at their schools. According to regulations established by the General Assemblies of 1914–1916, it was required of southern Presbyterian colleges that: (1) two thirds of the members of the boards of trustees be elected, nominated, or ratified by some church court; (2) the college president be a member of the Presbyterian Church in the U.S.; (3) faculty be "members of some evangelical Church, a majority being members of some Presbyterian Church"; (4) two years of biblical instruction be a graduation requirement; and (5) all teaching be in conformity with the doctrines of the Presbyterian Church in the U.S.[28]

Davidson College, one of the foremost schools of the southern Presbyterian church, maintained these standards by insisting that its faculty affirm the same vows required for elders and ministers in the church. In the 1920s new faculty were therefore required to answer publicly the following questions in the affirmative:

> a) Do you sincerely believe the old and new testament[s] to be the Word of God, the only infallible rule of faith and practice?
> b) Do you sincerely receive and adopt the confession of faith of the Presbyterian Church in the United States as faithfully exhibiting the doctrines taught in the Holy Scriptures?
> c) Do you solemnly engage not to teach anything that is opposed to any doctrine in the confession of faith; nor to oppose any fundamental principle of Presbyterian Church Government while you continue as a professor or teacher in this institution?
> d) Do you solemnly promise to be faithful in the discharge of your duties as a professor in this institution?[29]

By making such vows public events Davidson and other schools, such as Austin College in Texas, which adopted a similar discipline ensured that professors would understand that their faith was no strictly personal matter but of profound significance to the college and the church.[30] Faculty were engaged not simply to teach but to join faith and learning in the instruction of their charges.

Despite such efforts to maintain the orthodoxy of the southern colleges, and despite the conservatism of the South in general, controversy reared its head at Davidson in the 1930s. In 1934 Professor Kenneth J. Foreman was investigated for allegedly liberal statements he made in various published articles. Foreman had, for example, denied that the Creation narratives precluded an acceptance of evolutionary theory and maintained that the Presbyterian Church had "exaggerated man's present evil tendencies."[31] While Foreman's theology was influenced by historicist thinking, the Davidson trustees found that the professor did "not seem to be seriously out of harmony with the fundamentals of our standards."[32] The incident, while coming to a peaceful resolution, demonstrated that not even the South was insulated from the intellectual currents that had almost split the Presbyterian Church U.S.A. in 1925. Nonetheless, a survey of twenty-four southern Presbyterian colleges and junior colleges in 1941 concluded that these institutions "may take justifiable pride in the effectiveness of their religious emphasis." Significant numbers of students named Bible courses, faculty influences, and campus religious programs as contributing positively to the development of their religious lives.[33]

In the North signs of change were more often apparent in the interwar era. While regulations at Belhaven College in Mississippi still required students to attend Sunday worship and Sunday school in 1931, Waynesburg College in Pennsylvania, by the 1920s, only expected, but did not require, its students to participate in Sunday worship.[34] At Davis and Elkins in West Virginia, enforcement of daily chapel became more and more difficult in the 1920s, and the faculty regularly wrestled with means to encourage greater cooperation from the students.[35] Moreover, many schools, like Wooster, experienced a cooling of the religious ardor that had earlier characterized its students.[36] Though the most radical aspects of the moral revolution of the 1920s never made it to Presbyterian campuses, the cultural currents of post–World War I America did carry these schools away from their evangelical roots.

By the late 1930s the traditional orthodoxy that had undergirded most church colleges at the turn of the century had been superseded, at least north of the Mason-Dixon line, by liberalism. Writing in the 1940s, Merrimon Cuninggim celebrated the victory of liberal theology at denominational colleges:

> Such manifestations of a sectarian spirit are happily uncommon in the college picture today. Its frequent companion, fundamentalism, is still a problem in many of the churches across the land, and thus a factor which has to be taken into account in college programs of instruction in reli-

gion. But the colleges themselves have passed beyond such battles. . . . For sectarianism particularly, the trend has been strongly toward a more ecumenical and liberal point of view.[37]

Inasmuch as sectarianism, for Cuninggim, was roughly equivalent to concern for traditional doctrine, his evaluation is correct; by 1940 liberal theology dominated most northern mainline denominational schools. Thus Monmouth College, a United Presbyterian school, could offer a course on Jesus described as "A study of the life, character, and teachings of the greatest man that ever lived," and a professor at Park College, a PCUSA school in Missouri, could argue that Christians must be "ready to drop outmoded formulations of faith for more relevant formulations."[38] In an effort to maintain relevance and respectability in a world increasingly dominated by purely naturalistic thought, administrators and faculty of church-related schools accommodated their theological attitudes to the tenets of the day and thereby weakened the colleges' distinctiveness as specifically Christian institutions.

In the altered theological climate of the 1930s and 1940s the church was moved to redefine its relationship to the colleges. In 1943 the Presbyterian Church in the U.S.A., aided by the presidents of its affiliated colleges, dropped its requirement for mandatory worship but still required that faculty be "active members in good standing of some evangelical Christian Church" and that biblical studies be required for graduation.[39] The southern Presbyterian church, less influenced by liberalism, still required that two thirds of college trustees be elected by a church judicatory, the president be a member of the PCUS, faculty be "active members of an evangelical church, a majority being Presbyterian," and biblical studies be a graduation requirement. Significantly, the southern church, in 1947, dropped its stipulation that all teaching at its colleges conform to the standards of the Westminster Confession.[40] Though southern and northern schools were responding to theological and educational trends at different rates, both were becoming more theologically diverse.

The growing theological pluralism of the colleges led, by the 1940s, to an identity crisis among church-related schools. A statement issued by the Commission of Executive Secretaries of Church Boards of Education in 1941 noted that "there is a widespread conviction that in these disturbed and crucial times Church-related colleges must re-discover their distinctive and extraordinary functions as *Christian* institutions," and in 1944 the president of the Council of Church Boards of Education admitted that "there has been too much of a fade-out or a black-out of Christ on the campus of many a church-established college."[41] In 1942, Kenneth I. Brown, president of Denison University, acknowledged one key reason for this problem. At a national meeting of leaders of church-related colleges he noted that while many fundamentalist schools had not succumbed to the "dogmas of education," those in "the stream of liberal Christianity" (in which he placed himself and many of his listeners) had "sometimes welcomed the modern for the sake of newness" and "sometimes sacrificed great religious truths and experiences when they failed to conform easily and neatly with the assumption[s] of modern education."[42] Just as theological liberals adapted their faith to the dominant ideas of the day, frequently, for good reasons, they adjusted their educational assumptions to the ruling ideas of the university.

As secular research universities came to dominate the academic world in the twentieth century, church-related schools, determined to maintain the respect of the academic community, adopted many of the values of the university as their own. A stress on academic specialization, professionalization, research, and academic excellence, judged by university standards, increasingly determined the practices and policies of colleges related to mainline churches.[43] This is not to say that leaders of church colleges wanted to abandon their religious responsibility. President Lowry of Wooster, for one, in an address to the college students in the mid-1940s, declared, "You must not resent it if Wooster wants you to be a Christian and to accept the great fundamentals of the Christian faith. Any place once touched by Christianity must feel that way; otherwise, it would be a complete fake."[44]

Lowry, in fact, took the lead in calling for Christians to provide an alternative to the increasingly secular and government-dominated higher education of the day. In *The Mind's Adventure*, sponsored by the Board of Christian Education of the Presbyterian Church in the U.S.A., Lowry made a ringing call for Presbyterians to maintain and build a distinctive educational alternative to secular education.[45] Despite some enthusiasm at the time for such sentiments, in the years immediately after World War II Presbyterian laity seem seldom to have caught the vision, and competition with inexpensive government-funded schools was forcing colleges to conform to what the public wanted, which was largely to be like everyone else.[46]

Christianity was, by the 1950s, fighting a losing battle on the campuses of most church-related colleges. Despite rhetoric such as Lowry's, Christian schools were adopting the strategy of accommodation to the prevailing cultural currents rather than maintaining a strong Christian identity. A church committee to study Presbyterian-related colleges thus reported in 1952 that "in practice, church-related institutions seem to follow largely the patterns and policies of other colleges and universities which make no claim to be Christian. They reflect to a large degree the secular influences of our society."[47] John Dillenberger, then associate professor of religion at Columbia University, essentially agreed when he allowed that "church-related colleges as well as independent and state schools have become the victims of this process [secularization]. It is not unusual to find a church-related school in which religious dimensions have evaporated more than in the non-church school."[48] Though college presidents and catalogs continued to insist on the Christian nature of church-related schools, their statements reflected more hope than reality.

Indeed, in the 1950s some leading thinkers in the church began questioning the feasibility of Christian colleges. "I find it necessary in the name of Christianity," John Dillenberger argued, "to doubt that there could be or should be a Christian college or university unless circumscribed by more limitations than most Christians are willing to give. . . . In short, there can only be a college which is Christian if it is not too narrowly Christian."[49] Likewise Robert McAfee Brown, then professor of theology at Union Seminary in New York, argued in 1958:

> There are no final answers as to how a Church-related college is to conduct itself, there are no final criteria or standards by means of which we judge it to be Christian or less than Christian. One can sympathize with the fact that Boards of Christian Education, Church executives, individuals responsible to ecclesiastical authorities, and all the rest must have certain standards of performance by which they measure the work of the institutions under their control. But let them, and us, always remember that any external criteria would be ridiculous if made too absolute and dangerous if taken too seriously.[50]

Brown worried that an all-Christian faculty would result in an anemic faith, unfortified by the give-and-take of genuine dissent. As such, he claimed, unless the Christian college "has an open policy about hiring on the basis of academic qualifications rather than piety," then the school is neither Christian nor a college.[51] These ideas, while perhaps not widely held in the 1950s, would, by the 1960s, come to dominate discussions about the nature of church-related higher education.

Alterations in the social attitudes of the students in the 1950s and 1960s mirrored the changes in educational theory among Christian educators. Traditional regulations of student life came under growing fire from the increasingly cosmopolitan student body of the post–World War II age.[52] These trends culminated in the 1960s when, in the wake of the moral revolution and campus turmoil of the era, Presbyterian colleges virtually eliminated all behavioral regulations that set them apart from other schools. At college after college, rules regulating the use of alcohol, social life, smoking, and dress were abolished or weakened in the face of student and faculty protest.[53]

While colleges responded to student appeals for greater freedom and responsibility in social life, they also, in response to increasing pressure from students and faculty, and frequently in an effort to improve the quality of spiritual life on campus, ended their rites of communal piety. At Davidson the students staged a chapel walkout in 1961, at Westminster (Pennsylvania) students would study, play cards, or talk during worship, and at Illinois College the undergraduates stood up and sat down at the wrong time to register their opposition.[54] Under such conditions colleges tried to maintain their religious commitments while accommodating the demands of their clientele. Schools cut the number of required chapels, substituted convocations for chapel, and eventually did away with mandatory assemblies altogether. By the early 1970s Wooster, Illinois, Maryville, Westminster (Pennsylvania), Davidson, Southwestern at Memphis, and Westminster (Utah) had all abolished mandatory worship.[55]

The elimination of moral and religious regulations was, however, but a symptom of the deeper change that overtook the colleges in the 1960s. As Leonard Sweet has argued, the 1960s proved to be a decade of crisis for mainline Protestantism. Faced with the reality of a starkly secular culture and heir to a liberal theological tradition which sought to accommodate Christianity to the intellectual currents of the age, mainline churches—and their colleges—abandoned significant aspects of their traditional Christian identity. As Sweet notes:

> Old-line religion widely assumed that resisting the forces of secularization was like standing up to a steamroller. Since progress dictated that people become completely secular, this reasoning went, one must minister to them in secular ways. . . . Thus being secular was not a way of acknowledging defeat but a way of being authentically Christian in a new age. Churches willingly relinquished their creeds, rituals, pieties, and beliefs to accommodate new social attitudes. And many Christians began to downplay the Christian label and made being "truly human" and being a Christian the same thing.[56]

This attitude, combined with the ever-increasing concern for academic excellence judged by secular standards, finished off much of the vestigial Christianity that influenced many church-related schools.

The church, desiring to remain abreast of changes in the culture, did little to halt the secularization of its schools and, in some cases, aided in this move away from providing distinctively Christian higher education. In 1961 the General Assembly of the United Presbyterian Church in the U.S.A. adopted a major study on "The Church and Higher Education," and in 1963 approved a new set of guidelines for its colleges based largely on this report. These documents significantly altered the 1943 standards, thus setting the stage for the changes of the coming decade.[57]

According to the 1963 guidelines, the church-related school was to "seek to be a learning community which in word and act will provide for intellectual advancement and religious growth, and . . . undertake to carry out the ethical implications of the faith it represents." As such, faculty, rather than being "active members of some evangelical Christian Church" as required in 1943, were to be "dedicated to [the college's] declared institutional purpose and . . . faithfully serve the primary objective of academic excellence in a community which encourages true piety with integrity of thought and character." Instead of mandating a course in Bible, the church more vaguely required that each student be given "a mature classroom encounter with the Judaic-Christian heritage." Finally, the schools were to seek accreditation by a regional association as a "minimum indication" of academic quality.[58]

The change in faith requirements for faculty hiring, and the eventual abandonment of similar requirements by southern colleges, had important ramifications for the future course of Presbyterian-related colleges. Until the 1960s the insistence of the churches that the faculty of their colleges be members of evangelical churches at least preserved the appearance of a Christian community and, at best, actually resulted in distinctly Christian higher education. But, as noted above, by the 1950s and 1960s these requirements were coming under attack from some leading Christian thinkers. Such constraints, many believed, were anachronistic and even unchristian in a pluralistic age. As such these requirements were rejected in the North by the 1960s and in the South by the 1980s.[59]

The change in attitude toward concern for the beliefs of faculty members is demonstrated nowhere more clearly than in the history of Davidson College from 1960 to 1977. Because Davidson originally had strict faith requirements for faculty and because its change in policy was well documented, its story shows, in bold relief, what happened in a quieter way at most Presbyterian schools. In 1960 all faculty at Davidson had to be members of "some evangelical church" and, upon receipt of tenure, were required publicly to affirm, among other things, Jesus Christ as Lord and Savior, the "fundamental teachings of evangelical Christianity," and the Bible as the "only infallible rule of faith and practice."[60] In response to faculty claims that the tenure oaths hurt the college in its attempt to hire "top-notch faculty," the trustees, in 1965, abolished the public vows while directing the administration to seek "as permanent members of its faculty only those who, in addition to their academic qualifications, are committed to the Christian faith."[61]

In 1971, in response to yet further pressure from faculty, students, and alumni, the trustees again changed religious requirements for faculty, this time requiring that faculty "uphold and seek to increase [the college's] effectiveness as an institution of Christian learning" while also maintaining that all tenured faculty be active members of a Christian church.[62] This move failed to pacify faculty opposition to any religious requirement at all, however, and in a statement in 1973 the faculty charged that the tenure requirement was "likely to inhibit the recruitment of the best faculty and student body that could be obtained by suggesting that Davidson lacks intellectual freedom and diversity of opinion."[63] In response, the trustees, in 1975, moved to further loosen the religious requirements for faculty. While instructing the president to seek out Christian men and women for the administration and faculty, the trustees allowed that "in view of the fact that the Christian community has always had a place for the reverent seeker, the trustees may, in special circumstances, grant tenure to a person who respects the Christian tradition without commitment to all its tenets."[64]

The culmination of this series of changes came in 1977 when Davidson offered Dr. Ronald Linden, a Jew, a position as a professor in the political science department with the standard stipulation that faculty were expected "to uphold and seek to increase the college's effectiveness as a church-related college" and a reminder of the college's tenure policy. Linden accepted the job offer but condemned the college's hiring and promotion policies as "morally repugnant, socially anachronistic, and scholastically unwise." As such, he asserted, "I will strongly support any movement to eliminate such laws and practices."[65]

The president of Davidson, Samuel R. Spencer, took this response, upon legal counsel's advice, to mean that Linden, in fact, had turned down the position, and Spencer thus rescinded the offer. Immediately students and faculty erupted in a storm of protest. At a public meeting opposing the tenure policy of the college Dr. John Kello lamented:

> We are not being compared right now to Dartmouth et al., but to Bob Jones and to Oral Roberts. . . . The significance is clear. Many of our academic colleagues, regardless of their own religious convictions, are coming to view Davidson as a narrow-minded, anachronistic institution more interested in restrictive religious orthodoxy . . . than in academic freedom and freedom of speech and the pursuit of truths.[66]

Many students tended to agree. Davidson, because of its religious requirements, was being made a laughingstock. The choice, as many viewed it, was between religious criteria for faculty and academic integrity.

In response to the uproar, which was reported not only in the local press but in national papers such as the *New York Times* and the *Washington Post*, the trustees abolished all religious requirements for tenure.[67] Henceforth the president was to "seek out and secure as officers and faculty members non-Christian persons who profess a genuine spirituality, who can work with respect for the Christian tradition even if they cannot conscientiously join it, and who can conscientiously support the purpose of the college as set forth in the Davidson College Constitution."[68] Commenting on the trustees' action, one member of the trustees remarked, "I don't favor secularization. . . . It is my hope and prayer that the action we've taken won't have that result."[69]

No incident illustrates better the dilemmas of attempting to maintain a Christian identity in the modern world. In a pluralistic society, tolerance of others is an important virtue in public life. Since the days of the civil rights struggles of the 1950s and 1960s, mainline Protestant denominations had emphasized this moral imperative. Given this commitment, it appeared inconsistent to limit positions at one of the church's prestige institutions to members of a certain religious tradition. Moreover, maintaining such barriers stigmatized the institution in the academic world. On the other hand, once hiring is entirely open, virtually blind to religious considerations, then it seems only a matter of time until the majority of the faculty will be more loyal to their profession than to the institution and will vote to drop any residual loyalties to the institution's religious heritage.

The changes at Davidson, while more dramatic and better documented than developments at other Presbyterian schools, seem to be representative of the changes in faculty hiring that have occurred at most Presbyterian schools in the last thirty years. Usually with sincere theological justification, and almost always in the pursuit of academic excellence and academic freedom, the leaders of church-related colleges moved away from Christian commitment as a criterion for faculty hiring. As a result, fewer and fewer faculty approach their teaching and committee work with a Christian perspective, and colleges have drifted ever closer to their secular counterparts in mission and function. Though not all Presbyterian schools have followed this path, the overwhelming tendency has been toward a weakening of the impact of Christianity on the college campus.

The predominantly Black colleges now related to the Presbyterian Church (U.S.A.) have apparently followed the same path as most of the predominantly white schools in the course of the twentieth century. For example, Johnson C. Smith University, founded by the Presbyterian Church in the U.S.A. in 1867 to prepare "teachers, catechists, and ministers for the religious education of the colored race," had, by the 1980s, largely abandoned such specifically Christian goals.[70] At the turn of the century the Christian character of the school was clearly reflected in mandatory daily chapel and required courses in English Bible during all four years of study.[71] By the 1980s, however, worship was a purely voluntary activity, and there was no university-wide requirement in religion. Indeed, by the late 1980s, though some religion courses were still offered, the religion major had been dropped.[72] Though the predominantly Black schools were heirs to a cultural history different from their mostly white counterparts, the trends of secularization moved both types of colleges away from their traditional Christian roots.

By the late 1960s the United Presbyterian Church in the U.S.A. decided to renounce control of its colleges. The 1968 General Assembly, believing that the church-college relationship should be maintained by autonomous partners, recommended that all synods and presbyteries divest themselves of control of church-related colleges and form covenants with the schools. No one, apparently, dissented.[73] Moreover, new guidelines for church-related schools developed in 1973 lacked practically any criteria that were distinctively Christian. Henceforth church-related colleges were to stress "human values," offer courses in religious studies, and "support the struggle for full recognition of all persons as children of God." While the church, this statement declared, would "regard the colleges and universities as independent corporate institutions which aid in extending the outreach of the church," it insisted that "the colleges and universities are not under the control of the church."[74]

Though a 1980 study of UPCUSA-related colleges seemed to suggest that the church had perhaps gone too far in abandoning Christian criteria for its colleges, the General Assembly, in 1981, chose not to set requirements for Presbyterian-related schools but instead outlined several recommendations for the colleges. Church-related schools, the report declared, should strive for "academic integrity," assist in the development of "human potential," offer courses in religious studies, demonstrate a "commitment to Christian witness in the academic community," and "be sensitive" to the mission concerns of the denomination.[75] While some of these recommendations apparently sought to reverse the trend of secularization in the colleges, their nonbinding character gave them limited power to accomplish this goal.

The southern church, though formerly more conservative in its requirements for its colleges, had, by the 1980s, pursued the same path as its sibling denomination. In a document adopted by the General Assembly in 1982 entitled *Faith, Knowledge, and the Future*, the Assembly set no distinctly Christian requirements for college faculty, students, or administrators other than recommending that synods and colleges form covenants and that colleges "be encouraged to consider the implications for their mission of the Mission Directives of the Presbyterian Church in the United States."[76] Like the UPCUSA, southern Presbyterians had come to the conviction that the synod, not the General Assembly, should be the body to determine the terms of relationship between church and college.

The history of Presbyterian schools in the twentieth century is typical of the development of most mainline-church colleges in the past ninety years. These schools, founded, in large part, to nurture ministerial candidates and educate the Christian laity, now base decisions primarily on principles much like those of their secular counterparts. A study of Episcopal schools in 1969 concluded that the church relationship was essentially historical and that it "appears to have little impact on the everyday life of students on almost all of the campuses."[77] Likewise, a 1975 study by the Disciples of Christ found that the church and its colleges had an obscure relationship, and a 1976 evaluation of

United Church of Christ schools discovered that the schools were linked more by common humanistic values than by any distinctly Christian traits.[78]

While there are, of course, exceptions to this trend, it appears that most colleges related to mainline churches have lost much of their distinctively Christian character in the course of the twentieth century. Though most church-related schools provide an ethos open to spiritual ideals and constructive humanitarian concerns, they now rarely seek to unite Christian faith and learning in any explicit way. Given such a reality, it is no surprise that mainline Protestantism finds itself struggling to find its identity and role in the modern world. With few scholarly Christian academies attempting to address issues and ideas from a distinctly Christian perspective, and with ever fewer laity educated at distinctively Christian colleges and well versed in theology, the churches are suffering from weakened intellectual foundations and a blurred identity.

If such results were largely unintended, it is worth reflecting on how these changes came about. Many of the factors involved, such as professionalization, specialization, new intellectual currents, cultural pluralism, the rise of government-funded education, and changing cultural values and mores, were largely external to Presbyterianism. On the other hand, one feature of mainline Presbyterianism in America, the long-standing assumption that Presbyterianism would be part of the American cultural establishment, helps account for much of the response to such pressures.

From the early days of the republic, Presbyterians typically assumed that they, in alliance with other Protestants, would play a major role in shaping American culture. The founding of Presbyterian colleges was a major manifestation of this assumption, since colleges could train the nation's elite, thereby Christianizing the nation.[79] The broad features of this outlook continued at least through the World War I era, when a Presbyterian former college president, Woodrow Wilson, brought Christian idealism to the task of building a humane democracy that would be a model for the world.[80]

Already in Wilson's time, and increasingly during the rest of the twentieth century, it was apparent that the distinctly Christian dimensions of such laudable civilization building were problematic. In a pluralistic world such activity looked too much like cultural imperialism. Moreover, if a central feature of the democratic ideal was the equality of all persons, it was awkward to assert the superior wisdom of one group simply because of their religious heritage. Civilization building could continue, but explicit Christian reference would have to be toned down or abandoned.

Presbyterians, who were well represented among the nation's cultural elite, were not likely to see themselves as living in sharp tension with the mainstream developments of such a pluralistic culture. Even though they might have to drop some of their traditional theological concerns and emphasize social and moral values that persons of many traditions might share, they could promote these high ideals while retaining much of their traditional cultural influence. Most importantly for our analysis, they could continue to assume that there should be no essential tension between their Christianity and the best in American and Western cultural values. Liberal theology, in fact, emphasized the value of adjusting Christianity to the insights of modernity.

As long as something like a Protestant, or at least a Judeo-Christian, consensus played a strong role in American life, mainline Presbyterian colleges could bridge the gap between being Christian and being public institutions. It was easy enough to keep one foot in each camp, since the two had never been regarded as far apart. By the 1950s, this Judeo-Christian American way of life had often become rather bland, as Will Herberg pointed out in *Protestant, Catholic, Jew*, but at least it did not demand any sharp separation between respectable Christianity and respectable educated Americanism.[81]

In the crucial area of faculty hiring, for instance, it was still possible to rely on informal criteria and networks that would yield faculties largely sympathetic to the broad goals of church-related colleges. Intellectual positions that might be in conflict with basic Christian teaching were rarely seen as problems as long as there was not outright hostility toward the mainline churches or their moral values.

By the 1970s, however, the situation had changed drastically. Popular mores had moved far away from traditional Christian standards, and it was no longer viable to think of Western intellectual life as broadly Christian. Presbyterian colleges, however, remained firmly committed to their long heritage of maintaining cordial relations with dominant cultural trends. Faced with financial limitations, the need to broaden their base of student recruitment, and their desire to keep up with secular schools, they were not likely to change course and reassert a distinct Christian identity that would mark them as being outside the mainstream. Though keeping in touch with the cultural mainstream had always been an important part of the Presbyterian mission to America, by the late twentieth century the mainstream had diverged so far from the Presbyterian heritage that the strategy had lost its original function. Presbyterians were still serving the nation by providing it with some respectable schools, but no longer did this service, other than being a good in itself, have a clear relationship to the distinctive goals of the church.

In 1935 H. Richard Niebuhr had warned that "if the church has no other plan of salvation . . . than one of deliverance by force, education, idealism or planned economy, it really has no existence as a church and needs to resolve itself into a political party or a school."[82] By the latter half of the twentieth century most mainline Protestant church schools had resolved themselves into being simply schools.

Niebuhr's implicit challenge is still valid today, and perhaps more appropriate than ever. Twentieth-century mainline Presbyterians, assuming that they were part of the cultural establishment, have seldom seen American culture as a threat and so have trusted in education. Their colleges and universities, serving the public, have seldom effectively challenged the idols of mainstream liberal culture in ways that would offend potential constituencies or dominant academic opinion. Ironically, this course has resulted in the loss of a distinct identity, which in turn raises the question of the rationale for having church-related colleges at all.

Presbyterian schools differ widely as to how far they have traveled along the path here described. Many recognizably Christian aspects of their traditions remain, and there are some signs of increased interest in strengthening the Christian presence on campuses and in rethinking the educational philosophy that should guide church-related schools.[83] Given the long-term trends and attitudes, the challenges are formidable. Reassessment and renewal are certainly in order. Since church-related colleges depend on supporting constituencies, however, true renewal would have to arise more broadly in the church itself and would have to be based on a reassessment of where Presbyterians ought to stand in relation to American culture in the post-Christian era.

Fig. 3.1. Geographic Distribution of Presbyterian-Related Colleges and Universities, Showing Number in Each State

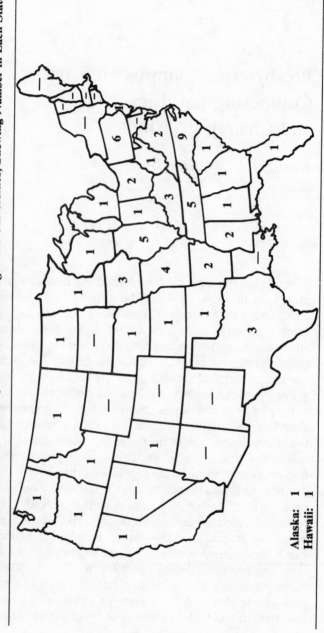

Alaska: 1
Hawaii: 1

4

Presbyterian Campus Ministries: Competing Loyalties and Changing Visions

Ronald C. White, Jr.

Presbyterians supported more than five hundred campus ministries in 1950. By 1989 the number had declined to 253.[1] Today there are calls from many quarters to rethink campus ministry as we have known it. The suggestions are wide-ranging and often in strong disagreement with one another. Before we can talk about the future, however, we need to understand something of the past.[2]

Presbyterian campus ministry is a broad stream with a variety of both tributaries and branches. As a child of the churches, the original impetus for campus ministry in the twentieth century came from denominational attempts to follow the church's students to the nation's colleges and universities. In ministering to students, Presbyterian campus pastors found themselves in the midst of a burgeoning new world of higher education. Its ethos served to transform the original conception of the task. Attempting to serve two institutions, the church and higher education, Presbyterian campus ministry came to have divided loyalties. The campus minister, sent by the church, often felt more at home in the university. Feeling called to relate to two worlds that had been growing apart, many campus ministers in recent decades have seen themselves in a ministry little understood by congregations, presbyteries, or the national church.

The purpose of this essay is fourfold. First, there is a need to sketch the historic tributaries of campus ministry. Second, it seeks to focus on four branches of Presbyterian campus ministry in the twentieth century. Third, it suggests just a few of the critical issues emerging from this historical sketch. Fourth, it provides a brief word about present conversations and future possibilities.

Beginning of Ministry

The churches have participated in campus ministry since the beginning of higher education in America. One hundred seventy-five of 182 colleges founded prior to the Civil War were under church sponsorship.[3] At the time of the Civil War, Presbyterians led the way among church-initiated institutions, with forty-nine.[4]

Campus ministry consisted primarily of the president and the faculty of these early colleges. The president operated as the *de facto* chaplain, and the faculty as Christian leaders who taught both physics and piety, history and values. These values were reinforced by daily chapel, Sabbath worship, and special days for prayer or mission emphasis, for example. In this context it did not occur to church leaders to designate a special person with specific responsibilities for the religious life of the students.

When presidents and faculties of colleges proved unable or unwilling to exercise ministry in the campus community, designated "chaplains" began to appear. The first chaplain was appointed at Yale in 1755. No other colleges had chaplains until after the Civil War. Colleges determined to hold on to their denominational connection frequently came to make college chaplains symbols of this church affiliation. The college chaplain functioned as a parish minister, conducting worship, offering counseling, encouraging involvement in evangelism, mission, and social service. Chaplains met academic standards expected of other faculty, and thus they could exercise some classroom responsibilities.

It is easy to overlook a third tributary in the stream of this history: congregations located adjacent to colleges and universities. Some, such as the Westminster Presbyterian Church in Wooster, Ohio, were started in the nineteenth century as the college churches of Presbyterian institutions.[5] Usually no formal tie existed to a Presbyterian college, but strong informal ties were there to administrators, faculty, and trustees. These churches, some with a "University" or "College" in their name, exercised significant ministries to students.

Ministry initiated by adult leaders—presidents, faculty, chaplains, parish ministers—was supplemented by a fourth tributary which flowed from the beginnings of American colleges: students initiated local voluntary associations. These associations were organized for worship, nurture, and service. They existed both in cooperation and sometimes in tension with the ministries provided by the adult leaders of the college. Clarence P. Shedd, in chronicling *Two Centuries of Student Christian Movements*, calculated that there have existed fourteen hundred local Christian student societies.[6]

The Young Men's Christian Association was formed at the beginning of modern campus ministry, through the union of several voluntary student associations. The YMCA was founded in London in 1844. The first YMCAs in North America were established in Montreal and Boston in 1851. Originally operating in the centers of larger cities, student YMCAs began at the universities of Virginia and Michigan in 1858. At many colleges older, independent associations joined the growing YMCA movement.

By 1875 there were over thirty student YMCAs flourishing in denominational and state universities and colleges—all organized locally. The student movement became national in vision and organization as an outgrowth of a dramatic spiritual awakening at Princeton in the winter of 1875–1876. Moved by a "college mission," which included the first appearance on a college platform of evangelist Dwight L. Moody, delegations of Princeton students traveled to other campuses to share the "great things the Lord had done at Princeton." Princeton student Luther Wishard initiated correspondence with two hundred colleges and universities to sound them out about forming an intercollegiate student Christian movement. Later he invited college leaders to meet with him at an 1877 meeting of the North American YMCA in Louisville. Out of that meeting the intercollegiate YMCA was born. Wishard became the organization's first student secretary or leader.[7]

A powerful missionary interest was also developing in these years. This interest became focused in 1886 at the first of the annual student summer conferences hosted by Dwight L. Moody at his newly constructed boys' school at Mount Hermon, across the river from Northfield, Massachusetts. Included among the delegates was Robert Wilder, who had been at the center of a group of Princeton students who had signed a pledge dedicating themselves to foreign missionary service. By the closing day of the conference, the one hundredth "volunteer" had pledged his life to missionary service. From Mount Hermon, the appeal for missions swept the college campuses, and over fifteen hundred students signed the pledge in the 1886–1887 academic year. In 1888, the Student Volunteer Movement for Foreign Missions (SVM) was officially organized.

Emerging as the recognized leader of the student Christian movement was a young recruit from Cornell, John R. Mott. Mott, a leader in the Cornell YMCA and active at Mount Hermon, became an associate national college secretary of the YMCA upon his graduation in 1888. His leadership abilities recognized by all, Mott assumed the position of secretary in 1890 and fulfilled those duties until 1915. He was also chairman of the executive committee of the Student Volunteer Movement from 1888 to 1920. With a world vision for Christianity, Mott was eager to establish ties between the student movements in various countries. Although he was a student secretary of the YMCA, Mott came to realize that it would be a mistake to bring together diverse student associations, not all with contacts with the YMCA, under one organization. He hoped, rather, for a "federation" of indigenous movements which would both preserve particularity and enhance understanding, missions, and the appreciation of the varied richness of the Christian faith. With Mott acting as the catalyst, the World Student Christian Federation was born out of a meeting of student leaders in Vadstena, Sweden, in 1895. Although just thirty, Mott was elected general secretary of the WSCF, a post he held until 1920.[8]

By 1900, when one spoke of the Student Christian Movement, it was understood to mean the intercollegiate YMCA and YWCA, the Student Volunteer Movement for Foreign Missions, plus a few smaller, more specialized associations. As the Student Christian Movement in the United States, these groups were affiliated with the World Student Christian Federation. It is important to understand these tributaries, for as Presbyterian campus ministries adopted new forms in the twentieth century they would see themselves as partners in the larger ecumenical Student Christian Movement.

Two Forms of Campus Ministry

There are at least four forms of Presbyterian campus ministry operative in the twentieth century.

First to be considered is the continuing presence of congregations in college communities. Even as we refer to church-related colleges, I choose to speak of these congregations as college-related churches. Some larger congregations, such as the University Presbyterian Church adjacent to the University of Washington, or the First Presbyterian Church of Berkeley, one block from the University of California, have full-time campus ministers on the staff, whose ministries touch hundreds of students. In some instances the chaplain of a Presbyterian college has been an associate minister of the local Presbyterian church. Davidson College in North Carolina is an example of this model. These college-related churches are not usually connected to one another. Their campus ministers have not usually been part of Presbyterian campus ministry associations. However, the story of these congregationally based ministries deserves to be chronicled in the history of Presbyterian campus ministry.[9]

A second branch of campus ministry is chaplaincy at Presbyterian colleges. Seymour A. Smith, in *The American College Chaplaincy*, reported that by 1951 chaplains were employed in 203 of 406 independent colleges surveyed. Eighty of these positions were created between 1945 and 1949. Of the 270 church-related institutions surveyed, 132, or 49 percent, had chaplaincies.[10] A survey of the ebb and flow of the chaplaincy at Presbyterian colleges would be useful.

In 1988 there were sixty-nine colleges and universities related to the Presbyterian Church (U.S.A.). The Presbyterian College Chaplains Association is a diverse group. Presbyterian college chaplains are full-time and part-time. Sometimes they see themselves as teachers with limited chaplain responsibilities. Their focus may be worship, counseling, or social action. They may have great or little relationship to congregations and presbyteries. Both national and Presbyterian college chaplains associations have encouraged an ombudsman style of ministry, where the chaplain is free to be concerned about campus life and thus reports directly to the president of the institution. Some exercise a theological function of helping the college think through its mission as an institution and its relationship to the Presbyterian Church. Many Presbyterian colleges no longer have a majority of students who are Presbyterian; and this is sometimes reflected by hiring a chaplain who is not Presbyterian.

University Campus Ministry

What is usually thought of when one says "Presbyterian campus ministry" are the ministries on large public and private universities that constitute a third branch of Presbyterian campus ministry. Formation of Presbyterian and other denominational campus ministries was a response to a new situation created by the growth of the great public universities after the Civil War. The Morrill Land-Grant Act of 1862 initiated a process that "caused the founding or further development of sixty-nine leading American colleges."[11]

A transformation in higher education came about in these years. The changes wrought were so far-reaching that Lawrence Veysey, in *The Emergence of the American University*, would declare, "The American university of 1900 was all but unrecognizable in comparison with the college of 1860." If the former colleges had been custodians of accepted truth, the new universities, utilizing a scientific model, operated from a mind-set where there were no assumed foundations. The metamorphosis was not just in ideas but in structures, so that Veysey observed that "the complexity of the university made the former college seem a boys' school in contrast."[12] What would the advent of the modern university, especially public universities, mean for the churches?

In 1881 Michigan Presbyterians expressed concern for students at the new state university at Ann Arbor. In 1887 the synod utilized a gift of property to establish Tappan Presbyterian Hall. The building was named in honor of Dr. Henry P. Tappan, the first president of the University of Michigan, who was a Presbyterian minister.

On March 20, 1905, J. Leslie French was called by the Tappan Hall Presbyterian Association to be the first Presbyterian student pastor. French would be a model for many future Presbyterian campus ministers. Educated at Hartford Theological Seminary, he had studied in Europe and received a Ph.D. in biblical studies from Hartford. At the time of his appointment as Presbyterian campus minister, he was also offered a part-time teaching appointment in the university. In those first years, French instituted the first religious census at the university, organized an interdenominational divinity club, worked closely with the Student Volunteer Movement chapter, organized Sunday evening groups, taught Bible classes, and traveled the synod acquainting the churches with his ministry. By his estimate the most valuable thing he did was "personal work." He meant by this "calling on new and old students (a case of wearing out shoe leather seven days a week)."[13]

At the national level, the General Assembly in 1905 recommended a strategy of appointing "special ministers," who would serve on college campuses even as chaplains served in the army and navy. "Student pastorates" were begun at Kansas (1905), Illinois (1906), Wisconsin (1908), Colorado (1909), Arkansas (1909), and Nebraska (1909). By 1910 the Presbyterian Church in the U.S.A. was well on its way to evolving a national plan of campus ministry. In that year there were ten full-time student pastors. In 1911 the Board of Education created the Department of University Work, the first denomination to do so. Richard C. Hughes was called as the first full-time director.[14]

Denominations in the South were slower in developing strategies to relate to students at non-church-related institutions. To be sure there were local initiatives. In 1904 the Presbyterian Church at Blacksburg, Virginia, called David J. Woods to a pioneering student ministry at Virginia Polytechnic Institute. This effort was supported by the Montgomery Presbytery and the Synod of Virginia. In 1905 the Synod of South Carolina voted to financially assist the Fort Hill church so it might appoint a pastor to work with students at Clemson College. The Synod of Alabama followed the same model at Auburn. By 1909 the University Presbyterian Church in Austin had instituted Bible chairs, following a model set up by the Disciples of Christ. Students were able to take courses in Bible that received university credit.[15]

Southern Presbyterians did not follow the campus ministry patterns of the great Midwestern universities until the 1920s. Dr. Henry H. Sweets, secretary of the Committee of Christian Education, reminded the churches continually of their obligations to follow their students. In 1922 he prepared a handbook, *The Church and Its Students at State Institutions of Higher Education.*[16]

The Presbyterian Church family embraced campus ministry with enthusiasm in the 1920s. Willard C. Lampe was appointed director of the Department of University Work for the Presbyterian Church in the U.S.A. in 1921. In 1923, as part of major reorganization of the northern church, all education ministries were placed under one board, the Board of Christian Education. In the same year southern

Presbyterians working on campuses met for the first time in what became an annual meeting. In 1925 Robert Miles, who had pioneered the work at Auburn, was called to be the first university secretary of the Board of Christian Education in the Presbyterian Church U.S. By 1925, fifty-two Presbyterian university pastors were employed by the northern board on fifty-two campuses of state and private colleges and universities.

The goal of campus ministry in these formative years was evangelism. In 1928 the northern Presbyterian university pastors declared evangelism the major focus of their ministry in a joint statement which articulated what had been their practice for a quarter of a century. But by now evangelism was conceived as ministry not only to Presbyterian students, but to all students.[17]

If the first quarter century was the period of formation, the next quarter century would be a time of rapid expansion. This expansion included not only numbers of students and campus ministers, but purposes and tasks.

In 1930 two meetings were held that would have long-term significance for the structures and purposes of Presbyterian campus ministry. At a convocation on ministry in higher education at Oxford, Ohio, was born the Association of Presbyterian University Pastors (APUPs). With twenty-four charter members, these pastors would attempt to bring focus and cohesion to Presbyterian campus ministry.[18]

In the same year the Conference of Church Workers in Colleges and Universities met in Chicago. This meeting took a hard look at precedents and possibilities. Hugh A. Moran, Presbyterian university pastor at Cornell, delivered an address about the priorities of "The University Pastor." He presented two models of campus ministry. The first model started with the church. The aim of the campus minister was "to mold the life of students in conformity with the established traditions and customs of" the church. The second conception was held, Moran said, by those "who place the student at the center of the picture." A lively debate ensued. Here was a question that would energize campus ministry conversations in the decades to come. In the beginning, many campus ministries were extensions of the local congregation. The patterns of ministry were congregationally based. Moran's question attempted to take seriously the unique nature of the life of students in the developing colleges and universities.[19]

Presbyterian campus ministry expanded during the Depression. Begun in the late 1920s, construction of Westminster Houses continued into the 1930s. Westminster Houses, or Foundations, became centers for a variety of ministries, including housing for women and for international students when university housing was not available.

The national strategy of expansion in the northern church was led by Maxwell (Max) Adams, director of the Department of University Work from 1934 to 1947. Under his leadership there developed a closer relationship with the denomination. Membership in APUPs moved from a voluntary to an almost required status. Large numbers of students were recruited for seminary and the ministry.

Social issues are central to the popular understanding of campus ministry. Although there was much discussion and action at the local level, it was not until 1940 that these issues were raised in a report at an APUPs meeting. The report commended this social concern, but issued a caution: "No one of the social issue items should be allowed to become the sole interest of study of the group to the exclusion of other items." The overriding concern was that "any ethical issue be allowed to appear to be the whole Gospel."[20]

At this same 1940 meeting the Presbyterian campus ministers reaffirmed the student focus of campus ministry. But the issues raised by Hugh Moran in 1930 would not go away. Moran asked whether campus ministry should ask students to conform to models derived from the parish or to models indigenous to the university. Now the larger question was becoming whether the focus of campus ministry could remain only students or whether the parameters needed to be enlarged to include faculty and administration—the total college or university.

This ideological discussion received a structural answer with a changing of the leadership at the national level. In

1947 Ken Reeves succeeded Max Adams and became the secretary of the Department of Student Work. Reeves was convinced that students were the link between the different
worlds of campus ministry—the church-related college, the
public university, and the parish. Hal Viehman succeeded
Reeves in 1949, and the name was changed again, this time to
the Department of Campus Christian Life. Viehman, a product of the YMCA and formerly a secretary of the Student
Christian Movement, brought with him a vision for ministry
in all dimensions of the university. In his years of service he
tried to convey a heightened sense of the Presbyterian campus minister as a "professional"—highly trained and qualified—who deserved the support of the whole church.

The decade of the 1950s was a period of unprecedented
growth for the Presbyterian Church. Campus ministry participated in this growth. In 1950 the Presbyterian Church
U.S. had less than fifty campus ministers. By 1962 there
were more than one hundred campus ministers on nearly
three hundred campuses.[21]

In the early 1950s Presbyterian campus ministers were
reading and discussing Sir Walter Moberly's *The Crisis in
the University*. Arising out of interaction of the Student
Christian Movement in the British universities, Moberly's
trenchant analysis spoke to the American situation as well.
His call to the modern university was that its necessary
neutrality should be "positive" and not "negative." Campus ministers received from Moberly the encouragement to
engage the university with intellect in the tradition of
Christian humanism.

If the 1950s began with campus ministry meetings devoted to study and reflection, by the end of the decade the
call was to action. In 1954 the *Brown v. Board of Education
of Topeka* decision became a catalyst to attack the segregation at the heart of American society. Martin Luther King,
Jr., called America to live out both its Christian and civil
creeds. Campus ministers were often in advance of the
churches in responding to King's call. Their involvement in
civil rights did not so much precipitate as symbolize a
growing estrangement from the churches that had sent

them to the campuses. Sometimes it almost seemed that as congregations hung back, campus ministers accelerated their social involvement. In these years, while the author of this essay was serving in a college-related congregation, he recalls talking with a Presbyterian campus minister at a public university in his state who told him he discouraged his students from attending "First Church" in his community. Why? "Too conservative." He meant conservative politically as much as theologically.

Phillip E. Hammond documented the changing profile of the campus minister in *The Campus Clergyman* published in 1966. In a section titled "The Unorthodoxy of Campus Ministers," Hammond provided the following comparison.

Fig. 4.1. The Percentage of Campus Ministers and Parish Ministers Who Agree with Various Statements[22]

Statement	Campus Minister (Number responding = 997)	Parish Minister (Number responding = 3,928)
Political Attitudes		
1. Strongly approve of the purposes of the United Nations	73%	57%
2. Strongly approve of the purposes of the AFL-CIO	21	11
Breadth of Interest		
3. Regularly read *Christian Century*	67	33
4. Regularly read *Christianity and Crisis*	44	6
5. Very interested in news of national and international affairs	75	62
6. Very interested in news of own denomination	35	68

Fig. 4.1. *cont.*

Statement	Campus Minister (Number responding = 997)	Parish Minister (Number responding = 3,928)
7. Very or quite interested in news of other denominations	57	68
The Church and Social Action		
8. Would very much like to see church-sponsored examination of major ethical issues	66	57
9. Agree own denomination is too conservative in the field of social action	53	17
Ecumenical Attitudes		
10. Agree own denomination is not sufficiently ecumenical-minded	53	17
11. Strongly approve of the National Council of Churches	51	42
12. Strongly approve of the World Council of Churches	59	44
Miscellaneous		
13. Agree own denomination does not have clearly defined policies	27	15
14. Have a Bachelor of Divinity degree	84	65
15. Have Ph.D. degree	13	2
16. Choose, as closest to own belief regarding the Bible, "an infallible revelation of God's will"*	8	24

*Other options: "inspired by God, but subject to historical criticism," and "a great history of religious experience, but not necessarily inspired by God." These two were chosen by 84 percent and 7 percent respectively of campus ministers, by 70 percent and 3 percent respectively of parish ministers.

Many forces were intersecting in the late 1950s and 1960s that challenged the traditional styles of campus ministry. The university was continuing to change. The "positive" neutrality that Moberly called for sometimes appeared to be critical attacks on traditional values, including Christianity. If local church folk were alarmed, campus ministers, appealing to their own prophetic task, called for understanding and engagement.

But the changes on college campuses were not just intellectual. Campus ministry began by providing many services not present in the fledgling public universities. As these services became available—housing, counseling, work with international students, departments of religious studies—the functions of campus ministry changed. These changes were occurring just as many Presbyterian campus ministers were turning away from some of the traditional activities of the past—worship, Bible study, evangelism. Worship was provided by congregations, who often told campus ministers not to duplicate what they were doing. Bible study, especially in an era given over to action, somehow lost its priority. Evangelism was being done aggressively by para-church organizations. Somehow the aversion to the methods of some of these groups seemed to justify an abandonment of evangelism as an appropriate part of Presbyterian ministry.

Out of these crises emerged some creative ministries: counseling with young men caught in the draft dilemma over the war in Vietnam, social justice ministries related to civil rights, training peer group counselors, and so on. In surveying and experiencing campus ministry in these years, however, what emerged often was the lone ranger. This was the campus minister who was out there on his or her own, following personal interests in developing a special-interest group or avenue of service that was attractive to only a small number of students.[23]

In these years the theater of ministry was continually enlarging. John Connor, former Moderator of the General Assembly, was a good example of a campus minister who had a ministry to a whole university. He earned the right to be

heard by those in governance at Oregon State University.
President Bob MacVicar listened to Connor and sought his
counsel. But Connor would gladly share credit with Leroy
Loats, Presbyterian campus minister at Oklahoma State
University, who built a special relationship with MacVicar
while he was in Stillwater.[24]

This kind of ministry was often called a ministry to structures. As Reinhold Niebuhr made clear in *Moral Man and
Immoral Society*, structures, as well as individuals, are responsible for both health and sickness. But how far to take
a ministry to structures? In 1971 the author of this essay
tried to visit the Presbyterian campus minister at a major
university in the West, but was told that he was not on campus. When would he be there? No one knew. Where was he?
He was at the state capital lobbying for higher education,
and the word was that he spent weeks at a time at the state
capital.

D. Keith Naylor, in "Liberal Protestant Campus Ministry: The Dilemma of Modernity," interviewed a veteran
Presbyterian campus minister who reflected on the widening theater of ministry in those years. "We ministered to
the students, to the graduate students, to the faculty and
staff, widening the circle and losing people all along the
way. Thus we ministered to the 'structures of the university,' whatever that means, and we were lost."[25] Lost is a
way of speaking of the crisis and confusion in the campus
ministry in the 1960s and 1970s.

Ecumenical Campus Ministry

A fourth branch of Presbyterian campus ministry is the
ecumenical campus ministry. Concurrent with the rise of a
new form of denominational campus ministries in the first
years of the twentieth century was the development of an
interdenominational campus ministry association. J. Leslie
French joined with his Baptist, Episcopal, and Disciples
colleagues at the University of Michigan to convene the Interdenominational Conference of Church and Guild Workers at State Universities in 1907. In 1910 this group

organized as the Conference of Church Workers in State Universities (CCWSU). In 1922 private colleges and universities requested membership, and the name was changed to the Conference of Church Workers in Universities and Colleges of the United States. True to historic Presbyterian practice, French and other Presbyterian campus ministers were leaders in this ecumenical endeavor.[26]

From the 1950s to the present, the ecumenical approach has moved from an association of individuals to the merger of denominational structures. In 1955 the United Campus Christian Fellowship came into being as a cooperative fellowship of four denominational campus ministries: Presbyterian, United Church of Christ, Disciples of Christ, and the Evangelical United Brethren. In an era of ecumenical enthusiasm and shrinking denominational budgets, the UCCF was hailed as the harbinger of the future.

Not all agreed. Retiring APUPs president Andy Armstrong, longtime Presbyterian pastor at Northwestern, spoke of a dilemma facing Presbyterian campus ministry. Yes, the new organization reflected oneness in Christ. But in just five years it was evident that campus ministry was losing strong Presbyterian institutional support.[27]

In 1964 the United Ministries in Higher Education was created. The same four denominations were now joined by the Moravian Church in a merger of denominational structures. In 1984 UMHE merged with United Ministries in Public Education to become United Ministries in Education, a merging of nine denominational campus ministries (UME).[28]

In the 1960s there was an attempt to revive the historic student Christian movement. Under Mott and others the SCM in the United States had been a vital force which took its place in the larger WSCF. But it began to decline in the 1930s as it lost the balance between personal and social faith. A group of students, supported by a cross section of campus ministers, tried to revive it by chartering a new University Christian Movement in 1966. Focused almost exclusively on a political agenda, they failed to attract broad support. No one was quite prepared for the announcement in 1969 that they were voting themselves out of existence. Robert Rankin, who had advocated a grant to the UCM from the Danforth Foundation, observed: "Its death certificate was signed by indifference to other modes of ministry."[29]

In 1966 the National Campus Ministry Association was formed as an umbrella organization for all of campus ministry. In the first full year of membership Presbyterians comprised 45 percent of the total membership (154 out of 339). Four of the first eight presidents of the NCMA were Presbyterians.

Throughout the 1960s and 1970s there were several attempts to revive a Presbyterian identity for campus ministry. With the coming of UMHE in 1964 the Association of Presbyterian University Pastors was asked to vote itself out of existence. But almost immediately efforts focused on creating a caucus within the larger, ecumenical structures. These efforts culminated in a 1978 pre-assembly convocation at San Diego and a meeting before the 1979 National Campus Ministry Association meeting. As a result of all those efforts the organization Presbyterian Ministers in Higher Education (PMHE) was founded. The goal was to redevelop support for campus ministry within the Presbyterian family, but at the same time remain a part of NCMA.[30]

Issues for Campus Ministry

In chronicling the story of Presbyterian campus ministry, some critical issues emerge, which are examined here in historical perspective.

1. Higher Education. Leander Keck, Dean of Yale Divinity School, addressing a joint meeting of the Association of Presbyterian Colleges and Universities and the Presbyterian College Chaplains Association in 1988, stated that the university and not the church is the source of salvation for people today. Keck emphasized that this is the reality we need to live with in implementing future campus ministries. The campus ministers, often "point" men and women for the church, recognized the reality before others in the church family.

This appreciation of the university, however, has had both beneficial and negative effects. Sensitive to their changing environment, campus ministers came to understand the need to encounter the university on its own terms. By comparison, you will hear Presbyterian campus ministers critique para-church campus ministries by saying that they do not take the university seriously.

But the question can be asked: Who sets the agenda? There has sometimes been an uncritical acceptance of ideas and agendas fostered by the university. Phillip Hammond speaks of "extravasation" in analyzing the dilemma of modern religious liberalism. Extravasation is a term used in pathology which refers to the escape of a substance from its proper vessels. Naylor applies this metaphor to campus ministry and the university. Starting from the premise that the sacred cannot be contained only in the vessel called the church has led to an embrace of the modern university as the "manufacturing plant on modernity." Campus ministers, Naylor argues, have often rushed to embrace the new. "Their activities ranged as far from the church as did their search for the sacred which found new vessels."[31]

The importance of the university is not just a matter of ideas. On the collegial level, frustrated by lack of support and understanding from both adjacent churches and presbytery, it is understandable why some campus ministers identify their closest colleagues as members of the university community.[32]

2. Denominational Identity. A continuing quandary has been the relation of Presbyterian campus ministry to the Presbyterian Church. A child of churches, often in advance of the churches, there has been an uneasy relationship with the church.

This quandary is reflected in the search for how campus ministry fits in the structure of the Presbyterian Church. Longtime campus ministers can tell stories of this organizational musical chairs which has led in recent years, in their eyes, to a downgrading of the status of the national leaders responsible for campus ministry. When Myrvin DeLapp, who had served both as a college chaplain and as a campus minister, succeeded Hal Viehman in the 1970s, there was no longer a Division of Higher Education or a Department of Campus Christian Life. With the reorganization of the church and the move from Philadelphia to New York, De-Lapp became part of Unit II of the newly created Program Agency.

Beyond structure, the issue is how to nurture students so that they will take their places in congregations after college days. Some have said that this is not an important goal, but such a sentiment undermines campus ministry's credibility with the churches. Many campus ministers believe it is important, and there are some new, or perhaps old, patterns on the horizon. For the first time in nineteen years a national Presbyterian student gathering was held in 1988. For years, seventeen thousand students have been gathering every four years for an Intervarsity national conference. Lutherans have worked hard at nurturing denominational loyalty in their students. Now Presbyterians are joining several other mainline denominations in reinstituting national student meetings.[33]

3. Ecumenical Patterns. The pull between denominational and ecumenical loyalties has been a constant source of tension. In an age of ecumenical enthusiasm campus ministers saw themselves as pioneers of new patterns of ministry. In his study, Naylor observed that "many campus ministers were high priests of ecumenism, often maintaining it as their chief religious principle."[34]

But some campus ministers saw warning signs on the horizon. They argued that ecumenical encounter grew out of denominational identity. If students were coming to the campus with even less sense of the Presbyterian Church, how could they be asked to make the leap into an ecumenical church? At the same time, those in campus ministry expected that denominations should support their efforts, without asking why enthusiasm and budgets were waning.

Several factors have challenged these patterns in recent years. Preliminary results of the Lilly Foundation study of the Presbyterian Church indicate that young people are leaving the church in their late teenage years—which has always happened—but now they are not returning when they are married and have small children. All segments of the church must accept responsibility for this pattern.

With limited budgets, Presbyterian college chaplains and campus ministers have had to choose between denominational and interdenominational associations. A compromise, which has had mixed results, has been to convene a Presbyterian caucus in conjunction with national ecumenical meetings.

Many persons are reevaluating ecumenical commitments and patterns. At the same time that there has been a rebirth of national student meetings, there is another effort to revive the student Christian movement. The Council for Ecumenical Student Christian Ministry (CESCM) planned a national gathering for December 1990. This movement has been energized by campus ministers and students who want the American Christian student community to again be a part of the WSCF. It remains to be seen how denominational and ecumenical loyalties can be balanced.

4. Finances.   Financial support has come from a variety of sources: General Assembly, synods, presbyteries, state and local councils and advisory boards, and congregations. Lewis Wilkins suggests that the recent ambivalence about funding ministries in higher education is directly related to the alienation many Presbyterians feel about the "new university" culture. Presbyterians know of their historic commitment to higher education, but "they also lack energy for raising the church's priority commitment to it."[35] Finding a way to turn this around will be a major challenge. Many campus ministers believe it is not fair to ask them to become fund-raisers. A vision for campus ministry has been lost. Finances will follow a compelling vision.

The Future of Campus Ministry

And what about the future? The context for campus ministry has changed dramatically in recent years. Students are older. The "ethnic minorities" are no longer in the minority on many campuses. The student population at U.C.L.A. was expected to be 50 percent "minorities" for the 1989–1990 school year! Many colleges are commuter campuses. How to minister in this changing environment? Conversations and literature about campus ministry differ markedly about the way forward.

One circle of conversation concerns the traditional roles of congregations. Neil W. Brown, executive of the San Diego Presbytery, declares that "campus ministry, as we have known it for 40 years, and its ecumenical version over the last 20 years, is over and done with."[36] Brown calls for congregations to reclaim pastoral concern for faculty, administration, and students. John N. Brittain, university chaplain at the University of Evansville, calls for a return of the church-on-campus model, "providing the campus the mainstays of our traditions, worship and study." Brittain criticizes recent campus ministers as content to offer broker services—matching students with concerns, but in the process not ministering themselves.[37]

Whatever the structure, the issue of the priority of personal faith and evangelism is usually present in any gathering. As in 1928 Presbyterian campus ministers affirmed evangelism as a primary task, in 1988 the new associate for evangelism, Gary W. Demarest, was a featured speaker at the national student gathering. But, speaking to the 1988 PMHE gathering, Hubert C. Noble, who served as chaplain at Occidental College for many years, warned those present that the present preoccupation with personal faith could do damage to the historic "two-way street" between faith and learning.[38]

One of the most difficult issues will be how to both retain denominational loyalty and instill an ecumenical vision. Dealing seriously with this structural question is important in any renewal movement among students in the Presbyterian Church. Clyde Robinson suggested in San Diego in 1988 that the ecumenical vision does not mean "investing heavily in ecumenical organizational superstructure." The better way is to infuse denominational events with "the presence of other traditions," which can thus serve to impart a global perspective.[39]

One senses a new concern for campus ministry even if there is disagreement on the best strategies. A child of the churches, in the twentieth century Presbyterian campus ministry has experienced both growth and crisis, enthusiasm and discouragement. Because there are many tributaries and branches there is no one answer. In discovering the way forward Presbyterians can be encouraged that there are creative precedents on which to build.

5

Presbyterians
and Their Publishing Houses

John B. Trotti and Richard A. Ray

When the United Presbyterian Church in the United States of America and the Presbyterian Church in the United States consolidated, they brought with them their publishing houses. This proved a historic union, joining traditions that had much in common. Once again, the major Presbyterian communion had a single program for publishing. This enterprise had, in one manner of speaking, passed through many convolutions to come full circle.

The new Westminster/John Knox Press differed quite radically from its original progenitors. Much had happened in American culture and publishing history since those early days. Even so, the two streams of publishing history that had flowed from those days into The Westminster Press and the John Knox Press had shared many commitments and faced similar challenges.

This essay only begins to plumb the depths and to evaluate some of the changes that were involved in the history of Presbyterian publishing. Even a cursory examination, however, shows that what began as an essentially evangelical endeavor came to serve a variety of purposes within the church's mission. It served the church's effort to minister in an increasingly complex culture from a Reformed perspective, and it provided a continuing flow of scholarly works that would have left both John Calvin and Martin Luther breathless. As time passed, it developed techniques and acquired the experience for entering successfully into commercial publishing. It made a name for itself wherever resources for the study of Christian life and thought were found. And, as a natural consequence of this successful adaptation to the new environment of belles lettres, popular marketing, and the most exemplary standards of technical scholarship, both Westminster and John Knox achieved unprecedented independence from their constituent denominations. But what kind of environment will the new, reunited Presbyterian Church now provide for its publishing enterprise?

Characteristically, Presbyterians have usually felt insecure and off balance when religious experience was not anchored securely in knowledge. Revivalistic excesses on the frontier could lead to unpredictable outcomes. Thus, the General Assembly of the PCUSA came to grips with this unsavory prospect in 1800 by purchasing large quantities of books for distribution. These books could be spread throughout the restless quarters of the frontier as proper antidotes to the theological controversies that threatened to distort the faith. Such books brought the Presbyterian confessions and the exposition of Presbyterian doctrines to the backwoods communities, of all places, as well as to the new urban populations of America.[1] A notable cultural event was occurring—religious perspectives, vocabulary, and coherence, which had emerged earlier in a European revolution of thought, were providing a welcome sense of order in the wilderness of the American religious quest.

This practice of brokering the production and distribution of books continued in voluntary societies—the American Bible Society, the American Tract Society, and others—which established their own imprints during the 1810s. Presbyterians played a significant role in the establishment of most of these single-purpose benevolent societies.[2]

In 1833, the Synod of Pennsylvania founded a Synod Tract Society to publish and distribute pertinent materials and books among its congregations and beyond. Its efforts were consolidated and widened when the Synod of Pennsylvania Tract Society became the basis for publications by the Presbyterian Church (Old School) in 1838, under a Board of Publication of Tracts and Sabbath School Books (in 1839 renamed The Presbyterian Board of Publication). Archibald Alexander's *The Way of Salvation,* a little book for young people, seems to have been its first release, followed in 1841 by Calvin's *Institutes of the Christian Religion.* Meanwhile, its competitor, the Presbyterian Church (New School), likewise began publication and distribution of its materials and books.[3]

Quite naturally, the Old School board seemed to have more energy for publication than its New School counterpart. In addition to pamphlets, tracts, and Sunday school literature, early publications from the Old School included an emphasis on music: *Psalms and Hymns* (1840), *Hymns for Youth* (1848), *Hymns for Young Children* (1848), and *Presbyterian Psalmody* (1853). Other publications in those early days included a fine edition of the works of John Bunyan (1844) and the multi-purpose Sunday school book *The Sabbath School Bell* (1860).[4]

Because postal facilities were not dependable and the frontier kept expanding at a rapid pace, the General Assembly requested that synods and presbyteries establish depositories of materials. Chief among these depositories were those in New York City, Chicago, Cincinnati, Nashville, Pittsburgh, St. Louis, and eventually San Francisco. Thus, a truly remarkable literary culture began to emerge among Presbyterians.

When that system did not function adequately, the PCUSA (Old School) established a system of colporteurs. These book distributors were not professional marketing experts so much as they were educated missionaries, spreading the faith and the culture of the Presbyterians from the settled East and Northeast throughout the land. In each community visited, they would seek to establish Sabbath schools and do other evangelistic work. In one striking account of their work, one colporteur swapped his tracts for playing cards. Then, before the eyes of those "converts" who made the trade, he destroyed the cards.[5]

In 1854, the General Assembly requested that the Board of Publication and Sabbath School Work publish popular biographies of John Knox, John Calvin, and other religious leaders. An appeal was issued for authors, and the program was launched. In 1855, the Assembly asked for development of a line of serious books for ministers with this argument: "One cannot lay the foundations of the Presbyterian church without books. Other churches may do without them, but we cannot." This gave expression to the distinctive character of Reformed theology—the view that faith invariably includes genuine growth and knowledge. Several substantial works resulted.[6]

Through 1860, the Board of Publication and Sabbath School Work was directed by William H. Engles, who served as editor for the publications. During his final year of service, fifty-one new books and nineteen tracts were published. The most outstanding among them was a four-volume set of the *Letters of John Calvin.*[7]

What is remarkable is that Presbyterians experimented so early with different systems and methods for producing and distributing books. It was a creative endeavor. In addition, the publications served as direct resources for the church, enabling the formation and growth of new congregations and Sabbath schools.

The Westminster Press

The official policies of The Westminster Press find their origin in the 1838 Old School action. Interestingly, we cannot locate the formal authorization for the use of the name Westminster or even the date on which the decision was made to employ it. Clearly, the term is a tribute to the Westminster Assembly (1643–1649) and to the Westminster Standards, which issued from that Assembly. The name appeared occasionally between the 1830s and the beginning of the Westminster Lessons in 1871, soon after the reunion of the Old and New School factions to form one PCUSA.[8]

The Westminster Normal Outlines were published in 1881, and the classic *Westminster Bible Dictionary* appeared in 1880, both typical examples of the importance of scripture. In the April 10, 1897, issue of *Publishers Weekly,* a brief story in the Literary and Trade Notes column marks at least one "official" origin of the name: "The Presbyterian Board of Publication and Sabbath School Work has adopted the imprint of *Westminster Press* for its undenominational books." In the 1940s, Westminster Press became an established imprint. Anna Jane Moyer reports that on August 5, 1941, the name was registered in the United States Post Office in Washington.[9]

After the devastating Civil War years, the reunion between the Old School and New School branches of the Presbyterian Church took place. During the war, publication had fallen drastically. In 1864, for example, only five books, three tracts, a packet of tracts for soldiers, two packages of leaflets, and two German hymnals were produced by the Old School. With the union, the Board began to respond again to pressures for books and materials of various kinds.[10]

By the turn of the twentieth century, John H. Scribner was serving as business superintendent or general manager of the Board, and he oversaw the progress by the PCUSA in publications.

The 1907 General Assembly criticized the Board for emphasizing Sabbath school resources, tracts, and periodical literature to the neglect of both leisure reading materials for juveniles and "serious" work for ministers. A total of 1,065 new congregations, however, attributed their origins to the work of the Board's colporteurs that year. Five years later the results were even more dramatic. In 1912, there were 1,500 congregations that pointed toward the influence of the distribution of literature as a signal event in their development.[11]

By this time, however, pressures had intensified for the publications to be offered in many directions—leisure reading, evangelism, teaching, and other related purposes. The PCUSA Board responded with a few titles in such new areas. The *Progress in Christian Culture,* by Sam C. Black, and *The World Work of the Presbyterian Church in the U.S.A.,* by David McConenghy in 1915, were examples of the way in which the concern for literature was moving more strongly into cultural and historical analysis. One can also find advertisements for The Westminster Press offering books that now seem to be extraordinarily relevant in their concern for natural and environmental resources. William C. Covert, the general secretary of the Board of Christian Education, had written two books which were not particularly religious in doctrine but which had found their way into the publishing program. They were *Wildwoods and Waterways* and *The Glory of the Pines.* While this may have delighted many readers, it must have seemed to show a somewhat confusing breadth of interest to others. Nevertheless, the majority of titles continued as before, feeding the immediate needs of Christian education efforts and evangelistic enterprises.[12]

Edward L. Sheppard noted that there was a general trend away from denominational materials in religious publishing. Between 1910 and 1930 "most denominational publishers dropped their sectarian label. The Methodist Book Concern became Abingdon Press . . . the Presbyterian Board of Publication became Westminster Press." According to Sheppard, this move represented the attempt of the presses to take a broader, more ecumenical stance while still serving the needs of their particular denominations.[13]

In 1924 a reorganization of the PCUSA denominational offices resulted in the location of the colporteur efforts under the Board of National Missions and the move to hire full-time book salespeople for the Board of Publication, now frequently called Westminster Press, lodged under the Board of Christian Education.[14]

Despite this change, which seems on the face of it to be a more businesslike way of doing the work of publication, Westminster Press continued to be largely a service press for denominational publications. The book selection committee of the Religious Round Table of the American Library Association listed no titles from Westminster Press among its annual "fifty best religious books" between 1925 and 1942. There is scant advertising by the Press until 1941, and it does not appear in the supplements of the *Publishers' Trade List Annual* in 1943. In the lists of total books produced annually through the years 1925–1941, there were only four to eight new titles per year. The Press was, as late as 1936, conspicuously absent from lists of established denominational publishing houses.[15]

Westminster Press did produce some significant worship resources during the first four decades of the twentieth century: *Forms and Services* (1905); a revised edition of *The Hymnal* (1911); *The Book of Common Worship* (1926); and another edition of *The Hymnal* (1933). Robert E. Speer's *Studies in Missionary Leadership* received some attention in *Publishers Weekly* in 1914, an exception to the general rule.[16]

In 1938, Walter L. Jenkins became general manager of the Publication Division and of Westminster Press. Jenkins, a minister, had previously served as field director of Christian education for the Board of Christian Education in Michigan. He had come to the circulation department of Westminster Press in 1936. His appointment to this position drew little notice outside the Presbyterian fold. However, he brought fresh ideas to the Press. With his leadership, a vigorous new era began, in many ways. He, along with other staff members, opened up broader involvement in religious publishing. Jenkins began to play an active role in the International Council of Religious Education, and Mae Shilock of the Press addressed the Publishers' Advisory Section in 1941.[17]

The emergence of Westminster Press as a significant religious publisher for America, however, seems to have been the result not only of an enterprising manager, but also because Presbyterian leaders, and perhaps church members, expected the church to produce good scholarship and quality fiction. It coincided as well with other changes in the life of American Presbyterianism explored in essays in this series.[18]

Again in 1941, Westminster Press conducted a survey of

literature available for young people. The results pointed to a strong need for well-written, moral fiction for youth. Consequently, a new line, Westminster fiction, was launched. Barbara J. Snedeker was charged with editing fiction, and William Heyliger was hired as her associate. Names of the Press's staff soon began to appear in *Publishers Weekly.*[19]

During 1941 also, *Publishers Weekly* began to carry advertisements from the Press listing eight books, and in 1942 seven issues of the periodical carried ads for the twelve new books from that year. "Biggest Promotion in Westminster Press History," boasted the ad, a claim no one could challenge.[20]

New titles began to appear by authors of quality, sophistication, and reputation: Emil Brunner, John Wick Bowman, Clarence Macartney, Andrew Blackwood, Floyd V. Filson, and Alan Richardson (not to mention John Calvin!). In 1945, the *Westminster Bible Dictionary* was revised, and a *Westminster Bible Atlas* published.[21]

By 1946 the *Publishers' Trade List Annual* showed ninety-two titles for Westminster Press. By 1950, the number had grown to 167. Prominent writers included H. H. Rowley, George Barclay, Paul Minear, Henry Sloane Coffin, Norman Snaith, Millar Burrows, Nelson Glueck, William Manson, Roland Bainton, H. Wheeler Robinson, and Russell Dicks. These writers possessed worldwide reputations in their respective disciplines.

In 1947, Westminster Press initiated an annual award for a work of fiction. The Novel Award drew entries but no prize the first year. In 1948, Nelia G. White won the eight-thousand-dollar prize for her *No Trumpet Before Him,* and in 1949 Dorothy C. Wilson won for *Prince of Egypt.*[22] The commitment of the Press to the stimulation of new, biblically oriented fiction is indicated by the remarkably large size of the prize for that day.

The Westminster Press has been well served by the diligent efforts and multiple talents of many people. Among these, Leonard Trinterud made significant contributions. In 1948, Paul L. Meacham became Religious Books Editor for The Westminster Press, and his appointment brought in additional influence and strength of lasting merit. By now the Press had moved to become a major force in American religious publishing. In 1951, the Press published a full catalog in the *Publishers' Trade List Annual,* an eight-page listing of 807 titles. Its offerings began to appear regularly among the "Top Fifty" books, selected according to the standards of the periodical. The Press began the scholarly series the Library of Christian Classics, drawing on reowned editors to offer critical editions of major works by Western religious leaders. Initiated with the collaboration of the SCM Press in Great Britain, it attracted as series editors Henry P. Van Dusen, John T. McNeill, and John Baillie.[23] Much of the credit for the remarkable renaissance in serious theological publishing is due to the unique abilities of Paul Meacham and his colleagues. Meacham's understanding of the pivotal importance of high quality in theological books was influential not only for The Westminster Press, but throughout the industry.

Under the progressive leadership of Meacham, the Press continued to grow in prestige and substance by offering English-language translations of major works that had been originally published in German and French. Edward L. Sheppard, in an article for *Library Trends,* described the ecumenical outreach of the Press in the 1950s:

> The Westminster Press has pioneered in the publication of sound theological literature (Layman's Theological Library, 1956) and Biblical commentary (Daily Study Bible, 1957) for laymen. Westminster Press authors are drawn from various denominations, and its materials for youth particularly are used widely by other Protestant churches.[24]

The classic *A History of Israel,* by John Bright, appeared in 1959. Alongside it and other more technical works, the Press offered Westminster Guides to the Bible for lay people. Early in the 1960s came more series: The Library of History and Doctrine; the distinguished Old Testament Library (begun in 1963 with Gerhard von Rad's *Genesis*) and the companion New Testament Library (begun in 1963 with Oscar Cullmann's *Christology of the New Testament* and titles by Norman Perrin and Günther Bornkamm).[25]

Westminster Press, with the merger of the PCUSA and the UPCNA, added the latter's Geneva Press in 1962 as a third publishing line, focusing primarily on larger markets than the Presbyterian Church itself afforded. From that time until the merger to form the PC(USA), The Westminster Press published between fifty and eighty new titles per year, about two thirds in religion and one third in literature for juveniles.

If the 1960s yielded wider ambitions and greater prestige to Westminster Press, they also brought a new kind of controversy and criticism. It was the fruit of adventurous publishing, the acceptance of a certain amount of risk entailed in providing an arena for the fresh discussion of varied religious ideas. In 1963 the Press offered J. A. T. Robinson's *Honest to God,* which became both a best-seller and a flashpoint for criticism. Three years later, Westminster published both Joseph Fletcher's *Situation Ethics* and Thomas J. J. Altizer's *The Gospel of Christian Atheism.* All three of the books sold well. In fact, the fast pace with which the books were purchased indicated that the Press had touched a nerve. People were interested in new thinking about the Christian faith, and most were not unduly frightened by innovative approaches. The publication of these particular titles also indicated that the Press was flexing its muscles and was willing to exercise a certain measure of independence from the denomination's ongoing task for the education of its own constituency in its own basic religious traditions.

At the same time, the publication of such books provoked questions. Some asked whether the Press cared for the welfare of the church as much as it seems to be interested in publishing sensational material. Scarcely noticed, during the heat of the debate, were the more substantial, less controversial books, such as the New Directions in Theology series and Charles R. Erdman's Commentaries on the New Testament series in paperback. The wide-ranging discussion of new ideas, from a variety of viewpoints, was going to mark the life of this denomination in many unpredictable ways in the decades to come. Some of the earliest signals of this change were first apparent within the publishing enterprise.

The 1970s saw Westminster Press churn out a remarkable flow of stimulating, scholarly theological work. This contribution should not be underestimated in its full historical impact. Its influence in the life of the denomination as well as its role in stimulating such publications in other denominations have been extremely important. A host of influential, often controversial, works became available to faculty and students alike within colleges and theological seminaries. These included works by Rudolf Bultmann, Wolfhart Pannenberg, Bernhard Anderson, John Cobb, Howard Clark Kee, John Hick, Bernard Lonergan, Oscar Cullmann, Paul Achtemeier, Elizabeth Achtemeier, James Luther Mays, and James Barr. While the perspectives of these scholars varied widely, they all expressed the commitment of this denomination to scholarship that would not flinch in the face of any cultural challenge. In fact, there was a subtle way in which the capacity to absorb and to debate the ideas in such books came to characterize the culture of the denomination's clerical leadership.

The board of the Program Agency of the UPCUSA in 1979 assessed the value of The Westminster Press and sought to answer critics: Westminster Press was intended to provide Christian nurture for the whole of the Christian church, not just for the denomination itself. The statement stressed the freedom of authors to express the truth as they saw it, declaring that the Press intended to provide stimulation for the mind of the churches and their educational institutions. The Press "encourages authors who make original contributions to religious thought and those who clarify religious ethical and moral issues." In addition, the goal of the Press was to ameliorate everyday life by advocating a "free, just, and peaceful society."

In the August 1979 issue of *Alert,* Charles Colman III, then general manager of The Westminster Press, addressed the relationship between Westminster Press and the Program Agency. He cited the Westminster Press Statement of Policy, which had been approved by the Program Agency board:

> The Christian church has responsibilities for the Christian nurture of its members and their understanding of the world in which they live as well as a wider concern for the needs of the world. The Program Agency of The United Presbyterian Church in the U.S.A. endeavors to discharge these responsibilities in various ways, one of which is a program of publishing. Some of its publications are intended for use primarily within the denomination; others are addressed to a wider audience. The work of The Westminster Press falls primarily into the latter category. Its publications are viewed as a contribution by The United Presbyterian Church to all Christians and to the human family of adults, young people, and children.
>
> The Westminster Press endeavors to stimulate the intellectual life of the churches and their educational institutions by representing the best thinking of the day on a broad range of religious and ethical concerns. It encourages authors who make original contributions to religious thought and those who clarify religious, ethical, and moral issues. The Westminster Press also contributes through its publications to the development and training of professional and lay leaders and members of the churches. Westminster Press publications enlarge the understanding of issues of everyday life in the community of humankind; they advocate a free, just, and peaceful society; and they foster the attainment of full humanity by individuals in their interpersonal relationships.
>
> In the interest of fostering creative exchange of thought and interreligious and intercultural dialogue throughout the world, Westminster Press publications represent a broad diversity of religious, social, and cultural points of view. Important concerns identified by The United Presbyterian Church may serve as focal points for discussion. Authors, however, are free to offer their own understandings of truth without being asked to subscribe to a particular creed or system of thought.[26]

The 1980s saw the publication of additional controversial and significant writers, under the leadership of Keith Crim, editorial director, and Robert McIntyre, general manager.

These included such Roman Catholic theologians as Hans Küng and Edward Schillebeeckx. Pioneering works in liberation theology and feminist thought also found expression through the Press. Though under pressure during the 1970s and early 1980s to be more closely tied to the denomination, Westminster Press remained an independent enterprise in many respects. At this point, the flow of dollars into and out of the publishing area of the denomination's life was not so much an issue. The production of many church supply items and curriculum resource materials carried with it the ongoing flow of the more scholarly, less widely sold books. This would be an issue that would surface in a particularly pressing way during the late eighties.

John Knox Press

One of the first actions of the Old School southerners was to establish an executive committee on publication. Following the lead of James H. Thornwell, who sought to guard Presbyterian governing bodies against the autonomous actions of "boards," the General Assembly of the Presbyterian Church in the Confederate States of America in 1861 kept mission and provision of resources in a committee structure. Soon they combined functions of education and publication in one committee, located in Richmond, Virginia.[27]

Despite great difficulty in securing paper and type, the committee produced fifteen tracts during its first year of existence. *The Children's Friend,* a small monthly paper, emerged to replace Sunday school materials that had formerly come from Philadelphia. By 1863, a monthly paper, *The Soldier's Visitor,* appeared along with twenty-eight tracts; forty-six more appeared in 1864.[28]

Following the Civil War, the PCUS was organized from the PCCSA, the remnants of New School Presbyterianism, and the Presbyterians in border synods of the Old School Assembly. Thus, the Presbyterian Church that emerged in the South felt a distinctive sense of responsibility and of regional identity. For instance, it could provide apologetic defenses of the schism and it could publish *The Distinctive Principles of the Presbyterian Church in the United States.* This was a relatively straightforward, rigid interpretation of Calvinism, which declared that no church is "loyal" to an earthly government and offered a partial defense of the South's peculiar institution of slavery. As later reports on the publishing enterprise in the South would recall, its publications were to be quite consciously "an evangelical agency." The PCUS Committee on Publication also offered serious tomes of orthodox theology which, frankly, did not sell as well as people might have hoped. Nor did they move far beyond the narrow confines of the denomination itself.[29]

In the 1870s, James K. Hazen became secretary and remained such until after the turn of the century. Although the Committee undertook the oversight of all PCUS Sabbath schools in 1888, the publications continued to emerge. They remained quite conservative both in form and in substance, reflecting an absorption with the question of denominational theological identity and rectitude. It could not have been a particularly happy time for those who were being influenced by the wider reaches of theological research and cultural thought. The Committee's publications also fostered the PCUS doctrine of the "spirituality of the church," selecting sermons for the *Southern Presbyterian Pulpit* (1896), for example, extolling and explaining the virtues of this particular doctrine.[30] The scholar passes lightly over that particular focus now, tending to look critically on it. Nevertheless, in spite of the cultural limitations operating in the doctrinal circumstances of the denomination at that time, the leadership of the PCUS had touched a nerve. There was, in the midst of the maelstrom of ideas that were beginning to challenge the identity of the church from a variety of perspectives, a strong if rather slender voice proclaiming that whatever else it might become, the church of Jesus Christ rested on a spiritual foundation.

With the death of Hazen in 1903, the committee structure reorganized and divided responsibilities for business affairs, Sunday school direction, and editorial work. R. A.

Lapsley became head of the editorial department, and though his leadership remained conservative, the work expanded greatly. Many of the books and leaflets from this period bear the name "Onward Press," but that seems to have been an informal imprint classification rather than a deliberate attempt to foster a publishing house.[31]

With the division of the Presbyterian community in America established, the southern church soon realized that it must develop a good deal farther its own publishing program. This began to emerge in the first half of the twentieth century. In 1931 Lewis J. Sherrill addressed the problem with these words: "The southern Presbyterian pen has almost run dry. We have prided ourselves upon intellectual leadership, but if productivity of the pen is even slightly related to the productivity of the mind, it might be plausibly argued that we have really ceased thinking."

The next leader of note, Edward D. Grant, assumed direction in 1934. He led the PCUS publications and other educational efforts, which produced a Board of Christian Education and a John Knox Press.[32] The Committee on Publication continued to develop, and it continued to use the name of the Onward Press. However, by 1938 it realized that the public seemed to identify the name "Onward" with a Sunday school curriculum publishing program. It thus changed its name, in what must be regarded in retrospect as a marketing decision, to the John Knox Press. It still had a Presbyterian ring to it, but it also had the feel of a broader publishing program.

General Assembly *Minutes* reported its official existence in 1939. "The name has been well received," the report indicated, predicting somewhat triumphally, "We propose to make it as well known through the country as that of any other church publisher." In 1941, however, the Committee report still indicated some hesitation in the use of this publishing imprint. Thus, in 1949, the report reemphasized the reason for using "John Knox Press." It was "to keep from being discriminated against in the open book market where church board publications are too readily branded as 'denominational propaganda.'"[33] Coupled with this, in the preceding years, was the authorization by the General Assembly of $125,000 as working capital. It was an unprecedented vote of confidence.

The first intention of this new publishing endeavor was limited to certain specific concerns. It was to perform evangelistic outreach; it was to support the youth programs and to provide resources for an educational ministry; it was to offer materials for Bible study, and to provide a new source for devotional material. The first book was Stuart R. Oglesby's *Prayers for All Occasions.* The second volume boldly set forth to offer an introduction to the book of Revelation, written by Donald W. Richardson. It was published in 1939 with the title *The Revelation of Jesus Christ.* A movement was under way, and this movement would inevitably bring about its own momentum for change. In the 1940 annual report of the executive committee of Religious Education and Publication, the committee said, "We are laying emphasis upon evangelism in the book store and publishing departments." The emphasis was on distribution and sales, however, of material that came to hand through recognized and accepted sources. The emphasis had not yet been placed on the concept that would soon shape the destiny of religious book publishing in America, the principle of intentional publishing. The 1941 report indicates the way in which Christian education concerns were shaping the publication program. Elizabeth Shields wrote *Guiding Kindergarten Children* and *Learning to Know God Better.* The values of home and domestic concerns received considerable emphasis as a broader vision began to emerge. The John Knox Press list in 1942 included Eleanor Millard's *Bible People Who Love God,* Nelle Morton's *Camp Leader's Guide,* Hunter B. Blakely's *Defending the Bulwarks,* and Elizabeth Shields's *Happy Times in Our Church.*

The authors were still those known to the publishing program, people who were serving recognized leadership roles in the life of the church. Nevertheless, the ebb and flow of an institution was beginning to emerge. Momentum, identity, financial structures, and sales strategy began to have their part in producing an institution, a publishing program with its own heritage and concerns. The optimism of this movement was recognized in 1946, when the report of the executive committee of Religious Education and Publication stated, "For the second time in our history our book sales ran ahead of periodicals. This shows an exceedingly healthy trend." The total gross income in that year for the sale of books and supplies was $359,978.83. When that figure is looked at in terms of the inflationary change in the value of the dollar, it was a very encouraging figure indeed.

It was in this year that John Knox Press was including more substantial theological volumes, such as *Guilt and Redemption,* by Lewis J. Sherrill, *Stewardship in the New Testament,* by Holmes Rolston, and *The Basis of World Order,* edited by E. T. Thompson. In this year, John Knox produced fifteen new titles. One may well wonder where the more seminal original works of literature were being produced. The groundbreaking works and the theology that were appearing in Europe had not yet been accepted in the programmatic, denominational concern of the publishing program. Changes were under way, however, and a new sensitivity to theological diversity meant that the clarification of the purpose of the publishing program was required. A statement of purpose in 1954 said, "The purpose of John Knox Press is to contribute to and stimulate the advancement of Biblical scholarship and Christian thought and living throughout the world by the publication and distribution of books and other printed materials." One notes that the arena had now been extended to the entire world, the purpose is put in terms of stimulating the advancement of scholarship, and the desired end is the development of Christian thought and living. There was still a word of caution, inasmuch as the authors were required to be "within the bounds of the evangelical Christian tradition."

In 1955, Dwight Chalmers, a graduate of Union Theological Seminary with a Th.D., came as editor of the John Knox Press. Chalmers brought to this position theological interest and commitments that were similar to those of Paul Meacham of The Westminster Press. Thus, the two major

Presbyterian publishing houses in the country were being led by editors with strong commitments to theological scholarship as well as to the ongoing needs of the local church. It was a unique situation in American religious book publishing. Both publishing houses were moving ahead in very progressive directions, and, taken together, were surely setting the pace for theological book publishing anywhere in the English-speaking world. Chalmers soon organized, along with the editorial direction of Balmer Kelly and A. B. Rhodes, The Layman's Bible Commentary. It was a very creative approach to both Christian education and biblical scholarship. This commentary series was designed from stem to stern so that it could offer men and women the best of current scholarship on the Bible in clear, concise, and readable fashion. Although there were critics who vigorously attacked the project as including liberal scholarship and surrendering to the dread specter of modernism, the commentary series was a smashing success. It sold widely throughout the world, was translated into several languages, and was to sell eventually over a million volumes. The readership of the John Knox Press had certainly extended now far beyond the limits of the denomination.[34]

This series was followed by the Ecumenical Studies in Worship and the Ecumenical Studies in History. These volumes clearly marked the intentional ecumenical philosophy that directed the publishing concern of the Press. They were written by scholars in different countries and denominations, and they were designed to offer fresh perceptions, which brought the best of classical Christian scholarship and understanding to the contemporary challenges before the church. The extraordinary theological depth in these projects is well illustrated by the character of the editorial leadership that was involved in recommending the authors for the series on history. The general editors for the Ecumenical Studies in History were A. M. Allchin of Oxford, Martin E. Marty of Chicago, and T.H.L. Parker of Cambridge. The editorial board included scholars from seven additional countries. Other important books were brought to the John Knox publishing program, including those by such theologians and scholars as Karl Barth and Johannes Munck. The John Knox Press was now, along with The Westminster Press, at the forefront of theological scholarship in the world. Together they provided a historical and ecumenical perspective for theological scholarship in America which was unprecedented in Reformed circles at the time.

In 1961, John Knox Press celebrated the one hundredth anniversary of the publishing efforts of the Presbyterian Church in the South. It expressly reaffirmed its place as "an evangelical agency," but it had also broadened its perspective on its responsibilities. Theological enlightenment was now found to be an essential ingredient for church leadership. The service of God included the lively and progressive use of the mind. Thus, John Knox Press had moved, as had The Westminster Press, to a position of theological independence and creativity on behalf of the denomination. It now saw itself as carrying forward the denomination's larger responsibility of providing theological leadership in the larger context of the church universal. It was one of the key ways in which the denomination made a theological and educational contribution to the world church, a contribution that expressed the particular genius and ethos of the Reformed tradition. At this point, John Knox Press was producing over sixty books a year.[35]

Each publishing season included contributions to a variety of intentionally designed series. In 1963, John Knox Press initiated the Aletheia paperback series, with the Chime paperback program to follow shortly thereafter. Both of these were designed to make the fruits of top-quality religious scholarship available to a more popular readership. The pinnacle of this point of sales in the popular book market was reached with the publication of *The Gospel According to Peanuts,* by Robert L. Short. This policy provided the somewhat intoxicating idea that popular publishing could take the sale of Christian books into the extraordinary reach of the world trade market. At the same time, it was hoped that the sale of large numbers of popular books could provide the financial resources needed for the

publication of such substantial works as Ernest Trice
Thompson's three-volume *Presbyterians in the South.* The
surprising sale of popular books, on the one hand, and the
windfall income generated by the development of new curriculum resources for church use, on the other, generated a
financial base that seemed to provide an enduring subsidy
for the more serious theological works, which could not
always be counted on to pay their own publication costs.
Unfortunately, this bonanza would be short-lived. The
challenge of securing a strong denominational commitment to the publication of theological works would surface
for both John Knox Press and The Westminster Press in
short order.

In 1967, the 107th General Assembly made a very influential and revealing change in the statement of purpose for
John Knox Press. Here it was recognized for the first time
that the purpose was to be identical with the 1954 statement, with one exception. The exception was that the reference to authors being within the bounds of the evangelical
Christian tradition was eliminated. What this meant was
that books concerning the thought of people such as Paul
Tillich, Rudolf Bultmann, Søren Kierkegaard, and so on,
could be published. This implied a greater intellectual diversity in the leadership of the denomination than was
probably found in the membership at large. Whatever else
the change meant, it was certainly a growing acceptance of
a broader theological mission and a perception that the
publication of books was particularly concerned with the
presentation of stimulating theological ideas, as well as sig-
naling the international and ecumenical form that theology
had assumed in the Presbyterian Church in the United
States. It was a significant change. It reflected the growing
identification of denominational leadership with the goal
of being at the front of positive cultural and intellectual
developments. The Enlightenment had been officially accepted. This step would substantiate a new vision of spiritual and intellectual freedom, and it would provide for the
exploration of critical biblical and historical methods.

This step also meant that John Knox Press, and the

Board of Christian Education from which it was structured, accepted the importance of trade book publishing. The distinctive distribution channels required for a diverse trade-oriented program would provide something distinct in the history of its publication program. John Knox Press was now understood as providing a forum for the free research and exploration of ideas. The general concept of academic freedom, associated with the standards in higher education, was readily embraced as a healthy and constructive way to pursue the truth. In this regard, it was widely recognized that a place for the free interchange of ideas was needed somewhere within the structure of the church's intellectual life. It was during this period of the fifties and sixties that the Board of Christian Education had recognized the importance of the free interchange of theological ideas with European publishing houses and had moved to develop this part of the publication program further.

The John Knox Press role in theological publishing was intentionally removed from that of providing an indoctrination in one particular confessional perspective. John Knox Press had become an instrument of the church for creative interaction with people of varying, thoughtful, and constructive points of view. It was now developing a new, freshly affirmed sense of tradition. This tradition would include the task of publishing for the overt pedagogy of the church and the explicit production of evangelical materials within a broader theological concern. An open-minded maturity was embraced with the following position:

> The statement of purpose of the Press makes clear that our books are not only to "contribute to" but are also to "stimulate," and that we are above all else concerned with "the advancement of Biblical scholarship and Christian thought and living throughout the world." At times the stress lies on stimulating and sometimes our books provoke discussion and even disagreement. . . . The only book of which our editors approve 100% is the Bible.

With this intention in mind, the publishing house moved toward a closer dialogue between Christianity and culture. Thus, 1967 saw the publication of *The Devil with James*

Bond!, Sunday Night at the Movies, Buddhism and the Claims of Christ, and *Auschwitz Trials: Letters from an Eyewitness.* Authors such as Sam Keen, writing on Gabriel Marcel, and Ronald Gregor Smith, writing on Martin Buber, began to appear. As the Board of Christian Education expanded its range of ideas, so John Knox Press kept pace with this widening intellectual horizon. While the publication program and the educational interests of the Presbyterian Church in the United States were now in the mainstream of intellectual currents, some must have wondered if the original purpose for the publishing house had now become obscure. Others felt that theological book publishing of the denomination had merely come of age.

It was in 1970 that the Board of Christian Education interpreted its policy to the General Assembly by stating that three kinds of resources were made available to its church constituency. The first included curriculum resources. These resources consciously and explicitly advocated the theological, ethical, and educational positions of the board. The second type of resource included material for leaders and others, produced by fellow Christians, involving Christian integrity, but not necessarily reflecting the Reformed tradition. It was in this area that John Knox Press fell. The third area of material included resources compiled by Christians that might or might not reflect an overt Christian stance, but which would better help the church to understand the world. In 1971 this report was accepted by the 111th General Assembly. In 1972, the 112th meeting of the General Assembly reaffirmed this approach, with the General Assembly Mission Board accepting the position in 1974. Thus, the church reaffirmed its commitment for a place in the life of the denomination in which even its own values could be critically addressed and explored.

During the years in which the Covenant Life Curriculum sales were growing, the income generated for the Board of Christian Education helped to support the developing sophistication of John Knox Press publications. When the Covenant Life Curriculum sales sharply declined, however, the heavily undergirded book publishing program had to

shrink. When the larger agency of the Board of Christian
Education felt financial pain, all its departments had to feel
the pinch, regardless of the particular virtues and requirements of the specific programs involved. This meant that
the importance of balancing current publications with the
development of a strong backlist of books faced the challenge from the financial weakness of the overall structure in
which John Knox Press was located. What was now seen
more clearly was that John Knox Press was organically dependent on a host of processes that were beyond its control.
What had been assumed, the official endorsement of a theologically sophisticated publishing program, was now revealed to have been an endorsement that still lacked
financial resources.

A new chapter in the life of John Knox Press had begun.
Keith Crim, a highly skilled biblical scholar, succeeded
Dwight Chalmers as editor. In turn, he was followed by Davis Yuell. The success of the Press in reaching the popular
market had caught the attention of the large commercial
publishing establishments in the United States, and Yuell
was soon invited to join the editorial staff of Harper & Row
in New York. Richard Ray came to the editorship and then
became managing director of the Press. The story of the
publishing program of John Knox Press was woven into the
amalgamation of the church's work at the denominational
level under the authority of the General Assembly Mission
Board. The process of restructure was far more complex
than had been envisioned at first. With the notable goal of
extending the theological witness of the church's faith into
the book world, the publishing house now faced the twin
obstacles of a shrinking curriculum sales base and a general
administrative structure at the denominational level that
was undergoing unprecedented reorganization.

In significant ways, a large mission board faces a unique
challenge when it must include within its work the oversight of a trade-oriented, commercially structured, competitive book business. Difficult questions immediately
surfaced. How were the administrative costs allocated to
John Knox Press from the parent organization, the General

Assembly Mission Board, to be assigned in ways that were fair to the denomination and distinctively appropriate for a commercial enterprise? How was cost accounting for John Knox Press to be distinguished from the kinds of accounting procedures used in managing the world mission, the educational, and the charitable responsibilities and commitments of the church? How were the charges for warehouse space, order fulfillment, and promotion to be shared with and distinguished from the costs that were involved in other Mission Board programs? Would this become the time when the entire denomination would have to learn more about the opportunities that lay before it with the publication of trade books?

Bringing together the different features involved in this process, the John Knox program began to recover its momentum and to expand. Following the increased stability in some of these areas, the Press approached the questions that would be part of its future life. To what degree should a denomination's program for serious theological publishing be financially self-sufficient? To what degree should it be undergirded by the denomination's mission budget or capitalized with denominational resources? Indeed, was it even possible to conceive of the free-market forces as the criteria that would determine the selection and publication of books in theology? Such questions, unprecedented in the church's publishing history, became critical issues. Would the denomination accept a responsibility for the production and distribution of books that might initially serve relatively few readers but that would carry out a long-term impact in the life of the denomination's leadership in many subtle and secondary ways? And, related to these questions, was the one that had often risen for both The Westminster Press and John Knox Press: To what degree should the church's trade publishing program remain an independent, protected arena, where the relatively free discussion of theological ideas could occur within the life of the denomination? Ross Cockrell, as publisher, began to move the process toward an independent Presbyterian Publishing House for the denomination.

When Richard Ray left to return to the pastorate in 1981, he was succeeded by Donald Hardy and then Walt Sutton. Adopting the independent publishing house model of Augsburg Publishing House, the newly separated Presbyterian program sought to stand on its own feet financially. As part of this new, independent organization, John Knox Press would report directly to the General Assembly and would be free to develop procedures and managerial processes appropriate for publishing. This new structural design remained in effect until the union of the denominations was achieved and the resources of The Westminster Press and John Knox Press were combined.

One of the most important publication ventures launched during this period, when John Knox Press was located in Atlanta with the General Assembly Mission Board, was the multiple-volume series of commentaries entitled Interpretation: A Bible Commentary for Teaching and Preaching. It was edited by James L. Mays, Paul J. Achtemeier, and Patrick D. Miller.

Marketing is always a significant challenge for small publishing houses. This is no different for those which must specialize in theological books. Before its move from Richmond to Atlanta, John Knox had worked out a sales representation program with the Religion Department of Harper & Row. Following the termination of this agreement, John Knox Press and The Westminster Press had their own separate sales organizations. With the union of the two Presbyterian publishing house programs, however, the marketing efforts could be combined under the aegis of the Westminster sales force, with marketing and editorial personnel from both houses involved in the newly united Press.

Westminster/John Knox Press:
A New Beginning

As the resources of both publishing houses were brought together under the leadership of Robert McIntyre, the new publishing organization would be given the comprehensive responsibility for producing church school curriculum, oc-

casional educational resources, periodicals, and other
print-related materials. In addition, it would carry out retail book sales and mail-order distribution. The Presbyterian Publishing House would be the parent organization for
the Westminster/John Knox Press. It would carry the line
of books from both publishing traditions, and it would continue to offer new volumes that were appropriate for the
new denomination's mission. In 1989, seventy new titles
were produced, with the Press catalog including the full
backlist of twelve hundred titles. With Davis Perkins as editorial director, the Press is currently moving forward with,
for example, several new series including the Library of
Theological Ethics, the Library of Ancient Israel, and Literary Currents in Biblical Interpretation, and several important reference works, such as the *Encyclopedia of the
Reformed Faith* and *The Women's Bible Commentary.* The
editorial team includes five other acquisitions editors and
one foreign rights specialist.

Challenges continue for the new publishing house. There
will be the publication needs the denomination itself will
have within its own program. There will be the challenge of
continuing to develop the tradition of scholarly publishing.
There will be the lure of attempting to publish for the popular market and to develop books that are responsive to popular spiritual interest. There will be the question of whether
all the books published should echo the theological and
ethical commitments of the General Assembly or of constituent groups within the denomination, or whether the
freedom of the Press to exercise critical scholarship would
be sustained in the face of denominational pressures.

The challenge before the Press, as the challenge will be
felt before the wider church, is the way in which we as Presbyterians must respond to opportunities to embrace the
free exercise of critical Christian scholarship. The Press
will also have to face the challenge that it faced in earlier
periods of its history as Presbyterians experimented with
first one method and then another, attempting to meet the
needs of the frontier and to develop its audience. If a new
balance combining independence, wide appeal, strong

scholarship, and a commitment to the original evangelical and spiritual goals can be sustained, a fresh new period of scholarship may well emerge. Another vital chapter in the saga of the Presbyterian press will emerge.

Conclusions

The development of the Westminster/John Knox Press brings us to the conclusion of this essay. What can the history teach? What reflections does it provoke?

First, history teaches us that the communication of serious theological discussion about the Christian faith is germinal to its ongoing productive life. The marketplace of ideas is an essential requirement for the fresh expression of the gospel message in appealing terms for each generation. This has remarkably little to do with conventional views of marketplace economics. The determination of the sales chart has never been successfully identified with the requirements for prophetic Christian publishing or with the educational requirements of the church. On the other hand, it has a great deal to do with the church's support of prophetic and hermeneutical dialogues in an open market for theological debate.

Second, it indicates that even though the Presbyterian publishing programs have not always enjoyed significant independence, they seem to flourish when they are granted greater freedom from the larger structures of the denomination. The presses have requirements for procedures and managerial processes that are unique to the book industry. This might also serve to preserve the way in which the church can speak, from within its ongoing concern in other programmatic areas of work, with the distinct evangelical witness that is always required for the church's life.

The church-related college may offer a model for comparison. Perhaps a formula can be found in this context. It might be a framework in which the Presbyterian Publishing House receives the guidance, support, and financial commitment of the denomination. It would also be a structure, however, that provides for increased autonomy under the general di-

rection of the General Assembly. In various forms, strength
and continuity from the parent denominations have blessed
the presses through the years. The responsibility to sustain
the confessional heritage, the rapport and the convergence
with its general sense of mission, and the nurture of writers
within the church have all characterized the presses' history.
On the other hand, the history of denominational restructuring, while seen as valid church reorganization, has been pre-
carious to publishing administration.

Such reorganization, as necessary as it is, rescrambles
priorities, mixes procedures, and jeopardizes the requirements of long-term planning that are indispensable for significant publishing projects. A more independent, yet
completely accountable Press might be better suited to the
managerial requirements, planning cycles, and cash flow
necessities peculiar to the publication business. Such a publishing organization might be better able to provide resources for the national market as well as for the broader,
missional thrust of the Press into the world market of ideas.

Two quite different studies of theological publishing
should be noted at this point. In 1969, The Westminster
Press assigned Roland Tapp, then its associate editor, to
conduct a study of publishing markets and trends. Nearly
twenty years later, in 1988, a grant from the Lilly Endowment enabled Christopher Walters-Bugbee and Barbara G.
Wheeler to produce "A Study of the Role of Denominational Presses in the Publication of Theological Books."[36]
Both studies point to the significant cultural changes that
will continue to make a lasting imprint on publishing decisions. Both also point to the ways in which pressures,
trends, and restructuring tasks within the denominations
have complicated and frequently obscured the unique responsibilities for the publication of books.

One of the remarkable results of the Tapp study was the
discovery that Presbyterians tend to honor the study of theology a good deal more than they actually practice it.
Clergy, it was noted, read surprisingly few works in theology. And, as a result, it could be assumed that the laity
hardly read any. The impact of this finding could have far-

reaching results. It could, for instance, affect the ways in which clergy are educated in theological seminaries and the way in which church school materials are prepared. Thus, in the final years of this century, the Presbyterians with their own publishing house may well have become the custodians of a great heritage that is more vulnerable than may have been realized. It may be in danger of becoming dissipated among the trends, the political pressures, and the managerial preoccupations in contemporary denominational life.

The more recent study by Walters-Bugbee and Wheeler corroborates this finding by Tapp. It reports that the real value placed on independent, courageous theological publishing may be in fact far less than many denominations realize. While an elite group of theologically informed readers have traditionally supported strong publishing programs, these few supporters can no longer provide all the assurance and guidance that are needed. The denomination that wishes to provide a serious publishing program must recognize the real cost and the basic requirements for fulfilling this mission, and it must give a very high priority and visibility to it. It must also be concerned to provide the publishing program with the measure of editorial privilege that good publishing always requires.

Thus both studies pointed toward decisions necessary for the new Westminster/John Knox Press. The Education and Congregational Nurture Ministry Unit, in which the Publications Service functions, moved in 1989 to address these areas of responsibility by adopting a policy statement concerning the Press as well as the other publication services.

"Guided especially by Reformed traditions of education and free and open inquiry, Westminster/John Knox Press is committed to the publication of serious works of high merit," the statement declared. It mentioned several goals of publications, the freedom of authors to offer "their own understandings of truth without being asked to subscribe to a particular creed or system of thought," and the presentation of "significant ecclesiastical materials for the Presbyterian Church (U.S.A.)."

The introduction to the policy statement clearly stated that "editorial autonomy is maintained with regard to manuscript evaluation and content." An accompanying "Vision Statement" also spoke of the "editorial freedom" necessary for the enterprise to maintain integrity.

Thus the formal statements and financial support structures have been put in place for the new Press.

Westminster/John Knox Press, Presbyterian Publishing House (the retail marketing operation), the Resourcing Division of the Education and Congregational Nurture Ministry Unit (church school curriculum development), and the *Presbyterian Survey* magazine all operate financially from the Publications Service Enterprise Fund. This Enterprise Fund receives the income from products produced by Publications Service and pays the salaries and expenses of the people in the areas listed above, as well as those employees in the Support Services and Central Treasury Corporation units who are responsible to the work and mission of Publications Service. A total of 220 employees of the Presbyterian Church (U.S.A.) are paid in full or in part from this fund.

While mission units of the church are to be financially responsible within approved budgets, the Press (through Publications Service) has a mandate to be financially self-sustaining through the Enterprise Fund. And yet the Press must utilize the Enterprise Fund according to the General Assembly Council policies that are applicable to the mission units that are not obliged to be financially self-sustaining. This state of affairs has been the occasion of much discussion among staff and the elected members of the Publications Service Committee, who have puzzled over how the Press can operate according to sound publishing industry practices and be financially viable without control over its own destiny in terms of policy and without fiscal autonomy in utilizing the Enterprise Fund. The discussion continues at present.

As the years have unfolded, both Westminster Press and John Knox Press found that they had to be increasingly competitive to generate sales in the international book market. Theirs was a unique mission of the church in the marketplace of ideas. Thus, their own distinctive contribution, within the combination of goals and values from the denomination, would not be duplicated by any of the large trade publishing houses such as Harper & Row, Doubleday, Scribner's, and Macmillan. Indeed, these publishing houses produced their works eclectically, expanding and reducing their lists of books in response to commercial sales requirements. The church's theological and publishing endeavors could not rest on influences external to them. On the other hand, the Presbyterian presses were conceived to be distinctive from the specialized publishing concerns of such houses as Zondervan, Baker, and Eerdmans. These had been determined largely by individual and family influences, along with denominational preferences that were not necessarily those of the Presbyterians. They were not accountable to particularly Presbyterian publishing standards or confessional heritage.

Thus, the particular role of the church-related publishing house has become clearer through the years. It has to provide basic research which undergirds theological education, the development of curriculum, and the materials for church professionals. It also has to provide for the integrity of ideas, for the freedom to explore and to test theological insights. It has to allow room for the criticism of ideas and commitments that have been accepted by actions of the church in the past. It has to be a forum in which ideas can be tried. It provides an opportunity for personal statements of faith as well as for those which are ecclesiastical. It provides a bargain for the church's external witness, for while other outreach programs are subsidized entirely by the church, and church-related sales, the sale of books in the broad book market involves public support for its publication program. It provides for a flow of ideas between lay and professional church leaders and interested parties which is essential to the life of the denomination. With the combination of John Knox and The Westminster Press, this adventure can now move forward with great promise. It must combine the passion for the gospel with the realization that our book publishing can now go farther into the world of trade sales, into the places where the witness of the church can have an impact, where it can meet the spiritual hunger that is widely present outside the church itself. As did the apostle Paul, the Presbyterian book publishing program can make a strong witness in the places where ideas are debated today.

The Presbyterian Publishing House will have the opportunity to serve the church's own needs with diligence and with care, but it will also have the responsibility to explore and to proclaim the Christian gospel in places outside the church where minds may be won for Christ. An independent, vigorous, and imaginative publishing house has been one of the ways in which our church has served both its own needs and the proclamation of the gospel at large.

6

A Brief History
of a Genre Problem:
Presbyterian Educational
Resource Materials

Craig Dykstra and J. Bradley Wigger

Introduction

The value of education is virtually unquestioned among Presbyterians. It is a tradition that has recognized learning to be an essential ingredient in the life of faith and therefore taken upon itself the task of building schools and providing the resources necessary for educating not only its clergy but all its members throughout its history.

In the light of this commitment to learning and education, it should come as no surprise that many in the Presbyterian Church (U.S.A.) today sense that its renewal and revitalization must be in significant part the renewal and revitalization of its educational ministry, institutions, and resources. The educational ministry of the Presbyterian Church is complex, involving congregations, judicatories at various levels, colleges and seminaries, and a variety of other institutions. Each of these educational settings is itself a complex interplay of factors and forces that include the persons involved, the relations they establish with one another, the materials they study and use, the patterns of language and symbol employed in their discourse with one another, the places in which they meet, and the organizational structures by means of which all of this is gathered together.[1] Renewal and revitalization of the educational ministry of the Presbyterian Church requires attention to all of this, in terms of both the present situation and the possibilities inherent in it. But neither the present nor the future can be understood without attention to the past. And every one of these educational settings, as well as each of the components within them, has a history.

We propose here to provide an outline of one such history, one that has to do with the changing shape or form of curriculum materials produced by the denomination for use in congregations. The education that goes on in congregations is hardly limited to what takes place in church classrooms with the aid of denominationally produced curriculum resource materials, but that is an important part of it. And the material resources themselves have both reflected and affected the basic meanings and patterns of education that have prevailed during any particular period. Yet we have few studies of these materials *as materials.*[2]

In this study, we examine how the materials themselves have changed from the early nineteenth century to the present. In doing so, we have paid more attention to the format of the materials published than to their content. We have done this on the hunch that shifts in basic form might reveal something significant about what teaching and learning are assumed to be. Curriculum resource materials produced by the denomination for use in Sunday school or church school (the name changes from time to time) have *looked* different during different periods. Substantive changes in how they appear in print turn out to mark substantive changes in how education in Christian faith has been understood in the Presbyterian Church. This essay is an attempt to chart out the important shifts, to discern some of the influences that have led to them, and to discuss some of the impact of these shifts on teaching and learning in the church.

We discern four major periods. The first is the period before "curriculum," dating from 1838, when the Presbyterian Board of Publication was established, to 1873. This latter date marks the creation of the first true "curriculum" (which we shall define shortly), the Uniform Lesson series. This series established the original and basic paradigm for curriculum in Christian education, one that dominated Presbyterian curriculum from 1873 to at least 1947. Despite some important changes in educational philosophy and in the scope of the denomination's responsibilities and interests in Christian education, the basic format of curriculum materials did not change significantly for seventy-five years or more. Indeed, the Uniform Lessons have continued into the present, even while other patterns have come and gone.

The third period lasts three decades from 1947 to 1975. It is a period of intense professional curriculum development, in which serious attempts to break the dominant mold were made. The years cover the period during which the *Christian Faith and Life,* Covenant Life, and *Christian Faith and Action* curriculum resource materials were produced by the PCUSA, PCUS, and UPCUSA, respectively. Most analysts argue that this is the period of greatest transformation in curriculum resource materials and that Presbyterians took the lead in creating quite new approaches to Christian education. And indeed it was so. But the basic genre of Sunday school literature was not successfully revamped, despite heroic efforts. This failure has led to the situation of the present.

The current period began in 1976 when both *Christian Faith and Action* and Covenant Life were replaced by *Christian Education: Shared Approaches,* a cooperative effort of a dozen denominations in which both the UPCUSA and the PCUS participated. Most recently, since CE:SA came to an end, the new Presbyterian and Reformed Educational Ministry materials have been produced. Both sets of materials have, in our view, given up the attempt to reform the basic curriculum genre. In this fact might lie some clues to current educational difficulties in the Presbyterian Church (U.S.A.) as well as to some of the educational challenges it faces.

Before "Curriculum"

The history of Presbyterian curriculum materials is tightly bound up with the rise and establishment of the Sunday school. When the first General Assembly convened in 1789, local Sunday school unions were just forming, and the influence of the evangelical Protestant Sunday school movement was beginning to spread.

Originally, Sunday schools were Sunday charity schools dedicated to teaching literacy to poor children in urban areas. They were important institutions, but the popularity of the Sunday school began to rise significantly only when its character shifted. From the colonial era to the beginning of the nineteenth century, education was accessible primarily to the middle and upper classes, and its subject matter was imbued with religion. Children learned to read and write using such resources as the *New England Primer,* which contained the Lord's Prayer, the Ten Commandments, the Shorter Catechism, and many "moral lessons."[3] With the advent of public schooling, education in literacy was made much more widely available, and Sunday literacy schools for the poor were less urgent. Only then did the Sunday schools take on a *religious* educational function and move into the middle and upper classes. Various evangelical leaders (mostly lay, though there were some clergy involved) seized the opportunity to turn the Sunday school into what Robert Lynn and Elliott Wright have described as "a prep school for the whole of evangelical America."[4] The Sunday school became a movement that spread across America and took on great prominence through the whole of the nineteenth century.

In 1824, the American Sunday School Union (ASSU) was formed. From the beginning, it published resources. It offered Bibles and Testaments, hymnals, catechisms, and question books used to guide discussion. In addition, the Union distributed a broad array of medals, picture cards, and reward tickets (blue, red, and white with scripture verses printed on them), all to be given to students as prizes for memorizing great portions of scripture, even whole books of the Bible. For a period of time, the Sunday school was oriented heavily to memorization as a basic learning strategy, and the Bible was its central subject matter.[5]

These were not the only resources, however. The ASSU had by 1859 managed to provide three-fifths of all American libraries.[6] The Union published thousands of books, inexpensively, and sent them out with colporteurs and Sunday school missionaries into "every destitute place."[7] Sunday school libraries far outnumbered school or community libraries. Subjects of the books ranged widely, but many of them were hard-cover, illustrated storybooks for children providing moral lessons enshrined in the worldview and doctrines of evangelical Christianity. Sunday school books provided the substance of much American reading at the time.

In addition, the ASSU distributed support books for teachers, such as *The Sunday School Teacher's Guide,* by the Rev. J. A. James.[8] This and others, such as W. F. Lloyd's *The Teacher's Manual* and Frederick Packard's *The Teacher Taught,* were not sets of lesson plans. Indeed, they gave little direct instruction about teaching at all. Rather, they provided inspiring messages concerning the teachers' high calling and counsel toward the improvement of their own spiritual lives.[9]

The beginnings of Presbyterian efforts to publish materials for the support of education in congregations must be seen in this context, for they were a response and reaction to what the ASSU was doing. In 1838 the General Assembly established "The Presbyterian Board of Publication of Tracts and Sabbath School Books." The formation of this board was the direct result of an overture brought before the Presbytery of Philadelphia in 1833:

> WHEREAS, It is at all times important, and peculiarly so at the present and in the existing circumstances of our Church, that effectual care be taken that our Catechisms and other doctrinal Standards, and also tracts and other publications in which correct views of Calvinistic truth are stated and defended, should be circulated abundantly among the people of our denomination; therefore,

> *Resolved,* That it be, and it hereby is, overtured by this Presbytery to the Synod of Philadelphia to take order for the establishment of a Presbyterian tract society within the bounds of the Synod, in order that the people of all our congregations may be furnished readily and at a moderate price with the standard and other authors of an orthodox Calvinistic character.[10]

The "present and . . . existing circumstances" had much to do with the *un*denominational character of the publications produced by the ASSU that were infiltrating Presbyterian churches. Because of the lack of doctrinal purity of these materials, the denomination would have to get into the act and produce and distribute a proper body of material of its own.

The very first of the board's publications was a moving if somewhat saccharine forty-nine-page dialogue written by Archibald Alexander, senior professor at Princeton Theological Seminary, entitled *The Way of Salvation Familiarly Explained in a Conversation Between a Father and His Children* (1839). Beginning in 1851, a semimonthly periodical for children called *The Presbyterian Sunday School Visitor* was published. The board's historian in 1888 said:

> Its pictorial illustrations are of a highly creditable character. Its matter, both selected and contributed, is strictly religious. Without sacrificing solidity to a simplicity which makes no demands of intellect, it presents the most useful and important truths in a style well adapted to engage the attention and arrest the affections of the young. Adults read it with pleasure and profit, and many have accorded to it an estimate of the highest grade as a paper adapted to all.[11]

Though the board faced some difficulties in its early years, by 1871 it was able to publish a 508-page *Descriptive Catalogue.* It listed 1,106 bound volumes, many written by the church's professors and scholars. There were, in addition, series of commentaries and biblical helps, collections of psalms and hymns, music books, juvenile picture books and packets, catechisms, question books, primers, spelling books and readers, various miscellaneous forms, cards, and engravings, plus a "Shorter Catechism in raised letters for the blind." Besides all this, one could obtain tracts, four to thirty-two pages in length, on over five hundred different topics, from "Miller on Presbyterianism" and "Perseverance of the Saints" to "Sabbath at Home," either singly or bound in one of four series. A number of these publications had been translated and were available in French, German, Latin, Portuguese, Spanish, and Welsh. And everything was specifically intended for popular use.

The important point for our purposes about this period in the history of curriculum resource materials is the form all these materials take. The ASSU and the Presbyterian Board of Publication were publishing *libraries.* These were not curriculum materials. They were reading materials. It is important to note the difference.

The word "curriculum" can, of course, be used to refer to any materials used in educational settings for educational purposes. Any printed resource can become curriculum in this sense, if it is used in this way. The producers of the materials we have been discussing certainly intended them to be so employed. But there is another, more specific sense in which the term "curriculum" is used when we refer to educational resources. The word refers to a particular genre of written material that has specific identifying features. We all recognize this genre when we see it. Curriculum, as a specific form of written work, is a printed book, magazine, or pamphlet *in which the material to be studied is accompanied by directions for the way in which it is to be studied.* Sometimes the material to be studied (say, a portion of scripture or a theological essay) and the directions for the educational process appear in separate places—perhaps a student's book for the one and a teacher's guide for the other. Often they appear in the same volume, and even on the same page. The point is that if the two are explicitly linked (and, usually, they are published and distributed together), they are curriculum in this narrower sense.

This genre or form of materials is now so commonplace that the word curriculum connotes such materials readily. But during the early years of the Sunday school movement and the Presbyterian Board of Publication, *no curriculum in this sense was published.* Libraries of material to read and study were published. Bibles, catechisms, question books, commentaries, hymnals, storybooks, tracts, and periodicals were published. But none of these were curriculum in the sense we usually mean it today. These materials were all read and studied by students and teachers, but directions for *how* they should be read and studied were not included.

So how did people know what to do with them? For the most part, it was obvious to teachers and students alike. Questions in question books were to be discussed and answered. Bible stories were to be told and talked about together. Catechisms and large parts of the Bible were to be memorized and recited. What "how to" help teachers needed came largely through informal "conversations with other teachers and discussions at teachers' meetings, where the agenda often included prayer, progress reports, and problem solving."[12]

More importantly, the question of how to teach was not nearly so central as the spiritual character of the teacher. The point of the early Sunday schools was the religious conversion of children, and this was understood to come more through the heart than through the head. As Anne Boylan points out, teachers "envisioned their work less as an intellectual process of imparting information and more as an emotional process of sharing spiritual experiences." Thus, the qualities most desirable in teachers had to do with their own religious vitality and whether they were "capable of appealing directly to their students' hearts." This was reflected in the content and approach of the teachers' manuals, which "emphasized qualities of heart over qualities of mind in the ideal teacher."[13]

These assumptions about the fundamental aims of the Sunday school and about the kinds of teachers needed are reflected not only in the teachers' manuals, but also in the content and form of the wider body of materials published. The function of study and the purpose of reading was to touch the heart and foster conversion. It was assumed that faith, both the teachers' and the students', could be stimulated and enhanced by the right kind of study, scholarship, and reading.[14] Study did not just form minds; it shaped souls. This was especially true of study of the Bible, but theology that was doctrinally correct, stories that touched the heart, and works aimed directly at the inspiration of the religious life all had important roles to play. The "Preliminary Notice" in the Presbyterian Board of Publication's *Descriptive Catalogue* (1871) claims that the materials described in it are the board's response to "the command of the Master, 'Feed my lambs.'"

> A whole library of volumes for the Sabbath-school is published by the Board, which, without claiming absolute perfection, challenges examination and comparison with the list of any publishing-house in the world. These books range comprehensively from the little book for the infant scholar up to the goodly volumes adapted to the reading of the members of our highest Bible classes. . . . Nor will the earnest Christian or the lover of deep Christian experience be disappointed in the study of this list. The rich thoughts of former generations have been conserved in the works of Baxter, Bunyan, Davies, Matthew Henry, Owen, Mead, whilst of more modern date the "Religious Experience" of Archibald Alexander, the "Daily Meditations" of George Bowen, the Biographies of McCheyne, Alexander, Walter M. Lowrie, Mrs. Sherwood, Samuel A. Rhea, and many others of similar spirit, will stimulate and feed the soul that hungers and thirsts after righteousness.[15]

In the beginning of Sunday school work as a whole and of the Presbyterian Church's efforts to provide materials to sustain education in congregations, the curriculum resources assumed to be needed were libraries of reading materials designed to nourish the spiritual life of scholars and teachers alike. "Curriculum," in the sense of published directions for the orderly study and teaching of a specific body of literature, simply did not exist. But its emergence as a new form was just over the horizon. The pivotal date is 1871, just as the *Descriptive Catalogue* was being published.

The Emergence of "Curriculum"

In 1871, twenty-nine representatives of denominational publishing houses and societies met and agreed to develop a "uniform" course of study based on the Bible.[16] The 1872 National Sunday School Convention approved the seven-year course they had agreed on, which ran from 1873 through 1879. These Uniform Lessons, though very simple in format, were the beginning of curriculum in the specific sense we have defined.

Later called the International Lesson System, its import was that for the first time a *system* of study would be provided. Though the Uniform Lessons consisted simply of an assigned Bible passage, a lesson title or topic, and a memory verse for each week, the crucial factor was that the publishers were moving beyond providing unsystematic helps and had started to organize the content and processes that would take place in classrooms all across the world.

The impulse toward "system" had a number of sources. For one, the Sunday school movement expanded rapidly after the Civil War, experiencing a "second birth." This expansion was accompanied and fostered by a kind of organizational boosterism led by some of the prominent merchants and manufacturers of the day.[17] Evangelical fundamentalists all, they were, as Lynn and Wright point out,

> rather indifferent to intellectual issues of the day. Their real interest was elsewhere. They found the problems of organization intriguing and fascinating. [They] took aesthetic delight in transforming an inchoate mass of men and resources into a cleanly developed, purposeful institution. To organize was not just a necessity; it was also the major creative act of life.[18]

The order and system that the boosters craved may have been excessive, but the rapidly expanding core of Sunday school leaders and teachers needed something. The calls for more help in organizing the content and processes of teaching had been rising for some time as the expansion of the movement grew too quickly for the local Sunday schools themselves to provide new generations of teachers out of the ranks of their own students.

Likewise, the goals and spirit of the Sunday school were changing under the impact of new visions of the meaning of childhood and the growing influence of an increasingly sophisticated public school pedagogy. Horace Bushnell's ideas on "Christian nurture" and his criticisms of the conversionism in orthodox Evangelicalism became increasingly influential. And the educational theories of Johann Pestalozzi were everywhere by the 1860s. The educational techniques he suggested emphasized the importance of the step-by-step, long-term development of the child's mind and personality.[19] Thus, the impulse to systematize at the organizational level was reinforced at the psychological and pedagogical levels.

The Uniform Lessons were not the first attempts at curriculum. There were a few precursors.[20] In fact, the Presbyterian Board of Publication (now of the northern branch of what was the recently divided church) itself had begun in 1871 to publish the Westminster Sabbath-School Lessons, which eventually would have "embraced a full curriculum of Bible study extending through eight years, and giving lessons on both the Old and the New Testaments."[21] These were never completed, however, because the Board halted its original plans and bought into the Uniform Lessons plan. Similarly, the "southern" branch (PCUS), disappointed with its own attempts to create a systematic course of study, began a set of Uniform Lessons in 1875 in cooperation with the Reformed Church in America.

Since the Uniform Lessons were nothing more than an uncopyrighted list, each of the denominations and publishing houses was expected to provide its own expositions and lesson helps as the material content of the new system. The first Presbyterian publication along these lines was *The Presbyterian at Work,* which in 1879 became *The Westminster Teacher.* This was a monthly journal consisting of approximately forty pages of expository articles for the benefit of the scholarship of the teacher. No regard was given to the age of the teacher's students. Typically, an issue would include six or seven general articles, including news, reflections on and suggestions for teaching, essays on the biblical texts, and perhaps some poetry and other literary supplements. Following the introductory section came the weekly lessons for the month.

For each week, the Uniform Lesson text, title, and memory verse were provided. In addition, seven more texts for home study, a catechism question and answer, lesson hymns, and a lesson plan were provided. The lesson plan for July 12, 1885, provides a good example. The text was 1 Kings 12:25–33, and the topic, "Idolatry Established." An outline was given: "1. The Lord Forsaken. 2. Idols Set Up. 3. False Worship Established. Time: B.C. 975. Places: Shechem, Bethel, Dan." Then came a one-paragraph "Explanation of the Lesson," which gave an overview or abstract of the text. The scripture passage was printed out, and after each verse references to related texts were provided. Next came a verse-by-verse exposition. This was followed by a section called "Application and Illustration," which made connections between the text and life situations. Then ten or more "Lesson Points" were provided, proverbial sayings through which students could be sure to understand the moral point of the lesson. For this lesson, one such point is: "To depart from God and to enter a sinful course is to start a train of evil, whose end no one can foresee." After all this, a section called "Suggestions for Teaching" appeared. This usually consisted of questions to be asked of the class members about the text. Sometimes the questions were left open; sometimes answers to them were provided. The questions were geared not only to help the students think about the text. They were also set up in such a way that the discussion of them would offer the teacher an opportunity to display some of the results of his or her own reading in the introductory essays. Then a suggestion for a blackboard picture was provided, in order that the students might have some visual image to go with the text. Finally, there was a section of suggestions "For Teachers of the Little Folks." Following the whole series of weekly lessons, *The Westminster Teacher* concluded with abstracts for a dozen or so new books published by the Board that could be ordered and used to enhance one's teaching and Christian life.

The Presbyterian at Work/Westminster Teacher was the beginning of modern curriculum in the Presbyterian Church. At first, curriculum was designed specifically and exclusively for the teacher. Students could depend simply on their Bibles. Soon, however, lesson materials to be put in the hands of the "scholars" were also made available. *The Westminster Lesson Leaf* was begun in 1873. *The Westminster Quarterly,* a lesson help for more advanced "scholars," appeared in 1880. Two sets of illustrated "lesson leafs," *Sunbeam* "for the very little people" and *Forward* for young people, were circulated by 1882.

Lesson helps in the hands of students were a significant development. With this innovation, Sunday school literature came to mean not primarily books and tracts to be read, but "lessons" to be done. The Bible continued as a mainstay, of course. But now parts of the Bible were picked out for study and inscribed on a separate sheet of paper. Furthermore, directions for the study of these Bible passages were available in what became an increasingly specific, ordered teacher's guide.

The pattern was set. Here we have, for the first time in the Presbyterian Church, curriculum materials in the modern sense. The paradigm had been established. Curriculum was now being produced in which the materials to be studied and the directions for their use accompanied each other. In the main, the modern history of Christian education curriculum is a series of elaborations on this basic form.

One of the important effects of the establishment of this new genre in the Sunday school was the fact that it gradually replaced books, tracts, and stories as the Sunday school's basic literature. Indeed, it can be argued that over time it also replaced the Bible. Thus the enormous variety of literature and styles that had been in the hands of teachers and students was reduced significantly, and control of the literature was held more tightly by the denomination.

A second important effect was that it formalized the role of teachers. Over time, the teachers' role subtly shifted from that of sharing their own evangelical faith to that of teaching the prescribed lesson. Each Sunday school class would be part of a large, national, even international enterprise, with everyone (or at least every Presbyterian) ideally doing the same thing every Sunday. Hence the abilities, technical skills, and knowledge of the teachers—and particularly their competence to function in their prescribed role—became a higher priority than the vitality of their faith or their evangelical fervor.

Both of these effects were to some degree intended and welcomed by the Presbyterian Board of Publication. The problem was that Sunday schools had been getting lesson helps of various kinds "from the most diverse sources—from voluntary societies, private publishing-houses, and not a few from denominational houses other than our own."[22] In Rice's history of the board, this state of affairs is cited as the rationale for producing the "Westminster Lesson Helps":

> This state of things was anomalous and every way undesirable. The evils were manifold. The effect on the schools was the opposite of unity and denominational co-operation. The tendency was directly toward disintegration—to the promotion of party and sectional feeling. The Sabbath-school Department from the beginning sought steadily and earnestly to bring our schools into communion and sympathy with one another and with the plans and purposes of the Church. . . . A community of literature, the use of the same helps and the singing of the same songs were believed to have a powerful influence in this direction.[23]

"Curriculum" was from the beginning a genre of literature specifically designed to control the relations and learnings so that they occurred in the Sunday school class according to a standard pattern.

Over the years, *The Westminster Teacher* became more elaborate and the student materials became somewhat more sophisticated. By the turn of the century, there were junior, intermediate, senior, and home quarterly lesson helps. In 1904, helps for beginners were added. In 1907, *The Westminster Teacher* became a weekly paper rather than a monthly magazine. International Graded Lessons were established by the International Sunday School Association and adopted by the PCUSA in 1909 and by the PCUS in 1914. A further refinement, the Closely Graded Series, commenced publication in 1915. But the basic pattern did not change. *The Westminster Teacher* continued in publication until 1929, fifty years.

The "Graded Series" publications were an innovation in the midst of continuity, coming as they did shortly after the turn of the century, under the influence of the burgeoning new child psychology and the related attempts by various scholars in the religious education movement to make Sunday school education more pedagogically sophisticated and theologically liberal. "Grading" and "closely grading" were partial responses. More radical was the move toward "child-centered" and "life-centered" curricula. This required something new. The PCUSA continued to make Uniform Lessons available, but in 1929 the "Westminster Departmental Graded Materials" moved off the Uniform Lessons track and became a set of materials designed to develop "Christian character" in children. According to a 1932 board report of the PCUSA, "the materials are child-centered, being built primarily on the basis of the interest, needs, and characteristics of the individuals in the age groups for which they are planned."[24]

Surprisingly, however, though the aims changed and the focus shifted toward the child's experience, the basic format of the materials remained the same. The Sunday school form of education that had been established by the late 1870s, and the basic structure of the materials that sustained it, were so entrenched that a whole new set of ideas about education and religion could not move them. And attempts to incorporate the new religious understanding and the new pedagogy into the old form simply did not work. Teachers became confused and complained about "the lack of Bible and doctrine" in the materials. By the end of their run, sales were off badly. At that point, the denomination had realized that something entirely different needed to be done. By then, too, liberal theology and progressivist pedagogy were coming under heavy attack, and Presbyterian scholars were among the leadership of the opposition.

The "New" Curricula

The "new" curricula were *Christian Faith and Life: A Program for Church and Home* (PCUSA), which began publishing materials in 1948, and later, in 1962, the Covenant Life Curriculum (PCUS). A "new" curriculum of another variety was *Christian Faith and Action* (UPCUSA), which succeeded *Christian Faith and Life* in 1970.

Christian Faith and Life was the pioneer. The story of its creation is superbly rendered by William B. Kennedy in an article entitled "Neo-Orthodoxy Goes to Sunday School,"[25] and we shall not repeat it here. There were many things new about it, including the new theology the curriculum tried to incorporate and communicate,[26] but of special interest to us is its somewhat ambivalent attempt to break the mold of the "curriculum" genre.

One important way in which it tried to do this was to publish *books.* The Board of Christian Education was returning in part to the pattern that had prevailed in the Board of Publication's Sunday school work before 1871. The Board of Christian Education was quite explicit in regarding The Westminster Press as a means by which it would discharge its educational responsibility, and committed it to "make available to the reading public books that offer a thorough, reliable, and readable interpretation of Christian faith and life."[27] This output would include an expansive literature for youth as well as adults. The *Westminster Study Edition of the Holy Bible,* which would bring modern biblical scholarship into the purview of the laity, was a significant component of the plan.

General publication was not enough, however. The curriculum makers wanted to put good books that children and young people could read at home directly into their hands. A whole series of hard-cover, four-color-illustrated home reading books were carefully prepared to convey to children and youth panoramic visions of the three great themes of the curriculum: Jesus Christ, the Bible, and the Church. The authors were recruited from among the denomination's theologians and biblical scholars, who were under the careful supervision of a group of editors, including some who were very well trained in children's education and literature. They attempted to make the church's story and message vivid and accessible while simultaneously informed and guided by the best of modern, theological scholarship. They were not uniformly successful, but some of these books were extremely popular. Robert McAfee Brown's contribution, *The Bible Speaks to You,* is still in print.

Why books? One reason was to provide a conduit to the home. If the books were good enough, the editors reasoned, children and youth would read them with their parents. This would help parents understand what was being taught and enable them to be participants in their children's Christian education. Other reasons are summarized in this published statement used to explain the rationale of the new curriculum:

> In the reading books on the life of Christ, the Bible, and the Church, it will be possible to overcome the fragmentariness which has dogged the Bible teacher and to give due attention to the great central and unifying themes. The interrelatedness of the different parts of the Bible can be clearly shown. But, more important, the constant emphasis will be upon what God is saying through these records to one who has to face life today. A consistent aim will be to give the pupil a working knowledge of his Bible and an ability to read it for himself. The reading books will remain with him as guides to help him in difficulties he meets in Bible-reading in later days.[28]

Ever since the beginning of the Uniform Lessons, "fragmentariness" had been the mark and bane of Sunday school education. This included not only a fragmentary approach to the Bible itself, but also the fragmentation of the Bible from the rest of Christian faith and thought as well as the fragmentation of Sunday school education from the kinds of education that could go on elsewhere—at home, for instance, in conversation with a family member, or by oneself, reading. The turn to books was an attempt to deal with this problem.

The publication of curriculum in the more restricted sense was not given up, however. The Uniform Lesson series continued, for one thing. And the *Christian Faith and Life* program included pupil's workbooks, picture and activity sets, and a teacher-parent magazine. The quarterly teacher-parent magazine in many ways reflected the style of *The Westminster Teacher,* except that now there was an issue designed specifically for each grade level. The magazine was intended to inform teachers *and parents* theologically and biblically, so they could be of substantive help to their pupils and children as they confronted the Bible and the stories and theology they learned from their reading. The editors hoped that in this way the magazine would aid in the process of reducing fragmentation and provide a different kind of helpful resource.

A typical issue contained a half-dozen or more general articles. Then two to three pages were devoted to each week's Sunday school lesson. For each week, the topic was given, together with scripture references (now no longer printed out; people could look them up), a one-line statement of the "purpose of the lesson," and then a general exposition, which wove together present-day issues and concerns with a Reformed theological interpretation of the topic and the scripture texts. Suggestions for structuring the lesson were sometimes built directly into the exposition, other times set apart. Sometimes these were quite directive, but often they were very loose, almost nonexistent. Over the twenty-year period in which these magazines were produced, they were continually "improved" in response to calls from teachers for more help until, by the end, a section on "Teaching Procedure" constituted approximately half of the week's materials.

With the return to permanent books and the attempt to provide a more flexible guide for teachers which would also be in the hands of parents, the *Christian Faith and Life* program attempted to take a different course from the one that had been leading to an increasingly fragmented educational approach. In many ways, it was very successful. The Presbyterian Church in the U.S. and the United Church of Christ basically followed suit a decade or so later. But for all three of these denominations, the struggle was difficult. Teachers often found the materials hard to teach, and it is not clear how many parents were able to be helpful interpreters of Christian theology to their children. Over time, more and more "how-to" helps were added, but the complaints continued. This curriculum simply did not fit easily into the normal Sunday school pattern.

William B. Kennedy has argued that the problem was deeply rooted in the basic educational strategy that places the Sunday school at the center of a church educational ministry. The Sunday school was originally an evangelical lay movement designed to pass a simple evangelical faith from person to person across generations. The original books and tracts were appropriate to that faith and strategy. "Curriculum," as it emerged through the Uniform Lessons, systematized, organized, and sustained that impulse. When the liberal religious educators tried to use it to make the Sunday school something different, the Sunday school itself and the curriculum genre that supported it were inappropriate to the task. Those educators had asked more of the teachers and the curriculum than they could bear. The new neo-orthodox educators did so as well.

The books published in *Christian Faith and Life* and Covenant Life overcame limitations the standard curriculum genre by itself could not. But these curricula tried to maintain and reform the old genre and the Sunday school strategy at the same time they attempted to transcend them. This may have been impossible. Says Kennedy:

> When the new curriculum further exalted the task of the teacher by providing a large amount of more sophisticated background material, many local teachers, even though positive in their response, felt that they were expected to become theological and biblical professors.[29]

Christian Faith and Life was not the last Presbyterian attempt to "sophisticate" and reform the old genre, however.

One more try was made, this time in a different direction. In the light of the difficulties with *Christian Faith and Life,* the United Presbyterian Board of Christian Education began a major Curriculum Reappraisal Project in 1961. Several years of intensive study led to a focus on what actually happens in classrooms and on what makes for a competent teacher. Teaching and teacher training, it seemed, were keys to reshaping the educational ministry of the church. If the previous "new" materials had counted on teachers and parents to be "theological and biblical professors," the next round would ask them to be "competent teachers."

The focus on teaching was fostered in part by the board's use of a number of professional secular educators as consultants. The new emphases on "programmed learning," "behavioral objectives," and breaking the teaching/learning interaction into identifiable parts ("micro-teaching") that had emerged in education schools in universities would be incorporated into church education. The curriculum would be constituted by "a tighter sequence of courses" (and a tighter sequence of actions within each course), leading toward specific aims, especially "Biblical literacy."[30]

The basic constituent of *Christian Faith and Action* would no longer be either the book or the lesson; it would be the "unit." The central curriculum resource consisted of a semipermanent teacher's guide for each grade, which was broken down into approximately nine units, each lasting anywhere from four to ten weeks. The notion of a "unit" had specific meaning:

> A block of material to be taught is a unit only if there is something that holds it together—something that makes it a unity. A number of Biblical passages selected at random is not likely to provide the basis for a unit. There has to be some common theme that runs through the passages, and each passage has to contribute to the achievement of *specific educational objectives* before the result can properly be called a unit.[31]

The unity was to be achieved through "concepts": "generalization[s] that we use to classify and analyze information and ideas."[32] The concepts were designed to be appropriate to the age levels of the students being taught, and the teacher's guide was a guide to organizing the teaching of these concepts.

The teacher's guide would typically begin with an introductory chapter, spelling out this new approach. It proceeded to a chapter on "Basic Procedures and Resources," which included multiple suggestions of teaching techniques (for example, field trips, role-playing, dramatization, crafts, puzzles) and resources that could be used to carry them out (such as audiovisuals, displays, books, games). Next the units themselves were presented. Each unit included six pages or so of theological, biblical, and historical background information concerning the concepts to be taught. Then followed another half-dozen pages on "Content and Objectives." These would cover certain ideas or smaller-scaled concepts that were integral to the larger unit (for example, "parable," "miracle," or "disciple"). In the light of the concepts, objectives were then carefully stated. An example would be: "Given selected references from New Testament writing that tell us facts about Jesus' life, the pupils should be able to describe and discuss a general outline of those facts from his birth to the final meal with his disciples."[33] Also in this section "Skill Development" was discussed; the section would list and describe the skills the student should now possess to reach these objectives.

The individual teacher was responsible for planning any particular lesson. The assumption was made that the teaching would become stronger and more personalized if the teacher would do this. "Curriculum" had come to mean neither a body of prose that students and teachers would read for their own edification nor a series of lesson plans that described how a group would study what was set before it. Rather, curriculum was now a construction manual to guide teachers in building an educational event. Out of a collection of concepts, objectives, background information, teaching techniques, and educational resources, teachers would construct unique learning events for each classful of students. The teacher's guides did provide a section in each unit on "Planning for Teaching," which outlined the essential features of the unit and gave suggestions on how to break down the unit into individual sessions (a sample "session outline" was often provided). And a section on "Techniques and Resources" provided many options for teachers to choose from as they planned. But the responsibility fell mainly on the teacher's shoulders to create education.

The need for "better teaching" had been identified as the central problem of Sunday school education, and this curriculum was designed to provide the kind of materials "better teachers" would need. "Better teaching" had taken on a rather technical meaning by this point, however, and the language of "expected outcomes," "identifiable pupil activity," and "overt response" began to dominate. Correlatively, better teaching depended on improved techniques, and the teacher's guides were loaded with them. The student workbooks reinforced this approach. The prose materials were bite-size, and colorful illustrations, fill-in-the-blank worksheets, puzzles, and games dominated. Whether and how they were to be used was left to the discretion of the teacher, but they were useless outside the classroom and the teacher's instructional leadership. Indeed, "curriculum," at least as a body of materials for students, had virtually disappeared. It had become almost entirely a collection of procedures and techniques that teachers could employ to shape the learning processes in which students would be engaged when they gathered under the teacher's guidance and supervision in the classroom.

Christian Faith and Action was obviously very different from either *Christian Faith and Life* or Covenant Life. But we group them together not only because the three were in print during a common span of time, but primarily because they were the Presbyterian Church's most concerted efforts to depart from the basic curriculum genre established in the nineteenth century. Two of these programs attempted more theological sophistication and published a large body of scholarship for popular reading in order to achieve it. The third went primarily in the direction of educational sophistication and raised educational process to a position of dominance. All of them were out of business by 1978.

The Eighties and Beyond

The story from 1978 to the present can be brief, for no major shifts in the shape of curriculum as a "literary form" have been attempted during this period.

Beginning in 1967, both the northern and the southern Presbyterian churches were involved in a cooperative interdenominational venture called Joint Educational Development (JED). Its initial purpose was joint research and a few cooperative educational activities. But by 1978 JED was publishing a curriculum called *Christian Education: Shared Approaches* (CE:SA), and the energies of twelve denominations were coordinated to produce it.

Four curriculum tracks or "approaches" were published. Churches were free to choose among them and, to a certain extent, to draw on them all. *Knowing the Word* was an extension of the Uniform Lessons. *Interpreting the Word* was the Presbyterian specialty. It focused on Bible study and built on what had been learned with CFL, CLC, and CFA. In doing so, however, it rejected both the publication of books and the unit system. Instead, it returned to the "lesson plan" approach. *Living the Word* focused on the Christian life and the experience of the church. Other denominations had primary responsibility for this approach, but it too depended primarily on the lesson plan format. The only approach to deviate from this was *Doing the Word*. It tried a variety of different strategies designed for use in various settings, mostly to undergird social action ministries on specific issues. In this approach, books were published, general study guides issued, "units" created, and even some "lesson plans" with student workbooks included. It was the least popular of the approaches, though it was not designed to provide a comprehensive Sunday school program.

When CE:SA returned largely to the "lesson plan" format, it implicitly recognized the inevitable constraints that a largely untrained, volunteer teaching staff and the Sunday school strategy as a whole place on the design of educational resources. The basic curriculum genre simply fits the institution better than any other, despite its limitations. The new Presbyterian and Reformed Educational Ministry materials (PREM), which succeeded CE:SA in 1988, continue this recognition. In these materials, the lesson-plan format of the genre developed in the late nineteenth century dominates even more heavily than it did in CE:SA. PREM and CE:SA are unlike their nineteenth- and early twentieth-century predecessors, however, in that they have maintained some of the educational jargon that was used to articulate the curriculum structure of *Christian Faith and Action.* Furthermore, the instructions for teaching each session have become considerably more concrete and direct than they were in the earliest "curriculum" materials. In the *Teacher's Guide, Grades 5–6, Year 1,* p. 48, of PREM's *Celebrate* series, for example, teachers are instructed to:

> Greet the students as they arrive. . . . Have students begin the "Meet the Prophets" puzzle. . . . Begin by singing "God of Grace and God of Glory." . . . Read the "Meet the Prophets" activity from the *Lifesigns* leaflet [and so forth].

Easily one half to two thirds of each lesson plan consists of this sort of instruction.

The story is one in which "direction for their study" takes up more and more of the printed page, and "materials to read" become increasingly brief and fragmented. With *Christian Faith and Action,* educational process began to dominate the materials, even though substantive portions of historical, theological, and biblical background and study material were included and suggested in the teacher's guides. All this proved too difficult for teachers. The reaction in CE:SA, and now even more so in PREM, is to simplify. The term "user friendly" is often employed to convey the idea.

Simplicity is in keeping with the nineteenth-century tradition. But the contemporary simplification has focused on teaching instructions and learning procedures. This is different from the nineteenth-century materials. In 1885, *The Westminster Teacher* provided fairly simple materials, but they focused on helping teachers gain a clear understanding of the Bible passage before them and its meaning for themselves and their students. That teachers understood and could carry out simple teaching procedures without step-by-step direction was assumed. Furthermore, during the period in which the old paradigm to which we have now returned prevailed, something of a "Christian America" still survived. The work of the Sunday school was reinforced by a larger cultural ecology. That is no longer the case, and it is an important question whether a concentration on procedure is adequate to the educational challenge.

One major issue the Presbyterian Church (U.S.A.) still needs to face is the problem of "curriculum" genre, the *form* its educational resources should take. It has faced this problem several times and tried several alternatives. How successful various attempts may have been is not the question we have tried to answer here. It does seem that we must face the issue again, however, before the next resources are produced. And when we do, the question of form will have to be considered in direct connection with the question of basic educational strategy. That problem is now more severe than it has been at any other time in our history.

7

The Use of the Bible in Presbyterian Curricula, 1923–1985

David C. Hester

Introduction

Last fall I was teaching an adult class at a Presbyterian church near the seminary where I am on the faculty. We were not studying the Bible, but members in the class—mostly older—appealed to the Bible, its sayings, its stories as they made their way toward understanding the questions of faith that were before us. For these folks, the Bible obviously still carried significant authority and had over the years become a resource and guide for Christian living.

After the class, conversation turned to their concerns for their children's and grandchildren's Christian education. Many expressed sorrow and disappointment that their grown children were no longer in Sunday school and, indeed, no longer active in congregational life, period. "Maybe they'll come back," they hoped aloud, " when they have children of their own." "Kids these days don't seem to care very much about the church," someone said. "And the children aren't learning the Bible anymore, either," another complained. Finally, one man asked the question I hear frequently in congregations I visit: "Why don't they teach the Bible in Sunday school anymore?"

The quick and probably defensive response to this question is that Presbyterians *do* teach children the Bible in church school today, just as we have throughout our history. Our newest denominational curricula continue our traditional practice of offering biblically grounded educational resources. In this commitment, Presbyterian and Reformed Educational Ministry materials are not new. Presbyterians have consistently believed in the centrality of the scriptures to the formation of Christian faith and the practice of Christian life, and, like the Reformers, American Presbyterians have worked to equip members with a knowledge of scripture adequate to this task.

But this response is too easy and inadequate to account for the truth that lies behind the question my Sunday school friend raised. The fact is, despite efforts at solid biblical education through well-conceived and -written church school curricula, contemporary American Presbyterians are largely biblically illiterate. That is, the Bible is not experienced as a guide for Christian faith and practice in contemporary life: adults in our congregations cannot read the Bible with understanding and do not find in the Bible authority for learning who they are before God and how God relates to the world they experience.

An answer that accounts adequately for this current state of affairs is, frankly, too much for the space of this essay. Such an answer would involve not only educational issues but social changes and attitudes toward authority and community life more generally. This essay can make a beginning toward an answer by tracing historically the use of the Bible in Presbyterian church school curricula during most of the twentieth century. We can examine, at least, what the church has meant during these years by a "biblically grounded" education for its members, what results were expected, and what assumptions about interpreting the Bible in light of contemporary experience were made by those who wrote and promoted these materials for the church.

During the sixty-year period we will survey, the boards of Christian education of the Presbyterian churches were committed to a historical-critical approach to the Bible, the theological centrality of scriptures in determining beliefs and practice, and the best methods of education advocated by secular educators and informed by developmental psychology. The inherent tensions between these three commitments—simultaneously embracing tradition and modernity—are woven into the fabric of the curricula produced by the church, as we shall see. Looking into the use of the Bible in our church school curricula promises to be a window opening onto the larger problem of biblical and traditional authority and identity for thoroughly modern secular Presbyterians.

Uneasy Beginnings: Westminster Graded Lessons

At the turn of the century, Presbyterian Sunday school curriculum consisted officially of denominational versions of the Uniform Lessons. These cooperative lessons, inaugurated by the Evangelical Sunday School Union at its 1872 national convention, began as bare outlines consisting of little more than an assigned Bible passage, the "Golden Text" for memory, and a topic named for discussion. Exposition of the Bible text, as well as any teacher helps, was provided by denominational writers, in harmony with their particular doctrine and tradition. This simple but captivating approach allowed for a kind of "unity through uniformity" with "every person, from infants to the infirm, in every Sunday school" studying the same Bible text, while simultaneously allowing each denomination to guard its own particularity.[1] Presbyterians participated in the Uniform Lessons nearly from the beginning, with the "southern" church joining in 1875, only three years after the PCUSA.

A typical Sunday morning found adults and children gathering for opening exercises, then dividing into graded classes for children and men's and women's classes for adults. The intention everywhere was to study the Bible. Helm Bruce, a dedicated teacher of the men's Bible class at Louisville's Second Church, put it succinctly: "The purpose of this class is to read the Bible and try to understand it as a whole." Bruce noted particularly "rules of conduct to live by" found in both Old and New Testaments.[2] The interpretation of texts was largely the task of the teacher, with only a modicum of curricular guidance. To understand the verses and convey their meaning was left to the hard work, past experience, and inspiration of devoted laity, many of whom received high honor and deep respect from grateful class members. Early in the century, however, winds of change began to reshape this familiar pattern.

In 1923 William Jennings Bryan made a bid to become Moderator of the General Assembly of the PCUSA on a platform pledged to drive modernism from the church. Though narrowly failing election, he campaigned for the Assembly to adopt a resolution denying financial aid to any Presbyterian school allowing Darwinism or any other form of evolution theory to be taught; again, he failed to persuade the Assembly to his point of view. In the same year, the Board of Christian Education was formed by the same General Assembly, consolidating the work of previous boards and agencies responsible for publication and Sabbath school work, secondary schools and colleges, home missions, the missionary education work of both foreign and home mission boards, men's work, temperance and moral welfare, and Sabbath observance. The same year, 1923, the General Assembly also reaffirmed the so-called "five point doctrinal deliverance" of the 1910 Assembly, which sought to make the Old School Princeton theology's doctrine of an inerrant and infallible scripture a test of Presbyterian orthodoxy.[3] The following year, more liberal Presbyterians published the "Auburn Affirmation," signed by 1,274 clergy, deploring the position taken by the previous Assembly, which the signers believed "impaired [the scriptures'] authority for faith and life."[4] In 1927, a commission established to address the dispute between the followers of Princeton's J. Gresham Machen and the signers of the Auburn Affirmation declared the "five point deliverance" without authority, on the principle that "no body, including the General Assembly, had the constitutional power to make binding definitions of the church's essential faith," a decision which affirmed diversity as an "enriching aspect of the denomination."[5] Two years later, Machen left Princeton, after the Assembly had approved a reorganization of the seminary intended to make it more theologically inclusive; and the still new Board of Christian Education introduced a brand-new curriculum to the church amidst the swirl of controversy.

The new curriculum, called Westminster Departmental Graded Materials, was "new" in several respects. First, it marked the first Presbyterian effort to create a comprehensive denominational curriculum intended for use by children, youth, "young people" and adults in a variety of educational settings. The Board report introducing the materials noted, as reason for their production:

> The rapidly expanding program of the Church School has created a demand for materials much broader in scope than the former lessons of the Sunday School, so as to include correlated materials for each organization, as the society, the Week Day Church School, and the club.[6]

The "former lessons of the Sunday School" refers to the International Graded Lessons, which, in graded form, had been in use as the Sunday school material since 1913.

Secondly, the curriculum was "new" because its authors intended to include in it the most "up-to-date" discoveries from general educational theory and practice concerning developmental needs and learning abilities of children at various stages of growth. To this end, the Board established within itself a Department of Educational Research, to be guided by three general principles:

> a. To keep the curriculum materials practical so that they will meet educationally the needs of the greatest number of churches.
> b. To make the materials educational, embodying the tested principles of scientific education.
> c. To see that all the materials contribute directly to the great Christian objectives of the Church's program of Christian Education.[7]

This "scientific education" approach included the assumption, already at work in the Graded Uniform Lessons, that the Bible was an adult book, written by adults for adults, and usable with children only in ways appropriate to their age and developmental interests.

That brings us to a third way the curriculum claimed to be "new." It offered a new approach to the Bible.[8] The curriculum contained the weekly Bible lesson approach, familiar from the Uniform Lessons, because "the Board believes that a knowledge of *suitable* Biblical material has supreme value for spiritual growth." [Emphasis added.][9] But, in addition, "life problem lessons" were written in the new quarterlies. On these occasions, familiar problems faced by learners in the process of growth were presented first, with the promise that "before the lesson is over . . . the pupil will be led to the Bible to discover some passage or verse that will help in the solution of the problem."[10] By this method, "the pupil soon comes to feel that it is a book which has very definite help for . . . learning to live in the Christian way."[11] So "school relationships" provide a "life lesson" for younger elementary children, for example, and "friendship" is the issue facing nine- to eleven-year-olds, for which the Bible is seen as a source of help. This inductive approach to the Bible is a logical, if innovative, outcome of a thoroughly "child centered" curriculum in which the Bible is seen fundamentally as "a guide for Christian living."[12]

With regard to use of the Bible, the curriculum designers clearly came down on the side of the "liberal" wing of the church. The desire for the "best" educational methods drew planners into the "progressive" education efforts of the day, already advocated for church education by the highly professional membership of the Religious Education Association, through prominent voices like those of George Albert Coe and William Clayton Bower. Indeed, advocates for the Westminster lessons saw their proposals as an effort to provide sound guidance through a maze of wildly competing psychological and educational theories. In its 1928 report, for example, the Board went to lengths to assure its constituents that, in the preparation of the new curriculum, "the staff on its way to the supreme spiritual ends of our editorial works accepts only the authoritative results of scholarship and the conservative theories of sound psychology."[13]

Christian education, as progressive education, was committed to encouraging the growth of individuals toward their highest goal, namely, "the fullest possible self-realization in Godlikeness."[14] The aim of Christian education was "to foster in growing persons a progressive and continuous development of Christlike character."[15] But development of character was not all that was intended; Christlike character moved toward the goal of a Christian social order, the realization of the realm of God on earth. The way to achieve God's rule, progressives contended, begins with Christian character being forged out of human experience—the place where "God is continuously at work in [the] world."[16] Thus education must begin with experience, and "curriculum" may be described as "experience under guidance."[17]

And what is the role of the Bible in this program? How is it the "Word of God" and the "rule of faith and practice" required by Presbyterian doctrine? The hermeneutical key for the curriculum designers was the concept of the individual child growing toward relationship with God. The "desired outcome of Christian education in the individual" was, as the 1929 board report stated it, "a developing Christian character."[18] Such development involved:

> a growing realization of God as Father; the personal acceptance of Jesus Christ as Saviour and Lord, and of his way of life as revealed in the Scriptures; the development of love, faith, a sense of responsibility, and moral strength as Christian controls of conduct in all life situations; fellowship with those striving for the Christian ideal and under normal circumstances, membership in a Christian church; wholehearted participation in, and constructive contribution to, the progressive realization of a Christian social order.[19]

Scripture served this process of growth in two particular ways. First, it provided instruction, knowledge about God,

Christ, God's plan of salvation for all humankind, and the Christian life. The Bible contained fundamental information for the realization of the high aims of living a spiritual life and developing a spiritual culture. In the scriptures, God had revealed the divine nature, the ideals for both individual life and community life, and the moral example in Christ of how those ideals may be realized through obedient love of God and love of neighbor. "Knowing God" meant growing in the knowledge of God through a growing knowledge of the Bible.

And the Bible served the growing Christian in another way too. It provided a treasury of what Paul Vieth called "the best religious experience of the race, as effective guidance to present experience."[20] Here were stories of other men, women, and children striving for spiritual ideals, whose experiences could help modern Christians reconstruct their own experience to achieve higher spiritual goals. It must be added quickly, however, that the Bible was not construed as the only means available for spiritual resource; natural laws, including those guiding individual growth and social development, were taken as divine reflection as well.

The hermeneutics of growth through knowledge toward Christian character in a Christian "democracy of God," to use Coe's ideal image, determined an approach to the Bible that treated it as an ancient, if unique and authoritative, book. Its historicity was fully granted, and prevailing biblical scholarship worked diligently at analyzing the ancient cultures and customs reflected in it as precursors to the modern age. Its authority rested in its ability to provide insight into the spiritual dimension of contemporary experience. The Bible was a useful tool in the human project of reconstructing experience toward greater unity with transcendent values.

That not all Presbyterians were at ease with this effort to wed progressive education with Reformed theology's *sola scriptura* principle is evident from an overture from the Presbytery of Monmouth to the 1931 General Assembly. Aimed precisely at the new materials, the overture requested:

that in the lessons of all grades much more evidence be given of belief in the Word of God as the only rule of faith and practice . . . and that Bible stories be much more used in the Beginners and Primary Grades, and that in the materials for the Junior, Intermediate, Senior and Young Peoples Grades provision be made for printing of the Bible passage for the day.[21]

The response to the overture affirmed the effort of the Board of Christian Education to follow the Assembly's directive of 1931 "To take the Bible for the general textbook on which these materials in all age groups shall be based, and to maintain throughout these materials an unmistakable emphasis on salvation by faith in Jesus Christ as Saviour."[22]

But subsequent annual reports of the board make it clear that the issue would not go away. The moving force in this curriculum, as we have seen, was frankly child-centered education for growth in Christian character, not biblical or doctrinal instruction per se. While the method included presentation of Bible stories, a survey of the Old Testament, a study of the Gospels and the letters of Paul, as well as training in using the Bible to address contemporary needs, how and what was studied depended on learner's interests and "readiness." Thus biblical passages were "selected" and narratives paraphrased or fragmented, leaving the user without a sense of a unified narrative or a biblical theology. The unity of the Bible was found in the common human desire for spiritual growth; that it spoke to needs and interests of various ages embarked on the mission of Christian living and social reconstruction gave its stories single purpose.

The effort at work in the Westminster Departmental Graded Materials was to join progressive education methods, most naturally at home with liberal theology in the steps of Schleiermacher, with a more conservative, traditional Presbyterian theology. The balance, always uneasy, collapsed with the national economy, the onset of world war, and a 35 percent decline in use of the Westminster Graded materials in Presbyterian Sunday schools that marked the decade ending in 1937. A change in curriculum seemed in order.

The "New Curriculum":
Christian Faith and Life

At least ten years after its introduction in the fall of 1948, Presbyterians were still referring to *Christian Faith and Life: A Program for Church and Home* as the "new curriculum," a point of pride for the editors who saw it as testimony to diligent efforts to constantly renew and refine the basic materials of the program. Recognition of the landmark character of this curriculum in Protestant church education is widespread, within both theological and educational circles; and the story of its development is already very ably told by William Kennedy in "Neo-Orthodoxy Goes to Sunday School."[23]

It is a fascinating story. It begins in December of 1937 with the general secretary of the board, Harold McAfee Robinson, proposing that future curriculum programs take a new direction, emphasizing with new urgency Christian community and basic doctrines of the church. The shift in emphasis from a child-centered, life-problem focus was supported by John Mackay of Princeton Seminary, who added his own concern for church history to the proposal. Movement and direction toward a new curriculum was under way.

After Robinson's death in 1939, Paul Calvin Payne, as the new general secretary, took up the task, which would eventually take nine years to complete. The world war, which by 1941 completely absorbed the United States, provided a somber yet zealous context for the work of curriculum development. The 1941 board report called attention to the church's "supreme missionary task" as the "chief educator of [humanity]" in the "present crisis of society." To meet this calling, the board determined "to present God's revelation of himself and his redemptive purpose in Holy Scripture in a more systematic form than is done at present"; to introduce the "cultural and spiritual heritage" from which Protestantism grew; and to provide "comprehensive and challenging presentations of the great Christian doctrines and their living message for today."[24]

These battle lines drawn, initial strategy was developed during the Staten Island curriculum conference of 1942, setting forth the principles that would guide future writers, including that scripture study was to be graded to the level of learners and was to be done, as the General Assembly of 1939 had directed, according to the "best scholarship." The conference also established three major themes, each to be emphasized for a year, by which the curriculum was to be organized: Jesus Christ, the Bible, and the Church—topics broad enough to include concern for doctrine and the social ethics of Christian discipleship. The staff eventually assembled after the 1942 conference would include educators, such as Edward B. Paisley and the educator-publisher W. L. Jenkins, and theologians James D. Smart and Leonard J. Trinterud, who would painstakingly work their way through countless controversies between sound educational principles and equally essential theological commitments until a solid curriculum was fashioned which could, as Smart put it, "develop and equip Christian disciples" for mission now.[25] Budget restrictions and strictly rationed paper supplies delayed introduction of the new curriculum until the world crisis that marked its beginning had ended and a different kind of crisis, that of rebuilding, took center stage.

But we must turn our attention now to a particular piece of this story, namely, what was "new" about the use of the Bible in the new curriculum. We may begin with the Board of Christian Education's perception of the state of biblical literacy in the church at the inception of the new curriculum. The board's annual report of 1947, entitled "Good Tools for Good Workmen," began its description of the situation: "One of the greatest problems in Christian teaching is that, while there is a great emphasis upon the Bible and attention to it in the Church School, few Christians seem to be able to read the Bible for themselves *with understanding* even after . . . fifteen years under the Church's instruction." [Emphasis added.][26] Factors named accountable for this regrettable state of affairs address the ways Bible had been taught in both the Uniform Lesson system and the

Departmental Graded materials. For example, a veiled charge against the Uniform approach complains that "much Bible-teaching has consisted merely of recital of facts and events as recorded in the Old and New Testaments without any clear indication of their importance for life today," thereby giving the impression that the Bible is irrelevant to contemporary life.[27] Or, against the "life lesson" approach of the Departmental materials, the "fragmentariness" of Bible teaching is scored, "the great unifying themes and sweep of God's redemptive purpose which gives meaning to all parts of the Bible being lost from sight."[28] Teacher ignorance of the results of good biblical scholarship is named as contributing to treating the Bible as "a book of intellectual problems" rather than "the Word of God for today." By the same token, the report cites the difficulty of even the best scholars' "getting at the real meaning of the text . . . for today" and the scarcity of books to help ordinary readers with problems of understanding. And, finally, attitude is noted as a problem, reflected in the "widespread idea that [persons] can know most of what one needs to know of God quite apart from the Scriptures."[29]

What the new curriculum offered as response to this state of affairs was an approach for which both the labels "Bible centered" and "pupil centered" were refused. "If one must speak of a center for the curriculum," the report declared, "then it is truest to say that Christ is the center—Christ as we know him only through the Scriptures of the Old and New Testaments, Christ the eternal Word of God."[30] The needs of the child, in turn, can only be known in light of relationship to Christ. The curriculum sought a way to teach children, youth, and adults that brought Bible and life issues together within the framework of biblical revelation. Rather than beginning with the child or selected biblical texts, *Christian Faith and Life* began with the experience that brought scripture and human need together—revelation of God in Christ. The educational task was the task of communicating this fact of revelation from one generation to another, from those inside the fellowship of Christ to those outside called to come in.

The fragmentariness of earlier biblical teaching would be overcome by the unity that revelation gave to the whole Bible. The Bible was presented as a drama of redemptive history, centered in Christ, the fulfillment of God's promises to Israel, and continuing in the life of the church. Thus, in the three-year cycle of materials, one year was devoted to presenting this unified story of God's revelation in history. The other two years, devoted to the themes "Jesus Christ" and "the Church," could then focus on particular biblical texts, always in the interpretive context of the revelation drama.

The same concept of God's revelation in history also provided perspective on the relevance of the Bible to contemporary life. The revelation of God, entrusted to the first disciples of Christ, to which the scriptures witness, continues through the church's teaching of the scriptures even to the present generation. Therefore, just as the revelation of Christ spoke to the deepest, most profound needs of the disciples, the scriptures, which bear witness to the Christ-event, call us to the experience of those disciples. The "essential content" of the curriculum is described in terms of the teacher's role in the continuing "widening circle" of revelation. Declared the report, "The word which the prophets and apostles heard and spoke and which for them had in it the decisive truth concerning the whole of life is the word which the Christian teacher must hear and speak today."[31] And, again, the pupil must "hear God speaking through the teaching of the Church, and it must be for [the pupil] immediately true that God redeems [God's] people, that God pardons sinners, that life can be transformed by God's grace."[32]

For *Christian Faith and Life,* neither "knowing the Bible" nor "developing Christian character" were sufficient educational objectives. The former ran the risk of confusing knowledge with commitment, while the latter tended toward moralism and a false sense of self-sufficiency. "Christian character" could be appropriately defined only in terms of the gospel emphasis on sin and redemption. The Christian character sought by *Christian Faith and Life* was one shaped to "the same mind and spirit, the same response to God and [persons], and the same outlook of life which Jesus sought to bring to life in his first disciples."[33] Bible study served the end of this disciple making, by inviting children and adults into the Bible's "new world under God's rule, in which all their experiences received new meaning."[34]

If "growth toward Christian character" provided the hermeneutical key in the previous curriculum, "becoming a disciple in Christ" fairly characterizes the use of the Bible in *Christian Faith and Life.* The authority of the scriptures rests in their possibility of becoming a Word from God calling people to new life in Christ, to community in the body of Christ, and to citizenship in God's eternal sovereignty. The power to effect this becoming lies outside the teacher or the church, in the power of the Holy Spirit. The authority of the scriptures, then, is finally God's coming through them to redeem the world. Church education, therefore, in *Christian Faith and Life* is inherently evangelistic, and every teacher an evangelist, opening the way into the scriptures and the life of discipleship for the student.

This view of the use and authority of the scriptures enabled—indeed, encouraged—full use of biblical criticism, in order to uncover as nearly as possible the world behind the text. But this was not disinterested probing. Rather, it was biblical criticism through eyes committed to faith, to a biblical theology that perceived a transcendent unity to the scriptures uncompromised by critical investigation. As Brevard Childs observed, this so-called "neo-orthodox" version of a biblical theology offered "an alternative beyond the liberal-conservative syndrome" and "the possibility of accepting biblical criticism without reservation as a valid tool while at the same time recovering a robust, confessionally oriented theology."[35]

Variations on a Theme:
After *Christian Faith and Life*

The introduction and remarkable success of the *Christian Faith and Life* materials in the PCUSA spurred new curriculum writing activity in other mainline denominations, all reflecting a remarkable Protestant consensus around the "neo-orthodox" biblical theology. Robert Wuthnow describes the postwar religious climate as a time of "promise and peril," a time of optimism "balanced with a sense of forboding," the mixed blessing of a war ended with an atomic bomb that launched a new age of unprecedented possibility and terror.[36] Religious response to this new age was marked by "an overwhelming emphasis on religious education. Leaders of all the major faiths expressed concern about the need to better educate the society in spiritual and moral values."[37] Coupled with this concern for education was a high priority for evangelism, which Wuthnow describes as "the issue on which religious leaders of all perspectives seemed to be most in agreement."[38] In this light, *Christian Faith and Life* provided an ideal model: well designed for serious and sophisticated education, its theological intention was avowedly evangelical. It provided a theological outlook that mirrored the prevailing mood of hope and crisis: through the church's teaching the scriptures, God confronted the contemporary world of human beings with its sinfulness and sickness, offering redemption in a new life in Christ, requiring a new way of looking at the world and living in it, and calling for an immediate decision. It seemed the right theology for the time: evangelical and traditional, yet thoroughly open to the modern world.

Covenant Life

Presbyterians spawned a second new curriculum in the postwar period: the Covenant Life Curriculum, developed by the Presbyterian Church in the United States and finally introduced in the churches in 1963. The beginning of the curriculum, however, is marked by the appointment of a special committee by the Board of Christian Education in 1955 to consider "how to describe a curriculum adequate to the task of communicating the Christian gospel."[39] The committee's task was to formulate a model curriculum by which the board could evaluate current materials and practice, in order to carry out a "curriculum improvement project" mandated by the General Assembly. But what began as a step toward evaluation became, instead, a leap of faith into production of a complete program of education which took the whole life of the church as its context for educational ministry.

The history of curriculum in the PCUS was parallel to what we have seen in the "northern" church. After initial reluctance, the PCUS had joined in the Uniform Lessons project in 1875 and adopted the graded series, again after initial hesitation, in 1915. At the time of a restudy of religious education in the church, authorized in 1944, Uniform Lessons provided one of two denominationally sponsored options for Sunday school use. The alternative available was the Presbyterian Graded Lessons, which, like the Westminster Departmental series, offered a thematic approach to study on a two- and three-year cycle. Lewis J. Sherrill's *Lift Up Your Eyes* offers a summary of the extensive restudy undertaken to test the adequacy of operating principles of Christian education in the PCUS and the desirability of initiating a new, single series curriculum for church school use.[40] The conclusion reached affirmed the continued use of Uniform Lessons and the Presbyterian Graded Lessons as options for churches, while providing additional material for special needs unmet by either of the two curricula.

The committee organized in 1955 to evaluate current materials was not a response to any widespread dissatisfaction with available curriculum. Rather, the impetus for another critical review and, ultimately, for change came from perceptions that a new age had dawned, hallmarked by the introduction of atomic power, new means of communication, a population explosion, increasing racial tensions, recession of the first wave of religious enthusiasm following the war, and eagerness on the part of professional Christian educators to incorporate new principles and practice into the pedagogy of the church.

The new curriculum was organized in a three-year cycle,

with year-long themes studied by all ages in ways suited to each group's learning needs and developmental interests. The cycle began with the Bible, the second year being devoted to a study of the Church, and the third year, Christian life. The "core" of the curriculum consisted of four books for adult study, underscoring the seriousness with which adult education was to be taken in the curriculum. Written by seminary faculty, these volumes were intended to provide "a balanced and scholarly library on the faith of the church."[41] The high quality of these first volumes also set an admirable standard for the whole curriculum.

Like *Faith and Life,* Covenant Life took God's revelation through the scriptures as the starting point. "The starting point of the Covenant Life Curriculum is the conviction that God has come and continues to come to [humanity] inviting [humanity] into everlasting covenant."[42] The church's distinctive task, in turn, is making God's revelation known. God's revelation of the covenant relationship God offers to all is the motive for the educational work of the church. And, therefore, the scriptures, as the witness to God's covenant with God's people, are central both to the curriculum and to the educational task of the church. In the core volume *Into Covenant Life,* William Kennedy wrote:

> We read the Bible, we study it, we go to it seeking to learn God's will for our lives. And, we believe, through its inspired words, God's Spirit speaks to us. . . . The inspired word illumined by the Holy Spirit to our hearts—that is how God reveals [God's self] to us today. This is the process by which we gain saving knowledge of God.[43]

In Covenant Life, as in *Faith and Life,* the Bible is central in two fundamental ways: first, as *witness* to God's revelation; and secondly, as *means* for contemporary men, women, and children to experience God's coming to the world to invite them into covenant relationship.

The hermeneutical key in Covenant Life was the image of the church as the "covenant community of God," responsible for communicating its faith "as it draws men and women and boys and girls into the life of the church *where the mystery of God's grace is brought to bear upon the fact of human need."* [Emphasis added.][44] Like the Bible, the church is both a witness to the covenant relationship God has revealed as God's intention for humankind and the means by which God calls people into that relationship. Bible, then, is studied to discover what God expects of God's people in covenant relationship.

Kennedy demonstrates the process of interpretation in a study of Philippians. It begins with listening to the text; then "we participate," trying, imaginatively, to get into the biblical frame of reference; thirdly, "we explore and analyze" our own times and circumstances, asking, "What do [these words] mean now?"; and, finally, "we undertake," since "God expects something to happen in us, and through us in the world" when we study the Bible.[45] Children, youth, and adults participate in this interpretive process in ways appropriate to their developmental characteristics, moving through what the curriculum described as "levels of communicating the Gospel," understanding that the full gospel is being communicated at each level. The youngest children experience covenant relationship primarily in nonverbal ways; elementary-age children are introduced to the biblical story verbally; youth are invited to commitment; and adults are addressed by the gospel primarily as witnesses. Interpretation "for covenant living" goes on at each and every level; and the whole process aims toward evangelization, witness to the gospel addressing the needs of the world. In Covenant Life Curriculum, biblical authority rests on the identification of the church with the covenant community called into being by God according to the witness of the scriptures, for the purpose of calling others into covenant through the church's active witness through the scriptures. The influence of "neo-orthodoxy" is evident.

Covenant Life Curriculum was visionary, designed to provide an educational approach that saw the whole life of the covenant community as the true setting for learning. This vision, however, was never successfully communicated to churches, which seemed unable to move past the schooling model of systematic study to decision making that engaged the social issues of the day. From the outset, Covenant Life was caught up in the maelstrom of political and social crises beginning in 1963—including the assassination of a President, a march on Washington for civil rights, and the war heating up in southeast Asia—and which swirled uncontrollably until publication of the curriculum ceased in 1978. The days of consensus in the church, theological or political, were gone and, with them, the means for supporting such a comprehensive and unified educational effort.

Christian Faith and Action

At the time of the formation of the United Presbyterian Church in the U.S.A. in 1958, *Christian Faith and Life* was adopted by the former United Presbyterian Church of North America, and thereby became the "official" curriculum of the new denomination. In 1961, a major project of evaluating the curriculum was initiated, which resulted in the introduction in 1968 of *Christian Faith and Action: Designs for an Educational System.* In an address to the 1967 General Assembly introducing *Christian Faith and Action,* Ellis Nelson outlined the reason for change, as well as the direction. First, Nelson noted, the world had changed dramatically since the introduction of *Christian Faith and Life* in 1948, and there was thus an inherent need for the church's educational materials to change, if they—and the church—were to be responsible in a rapidly changing environment. After a depressing analysis of social conditions in 1962, the board report for 1963 had concluded, "American society has lost the Lord of life." National skepticism about the trustworthiness of centralized power in public institutions raised doubt about the wisdom and effectiveness of national church agencies too. And, by 1964, the Board of Christian Education of the UPCUSA had begun a process of decentralizing responsibility for educational ministry decisions. The report for that year described the board as "a means by which the resources of all parts of the church can be brought together and . . . made available to the entire church."[46] Congregations and presbyteries were encouraged to take educational ministry design into their own hands, adapting and creating resources to address the world of issues as manifested locally, since a national curriculum could neither keep up with rapidly changing needs nor address those needs in ways appropriate for every local circumstance.

The second reason Nelson gave for the development of *Christian Faith and Action* spoke to changing assumptions about educational strategies. *Faith and Life* had assumed, Nelson observed, that (1) church education strategy started with the children, (2) better materials would lead to better teaching, and (3) parents would use materials at home to educate their children in partnership with the Sunday school.[47] The appraisal project had shown these assumptions to be mistaken. *Faith and Action* was an effort to initiate a different approach: (1) It began with adults, or at least the abilities that adult Christians could be expected to demonstrate; (2) it took the teaching-learning process as a focus of attention, writing specific goals, objectives, and procedures for evaluation into every unit of study; and (3) it identified the congregation's instructional task apart from the nurturing responsibility of family.

What was not at issue, officially at least, was the theological direction and motivation of the curriculum. *Faith and Action* took up the same general outlook as *Faith and Life*. The Bible as the "unique vehicle of God's address to [humanity]" remained at the center.[48] God's address calls the church to a ministry of reconciliation, a key concept in the Confession of 1967. The scriptures were united in their unique and authoritative witness to Christ, and through them God "confronts us, with [God's] will," making God "personal demand to us as persons."[49]

Nevertheless, the theological atmosphere in 1967 was considerably more diverse than it had been in 1948. Neo-orthodox biblical theology, particularly in its most self-assured form, had already felt the qualifications imposed by form and redaction criticism, by the challenge of Harvey

Cox's *Secular City* and Bishop Robinson's *Honest to God* and the continuing theological insights of Paul Tillich. *Christian Faith and Life* had imposed a normative theological position through which biblical interpretation was filtered into the curriculum materials. *Christian Faith and Action* enacted an important shift in approach that had the effect of allowing for more theological diversity in interpretation.

Faith and Action focused on developing certain abilities among Presbyterians, rather than on seeing things from a common perspective, which diversity of opinion generated by the political and social crises of the day would make extremely difficult. First among the desired outcomes of the new venture in church education was this one:

> The ability intelligently to interpret the Bible as the unique medium through which God chooses to speak to [people], thereby calling [God's] people to active response in the worship and mission of the church in the present world.[50]

To this end, the curriculum was intended to provide as resource the best of critical biblical scholarship. However, interpretation was to be the responsibility of every church member; dependency on scholars and preachers was particularly criticized. The curriculum could provide the process, but church members would have to provide their own decisions about meaning and response. And, in addition to exegetical process, church members would have to listen very carefully and fully to "voices of concern from persons outside the institutional church." As the designers put it,

> The ability to discern what God through Scripture has to say in our age, and to discern this not apart from but in relation to the many voices of contemporary society, opens the door to understandings essential for the renewal of the church.[51]

The previous image of returning to the perspective of the prophets and apostles is still there; but now there are contemporary perspectives that must be seriously engaged too, and interpretation has become a more dialogic event. The hermeneutical key in *Faith and Action* is "God, the recon-

ciler, who has given the church a ministry of reconciliation"—a powerful and timely image in the chaotic period
for which *Faith and Action* was designed.

Christian Education: Shared Approaches

The emerging pluralism in Presbyterian life took one
more turn heading into the eighties with the four-approach
effort of *Christian Education: Shared Approaches.* Presbyterians participated in this Joint Educational Development
project (JED) from its beginning in 1972, and replaced
Christian Faith and Action and Covenant Life with the new
materials beginning in 1978, with a choice of *Knowing the
Word, Interpreting the Word, Living the Word,* and *Doing
the Word.*

All these approaches were centered on the Bible, with
Knowing the Word continuing the content-oriented approach of the Uniform Lessons tradition, while *Interpreting the Word* focused on understanding and responding to
the meaning of the Bible. *Living the Word* addressed issues
of the Christian community, while *Doing the Word* was intended to enable groups to struggle with issues of the
church's mission in the world, in the face of social crises.
These resources were intended to enable congregations to
design an educational approach tailor-made to the local situation, and which, because it was an ecumenical curriculum, would invite shared activity in the local community
between congregations of the participating JED denominations. In a day of scarce budgets and declining congregations, CE:SA hoped to be a flexible, Bible-centered
curriculum that could satisfy widely divergent needs without unnecessary denominational duplication of resources.

Initial response to CE:SA in the UPCUSA, judging from
the *Minutes* of 1979, was favorable: 86 percent of the denomination's congregations had ordered material from at
least one of the four approaches. At the same time, diversity within the Presbyterian family was raising the thorny
question of where, if anywhere, the boundaries lay that
identified a "Presbyterian position." For example, the 1978

General Assembly, meeting in the summer before the introduction of the new curriculum in the churches, established
a task force

> to engage in a study of the diverse ways of understanding
> biblical authority and interpreting Scripture that are now
> prevalent in our denomination; that components of the study
> include an exploration of our theological heritage in the Re-
> formed tradition . . . ; and that a result be recommended
> guidelines for a positive and not a restrictive use of Scripture
> in theological controversies.[52]

CE:SA's fourfold approach and nondenominational character added to the sense of disunity and factional interests
already abroad. So, while materials may have been widely
used, particularly *Knowing the Word, Interpreting the
Word,* and *Living the Word,* general acceptance was far
more halfhearted than enthusiastic. The dialogue possible
because of pluralism and diversity was never a necessity;
critical tension, a possible virtue of a four-dimensional approach, could always be disengaged by a congregation simply "doing its own thing." CE:SA could be thoroughly
reflective of the individualistic mood of the day.

Presbyterian and Reformed Educational
Ministries (PREM)

The formation of the reunited Presbyterian Church
(U.S.A.) in 1983 became the catalyst for the most recent
effort to create a new "biblically grounded" curriculum.
Two overtures to the 1984 General Assembly were directed
explicitly to concerns linked to continued use of CE:SA.
One overture, from the Presbytery of Eastern Oklahoma,
asked that the General Assembly "place a high priority on
Christian education" in the new church's mission statement in keeping with Presbyterian tradition, which "has
always put a major emphasis on the teaching of the Word."
The overture argued in light of the fact that "in recent years
materials and other resources were not originated by the
denomination" and "much of that curriculum was not
compatible with the Reformed tradition."[53]

A second overture, from the Presbytery of the Piedmont, requested directly that the General Assembly ask its agencies "to develop a program in Christian Education including a curriculum that will address Reformed theology, polity, and mission of the church, and encouraging these bodies to place a high priority on inclusiveness." Again, need for such action was felt to be warranted by "widespread ignorance of the reformed heritage among members of the Presbyterian Church (USA)," traced to the failure of CE:SA materials to "emphasize any one tradition."[54]

General Assembly responses to these two overtures led to a consultation at Montreat in the summer of 1984 at which 120 representatives of various agencies and interested groups discussed how a comprehensive educational ministry might be designed for the reunited church. Out of that consultation came a church-wide study paper, *Educational Ministry of the Presbyterian Church (U.S.A.),* and a proposal:

> To create a new Reformed and Presbyterian educational ministry, including curricular resources and pastor and teacher development components, for the equipping of the whole church, the "laos," for ministry in the world; the entire program to be biblically based, expressing a holistic approach to the church's ministry of education and in full recognition and celebration of the diversity of the Presbyterian Church (USA).[55]

This proposal was approved when the Program Agency and Mission Board met in January 1985. Creation of a new educational design was under way.

From the beginning, PREM has always been more than printed curriculum, representing an approach to educational ministry that is fully aware of the interdependence of the church's various ministries. People learn and teach through a variety of experiences in many different settings, including worship, Bible study, prayer gatherings, at work, at home, and in community service and social action. All these opportunities for growing in the life of faith are the proper concern of PREM.

Nevertheless, PREM also includes printed curricula for church school use. Two choices are currently available: *Bible Discovery* and *Celebrate,* each offering materials for children, youth, and adults. And both approaches share in the PREM commitment to be "biblically grounded, historically informed, ecumenically involved, socially engaged, and communally nurtured." *Bible Discovery* continues the Uniform Lesson tradition organized by biblical content, by theme or by Bible book, with Old Testament texts predominating in the fall and New Testament texts beginning at Christmas and continuing through spring. The focus is on Bible content and learning the biblical story. *Celebrate,* by contrast, is organized to be compatible with the Common Lectionary, with the intention of better integrating worship with the Sunday school experience. The study paper reasoned:

> To be a nurturing community, the church is called to develop a life together that includes worship, teaching, evangelizing, and mission involvement, related to the theological emphases of the church year and focused on justice and peace. This effort may be facilitated by creative use of the ecumenical lectionary as a parish discipline.[56]

In both curricula, Bible, theology, and mission interact throughout the lessons, so that Bible is studied in the context of theology and mission and mission is undertaken from a biblically and theologically informed perspective.

The hermeneutical approach of PREM is guided by the theological *regula fidei* found in the church's Confession of 1967 that "the Bible is to be interpreted in the light of its witness to God's work of reconciliation in Christ."[57] This work goes on, through the power of the Holy Spirit, in our own day. Thus, to discern the word of God for our time is to recognize scripture's witness as witness to us, to understand its meaning as meaningful to us. The hermeneutical expectation is that "the present meaning of each passage will emerge from a dual understanding of what the biblical writers meant *then* and the situation in which we read it *now*." And, for PREM, the "now" is particularly informed by "the voices of oppressed and excluded peoples," because "Christ came to set humanity free."[58] Earlier emphases in curricula that saw the task of interpretation as encountering Christ or deciding for covenant living have shifted in PREM to reforming the church and guiding its mission of liberating service in the world.

The present meaning of the biblical story is found in the "images and concepts of the ancient world translated into pictures and ideas which are (1) meaningful to us, and (2) which do not violate the original meaning of the text."[59] Thus, Bible study is an effort to retell the Bible story in our own age and in our own words, but in a way that retains its witness to God's reconciling and liberating work in Christ. "The Bible is the story of a human journey, of a search for what it means to be God's people in God's world."[60] That is our bond with those whose lives are told in the ancient story; we identify with their experiences and take from them a sense of direction for our own lives. In this dialogue between the scriptures and our own lives, we may hear God's word speak to us. The role of PREM resources is to help us engage faithfully in this dialogue, in order to respond to the word we hear.

It is, of course, too soon to tell how effective the comprehensive approach of PREM may be for biblical education in the church. The choice of lectionary compatibility for *Celebrate* will dictate significantly the scope and relationship of texts studied in that curriculum, as does the Christocentric pattern discernible even in the *Bible Discovery* pattern. Moreover, the intended integration with worship via the lectionary will depend on cooperation and planning between congregational leaders far beyond the usual pattern. And it will be critical to see how noncurriculum materials—print and video—develop the PREM concept. The attention paid to voices of oppressed or marginalized people is a critical addition to the dialogue of interpretation set before a largely privileged-class church; likewise, the commitment to a global perspective for understanding the church and its mission. How these commitments may be authentically carried through, how thoroughly a proper "hermeneutic of suspicion" may be exercised, remains to be seen but certainly can be expected to be a constant challenge. Teaching church members to interpret the biblical story in images and concepts consistent with the biblical witness yet sensitive to contemporary experience across national, economic, and racial borders will take remarkable teachers, as well as excellent curriculum and learners eager to be involved in the process. Therein lies the threat and the promise of a Presbyterian and Reformed educational ministry.

Afterword

Are there clues for the future in this historical survey of Presbyterian use of the Bible in educational resources? At the end, what can we say about the prospects of Presbyterians' "knowing the Bible" in the next generation? That, after all, is a primary commitment of Christian education: for one generation to give to the next that which it received—the community's sacred scripture.

We have seen that "knowing the Bible," for Presbyterians, has always been a fundamental commitment, connected particularly with faith and practice. That is to say, Presbyterians have claimed historically that knowing the Bible was essential to self-identity, to knowing the nature of reality, including God, to forming our worldview, and to making ethical decisions appropriate to a Christian way of life. Faith and the practice of faith, we have said, are grounded in the Bible. Moreover, as Reformed Christians, we have said that faith and the practice of faith must be interpreted from the Bible in light of the plain sense of the biblical text, in the context of different and changing human conditions and in the full glare of scientific and secular learning, because truth is whole and cannot be ignored whatever its source, since all that is true has its being in God. And the task of interpretation, of knowing how the Bible authorizes faith and practice in the present day, belongs to the church, taught by the Holy Spirit. Thus education in the Bible, in the historic traditions of the church, and in the liberal arts and sciences of the day has been presumed preparation for the Presbyterian practice of interpretation since the days of John Calvin. The curricula we have examined stand in that line.

Curriculum is an effort to provide guidance for the church to carry out its interpretive task, to enable formation of beliefs, and to encourage a life of discipleship. In our survey, we have moved from a time at the turn of the century when biblical education was guided by little more than a selection of texts or topics, interpreted through the wisdom and piety of dedicated teachers mindful of the needs of their students, needs first determined more by theology than psychology or pedagogy. Progressively, the task and the curriculum became more complicated and more removed from the knowledge and skills of the untutored church member. These changes mirrored the growing complexity of biblical scholarship and educational and human development theory, as well as changing tides in theology. Our world has changed rapidly during this century, and the church's curriculum, in good Reformed fashion, has tried desperately to respond to those changes. We have become a world dependent, for better or worse, on experts; and that dependency is a fact of church life too, particularly for biblical criticism and interpretation in educational practice. Now we are committed to teaching church members how to interpret the biblical texts once presumed to lie so open before them, and we expect our teachers to learn a variety of methods appropriate to various ages in order to make faith known to the children of faith.

Other changes have occurred to complicate matters further. Biblical education is nearly limited to Sunday school, without reinforcement or supplement from contributing institutions of former years, such as the home, the school, and even a general, cultural ethos. That is an enormous, indeed impossible, burden for which the Sunday school has never been equipped. Assumptions about the Bible as an essential source for our self-identity, our worldviews, or our ethics no longer hold in our cultural climate, even among active church members.

There are no quick fixes on the horizon. Reformed faith has never been a simple matter, and if biblical education is at its heart, we should not be surprised by the challenge a modern world presents us. It will not help us to long for some easier day when "knowing the Bible" seemed an obvious and natural expectation for anyone who went to Sunday school regularly. We shall have to do the hard work of enabling secular Presbyterians to interpret the Bible for faith and practice and of teaching them, in turn, how to help their children do the same.

We can begin at the seminary level. Pastors must be equipped not only to interpret texts for the sake of sermon preparation but also to teach church members the skills needed to open the Bible as a resource for reflection on faith and for guiding personal and family decision making. Also, pastors and educators need to be able to teach teachers how to teach, and particularly how to interpret biblical texts presented in their teaching materials, to enable teachers to use curricula critically and creatively so that it serves the end of education for discipleship, for which it is intended.

In the congregation, we will need to devise a variety of opportunities for learning the Bible—far more than some part of one hour in a Sunday school classroom. For example, Ellis Nelson has suggested the formation of a "central study group" made up of church leaders representing the whole life of the congregation, whose task it would be to meet regularly, under the guidance of theologically trained leaders, to reflect on how the church may be faithful to God's calling today.[61] This would not be a Bible study group per se, but it could not help being a group committed to interpreting the Bible for faith and practice.

Other strategies might gather parents and children to discuss how the biblical story can inform family life and personal decisions. The point here is to find ways to model biblical authority and the practice of interpretation in a variety of everyday settings, rather than reserving Bible study for classroom exercise.

In an era of increasing numbers of adults doing graduate

study or continuing adult education, the church's educational program needs to be intellectually challenging, socially critical, and systematically planned. Current practice is typically hit-and-miss, without opportunity for participants or planners to build on prior experience, and study is frequently uncritical and bland. If we intend that adults should take church education seriously, then we will have to plan for serious and significant learning.

The last word here is a personal one. Wherever I go to teach in congregations, I find women and men eager to talk about what they believe, eager to talk about the world we live in and to wonder and argue about what God may be doing here. And, at the center of this search, I find people anxious to believe that the Bible can inform their faith, can help them make decisions faithful to their commitments to Jesus Christ and the church. They want to be able to affirm the authority of the Bible without abandoning modern knowledge and know-how and in the company of others with whom they share religious traditions and experiences. Schedules may be hectic and time limited, but the desire to know the Bible and how to interpret it for daily bread is still strong. We shall have to be steadfast, patient, and imaginative if we are to find our way to respond in the future. But we have a cloud of witnesses, among them the creators and critics and benefactors of a century of curricula, urging us on.[62]

8

Changing Leadership Patterns in the Presbyterian Church in the United States During the Twentieth Century

Richard W. Reifsnyder

During the twentieth century, North American Christian denominations have emerged as large-scale bureaucratic institutions whose character has been transformed by changes as much in organization as in formal theology. As Christian communions became more intentional about management, this concern affected the leadership styles that predominated. The changing styles of leadership both reflected and accelerated transformations within the church and the culture.

Leadership traditions in the Presbyterian Church in the United States (PCUS) differed from those of the United Presbyterian Church in the United States of America (UPCUSA) and its antecedents, the Presbyterian Church in the U.S.A. (PCUSA) and the United Presbyterian Church of North America (UPCNA). Certain historical reasons account in part for this difference, but the PCUS remained a much smaller church, where people were better known to one another, and so personal ties were significant factors in developing church policy.

In the South, Baptists and Methodists greatly outnumbered Presbyterians and created an evangelical climate for church life. Nevertheless, the PCUS, according to religious

historian Sydney Ahlstrom, "extended a disproportion-
ately large influence in Southern affairs, on account of the
social prominence of its members, its extreme inner cohesiveness, and its demand for a learned, doctrinally orthodox clergy."[1] The denomination, although it refrained from
popular social and economic movements because of its distinctive doctrine of the "spirituality of the church," developed a quasi-establishment outlook in the Southeast. As it
moved into the Southwest, the PCUS tended to coalesce
into eastern and western wings. Gradually during the twentieth century the PCUS moved away from its regionalism
and into the mainstream as contacts with northern Presbyterianism and other traditions increased. As the crucible of
cultural change refined practices in both the PCUS and
UPCUSA during the last several decades, leadership patterns became very similar.

The leadership patterns in the PCUS do not conform
neatly to generational divisions. For the sake of comparison, however, this paper analyzes the leadership in approximately the same time frames as will be looked at in the
UPCUSA stream: 1920–1935, 1935–1959, 1959–1973,
1973–1983. Transitions were marked by the selection of a
new Stated Clerk of the General Assembly. Biographical
data from ninety persons who served in major administrative roles were examined according to specific questions:
date of birth, gender, racial ethnic identity, educational
background, ecclesiastical status, and pattern of work experience prior to and after agency service.[2]

Leadership in the Thornwellian Tradition:
1920–1935

The PCUS was not only a much smaller, regionally oriented church, but it also had a different ecclesiological basis than its UPCUSA counterpart. Opposition to the usual
mainstream Protestant pattern of undertaking the mission
of the church through boards had developed in Old School
Presbyterianism in the South in the years prior to the Civil
War. James Henley Thornwell, professor at Columbia

Theological Seminary, argued that boards were not explicitly commanded by scripture. He had the opportunity to influence the church along his lines of thought when the Civil War precipitated the formation of the Presbyterian Church in the Confederate States of America in 1861. The General Assembly established four executive committees directly responsible to it, each with members and staff elected for only one year at a time.

Moreover, Thornwell remained suspicious of centralized authority. He argued that presbyteries and synods served as the primary agents of mission, rather than a General Assembly. The desire for decentralization also led the church to disperse geographically the executive committees, a pattern that remained in effect for nearly ninety years.[3]

The thirteen leaders who served the PCUS in major administrative roles following World War I were all born about the time of the Civil War and reflected the cultural assumptions of the time. Samuel H. Chester, for example, secretary of the Executive Committee of Foreign Missions from 1893 to 1926, belonged to the Ku Klux Klan, as did all the elders and deacons of his home church.[4] To an even greater extent than in the PCUSA, education of the leaders took place in denominational schools. This was true of the undergraduate education of eleven of the thirteen and of the seminary education of all nine of the clergy. The common, though somewhat parochial, educational experience helped to maintain a staunchly conservative unity. Although there was occasional theological squabbling, the PCUS was not badly affected by the fundamentalist controversy which sundered the PCUSA.

Nine of the thirteen key leaders were ministers and four were laypersons, of whom three were women. The nine clergy averaged more than twenty-two years of pastoral experience before becoming administrators. Invariably the executive secretaries went directly from the parish and stayed in that position as the culmination of a career.

The work of the executive committees remained modest in scope, and Foreign Missions was clearly preeminent. Committee offices were dispersed geographically, which served to limit the power of executives, but which also made coordination difficult. In 1927, the Assembly sought to remedy this deficiency when it established the Committee on the Assembly's Work as a coordinating body, with the different program functions as subcommittees of it. Many in the church viewed it as far too centralized an organization. Giving declined, and the experiment was abandoned in 1930.[5]

Although being an executive secretary required administrative skill, promotion became the primary task of these officers. They needed to be popular and inspiring speakers in order to stir up enthusiasm and financial support for their cause. Executives tended not to be theological innovators or controversialists, but persons skilled at developing a consensus for the mission of the church.

During this period, women made some major breakthroughs in leadership in the church, largely due to the extraordinary abilities of Hallie Paxson Winsborough. Daughter of the manse, valedictorian of her class at college, married to a lawyer, she raised six children and devoted herself to church work. In 1912 she organized the Women's Auxiliary of the PCUS and became its first superintendent. The executive secretaries of the four major committees, however, carefully supervised the auxiliary. Only in 1927 did Winsborough win permission to give her own report at the General Assembly. The executive secretaries supported this effort and in general were sympathetic to an increased, though limited, role for women. Women gained influence largely through this specialized arena. Women's involvement also came through contributions to publications, especially for children.[6]

During this period, despite the Thornwellian intention of curtailing the independence of the mission structures, the executive committees in practice functioned largely as did the boards of the PCUSA and UPCNA. They had to raise their own support, and they operated on their own when General Assembly was not in session. Moreover, the principle of electing executive secretaries by the Assembly, rather than by boards as was the northern tradition, seemed to have the unintended effect of making them more independent of the committees they served. A Methodist bishop is reported to have told one executive secretary in the 1930s, "No Methodist bishop has anything like the power or independence of a Southern Presbyterian Executive Secretary."[7] The institutional realities modified ecclesiological theory, but the theory still possessed a mythic hold in the denomination.

Respected Leadership in Organizational
Transition: 1935–1959

During this period, marked by the Stated Clerkship of E. C. Scott, the PCUS remained a regional, largely insular church, held together in part by Calvinistic theology but even more importantly by personal ties. It was a period of spectacular numerical growth. During the first half of the twentieth century the PCUS tripled in size. Church membership was growing faster proportionally than the population. The leadership reflected an era of confidence. People knew the leaders, who were dynamic figures and who exercised authority through the force of their personalities. A few voices advocated a more social gospel, but on the whole the conservative consensus prevailed.

Of the thirty-one people who formed the core of leadership, only four were laypersons, two of whom were the women who served as executive secretary of what was now known as the Women of the Church. Lay leaders remained scarce, despite the periodic concern of the General Assembly that too many clergy were being drawn into executive service. Invariably the Assembly urged that more laypersons be hired, but admitted that qualified clergy were less expensive than laity.[8]

The church realized imperfectly its conviction that ministers should assume administrative leadership only for a limited time and then return to parish ministry. Of eleven persons who served as executive secretaries or Stated Clerk during this time, only one returned to the parish. The pattern prevailed more substantially for the second-level leadership, nearly half of whom returned to the pastorate. Significant parish experience prior to executive service was the norm, though it averaged only fifteen years, less time than in the previous generation. In most cases, a person did not go directly from the parish to be an executive secretary, but rather served first in another administrative capacity.

Educationally, the vast majority of the leaders received formal training in southern Presbyterian schools. Indeed, 25 percent went to Davidson, and 50 percent of the clergy came from Union Seminary in Richmond.

As in the North, this was a time of "ecclesiastical giants." Charles Darby Fulton, for example, the executive secretary of the Executive Committee of Foreign Missions, was born in Japan and educated at Presbyterian College in Clinton, South Carolina, and Columbia Seminary. He returned to Japan as a missionary under the auspices of the PCUSA board. He served as a field secretary before becoming executive secretary in 1932, a position he held for thirty years. One of his successors described Fulton as a "dynamic leader, as was the style in those days . . . an orator and great story teller, who could sway people." Fulton personified a church confident of its cultural hegemony and the validity of its mission.[9]

Edward D. Grant demonstrated similar qualities. Born in Scotland and orphaned at an early age, Grant went to work as educational secretary for the Executive Committee on Foreign Missions after he graduated from Austin College. At the age of thirty-seven he became executive secretary of the Executive Committee of Religious Education and Publication, a position he held for more than twenty years. Grant was widely known and loved. He was an able Bible teacher and a passionate advocate for evangelism, who provided "brilliant and dynamic leadership." Not only the church recognized his leadership. After he retired from the executive committee, he became head of the Louisiana state prison and hospital system, and later he headed several other business and charitable concerns. Although atypical of the church's administrative leadership in being an elder rather than an ordained minister, he had that highly prized quality of being able to combine deep piety and evangelical fervor with devotion to administrative leadership.

These leaders served as ardent advocates for their cause. The church acknowledged its admiration for their leadership by electing Fulton, Grant, and two other executives as Moderators of the General Assembly.[10]

This was an era of confident expansion within Protestantism generally, and the style of leadership in the PCUS reflected that expansiveness. Although the distinctive southern Presbyterian perspective was fervently maintained in theory, the church modified its practice and became more like its PCUSA counterpart. In 1949 the General Assembly abandoned the fiction of the executive committees and created boards, which elected their own secretaries, subject to General Assembly approval. The church created a General Council to facilitate stewardship and coordinate the budget. The role of the Stated Clerk was expanded slightly and the office moved to Atlanta, in the first step of an effort to consolidate the administration of the church. The major personnel remained the same, but the restructuring had implications for the style of leadership that would be sought in the next several decades.[11]

A Time of Broadened Church Vision: 1959–1973

As the church moved into its second century, it also began to move gradually into the broader religious and cultural life of the nation. The catalyst was the challenge of the civil rights movement, and to a lesser extent the needs of the cities and the debate over the Vietnam War. Advocates within the church argued for a modification of the church's traditional adherence to the "spirituality of the church" and a greater involvement in social action. Others, influenced by neo-orthodoxy and encouraged by changes in the UPCUSA leading to the adoption of a new confession in 1967, sought modifications in the denomination's rigid adherence to the Westminster Confession of Faith. Moreover, the PCUS began to move beyond its regional base as resistance to involvement in organizations such as the National Council of Churches began to wane.[12]

A sign of the trend was the fact that of nineteen persons considered for leadership positions, six were trained in non-PCUS schools. Although Davidson College still graduated 25 percent of the leadership and Union Theological Seminary in Richmond graduated more than 50 percent, six of the ministers also did graduate work at Princeton, Yale, or Union Seminary in New York.

Clergy continued to dominate in administrative positions, despite the pleas of the General Assembly to consider more laity. With the exception of three women, all the major staff roles were filled by clergy. Lawrence Bottoms became the first Black executive, serving the Board of Church Extension, first as secretary for Negro work and from 1964 as associate secretary of the Board of Church Extension. For many years he was the only Black in a leadership role. Later he became the first Black Moderator of the PCUS, one of only two Moderators to come from the ranks of church administrators during this time.[13]

Pastoral experience continued to be the primary training ground for administrative leadership. The nine ministers who served as chief executives or Stated Clerk during this period averaged nineteen years pastoral experience. Although the image was carefully maintained that administrative service was a temporary call away from the parish rather than a career pattern, the reality was quite different. Only four of sixteen clergy who held major administrative posts during this period ever returned to parish life after service for a board.

Most of the clergy who were called to executive service were pastors of sizable churches who had served on the board to whose service they were called. But academic life also figured prominently as the immediate background for administrative positions. James A. Millard and T. Watson Street were professors at Austin Theological Seminary when called to be Stated Clerk and executive secretary of the Board of World Missions, respectively. William H. Kadel became executive secretary of the Board of Christian Education in 1968 following a ten-year stint as president of Florida Presbyterian College.

The desire for a decentralized church meant that the boards remained geographically separated, but this also had the unintended effect of helping to create strong, independent executives, who developed networks of support. Because the General Assembly was the one place where the church as a whole could speak, the executives worked hard to fight for budget and develop a platform where they could be heard. The annual conference sponsored by each board at Montreat served as an arena for garnering support, if not competitive advantage.

Leadership began in the 1960s to respond consciously and intentionally to changes in the social context. T. Watson Street, in many ways continuing the highly visible, decisive style of Darby Fulton, maintained the delicate balance between responding to thoughtful voices calling for essential changes in mission strategy and sustaining the loyalty of a large conservative constituency who saw missions as the chief work of the church. He developed ties to the Commission on Ecumenical Mission and Relations (COEMAR), which had begun wrestling with these changes a few years earlier.[14]

Important connections with the northern church were made as well by John Anderson, who left a thirty-five-hundred-member church to become executive secretary of the Board of Church Extension in 1965. The board changed its name to National Ministries, reflecting Anderson's new priorities. He intentionally began to utilize the reserves of the board, with their full support, in order to move beyond building new churches into social action. Some of the most controversial actions gave the apparent power of the executives high visibility. In particular, when Martin Luther King was assassinated during a Memphis garbage workers strike, Lawrence Bottoms urged Anderson to take immediate action on a request by Memphis Presbytery to provide $10,000 for the churches to feed workers' families. The action gave the PCUS credibility, but stirred fears of too much centralized power. In Anderson's view, the board and the General Assembly were way ahead of the grass-roots church on social concerns, and although overtures attempted to censure the board and its executive secretary, the General Assembly responded by commending their work.[15]

This new cadre of top leadership in the boards, which included not only Street and Anderson but Evelyn Green of the Board of Women's Work and Lawrence I. Stell on the General Council, intentionally sought to move the church out of its regionalism. They trusted one another and cooperated in responding to national and world movements. Because the boards were separated geographically and because the staffs were kept small in order to prevent what one executive called a "critical mass" from forming, they could be penetrated and persuaded almost at will by a strong executive. The leadership during this time used that leverage of the church structure to move the PCUS in new directions.

The leadership of the boards became a focal point for addressing the social and cultural change that was impacting the church. A desire for better coordination and efficiency in the work of the boards provided the catalyst for a restructuring, which occurred in 1972. A keen interest in drawing on the insights of certain management techniques and processes also stimulated the restructure. But, at least in the opinion of some of the executives like John Anderson, the church reacted against the strong leadership of the boards with the feeling that they had gotten "too far out in front." In an ecclesiastical counterpart of a states' rights emphasis, the General Assembly sought officials who "shouldn't lead, but simply serve."[16]

The executives during this transitional period harked back to a style of strong, visible, authoritative leadership of an earlier generation. But in terms of issues and vision, these leaders adopted a broader agenda. As in the North, the top executives of the PCUS boards assumed there would be an ever-expanding church program. This assumption proved faulty, as membership peaked in 1968.

Leadership in the Collaborative Style:
1973–1983

Reflecting a more egalitarian ethos and desirous of expanding the emerging social agenda, the church adopted a new structure in 1972, which was inclusive and participatory by design. The organization was not only to coordinate and integrate the program, but to transcend the tendency of particular groups or highly public leaders to advocate uncritically their particular interest. As in the UPCUSA, synods and presbyteries engaged in an increasing variety of forms of mission and employed staff to assist them. General Assembly staff had to adopt new expectations and patterns of operation.

This was a turbulent decade in church and nation. The nation reeled under Watergate, the Vietnam defeat, and the Iran hostage crisis. Church membership began to decline. New perspectives, especially that of liberation theology, challenged traditional concepts of the church's mission. Calls for accountability and fair representation increased. The new structure reflected these changes.

At the center of the new structure was the General Executive Board (GEB), "designed to reflect the church in microcosm." Instead of the "high steeple" preachers and the semipro laypersons who traditionally had constituted the boards, synod nominees made up more than half of the GEB. The General Assembly nominated twenty more, "assuring adequate representation of women, youth, Blacks, and Hispanic Americans." Moreover, the five divisions of the GEB were not to be functionally autonomous, but related and integrated. The church hoped for a "collaborative style of operation," with all divisions having input and coming to consensus on any important decision.[17]

Moreover, restructuring accomplished the often-resisted goal of centralizing the offices. The one mission of the church would be more readily coordinated through the management team and, in the eyes of William Fogleman, chair of the restructuring committee, would enable the PCUS to take seriously Presbyterian connectionalism.[18]

This approach required a very different kind of leadership from that which the church had traditionally cultivated. The general staff director and the five division staff directors provided administrative coordination through a GEB management team. One member of the team served as chair on a rotating basis. By limiting service as a division head ordinarily to no more than two four-year terms, the church institutionalized what had been an elusive ideal, making executive service a temporary diversion away from one's primary ministry. Process and procedure were elevated over strong, dominating, visible personalities.

It is clear that calling people into administrative work at a younger age and with less pastoral experience became a trend. Of eighteen persons who served as chief administrator or division heads during this period, fourteen had parish or chaplaincy experience, which averaged twelve years. Nearly all those who became division directors had experience in some administrative capacity before undertaking that major role, although not necessarily in the same field. Clifton Kirkpatrick, for example, had no parish or missionary experience when he was called to be director of the Division of International Mission. But he had significant administrative background in ecumenical ministries in Houston. He proved himself an effective administrator committed to the mission cause, but he personified an emerging career pattern which emphasized specialized administrative skill. The ideal of having people move in and out of administrative positions became more of a reality in this period than in others, as seven persons returned to the parish or other ministerial duties after their term or after their position was otherwise terminated.

A similar pattern impacted the office of Stated Clerk, which never was the focal point for the church's life as it was in the North. Whereas Eugene Carson Blake and William P. Thompson served ex officio on nearly every significant General Assembly committee and had broad ecumenical responsibilities, the Clerk in the PCUS did not have comparable responsibilities. In 1973, reflecting the traditional PCUS concern but also reflecting a culturewide tendency to curtail the power of individual leaders, the General Assembly determined the Clerk would be elected for a three-year term, with eligibility for election to two additional terms. James Andrews had been a pastor for only two years before serving in administrative capacities at the World Alliance of Reformed Churches and Princeton Theological Seminary. He returned to the PCUS in 1971 as assistant to the Stated Clerk before taking over in 1973. The church desired in its leadership those who had management experience.[19]

Women began to play a more prominent role in the church's administrative life. Three women were among the eighteen key leaders, including the first clergywoman in an administrative post, the Rev. Patricia McClurg. The restructuring stipulated that at least one of the division heads would be a woman. Evelyn Green, who had been executive secretary of the Board of Women's Work since 1960, became director of the Division of National Mission. In order to stagger the terms of staff, the initial team was elected at random to two-, three-, and four-year terms. Green drew a two-year term and, after a performance review, was not invited to serve another term. The church, and especially the women, loved Green and found this decision painful and confusing.[20]

Green's ties were with an earlier generation of leaders. By and large the top leaders had been born in the late 1920s or 1930s. Many trained at PCUS colleges. Union Theological Seminary in Richmond graduated six of these leaders, though significantly eight did some form of theological training at Union (N.Y.), Princeton, or Yale Divinity School. The PCUS began to move beyond its regionalism.

Major difficulties in the collaborative management team led to a significant readjustment in 1976. The church faced budgetary difficulties as more money was kept at the local level. People in the PCUS tended to trust people more than structures, and the church found that even the nomenclature made it difficult to grasp. The original design anticipated the need for ongoing adjustment, but administrative chaos forced changes earlier than planned.

The management team approach required a lot from its personnel. Administrators needed to be advocates for their piece of the work while being equally committed to the welfare of the whole mission. John Evans, the general staff director, admitted he found corporate decision making very difficult. Meetings consumed an inordinate number of hours as the team sought consensus. No single leader was to make executive decisions. Considerable difficulty occurred because of a rush to implement the restructuring more quickly than the committee had recommended. A group of persons, including several former Moderators, made many of the selections of top echelon leadership. They sought continuity from the old boards while ensuring that the staff would be broadly representative and include women and ethnic minorities. Politics influenced the selection of personnel and did not necessarily produce people committed to a similar vision of a management team.[21]

Consciously backing off from some of the management terminology in favor of ecclesiological language, the General Executive Board received a new name, the General Assembly Mission Board. At the same time, the management team and priority-setting approach was modified in favor of a more traditional hierarchical, CEO model. The Rev. Patricia McClurg became the administrative director in 1977, after a prolonged search process. Morale was poor and McClurg, who favored a collaborative leadership idea, worked hard to develop a team who could cooperate. With her balance of toughness and efficiency, McClurg helped to stabilize and to heal the administration. She greatly reduced the amount of time spent in meetings, emphasized the responsibility of the directors to their divisions, and focused the team on long-range planning. McClurg made the structures work effectively, according to those interviewed. But the structures themselves and the context of the times also called for a style of leadership which placed a premium on management process and personnel skills.[22]

Conclusions

A simple chart can illustrate some major characteristics of the chief executives of the Presbyterian Church in the

U.S. Certain patterns emerge when leadership is viewed from the perspective of more than a half century.

Fig. 8.1. Chief Executives of the Presbyterian Church in the United States

	Total Number of Chief Executives	Number of Clergy	Number of Women	Racial/ Ethnic Persons	Moderators Formerly G.A. Staff
1920–1935	7	5(71%)	1	0	1
1935–1959	11	7(64%)	2	0	4
1959–1973	9	8(89%)	1	0	3
1973–1983	18	15(83%)	3	1	0

	Denomi- nationally Connected College	Denomi- national Seminary/ Chief Seminary	Years of Pastoral Experience Prior to Administrative Work	Average Age When Entered Administrative Work
1920–1935	4(57%)	5 (3 UTS, Va.)	22	47
1935–1959	7(64%)	6 (4 UTS, Va.)	15	42
1959–1973	6(67%)	7 (4 UTS, Va.)	19	50
1973–1983	10(56%)	9 (6 UTS, Va.)	12	37

Despite certain philosophical objections to administrative service as a career pattern for clergy, that pattern nevertheless occurred in the PCUS tradition. The need for a specialized, expert administrative leadership accompanied the emergence of a bureaucratic church organization during the twentieth century. There are some contrasts to the UPCUSA tradition, however. Although the years of parish

ministry experience prior to entering General Assembly
staff positions declined, the drop was not as precipitous in
the PCUS as in the UPCUSA. A significant change did occur with the reorganization in the early 1970s. People began entering administrative service at an earlier age, with
less pastoral experience. The church was seeking leaders
with specialized skills in management process and human
relations.[23]

The statistics confirm what was readily apparent: women
and racial ethnic persons held no significant administrative
positions in the church until very recently. A commitment
to affirmative hiring practices became part of the restructuring in the 1970s. A major milestone occurred when the
General Assembly Mission Board selected the Rev. Patricia McClurg to be its administrative director in 1977. She
became the first woman to be the chief executive of the
denomination's organization, and she won the church's respect for her accomplishments.

The PCUS followed the UPCUSA trend in selecting
fewer Moderators from the General Assembly staff in its
later years. Whereas during the first two thirds of the century the heads of the executive committees and the boards
earned credibility by being highly visible and articulate
spokespersons for their particular causes, administrative
leaders in the 1970s became, by design, more anonymous.
The church desired skills in managerial processes in order
to involve broad participation in the decision making and
to ensure a high level of accountability. The times discouraged domination of church life by great personalities. Indeed, there was a conscious attempt to move away from
what some perceived as a hierarchical, authoritarian style
of leadership. In the view of longtime PCUS synod executive William Fogleman, restructuring attempted to restore
the church to a more serious commitment to Presbyterian
polity in its administrative decision making.[24]

Because the PCUS was a smaller church than the
UPCUSA, personal ties mitigated some of the effects of
the changes in leadership style. To a greater extent than in
the UPCUSA, the denominational colleges and seminaries

provided the training for church staff and helped create a certain cohesiveness.[25] Nevertheless, the church during the 1970s made significant changes in its manner of securing personnel. Some lamented the loss of those widely known and trusted leaders who were readily identified with particular mission causes. It was not always clear to the church what those who worked in areas such as "court partnership services" did. But there were important gains, particularly new opportunities for women and racial ethnic persons to exercise leadership in the church.

The organizational revolution deeply penetrated the PCUS, and despite the tradition of leadership built on personal ties with dominant personalities, the collegial, egalitarian style reflected the new context in which the church found itself. Church leaders earlier in the century were confident of the ongoing growth and expansion of the church. Dominant personalities reflected those assumptions. During the 1960s and 1970s the cultural context changed. Membership in the PCUS peaked in 1968 and began to decline thereafter. A certain loss in confidence permeated the church. Restructuring institutionalized certain desired changes in leadership style, but, just as in the case of the UPCUSA, it is unlikely that the old style leadership could have been maintained. Church members had lost their confidence in being led and desired instead to find ways to be included in the process of decision making. Competent managers replaced charismatic vision builders as the primary model for leaders in the denomination.

9

Transformations in Administrative Leadership in the United Presbyterian Church in the U.S.A., 1920–1983

Richard W. Reifsnyder

During the last several decades the perception of leadership in America's mainstream Protestant traditions has been transformed. To some it is a sign of decline. More anonymous, even faceless leaders seem to have replaced administrative leaders who once held positions of considerable ecclesiastical and cultural influence. Whereas formerly denominational administrators were much-respected personalities in the church and influential in the culture, now ecclesiastical leaders are viewed as bureaucrats and managers.[1] Others view the changes in less disparaging ways. Opportunity for leadership in administrative structures has opened up significantly to those who were previously on the margin of the church. They argue that a new breed of leadership whose style is responsive, collegial, and participatory has replaced an older, more hierarchical leadership, strengthening the church's witness.

However evaluated, many observers inside the church and out agree the nature of leadership has changed. This essay analyzes some of those changes over a sixty-year period within the United Presbyterian Church in the U.S.A. (UPCUSA) and its predecessors, the Presbyterian Church in the U.S.A. (PCUSA) and the United Presbyterian

Church of North America (UPCNA). What can be said to characterize those who have been administrative leaders of the national agencies of the church? What changes can be discerned in their backgrounds and experience? How have expectations changed concerning the nature of Presbyterian leadership?

From the colonial period well into the twentieth century, the Presbyterian Church exercised considerable influence in shaping American culture. By the mid-nineteenth century other denominations, such as Methodist, Baptist, and Roman Catholic, were growing more rapidly than the Presbyterian. Nevertheless, the authority granted Presbyterian leaders far exceeded the denomination's numerical strength. A strong educational tradition contributed to this, as did the conviction Presbyterians held that Christians should seek to transform culture.[2]

During the last century, forces in the society, and especially in business, have shaped American Protestantism in significant ways. The church became a large-scale bureaucratic organization, with shifting organizational needs and expectations. The Presbyterian Church, in particular, has led the way in adopting changes in organization and leadership style. The changes that took place in leadership are complex, reflecting forces both in the society at large and in the church itself.

In essence, this is a collective biographical study, or a prosopography, to use the technical term. Biographical data were compiled concerning more than a hundred top or second-level administrators in the national agencies. The biographies were studied according to certain specific questions: date of birth, sex, racial ethnic identity, educational background (college and seminary), ecclesiastical status (lay or clergy), and pattern of work experience prior to and after agency service.[3] Selected interviews and correspondence with men and women who have served as administrators or were close observers of the changes of the last quarter century supplement the biographical data. Some historical "periods" emerged, and during each period leaders bore distinctive characteristics.[4]

Four periods, or "generations," of leadership can readily be identified: 1923–1937, 1937–1959, 1959–1973, and 1973–1987.

The Era of the Christocentric Moderates: 1923–1937

In an effort to provide more efficient coordination and coherent planning for its mission program, the church reorganized itself between 1921 and 1923 into four new boards: The Board of Foreign Missions, the Board of National Missions, the Board of Christian Education, and the Board of Relief and Sustentation. The establishment of these boards and the creation of the staff to administer their work marked the culmination of the church's transformation into a large-scale bureaucratic organization.

World War I generated considerable energy not only to make a world safe for democracy, but also to fulfill the century-long effort to create a Christian America. Although the enthusiasm for ecumenical cooperation waned in the collapse of the Inter-Church World Movement, the administrative transformation prepared the denomination to expand its own mission. This was a time of theological conflict between fundamentalists and moderates within the church. The leaders of the boards tended to be theological conservatives who not only were administratively competent but also sought to focus on the mission outreach of the church as a way of overcoming theological division.[5]

For our purposes, thirty-eight persons have been identified by me as having their chief administrative experience in this "generation," which ended with the retirement of Robert E. Speer as secretary of the Board of Foreign Missions in 1937.[6] Speer had been the chief spokesperson for foreign mission for a generation. The Board of Foreign Missions under Speer became the focal point for discerning and accomplishing the church's mission, as would the Board of Christian Education under Paul Payne in the 1940s and 1950s and the Board of National Missions under Kenneth Neigh in the 1960s.

The leaders of this period, 1923–1937, came of age during the latter part of the nineteenth century, as America came of age as an industrial and world power. Despite the challenges posed by Darwinism, biblical criticism, urbanization, and immigration, the church retained tremendous confidence in the expansion of God's sovereignty under Protestant leadership. The boards of the church emerged as important instruments in that expansion.

The thirty-eight top administrators in this period had similar backgrounds. Thirty-one were ministers, thirty-six were white, and thirty-three were male. Of the five women, nearly all had previously served as staff for the Woman's Board of Home Missions or Woman's Board of Foreign Missions, which had lost their separate identities in the restructured church. Similarly, the Blacks who had previously served the Board of Freedmen became administrators of related divisions in the new Board of National Missions. But no woman or Black served in any high-level administrative position.

Two thirds of the leadership graduated from small Presbyterian-related colleges. Seven were College of New Jersey (Princeton) graduates, one of whom became Stated Clerk and two of whom became general secretaries.

Within the much smaller and more conservative United Presbyterian Church of North America (UPCNA), the formative role of the denominational college is especially clear. Four of seven had attended denominational colleges, and all graduated from a denominational seminary.

Four of the eight persons who became chief administrators in the PCUSA tradition had attended Princeton Theological Seminary, but that seminary's dominance was not found to be nearly so great among the backgrounds of subordinate level administrators.

The career patterns of those who served as staff are striking. Of the thirty-one who were ordained, all had spent significant time in either pastoral or mission work. In fact, the Stated Clerk and seven general secretaries in the PCUSA during this period spent an average of nearly twenty years as pastors or, in two cases, college teachers, before entering service as administrators. Lewis Mudge, for example, spent twenty-six years in the parish ministry before leaving an eighteen-hundred-member church to become Stated Clerk in 1921.

In most cases the chief administrative leaders went directly from being pastor of a very large church to being head of a board. Serving as Stated Clerk or general secretary was viewed as the crowning achievement of a distinguished career in parish ministry. These men were not part of a specialized career pattern, although many secondary-level administrators developed more of an administrative career pattern. Warren Wilson, for example, after fourteen years in the parish, devoted the rest of his career to administering the Department of Rural Church in the Board of National Missions. The women, who, of course, were not ordained, developed patterns that often began with teaching or missionary service, followed by lengthy administrative service. Ann Taylor taught for five years and worked as a student secretary for the YWCA for another seven before serving the Board of National Missions, first as a field secretary, then for twenty-two years as secretary for Woman's Work and Promotion.

The career of Robert E. Speer is unique for its absence of pastoral service. His organizational genius, his devotion to his work, his high energy level, and his attention to detail made him an able administrator. But to the church at large he remained above all an advocate for the foreign missions cause. A gifted preacher and prolific writer, he served no particular congregation, but rather the whole church. Speer personified the role of "leader" in this period. He was a charismatic spokesperson for a particularly important cause, challenging the church with a vision and prodding it to fulfill its responsibility. In significant ways, his model for leadership continued until the 1970s.[7]

The church venerated its leaders during this period. Five of the seven general secretaries, as well as the Stated Clerk, were elected Moderators of the General Assembly, either before or during their term in office. A comparable pattern held true in the United Presbyterian Church of North

America, with three of the six chief administrators being elected Moderator of that denomination.

Ecclesiastical Giants and the Church Ascendant: 1937–1959

During this twenty-plus-year period, the pattern of highly visible, well-respected, and powerful leadership continued. The suburban population expanded following World War II, and the denominationally supported new church developments fostered steady growth in church membership. Strong national leaders for the church became a reality only after the restructuring in 1923. Before that the boards, with the possible exception of the Foreign Mission Board, were fragmented and geographically limited in their appeal. The establishment of four boards centralized authority and created the machinery for a truly national organization. During the 1940s and 1950s the organizational potential exploded during a period when the Protestant churches assumed cultural dominance and continuous expansion. Church leadership during this era of Billy Graham crusades and the appeal of Norman Vincent Peale's power of positive thinking kept clear focus on the church's organizational growth. Sydney Ahlstrom declared with considerable justification that it was not until the 1960s and the election of John Kennedy as President that the Puritan era in American history came to an end.[8]

The leadership fit the assumptions and expectations of the times. A publicity piece honoring Paul Calvin Payne quoted Genesis 6:4 (King James Version): "There were giants in the earth in those days." It seems an apt description of him, and also of the leadership more broadly. Those who headed the boards expected to use their platform to influence the church. As an admirer wrote of Stated Clerk William Barrow Pugh after his death in 1951, "He was anything but the secretarial temperament. He was a leader . . . indisposed to neutrality." A certain reverential awe surrounded these dominant personalities.[9]

The senior leadership during this period continued to be

white male ordained ministers. Of the thirty-six people examined in this generation, twenty-eight were white males
who had been ordained as clergy. Of the eight lay leaders,
six were women. Perhaps significantly, three of those
women served the Board of Foreign Missions, where it was
not uncommon to have women who had served on the mission field undertake administrative responsibility. There
was also a woman administrator, Evelyn Fulton, on the
UPCNA Foreign Mission Board. Toward the end of the period more women came to serve on the staffs of the Boards
of Christian Education and National Missions, but almost
exclusively in the publications area or in women's work.
Men or women identified as Black or another racial ethnic
minority seem practically nonexistent in upper-level leadership positions.

Educationally, the leadership of the UPCNA boards
came trained almost exclusively at denominational colleges
like Muskingum and Westminster in Pennsylvania and at
the denominational seminary, Pittsburgh. There was a
greater representation of Ivy League schools in the PCUSA
stream. Charles Leber, general secretary of the Board of
Foreign Missions, studied at Johns Hopkins, while Stated
Clerk Pugh and Board of Pensions general secretary Reid
Dickson studied at the University of Pennsylvania. All
three learned their Presbyterian theology at Princeton
Theological Seminary.

Three of the five general secretaries in the PCUSA, plus
the Stated Clerk, had pastoral experience, averaging fifteen
years. Hermann N. Morse, like Speer, was an exception to
the pattern. He spent his entire career working for the
Board of National Missions, serving as a researcher and
associate before being elevated to general secretary in 1949.

Extensive pastoral or mission experience remained the
norm. Often a board called a minister directly from the
pastorate to administrative leadership. Pugh went directly
from a Philadelphia pastorate to be Stated Clerk, although
he had served as an assistant to Lewis Mudge while in the
parish and was well connected as the nephew of the first
full-time Stated Clerk, William Henry Roberts. Paul Calvin

Payne served five different churches before the Board of Christian Education called him from the thousand-member First Presbyterian Church of Ithaca, New York. Charles T. Leber was only thirty-six when the Board of Foreign Missions called him from a twelve-hundred-member church in Scranton, Pennsylvania, to become its general secretary.

A similar pattern prevailed in the UPCNA. Youth was valued. Glenn Reed returned from the mission field at the age of forty to head the Foreign Mission Board. T. Donald Black, who has been at the center of the church's national life at several major transition points, became the first nonmissionary head of the UPCNA Foreign Mission Board when he was called from the pastorate in 1954 at age thirty-four. Black moved to his position while serving as president of the Philadelphia-based board. Elected boards frequently recruited staff from among their members during this period.[10]

Ordinarily the church called people to leadership on the boards after they had demonstrated effectiveness for some years as pastors or missionaries. But general characteristics can only tell part of the story of leadership in this era which was so dominated by strong personalities.

Paul Calvin Payne, general secretary of the Board of Christian Education from 1940 to 1957, one of those dominant personalities, made Christian education the focal point for much of the church's energy. Charged with developing a new Sunday school curriculum, he summoned the resources of the church to spend a million dollars developing the *Christian Faith and Life* curriculum, designed to draw on contemporary biblical scholarship. Most church leaders viewed the expense as a gamble, but within six months of publication $1.6 million worth of orders provided an indication of acceptance. Eventually the curriculum was used by 90 percent of the PCUSA churches.[11]

Those who worked with him described Payne as irresistibly persuasive. Although he kept authority in his hands and expected the staff to support his decisions, subordinates say he also gave considerable latitude to them to develop ideas and become part of the creative process. In part he exercised leadership because of the rapid expansion of staff to support the Christian education needs of a burgeoning suburban population. During Payne's tenure the number of staff increased from eighteen to over one hundred, and the budget from $750,000 to $4 million. Field directors not only disseminated and promoted programs created by the national staff, they also surveyed effective candidates for the board itself. While the general secretaries were responsible to their boards, they also helped shape them. Payne saw to it that the Board of Christian Education was strong. Eugene Carson Blake served while a pastor. So did Edler Hawkins and Thelma Adair, two strong Black leaders who became Moderators of the General Assembly.

Payne used his platform to articulate powerfully the cause of Christian education. True, his vision coincided with the needs of a growing suburban church confident in its cultural position. But his forceful personality proved essential in capitalizing on the opportunity. The leaders of this period tended to be well connected to the dominant cultural leadership. One later executive labeled them "epic, entrepreneurial, elitists," who assumed the value of American culture and Christianity. William Barrow Pugh served as chairman of the General Commission of Army and Navy Chaplains during World War II and received a Medal of Merit from the Secretary of War for his efforts. His successor as Stated Clerk, Eugene Carson Blake, was frequently pictured with President Eisenhower, who became a Presbyterian shortly before his election.[12]

In contrast to the earlier period, only one Moderator of the PCUSA and two of the UPCNA were drawn from among the general secretaries. Although the church venerated these charismatic leaders, it appeared less eager to honor them with the position of Moderator as well.

Challenging the Kingdom Builders: 1959–1973

In 1958 the PCUSA and UPCNA churches merged to form the United Presbyterian Church in the U.S.A. The staffs of the boards merged harmoniously. For the first part of this period, the leadership patterns of earlier periods were maintained. Strong executives, especially in the Commission on Ecumenical Mission and Relations (COEMAR), created to reflect new approaches to mission, and the Board of National Missions, used their platforms effectively to secure support for the programs of their semi-autonomous boards. Enormous changes took place in the world and nation during this time. Newly independent nations in the third world provided a different context for missionary work. The slogan "one mission on six continents" reflected the desire to integrate mission. During the 1960s, American society grappled with the challenges of civil rights, poverty, urban conflict, the Vietnam War, the new morality, the death of God and secular city theology, and the questioning of authority of all types.

By the end of the period the powerful, hierarchical leaders faced challenges to their positions as new expectations for leadership emerged. In part this was an intentional effort made by the staff to respond to the changing social climate of the 1960s; in part, the changes in the kind of leadership desired was imposed by the new social context.

Biographically, the leadership began to shift. Of the thirty-one persons examined, seven were lay people, four were racial ethnic, and four were women. For the first time a woman held a significant administrative post. Margaret Shannon, a missionary teacher and campus worker before joining the Board of Foreign Missions in 1940, became associate general secretary of COEMAR in 1958.

The leaders of this generation were born in the first decades of the twentieth century and matured during the period of the Depression. Educationally, those whose background was UPCNA had studied almost exclusively at a denominational college and seminary. But for those in the PCUSA stream, the denominational college was no longer the primary training ground. Less than half went to denominational schools. Moreover, no seminary dominated the executive field. Five attended Princeton, three McCormick, and the rest graduated from other seminaries.

Noteworthy in the career pattern of these executives is a

decline in the number of years spent in parish ministry. Of the nine persons who served as chief administrators during this period, eight had parish or mission experience, but it averaged only thirteen years.

Other administrative work was becoming a prerequisite for the highest levels of service. John Coventry Smith, after spending nearly two decades as a missionary to Japan and pastor, joined the staff of the Board of Foreign Missions and was elevated eleven years later to general secretary of its successor, COEMAR, at the death of Charles Leber in 1959. Kenneth Neigh had been a pastor for nine years, but was called to the Board of National Missions after a ten-year stint as executive presbyter in Detroit. In 1951 Glen Moore became secretary of the General Council, a position designed to help coordinate the work of the boards, after fifteen years as an executive for the Presbytery of Los Angeles and the Synod of California. James Gailey, after eleven years in the parish, in 1944 became a field director for the Board of Christian Education, and then worked his way up through the ranks, becoming general secretary in 1971.

The statistics and these illustrations suggest that administrative service became less a responsibility undertaken toward the end of a career devoted primarily to the parish and more of a specialized calling within the ministerial profession. Few of the leaders had any specialized management training, however, and often picked up what they knew on the job or through reading and seminars. Lack of formal training did not preclude competence. Yet at least one general secretary lamented not being taken seriously as an administrator by laymen who "just don't believe that clergy have any management skills."[13]

The church depended on the "old boy network" to obtain administrative staff. Kenneth Neigh was never interviewed when he was selected to be general secretary of the Board of National Missions. Asked to served on a committee designed to consider the church's mission in the 1960s, Neigh realized Hermann Morse was making his decision about who would be his successor. John Smith asserted he knew "of no one, myself included, who was interviewed for the position [of general secretary] or who applied." By the same token the executives procured their staffs simply by hiring whomever they desired, without having to advertise positions or formally to interview.[14]

In 1968 John Coventry Smith became the last executive of a national church agency to be elected Moderator. The 1960s were a turbulent period for the society and the church, and a call for a new type of leadership in the church emerged from this period.

Much of the ferment in the church came in the Board of National Missions. General Secretary Neigh, committed to the principle of decentralizing mission so that it could be done at the most effective level, sought to avoid directing everything from a national headquarters. He assembled a team, including Bryant George and David Ramage, who had urban experience in Chicago, and Max Browning, a forward-looking management consultant. They tried to carry out this decentralization and to foster social-action initiatives.

Although strong leaders had always pressed the church in new directions and had evoked some criticism for their power and methods, the setting had been one in which the church felt confident and assured of its position in society. Now, as mission became less clearly identified with traditional means for fostering church growth, a perception emerged in the minds of some that, as Browning put it, the "leadership of the last ten years were rejecting the teachings of Christ by their total commitment to social action issues."[15]

This shift of power away from the center took place in COEMAR as well, and church members did not always understand the new approach to mission. Elected board members, reflecting the tenor of the times, believed they should be as visible as the staff, if not more so, in speaking for the board.

In a time of radical questioning of the basic nature and purpose of the church, some began to resent the power of leaders who held control over money and programs. An incident in 1970 galvanized the feeling. In order to salvage a fragmented General Assembly, Smith and Neigh proposed providing $1.25 million from their reserves to initiate a program for the self-development of peoples. The proposal received a standing ovation from the General Assembly, but as the two left the stage, someone muttered to a National Missions board member, "We're going to make sure there will be no more Ken Neighs and John Smiths."[16] Both Neigh and Smith had to get the approval of their ordinarily highly supportive boards. They did so, with some difficulty. But the perception grew that they had too much power over how monies were raised and spent. In fact, their power lay in their ability to create a vision for the church and to implement it with the support and encouragement of the boards. The challenge to their leadership resulted in part from their theological convictions. "Out of their understanding of the gospel," Donald Black asserts, "Smith and Neigh tried to identify with our efforts to empower the minorities. Once you identify with a minority, you are the target of the same antagonisms facing the minority." Moreover, despite the theological concern for decentralization, their administrative style remained closer to a hierarchical and authoritarian style which had characterized earlier periods.[17]

Eugene Carson Blake personifies this transition to new expectations for leaders. Coming to the office of Stated Clerk from one of the Presbyterian Church's largest congregations, he determined "not to let the unpretentious title 'stated clerk' keep him from recognizing the position's influence and inherent authority," as his biographer Douglas Brackenridge put it. The first Clerk from a synod other than Pennsylvania, he sought to be a national figurehead for the church. Brackenridge relates that Blake interpreted the task of carrying on the "general correspondence of the Church" to mean, "If you want to talk to Presbyterians, you have to talk to the Stated Clerk. In other words, it's the top job." He expanded the Stated Clerk's role in two particular areas, becoming the church's chief spokesman in the ecumenical arena and using his position to act as an intermediary between the church and political power structures. His sermon in 1960 in an Episcopal cathedral proposing church union with other denominations, which he somewhat disingenuously claimed he was giving as an individual minister and not as Clerk, earned him that visible confirmation of cultural significance, his picture on the cover of *Time* magazine. His strong support of the civil rights movement culminated in his being arrested in an effort to desegregate a park in Baltimore in 1963, an action that won him both admiration and animosity.[18]

Blake's leadership in creating a broadened vision for the role of Stated Clerk evoked objections from others who thought the office was vested with too much power. An indication of the transformation of the church's expectations of its leaders and especially its disillusionment with ecclesiastical giants was the humiliation suffered by Blake when he ran for Moderator in 1973 and came in fifth of five candidates. His defeat can be explained in part because his absence while serving for seven years as general secretary of the World Council of Churches made him less well known within the church at home. It was also a sign of a growing discomfort with powerful leaders in his mold.[19]

The organization of the General Assembly boards during this period provided a platform from which a strong leader could project a vision before the church and develop the means to implement it. Although there was a General Secretaries Council which met regularly for mutual exchange of ideas and for budget consultation, each board for the most part operated independently, developing its own constituency and appealing for its own support. In certain cases these leaders developed strong ties, such as those between Blake and Neigh or Neigh and Smith, which enabled them to cooperate effectively. But they remained chiefly independent entrepreneurs, whose prime concern was fostering the well-being of their own enterprise.

The Participatory Model of Leadership: 1973–1983

Wholesale reorganization of national church structures in 1971–1973 led to dramatic changes in the leadership

profile. What began as an effort to develop regional synods
and provide for an administrative organization more responsive to the mission needs of an urban population led to
a restructuring which eliminated the three major program
boards. In an effort to emphasize the unity of the mission
worldwide, the church created three new agencies, distinguished by function. The Program Agency, by far the largest agency, included all the programmatic emphases. The
Vocation Agency handled personnel for the mission. The
Support Agency served the functions of stewardship, publicity, and interpretation. A General Assembly Mission
Council provided coordination and financial oversight.[20]

The new structures had significant implications for leadership. Kenneth Neigh and others are convinced that the
reorganization was an intentional effort to prevent strong
leaders from having a platform from which to advocate and
implement bold programs.[21] More positively put, the
church developed a process of decision making that intended to be more participatory and to ensure a hearing for
a greater variety of voices within the church.

The times also had a significant impact on the changing
pattern of leadership. A heightened concern for the rights
of groups that felt excluded from power marked the society
at large. Liberation and empowerment became central
theological and political themes. Disillusionment with national leadership following Watergate and the Vietnam experience eroded authority granted to all institutions and
individuals. Developing clearer lines of accountability and
ensuring fair representation were viewed as important
ways to secure justice. Groups within the church that felt
excluded from significant decision-making responsibilities,
such as women and racial ethnic persons, challenged the
church to take seriously its own profession of inclusiveness.
Moreover, certain trends in management, such as management by objective, and the human relations movement,
penetrated the church. Leaders for the church needed different skills from those previously required.

The profile of this generation of leaders reflects these
changes in expectation. Twenty-one persons were consid-

ered, namely the Stated Clerks and those who served as agency heads or chief associates. Nearly all were born in the decade following the First World War. Clergy still dominated, with only five laypersons in the leadership cadre. Three were of minority racial ethnic identity. Two were women. Farther down the organizational hierarchy there was greater inclusiveness.

When one looks only at the ten persons who served as chief executives, there are some significant patterns. Four of the ten were laypersons. William P. Thompson, a lawyer from Kansas, had served as Moderator of the General Assembly before being elected Stated Clerk in 1966. Thompson's skills mirrored a church that increasingly needed a legal interpreter, not only for its own complex rules, but in relation to civil issues. His extraordinary knowledge of church law, coupled with his decisive interpretations, made him an effective Clerk. Nevertheless, he reflected in his personality a different era of leadership from that of his predecessor. Blake was charismatic, a commanding presence who would be noticed when he entered a room. He personified a confident, expansive, growing church, just as Thompson personified a church in transition, seeking to manage its affairs effectively in more turbulent times.[22]

Laymen served as heads of the Board of Pensions and the Support Agency, areas of the church's work requiring significant managerial expertise.

A commitment that racial ethnic persons would be more highly visible in leadership positions led to the appointment of two Blacks in major administrative roles. Oscar McCloud was only thirty-six when called to head the Program Agency, although he had administrative experience in all three of the previous programmatic boards. Leon Fanniel was executive director of the General Assembly Mission Council, though he resigned after only a year and a half, realizing his skills were in different areas.[23]

Margaret Thomas became the first clergywoman to have a major administrative role in the UPCUSA when she was appointed deputy executive director of the General Assembly Mission Council in 1977. She had served as a research

specialist for the Presbyterian Church in the U.S. and for
the Support Agency before moving to a broader responsibility handling the details of coordinating, planning, and
budgeting for the Mission Council. Women had long
played significant roles in church administration, but only
now began to move beyond writing or editing publications
for women or children.[24]

Educationally, the administrative leaders had varied
backgrounds. Although three had Princeton training and a
half dozen others had training in Presbyterian colleges, the
majority had received education in state schools or small
liberal arts colleges. One, Oscar McCloud, received his secondary school education in a Presbyterian school, Boggs
Academy. Although it is difficult to make inferences on the
basis of education, in general this generation had less connection to denominational schools or to schools that have
traditionally been involved in training America's cultural
establishment.

Statistics confirm the emergence of a different career pattern, with administrative service increasingly recognized as
a specialized ministry. Five of the six clergy who served as
chief executives of the agencies had pastoral or missionary
service. However, it averaged only nine years. Increasingly
executive service in the UPCUSA was seen as a career pattern, an ecclesiastical version of civil service, begun relatively early in one's ministry and maintained throughout.

The 1973 reorganization mandated that leadership be
chosen in participatory and inclusive ways. Search committees committed to an open hiring process replaced the
"old boy network." The reorganizers desired a clean break
with the old structures, both in order to eliminate some
staff who were viewed as inefficient and also to seek leaders
with different styles. In what was later regarded as an inhu-
mane procedure, all staff members were asked to resign
from their positions and then invited to apply for new positions.[25]

Some strong leaders either did not apply or were not
hired. The Agency boards were themselves inexperienced.
Their composition reflected a new concern for geographical

diversity and inclusiveness, in contrast to the tendency of the previous boards to be dominated by "high steeple" pastors and elders who were concentrated in certain synods. One seasoned observer of national church life charged that the synods did not care enough and "sent some of their worst people to be on Agency Boards," people who did not fully grasp the way to hire competent staff. There was a tendency to hire those who had worked on the design to implement the new structure.[26]

Both the new structure itself and the spirit of the times led the church to seek managerial competence rather than strong individual charismatic leadership. Even those who served in the new structures sensed their role was diminished. Oscar McCloud, who headed the Program Agency, maintains that the structures, and all the expected processes and procedures, were intended to "prevent leaders."[27]

Expectations of how the leadership would function were transformed. The more managerial-sounding "general director" or "executive director" supplanted the old ecclesiastical term "general secretary." Staff people were no longer called without competing in an extensive and open interview process. For example, when Oscar McCloud expressed an interest in having Donald Black become his associate in the Program Agency, he made it clear to his former boss that Black would be interviewed along with a number of others and that it was not a foregone conclusion that he would be selected or would even be McCloud's first choice.[28] Personnel policies were clearly set and procedures for annual reviews systematized.

In essence, the church confessed its past neglect of inclusive hiring practices. In the late 1960s, under the prodding of the Council on Church and Race, the church conducted a major study of personnel in the boards and staff, which revealed the paucity of Blacks in leadership positions. Conscientious leaders like Donald Black realized they had relied on the old-boy network for so long they really did not know how to rectify the error. When the church was reorganized in 1971–1973, minority racial ethnic communities and women convinced those in the selection process that simply to carry over staff would perpetuate injustice. All the jobs had to be considered new and open to affirmative action hiring procedures. Though many staff thought this was morally correct, it had a devastating effect on personnel. Many white males over fifty felt they came out on the short end of every interview.[29]

A number of other factors converged to make leadership in the 1970s and early 1980s problematic for the church. The tendency to question authority of all types and the hesitancy to defer to experts not only made the executive leadership suspect, but also led to boards to monitor the staff more closely than in the past. The former ecclesiastical "giants" were not "Lone Rangers," operating independently of their boards; they were skilled managers of the boards and often worked to secure strong people supportive of their approach. The new structure virtually eliminated that kind of influence by the staff. Indeed, one of the frequent complaints of the national staff was that board members were not clear about their role. Board members tried to involve themselves in management rather than simply to set policy.[30]

Moreover, these leaders presided over a church that was declining in membership. Shortly after the restructuring, a financial crisis necessitated the termination of a number of staff. A deliberate attempt to decentralize meant that mission was no longer the initial prerogative of the General Assembly but was taken on increasingly by synods and presbyteries. That meant, however, that General Assembly executives simply had fewer people and resources to manage. In addition, they did not have access to reserve funds which gave the former executives considerable clout. The General Assembly Mission Council controlled the finances so as to coordinate the one mission, but the system of planning, budgeting, and evaluating which was to accomplish it became a constant source of contention.

Collegial leadership replaced the authoritarian, hierarchical style. The structure relied heavily on particular management processes and required frequent and long consensus-building meetings. The efforts to be effective managers frequently dissipated creative energy.[31]

Many of those in major administrative positions in the 1970s acknowledged the structural flaws that inhibited the emergence of strong, visible leaders. Working relations between the agencies and the GAMC were constantly being renegotiated. Turbulence marked the early years of the GAMC because of constant personnel changes, including the appointment of five different executive directors. The determination not to perpetuate the old regime was so strong that, in the view of Daniel Little, it was not until he was named head of the GAMC in 1975 that an "insider" from the staff was a possibility.[32]

Significantly, even some of those who benefited most from the restructuring acknowledge that the reaction against strong individual leaders went too far. For Oscar McCloud, the assumption that the old boards were broken and had to be fixed was an overreaction that ultimately diminished rather than strengthened the church. George Hunt, editor of *The Outlook,* observed that though the church had often chafed under the leadership of those dominant personalities, in retrospect much seems positive about the patterns of those earlier periods.[33]

Conclusions

Certain patterns emerge when leadership is examined from the perspective of more than half a century. Some of these can be seen when statistics for the chief executives are graphed.

A major trend during the twentieth century has been the emergence of administrative service as a specialized career pattern for the clergy. The average years of pastoral experience prior to entering General Assembly staff positions declined significantly, indicating that clergy who became administrators began that service earlier in their careers. By the 1970s and 1980s, the average age at which a person began administrative ministry dropped into the thirties. This was in marked contrast to a time earlier in the century

Fig. 9.1. Chief Executives of the
United Presbyterian Church in the U.S.A.

	Total Number of Chief Executives	Number of Clergy	Number of Women	Racial Ethnic Persons	Elected Moderators of G.A. Staff
1923–1937	15	12(80%)	0	0	9
1937–1959	11	11(100%)	0	0	3
1959–1973	9	8(89%)	0	0	1
1973–1983	10	6(60%)	0	2	1

	Denominationally Connected College	Denominational Seminary/ Chief Seminary	Years of Pastoral Experience Prior to Administrative Work	Average Age When Entered Administrative Work
1923–1937	10(67%)	13 (3 Princeton Theological Seminary)	19	50
1937–1959	8(73%)	9 (4 PTS)	15	42
1959–1973	5(56%)	7 (3 Pittsburgh)	13	41
1973–1983	2(20%)	5 (4 PTS)	9	34

when administrative work marked the culmination of a pastoral career. During the last fifteen years, the church sought leaders skilled in management process and human relations experience.[34]

The statistics confirm what was apparent to all but only recently questioned. Women and racial ethnic minority persons held virtually no top positions until the 1973 reorganization, when the church made a conscious effort toward affirmative action. Simply being brought into the leadership did not resolve all issues for members of racial ethnic minorities and women, however. Black recalled one woman in an important administrative post saying to her male colleagues, "You make the decisions in the men's room, and I'm not allowed." The restructuring in the 1970s was intended to develop a decision-making process that would be truly participatory.[35]

The precipitous decline in the number of General Assembly Moderators who came from the ranks of General Assembly staff reveals the changing expectation of leadership. Instead of being highly visible personalities who made reassuring speeches to the church and developed a constituency for their programs, denominational executives in the 1970s, by design, became almost anonymous, much less visible. Kenneth Neigh commented that in the old days "mission and the gospel were transmitted through great personalities." That expectation has not only changed; it is frowned on. As we noted, the church consciously attempted to move away from what some perceived as a hierarchical, authoritarian style of leadership.[36]

Creating a structure that deemphasized individual visibility had negative consequences, however. The acute concern for accountability meant the church spent considerable energy simply defining lines of authority and delineating areas of responsibility. Many felt the structure discouraged individuals from taking bold initiatives.

Moreover, the church consciously sought broader participation from its diverse constituency, in particular from those who had been on the margins of church leadership—racial ethnic persons and women. One staff executive acknowledged that part of the rationale for securing a totally new staff following the 1973 reorganization was the assumption that "everyone has to have a crack at it." This commitment to open hiring reflected the times. While the intentions were good, not everyone applauded the results. James I. McCord argued that the period was pervaded by a romanticism which suggested that "anyone can do anything as well as anyone else." One staff person, commenting on the contrast to the era of the "giants," lamented, 'We're up to our knees in pygmies!" Max Browning suggested that some of the personnel policies intended to open up the church have actually dampened the possibility of securing creative leaders who combine creativity with the know-how and determination to carry out the vision. Browning complained, "I think we're paying the price of a personnel process that will not give us that kind of leadership. . . . At some point we're going to have to revise our whole approach to this open hiring thing because it is keeping us from getting the right people in." The best leaders, in his view, "are not going to fill out a bunch of silly forms," and, in fact, tend to "scare the committees who are doing the interviewing."[37]

In changing its perspectives on leadership, the church responded to a new cultural circumstance, the full significance of which it was only dimly aware of. In important ways, the mission of the church has been tied up with the mission of the nation. The expansion of American influence in the world characterized the first two thirds of the twentieth century. The optimism of the mission agencies of the church paralleled the optimism of the nation. Leaders assumed the Presbyterian Church and its influence would grow. Church leaders in this period were "giant" personalities who gave reassuring speeches and presided over an expanding program. They perceived that the church played a dominant role in the culture, even as it modified its understanding of mission. While it might be expected educational background would have been a factor in that perception, the statistics are ambiguous. What can be said is that there has been a significant decline in the impact of denominational schools in the training of leaders during the past thirty years.[38]

A number of factors coalesced in the 1960s and 1970s to modify the cultural assumptions. Turbulence surrounding the Vietnam War, the civil rights movement, and urban unrest undermined national self-confidence and challenged the authority of traditional leaders. In 1967 church membership reached its high point and began to decline. Then the UPCUSA reorganized itself structurally. Even without restructure it is doubtful that the old-style leadership could have been maintained. Assumptions about the church and its place in society had changed too much. A certain suspicion about leadership emerged in the nation which has made it more difficult for leaders to create a constituency for their vision of the church.

10

Looking for Leadership:
The Emerging Style of Leadership
in the Presbyterian Church (U.S.A.),
1983–1990

Richard W. Reifsnyder

In 1983 a cautious euphoria accompanied the reunion of the General Assemblies of the two largest branches of American Presbyterianism. Leaders hoped that a larger, reunited denomination could recapture some of its lost influence and expand its mission creatively. But they also recognized that each of the previous churches had been declining in membership, and the perception that they might be presiding over a church that would make a witness but not be a power chastened their optimism.

Leadership posed a crucial challenge for the reunited church. During the previous twenty years both churches had expressed a deep ambivalence about strong individual leaders within the church, and that ambivalence pervaded the new structure.

Reunion took place during a time when expectations in American society were changing. The Reagan revolution sought to deemphasize the role of the federal government in social and economic matters and to restore some of the initiative to state and local authorities. Deregulation and the emphasis on defense buildup and business expansion provided enormous economic opportunity for some. At the same time, social problems such as homelessness, environmental pollution, and drug abuse became exacerbated. The prevailing ethos, which was skeptical of governmental solutions and desirous of moving decision making away from the center, affected numerous institutions including the church. People found new reasons to mistrust the higher governing bodies and retain resources close to home. Moreover, renewed interest in the churches during the 1980s on personal piety and individual spiritual quest became part of the context in which the reunited church sought to forge a common mission.

Bringing two churches together unavoidably required creating new administrative machinery. The structures created in this transformed social context reflected the desire to move away from centralized planning without abandoning the commitment to inclusiveness and effective coordination. Beyond that, however, church leaders utilized reunion as an opportunity to remedy earlier flaws and to improve the structures by which the church accomplished mission. A concerted effort was made to engineer the restructuring with a minimal amount of disruption. A General Assembly Council (GAC), made up of equal numbers from the PCUS and UPCUSA, undertook to redesign the church during a five-year period while also administering the ongoing mission. Members remained on the GAC for five years before classes were established and some members began to rotate off the Council.[1]

Considerable discussion pervaded the church about supposed differences in styles of decision making between the former denominations. The PCUS usually was characterized as using a "behind the scenes," political style based on personal relationships. The UPCUSA was characterized as employing a more confrontational and mandate-oriented style. The communions had, however, in fact become more alike than different, particularly in their utilization of managerial processes. The Structural Design for Mission, adopted in 1986, confirmed the basic administrative perspective of the previous twenty years while making some effort to reclaim some of the strengths of an earlier period of leadership.

Currently nine functionally identifiable ministry units form the heart of the Structural Design for Mission. On the one hand, by lodging particular aspects of mission with particular units, the church appeared to disseminate authority more broadly and to meet the criticism that people could not understand what the General Assembly entities did. The tasks of the Global Mission or Social Justice and Peacemaking or Evangelism and Church Development ministry units are apparent from their names. Harking back to the days when the boards were led by dynamic, hierarchical leaders, the units present an opportunity for people to identify with certain work of the General Assembly and certain leaders who personify that work.

On the other hand, the units do not operate independently. Their very name, units, imply they are part of something larger. A series of linkages ensures that each unit will develop its program in the light of the whole. The General Assembly Council provides coordination. Certainly the existence of nine separate units suggests some of the ambivalence about strong leaders. Each unit's having to fight for its particular turf and budget has resulted in dispersing leadership and preventing any small number of individuals from accumulating too much power.[2]

The New Leadership

Structure would determine in significant ways the type of leadership required. The Structural Design for Mission, consolidating the developments of the 1970s, called for leadership that was open, inclusive, and collegial. There could be no return to the older, authoritarian, kingdom-building style of administration. Good administration would mean developing a spirit of partnership while avoiding patterns of domination and control.

Significantly, the General Assembly Council chose a professional management consultant as executive director. Elder S. David Stoner, who received an M.B.A. from Harvard in 1960, spent twenty-seven years with a firm specializing in human resources management before becoming

head of the GAC staff in 1987. He had served the church in
a number of volunteer capacities, including as a member of
the commission that implemented the 1973 reorganization
in the UPCUSA.

Stoner has had the difficult task of leading the church
without trying to direct it from above. He has the responsibility of coordinating the work of the units in the light of
priorities set by the General Assembly, but without exerting authority in ways analogous to being a chief executive
in a corporation. Conscious of his position in a highly diverse and pluralistic church, he describes his task as working in a conciliar and collegial fashion to build consensus.
In Stoner's view, the structure of the new church is not
without flaws and will require special effort from a management point of view. The structure requires competent managers, trained in human-relations skills and group
processes by which decisions can be made. By contrast, an
earlier generation, in a different structure, looked for theological perspective and oratorical and promotional profi-
ciency.[3]

The executive director of the GAC is to be chief manager, not chief spokesperson for the church. The Council
itself has assumed enormous responsibility as it has sought
to implement the reorganization necessitated by reunion. It
has kept close oversight of the work and has undertaken
numerous tasks which in other times would have been the
responsibility of the staff. The tendency of the elected persons to exercise more oversight of the work of the administration rather than merely to set broad policy had been
developing for a number of years. That trend blurs the lines
of responsibility. Often the Council wanted to announce its
decisions through one of its members, rather than through
staff channels.

Donald Black, who served as first executive director of
the GAC, suggests that an assumption has been made
over the last two decades, perhaps erroneously, that the
church trusts elected councils or boards more widely than
the staff they select. The assumption leads to the deduction
that the elected persons should be intimately involved in

management. In the view of one participant there has been a "deep sense of suspicion about the staff" combined with a "deep appreciation" for what they do. This ambivalence may impede the effective functioning of a staff who should be expected to create a vision for the church. During interviews with GAC members, it was said that they recognize the need for those who have been so heavily involved in establishing the new structure to pull back and allow the staff to do what they have been called to do. But the relationship between elected members of the GAC and ministry units and the staffs of those units remains one of the unresolved questions of leadership. The confusion concerning areas of responsibility reflects some of the ambivalence within the church about the kind of leadership it desires. Power in the new structures seems to be lodged not in individual leaders, but in conciliar bodies.[4]

In selecting the directors of the ministry units, the church sought persons with management skills to make the structure it created work. Although some viewed the selection of five of the nine unit directors from the smaller PCUS as evidence of that stream's domination of a highly political process, other factors influenced the decisions. For example, many of the most experienced administrators in the UPCUSA stream were nearing retirement, while those from the PCUS were younger. More important than geography were skills and experience. Seven of the nine were already working in the existing structures and had considerable experience with the participatory, collegial, process-oriented management common to both churches. An eighth, George Telford, came to the Theology and Worship Ministry Unit from a parish, although he had served eight years as director of the Division of Corporate and Social Mission in the General Assembly Mission Board (PCUS).

The directors of the ministry units had come of age professionally in the 1950s and 1960s and experienced the theological and social turbulence that led to the transformations in the church's organizational style.[5] As a group they defy the century-long trend of the declining influence of denominational colleges in training denominational leaders. Six of the nine attended denominational schools, although most had graduate education beyond denominational bounds. A third of the directors are elders (40 percent if David Stoner is included). This continues the trend toward greater participation of elders in the top administration of the church. George Hunt, editor of *Presbyterian Outlook,* observed that at the national level laymen and laywomen have recently been among the most influential leaders. This has been true not only of staff, but also of the General Assembly Council itself, where five of the first seven chairpersons were elders. Moreover, elders chaired the crucial committees on the Structural Design for Mission and Mission Priorities. Significantly, too, the clergy who do serve on the Council and units and as staff rarely are pastors from very large and influential congregations, from whom the bulk of national church leadership was called in a former day.[6]

Diversity in Background

The church maintained its determination to be open and inclusive in its hiring practices, rectifying past injustices and neglect by setting goals of 40 percent women and 20 percent racial ethnic persons in management positions. Women filled three of the nine chief positions, and racial ethnic persons two. David Stoner reported in 1988, after the nearly six hundred positions in Louisville were filled, that 47 percent of the professional staff were women and 24 percent were racial ethnic persons. These figures surpassed the goals for inclusiveness by gender and race.[7]

Diversity and inclusiveness played an important role in the Structural Design for Mission. Although a concern for theological pluralism did not seem to influence the selection of ministry unit directors, care in selecting subordinate administrators, including several well-recognized leaders from the self-consciously evangelical wing of the church, sought that diversity.

Five of the six directors who were clergy had considerable parish experience. Three served more than fifteen years before entering administrative work. In that regard, these directors vary slightly from the trend during most of the twentieth century of beginning administrative service after fewer and fewer years of pastoral experience.

Nevertheless, nearly all had considerable administrative experience before being called as ministry unit directors. Highly developed managerial skills topped their lists of qualifications. In some cases, nearly all of their experience was administrative. Clifton Kirkpatrick, although the youngest unit director, had twenty years of experience directing several ecumenical ministries and the International Mission division of the General Assembly Mission Board (PCUS) before becoming director of the Global Mission Ministry Unit. John Coffin had served previously as pastor and missionary, but for more than twenty-five years headed various aspects of the Board of World Missions and the GAMB before becoming director of the Stewardship and Communication Development Ministry Unit.

Edgar W. Ward, after serving parishes for sixteen years, was on the staff of the Presbytery of Chicago, the Board of National Missions, and the Vocation Agency. He developed a number of programs for the Black church and for the placement of racial ethnic persons before being called to head the Church Vocations Ministry Unit. James Foster Reese, who heads the Racial Ethnic Ministry Unit, developed administrative expertise in a number of General Assembly entities in the UPCUSA, including the Board of Christian Education, the Vocation Agency, the GAMC, and the Council on Administrative Services.

Belle Miller McMaster, director of the second-largest ministry unit, Social Justice and Peacemaking, has deep roots in the PCUS. Wife of a PCUS pastor and daughter of Patrick Dwight Miller, who served for ten years as executive secretary of the Board of Church Extension and was later elected Moderator of the General Assembly, McMaster administered various aspects of the church's corporate witness, including the Division of Corporate and Social Mission of the GAMB from 1981–1988. Robert D. Miller, whose father was a prominent PCUS elder who pressed the church to oppose segregation, pastored three churches and headed the Division of National Mission of the GAMB before serving briefly as the director of the Education and Congregational Nurture Ministry Unit.[8]

The remaining two ministry units were originally headed by women from the UPCUSA tradition. Patricia Roach, whose background included teaching and dental-hygiene work and who received an M.B.A. from Wright State University, served as coordinator for the Metropolitan Urban Ministry and as associate general director of the Program Agency before being called to head the Evangelism and Church Development Ministry Unit.[9] Mary Ann Lundy, a teacher who served the church in a number of different capacities, including being director of communications for the Presbytery of Twin Cities, gained considerable administrative experience as coordinator of the National Student YWCA from 1982 to 1987. A strong advocate for human rights issues, Lundy directs the Women's Ministry Unit.

Each of the first nine unit directors was a competent administrator who had demonstrated skills in managing aspects of the church's ministry according to the processes developed during the previous decade. They did not necessarily have particular expertise or theological background in the field to which they had been called. But that was not deemed critical to the successful functioning of the new structure. Experts could be hired. The unit directors needed to be competent managers above all, overseeing the process, rather than presuming to be experts themselves. In many cases, the unit directors were passionately committed by temperament and background to the issues their unit brought before the church; but experience in a particular aspect of mission was not as crucial as managerial skill.[10]

The units have had several years to set their agendas before the church and make their case for their share of the budget. The presence of nine ministry units gives the impression that they are equally weighted in priority for the church, though clearly their budgets indicate otherwise. The Global Mission and Social Justice and Peacemaking ministry units each spent approximately 20 percent of the

church's 1989 mission budget, while the other seven combined spent only 25 percent.[11]

Presumably budget should be set in light of the priorities
adopted by the General Assembly in 1989. Despite the attempts to see the church as one integrated whole, it may be
that ministry units will focus primarily on securing an increased portion of the overall share of limited resources
rather than expanding the vision of the church.

Expectations of Leadership

What does the church expect of the professional leadership of its ministry units? The semiautonomous leaders of
the boards in a previous generation operated to promote
their own vision of the church and to secure the resources
to accomplish tasks related to the vision. The Structural
Design for Mission clearly does not intend that the church
modify its commitment to unified mission or return to
leaders who operated as entrepreneurs to secure their own
programs. These leaders were in part a product of an expanding church, in an era of national expansion. Despite
the often-stated desire for renewal, an assumption seems to
remain that we live in a different era, in which the church
will not expand but will learn to manage its limited resources so as to be an effective witness anyhow.

Some voice the belief, however, that to be effective the
ministry units must reconstruct at least part of that older
pattern, so that strong directors might be able to present
their cases creatively to the church and build their own
constituencies. Budgetary problems have already con-
strained the work of the ministry units in the first years of
their existence.

Considerable discussion centers on why people have
not been contributing more money to the work of the
General Assembly. In part, of course, this is because more
mission is being done in congregations and in the middle
governing bodies. But it also may reflect the reality that
people tend to identify mission with personality. An older
style of leadership, often through force of personality and

effective promotion, won support for their visions of mission.

The church no longer exists in a context of expansion. That is to say, it is no longer assumed, as it once was, that the church's or nation's influence will increase either ecclesiastically or nationally. Nevertheless, the vitality of the church's mission may depend on the leadership ability of ministry units to dramatize their need and create enthusiasm for particular aspects of ministry. The structure may have called for managers, but the well-being of the church necessitates managers who create an identity and an excitement. Individual personalities remain important. Nearly every person interviewed for this essay mirrored the sentiments of former UPCUSA executive Kenneth Neigh: "A leader with savvy can make a poor structure work and one without savvy cannot make a good one work."[12] The question is whether the church would welcome the emergence of individual personalities from the ministry units.

The church's evaluation of the Office of Stated Clerk of the General Assembly and its present occupant, James E. Andrews, offers a cogent illustration of the ambivalence the church has about leadership. Following reunion, the church developed a new position description which recast the office according to the norms of collegiality and accountability. Perhaps reflecting a perceived desire to make a break with the past, a Special Committee on Nominations for Stated Clerk indicated it would bring the name of the Rev. Patricia McClurg, administrative director of the GAMB, to the 1984 General Assembly. That Assembly's Standing Committee on Nominations for Stated Clerk chose to nominate instead the Stated Clerks of the previous denominations, William P. Thompson and James E. Andrews. McClurg withdrew, but two others were nominated from the floor. After four ballots, Andrews finally won, but the *Presbyterian Outlook* said at the time the decision represented "the rejection of a leadership style . . . a signal that the Presbyterian Church is changing . . . and doesn't want a leader."[13]

Four years later, Andrews received a less than enthusias-

tic end-of-term performance review, and the Assembly
Committee to Nominate a Stated Clerk proposed elder
Harriet Nelson instead. Nominated from the floor, Andrews defied expectations and was elected by a twenty-five-
vote margin. Asked afterward what he thought was the
reason he had won, he pointed to his experience, but then
admitted, "I don't really know." That comment may reflect
accurately the church's own uncertainty about what kind of
leadership it expects of the Clerk, not only at the Assembly
meeting itself but as a representative of the church to the
larger community. Does it desire a strong, forceful Clerk, to
represent the church in the world, or an administrator to
facilitate its processes? The General Assembly Council's
proposed changes in the Structural Design for Mission regarding the Stated Clerk's office reflect the ongoing effort to
define the kind of leadership the church expects. Andrews
staunchly opposed the changes, and they were defeated by
the 1989 General Assembly.[14]

What kind of leadership does the church expect its professional staff to provide? Are James Andrews, David
Stoner, and the ministry unit directors to be primarily
managers of a particular part of the work? Or are they intended to be leaders who generate confidence and trust
among members of the PC(USA) and more widely, and
who will inspire the church with a particular vision of mission?

The kind of leadership the church desires depends in
large measure on its own theological vision of the nature
and purpose of the church. In a period of expansion, the
mission of the church seemed clearer. The boards of the
church clearly identified certain tasks and labored hard to
develop a constituency for accomplishing those tasks. Despite theological differences, consensus remained that the
church should expand, and the mission apparatus provided
a unifying focal point for that expansiveness.

Certainly part of the current dilemma about leadership
has been the lack of a clear vision about what the church
should be doing. The contemporary PC(USA) is highly diverse. It incorporates widely varying perspectives about its

primary mission. Indeed, this was clear when the 1989 General Assembly adopted two priority goals and sixteen nonprioritized continuing goals. Perhaps it is natural, in a highly pluralistic church that lacks clear theological consensus, that leaders who are primarily managers would become predominant in church structures.[15]

The question is whether the church has gotten too caught up in process at the expense of substance, preoccupied with managing the resources rather than creating the vision. The context has changed. Although the church no longer accepts the older, elitist style of leadership which seemed to work effectively earlier in the century, it gropes for a suitable alternative. Church organizational theorist Robert Worley of McCormick Seminary suggests that when traditional sources of empowering leaders vanish, as has happened in the church in recent years, leaders must build their own legitimacy. "There are no mandates around," he argues, "so leaders must generate their own mandates or they will be dead." Contemporary religious leaders need both to understand modern large-scale organization and to have a sense of direction. They must help people accept their leadership, since people will not grant it automatically, simply because of the office.[16]

The church created a structure in 1986 that called for skilled managers in order to implement it effectively. The challenge for the church in the next decade will be to build on the open and inclusive style but then move beyond that to where leaders will be encouraged and facilitated to create a mandate for their vision of the church.

A major and unresolved factor in the denomination's future is the deep ambivalence about strong leadership which has existed in the PC(USA) and its predecessors for the past twenty years. On the one hand, there has been a frequent lament for the loss of strong leaders capable of creating a vision for the church and the capacity to carry it out. On the other hand, there has been a deep suspicion of lodging too much power in the hands of individuals. In part this is a logical outgrowth of Presbyterian polity. But it is also a widespread North American cultural attitude. The church has consciously built structures that mitigate against small groups or individuals exercising significant power.

Perhaps there is a tendency to resent strong leaders when they are in power and to long for them when they are not. Returning to an older style of leadership is not an option for the church. The church must continue its commitment to be representative, inclusive, and collegial, while being able to discern leaders who are not only competent managers but also seek to inspire and motivate the church. This will require moving beyond the church's deeply rooted ambivalence and even our suspicion to provide room in the church's structures for the Holy Spirit to call forth from among present personnel and those to come people of contagious faith and strong vision to lead the church in new directions in mission.

11

Presbyterian Women Ministers: A Historical Overview and Study of the Current Status of Women Pastors

Lois A. Boyd and
R. Douglas Brackenridge

Thirty years ago the Presbyterian Church and other mainstream Protestant denominations were just beginning to be concerned with the subject of the status and acceptance of ordained women. Presbyterian women gained ministerial ordination privileges only in 1956, although the Presbyterian Church in the U.S.A. (PCUSA) had approved their right to ordination as elders and deacons in the 1920s.[1] The Presbyterian Church in the U.S. (PCUS) did not approve ordination for women as ministers, elders, and deacons until 1964. In 1959, however, women still comprised a very small percentage of the eldership, and there were only about twenty-five clergywomen in the PCUSA. Women's representation at presbytery, synod, and General Assembly was minimal or nonexistent. No woman had ever been nominated, let alone elected, to the position of Moderator of the General Assembly. Female seminary students were still a novelty, and the faculty and administration of the seminaries were predominantly male. Sexism, sexist language, feminist theology, equal opportunity, and affirmative action were issues yet to develop in the church.[2]

Today the Presbyterian situation is different in many ways. There is an increased number of women clergy working in the local church and of women, ordained and lay, serving on boards, agencies, committees, and university and seminary faculties and administrations.[3] Women have recently been contenders for the offices of Stated Clerk and Moderator of the General Assembly. Seven have been elected as Moderators since 1971 (as of 1990). Governing bodies seem sensitive to denominational commitments to ensure women a fair and equitable participation in all aspects of church life, and most have recognized special needs on the part of clergywomen.

Nevertheless, despite the high percentage of female students in seminaries, the church pronouncements, the organizational support, and the relatively larger number of clergywomen,[4] a woman in congregational ministry is seen as unusual by many persons. There are still proportionally few females in the formal leadership of the Presbyterian Church (U.S.A.). Thus, in discussing women clergy, one is dealing with an "exceptional," although certainly not unimportant, group of persons who necessarily have their special concerns.[5] The interesting component in studying women's ministry is that women, in numbers and support, have played a large part in American religious history. But with continuing polarization over whether women indeed should be ordained—and, if that is no longer a real issue within most Protestant denominations, then whether congregations are going to accept women pastors—one finds confirming studies by Protestant denominational units and by ecumenical bodies that show women clergy still experiencing nonacceptance, especially at the regional and local levels, on cultural, social, and theological grounds.[6] The Presbyterian Church, for one, has made strenuous efforts in recent years to reshape denominational polity in order to remove inequities, but indications are that legislative enactments have not fully influenced behavioral patterns.[7]

This essay examines the current situation of Presbyterian women within the context of a two-century struggle to attain equality within their denomination. This case study particularizes one denomination's experience, yet this story might prove relevant to where contemporary Protestant women now stand in the light of their forebears' struggles and successes.[8]

Historical Background

Eighteenth- and nineteenth-century Presbyterian churchmen almost without exception held that women should be silent in the church, subordinate to male authority, submissive to doctrine and church order, and satisfied to function within their proper "sphere." That sphere was defined in terms of domesticity, femininity, religious inclination, and moral influence, resting heavily on themes of nature and nurture. In sermons, tracts, and books, pastors and theologians argued their case on the "woman question" at length, using selected biblical passages to undergird their theological rationale, especially concerning women not praying and preaching in mixed assemblies, and the denomination concurred. Women had virtually no acknowledged influence other than that exercised in the home, no status in that they must remain silent in church councils, and no authority in that they were by definition subordinate to male decisions.[9]

Although the early literature offers limited information from women themselves about their situation vis-à-vis the church, in the latter part of the nineteenth century Presbyterian churchwomen in the United States began to gain considerable visibility through their participation in denominational, educational, and mission-oriented groups, by serving as missionaries and teachers, and by engaging in various ecumenical endeavors. Influenced by the women's rights debate and by churchwomen's evolving power in Protestantism, Presbyterian women sought changes in denominational polity that would enable them to participate in the church's decision-making processes. In particular, they claimed the right to prepare themselves to function as ministers of the Word and sacrament should they be called to do so.[10]

The office of "deaconess," approved in 1892, had opened specialized positions, such as directors of Christian education and commissioned church workers, but none of these

designations granted official status in governing bodies. In
the 1920s the PCUSA modified its constitution to permit
ordination of women to the diaconate and eldership but,
with the exception of the small, dissenting Cumberland
Presbyterian Church, withheld ministerial ordination.[11]
Very few women were elected to serve on sessions; consequently female representation at presbytery, synod, and
General Assembly was not proportionate to the numbers of
women who were church members.[12] Discussion of
women's ordination to the parish ministry subsided during
the Depression and World War II, but was renewed in the
1950s by church leaders whose theological and social con-
victions favored a more inclusive church and ministry.
Furthermore, at that time the church faced a critical short-
age of ministers. In 1956, the PCUSA (to become the
United Presbyterian Church in the U.S.A.) amended its
Form of Government to add the right of women to be ordained as ministers as well as elders and deacons, and in
1964 the PCUS granted women the right to serve as deacons, elders, and ministers.[13]

Many denominational leaders saw such constitutional
changes as the end of the active quest for gender equality.
Eugene Carson Blake, Stated Clerk of the UPCUSA, for
example, told churchwomen that he saw no need to "lift a
hand" beyond changing the Form of Government, since he
believed that when all legal impediments had been removed "the churches and their councils will gradually
make fuller use of women's leadership." Although he
strongly believed in the changes, Blake privately shared the
view that only a few women would actually seek ministerial
ordination and that females would not easily be included so
long as church executive positions were dominated by
males.[14]

In the absence of specific vehicles to implement the actions of General Assembly, some churchwomen cautioned
that *de jure* equality did not guarantee *de facto* equality.[15]
Their prediction proved accurate. More than a decade after
the 1956 ordination decision, women comprised only
0.533 percent of the UPCUSA ordained clergy (69 females

and 12,865 males in 1969), and nearly forty years after the same denomination allowed women to be elected elders, only 15.7 percent of the eldership were women. In the diaconate, where ordination did not entail status in the presbytery, synod, and General Assembly, women showed substantial gains (40.8 percent female).[16]

Recent Decades

In the 1960s clergywomen experienced considerable difficulty in their search for a pulpit. Most were offered pastoral charges of small, often weak congregations or assignments as assistant ministers that were session-hired and thus not subject to presbytery minimum salaries or pension payments. In 1969, for example, about half of the sixty-nine clergywomen functioned as pastors, but that number included associate pastors, assistant pastors, chaplains, and stated supplies. The remainder served in foreign or national missions, colleges, seminaries, and denominational boards and agencies. Five were engaged in postgraduate studies. Initially, the largest percentage took positions as assistant pastors, and a few advanced to associate pastor status. Those who were called as pastors served in churches whose membership ranged from 22 to 294, but most fewer than a hundred. These figures also showed low mobility and lengthy periods of unemployment between positions for women, interpreted to be due to cultural, social, marital, and familial pressures but probably also because women found it so difficult to get calls that they tended to rely on their spouse's vocational opportunities. Not surprisingly, women reported that some seminary professors advised female students not to enter the parish ministry because of the problems involved.[17]

In the 1960s, a group of women church administrators in the UPCUSA organized to fight the pervasiveness of inequality and proposed to the General Assembly in 1967 a study of women in church and society. Chaired by Priscilla Chaplin, the Special Committee on the Status of Women in Society and the Church conducted extensive research and produced a landmark study that documented widespread inequality and made visible women's issues.[18] The report also precipitated various theological and sociological studies, the creation of women's support groups at regional and national levels, and a series of overtures to guarantee women equal participation in church life. Concurrently, the denomination sponsored workshops and study sessions that examined problems facing women, discussed sexist language in theology and liturgy, addressed issues such as the Equal Rights Amendment and abortion, and actively sought women for executive positions and committee assignments.[19] Comparable activities occurred in the PCUS, as both denominations committed themselves to promote and implement equal-opportunity policies.[20]

Female and male church leaders agreed that pronouncements alone would not change long-established cultural and theological attitudes and moved toward establishing administrative structures devoted to mobilizing resources toward a greater inclusion of women in the church. During denominational restructuring in the 1970s, churchwomen in the northern and southern churches applied sophisticated political strategies to obtain official status; as a result, the PCUS Committee on Women's Concerns held its first meeting in Atlanta in 1973, and the UPCUSA Council on Women and the Church organized in New York in 1974. These advocacy groups gave priority to assisting women in their preparation for and placement in pastorates. Other specialized groups, such as Church Employed Women and the Third World Women's Coordinating Committee in the UPCUSA and the Committee for Racial Ethnic Women and the Committee on Church Employed Women in the PCUS, focused on equal-opportunity issues for lay, clergy, and marginalized women.[21]

A major project of the seventies and eighties, begun in 1978 under the aegis of the UPCUSA Vocation Agency, was a five-year, half-million-dollar Women in Ministry project directed by Ann DuBois and Penelope Morgan Colman to facilitate the placement, acceptance, and support of women employed by the church.[22] Research projects, including questionnaires sent to Presbyterian clergywomen, gave overwhelming evidence that attitudinal change, particularly at the presbytery and congregational level, was essential for the progress of women in ministry.[23] An outgrowth of this program has been an ecumenical program called "Blindspots and Breakthroughs," designed to help individuals understand and change their attitudes regarding the employment of women and other minority persons.[24] Such an approach represents a change in a continuum of efforts: the pressure toward inclusion being to be directed toward the individual—the church official, the lay member, the clergy—as well as the "denomination" in abstract terms.

Largely because of the advocacy atmosphere, concerns about denominational support for women clergy and female lay employees prompted the Program Evaluation Committee of the General Assembly Mission Board, the Vocation Agency, and the Advisory Council on Discipleship and Worship of the Presbyterian Church (U.S.A.) to address the questions in 1986. While acknowledging aspects of the denomination's acceptance of women in ministry, the combined reports of the three groups concluded that the continuing preference of a majority of congregations for a "white, male, married clergyperson" precludes an inclusive church.[25] And, indeed, if one examines the historical context and the events of the past few decades, one could paint either an optimistic picture of the strides made since the early 1970s or a less positive assessment based on the intransigence of the church, especially on the regional and local level, to unequivocally accept women in ministry.[26] Our intent in this study is to present both positive and negative evidence and to raise questions that still need documentation and appraisal.

Evidence Concerning Acceptance

On the positive side, churchwomen are much better anchored in denominational structures. Rather than being provisionally represented, they have emerged through two denominational reorganizations with permanent structures for women's concerns and balanced representation on all boards, units, and committees. The new mission design approved by the Presbyterian Church (U.S.A.) in 1986, for example, provides for a Women's Ministry Unit and specific committees (Justice for Women, Women Employed by the Church, Women of Color, and Presbyterian Women) and linkage with other units and committees.[27] Outside of formal structures, a group of Presbyterian clergywomen have formed the National Association of Presbyterian Clergywomen to provide additional support for clergywomen and to explore ways of relating to denominational structures through the Women Employed by the Church Committee.[28]

Women are increasingly entering the pastoral ministry and are being called by congregations of various sizes throughout the country. Figures from 1989 showed a total of 2,098 women ministers, with 1,197 serving local congregations (pastor, co-pastor, associate, assistant, stated supply), 281 holding ministries such as presbytery/synod staff, pastors at large, and chaplains, and the remainder in non-PC(USA) professional or unclassified positions or retired. In five years, the number of female ministers grew by 80 percent, from 1,168 to 2,098.[29] Governing bodies, responding to denominational guidelines and the pressures of women's advocacy organizations, have addressed the needs of women students, candidates, and pastors. A number of synods and presbyteries have instituted programs and procedures to assist the acceptance of female clergy. The technique of putting women into pulpits as interim pastors-at-large has been successful in facilitating personal encounters on a continuing basis between women clergy and congregations.[30] For the first time in denominational history, some large congregations of a thousand or more are seriously considering women candidates for senior pastorates, which are associated with denominational influence, authority, and status.

The student population of Presbyterian seminaries has changed considerably from the early 1970s, when women constituted less than 10 percent of seminary candidates for the Master of Divinity degree.[31] In recent years, women have represented from 30 to 50 percent of specific seminary enrollments; for example, in 1986 they constituted 42 percent of Presbyterian seminary graduates. Graduates generally have found positions as quickly as their male counterparts.[32] Responding to this new constituency, seminaries have modified curricula to include courses dealing with women's studies (historical, theological, and practical), have employed women as professors and chaplains, and have maintained specialized programs and support groups.[33] They have expressed their desire to increase the number of female faculty and administrators. Indicative of future developments is a comprehensive study of Presbyterian theological institutions, approved by the 200th General Assembly in 1988, which will address women's issues as well as other topics.[34]

Surveys conducted by the Special Office of Research of the Support Agency (UPCUSA) in 1980 and 1986 indicated that Presbyterian pastors and laypersons had more positive attitudes toward women clergy than they had in the previous decade. Eight out of ten panelists in each sample felt that members of their congregations were "more open to the idea of women in the ministry than they were five years ago." Given a list of pastoral activities such as preaching and administering the sacraments, more than 75 percent of the panelists said that it would make no difference if the minister were male or female. When asked to rate a number of stereotypical statements about women in ministry as being either correct or incorrect, panelists tended to view the positive statements as being correct and the negative statements as being incorrect. While the positive attitudinal changes in the survey were not matched by corresponding changes in actual hiring practices in the churches, they did indicate a more receptive atmosphere than had previously been shown.[35]

Encouraging evidence also emerges from Edward Lehman's study of attitudinal dynamics in local Presbyterian congregations relative to the acceptance of women clergy.

He finds a correlation between a congregation's having a woman as a minister and its acceptance of women in ministry. The contact with women clergy, however, has to be more than minimal, such as hearing a visiting female speaker or having an occasional conversation with a woman minister at presbytery.[36] His earlier research also showed that "analysis of data from the members of churches where clergywomen actually served as pastor indicate that the predictions of doom for the congregation as a result of the clergywoman's presence did not materialize."[37]

Negative findings must be placed alongside the positive. There is no question that the denomination is on record in support of inclusiveness, but its executive positions, seminary presidencies and deanships, and key political appointments are predominantly male. Women administrators almost without exception speak of gains but describe continuing programs of advocacy. In a few instances, presbyteries have voted to ordain men who openly express their opposition to the ordination of women. And certainly the "woman issue" prevails among the most conservative elements of the denomination.[38]

Women have stated privately to us, and in other more public interviews, that some presbytery committees, while following the letter of the law, frequently fail to give them personal and professional support. Others have felt isolated from the presbytery and angered by lack of communication or "lost paperwork."[39] Moreover, some presbyters, both male and female, have expressed frustration that although sessions endorse female candidates and presbyteries take these women under their care, the congregations themselves often will not consider a woman minister when their pulpits are vacant and the presbyteries do not follow through on supporting their placement.[40]

A particularly descriptive figure is that Presbyterian clergywomen now (1989) constitute only some 10 percent of the ordained clergy. Admittedly the proportion has increased since 1984 when it was 6 percent, but during the same five-year period the number of male ministers grew by less than 0.2 percent. Although the number of female candidates has dropped by 13 percent since 1984, women's share of total number of candidates has increased because the number of male candidates has dropped by an astounding 51 percent.[41]

Equally descriptive is that, even with the positive attitudinal changes reflected in the 1986 Presbyterian Panel study mentioned earlier, that Panel also indicated an increase of fewer than 8 percent of panelists who responded affirmatively when asked if members in their congregations would accept a woman minister. Most panelists, when asked the sex, race, age, and marital status of a pastor who would be most compatible with their congregation, responded: a married white male between 40 and 49 years old.[42]

The Hesitancy to Change

Edward Lehman's research has led him to conclude that church members are not always consistent in their response to clergywomen, "numerous members [saying] that they had no preference for men (or women) concerning specific functions clergy perform—leading worship, preaching, administering sacraments, counselling—virtually every task for which clergy are traditionally responsible. At the same time they indicated that they prefer a man as the individual with the title of 'pastor' of their congregation." Here Lehman sees a hesitancy to change in relation to two basic symbols conjoined in one movement—the distinctions between the sexes and religious tradition.[43]

The number of women leading large congregations of a thousand members or more presently is small. Women as heads of staff of any size in 1986 were listed as only 389, while in 1988 that number was 405.[44] Although the selection processes for the larger pulpits are very competitive, evidence indicates that the typical pattern is for large, affluent congregations to resist the idea of women in ministry more than smaller and organizationally weaker bodies.[45] One clergywoman saw the Presbyterian church of the 1980s as not much farther ahead than that of the 1960s in

terms of a woman's being hired as a head of staff. This is
where, as she put it, "competence, personality, experience,
credentials, authenticity are meaningless if people have not
struggled with their own attitudes about female power and
authority."[46]

In the case of preaching, pastoral psychologist and theological educator Maxine Walaskay has compared women's
acceptance in the pulpit with generalized patterns based on
empirical studies of the impact of gender on role performance and on perceptions of performance. She writes that
studies show that both women and men perceive and evaluate the performance of women differently from that of
men, and often women are more negatively evaluated for
equal performance of a like task, except with regard to written presentations of men and women of high accomplish-
ment; that women and men are responded to more
favorably when they perform tasks in ways that are seen as
congruent with their gender; that women are evaluated
more critically for certain qualities in nonverbal performance than are men. Walaskay suggests that resistance to
the authority of a woman in the pulpit is to be expected
since the congregation is not likely to have had much experience in listening to female preachers and are probably
ambiguous about what they feel. She gives a personal example in which a colleague, in critiquing one of her sermons, said, "When you come right down to it, it's just that
I don't want a woman to tell me what to do."[47]

Various clergywomen have speculated to us about gender-
related differences in preaching and pulpit presentations.
They have described how they believe they are perceived in
terms of the powerfulness of their delivery, their dress, the
timbre or volume of their voice, their gestures, and, of
course, the content of their sermons. They also have discussed the traditional homiletical instruction received and
some particular problems of application when women try to
implement it. In such conversations, the observations are
descriptive only; no conclusions are drawn.[48]

Even though figures indicate that females generally find
first calls as readily as males, other numbers show that

older women or those not able to change locations to take a position search longer for a new or first call. Furthermore, it appears that women in general have more difficulty in securing appropriate positions in their second or third call.[49] Moreover, Lehman suggests that while the percentage of congregations and individuals open to accepting women ministers is increasing, the success of one woman minister does not necessarily carry over to others.[50]

A statistic that is curious, and which may have negative implications, is the large number of ordained women classified in past General Assembly *Minutes* as being unemployed, not seeking a call, or engaged in occupations that do not fit other Assembly listings (this would include secular employment). The 1987 statistics list 387 women in this classification. The 1989 statistics have 394 women under a designation of "Unclassified" and 153 as non-PC(USA) professionals, which presumably is similar. The Women's Unit has indicated that it plans to try to determine the location and status of these women. Substantive data is necessary, because circumstances seem complex. One possible line of inquiry might rest with the woman student's goal when she enters seminary. Some evidence indicates that women seminarians are more undecided about future goals or, after enrolling, are less likely to see themselves as a parish pastor than are men students.[51]

Concerning equal pay, reports have shown that women consistently earn less than male clergy in all full-time categories of pastor, associate, and assistant. A 1982 study of eleven Protestant denominations revealed that the median salary for males was $20,000 to $22,000, while only $14,000 to $16,000 for women. None of the female clergy had a salary above $28,000. Where men tend to garner peak earnings between the ages of 35 and 54, women have experienced no notable increase in salary range with age.[52] A more recent ecumenical salary study conducted by the National Council of Churches in 1986 reported that qualified women earn $2,000 to $4,000 less than men in similar positions.[53] The Presbyterian Church (U.S.A.), however, has taken a major step to close this gap by approving a compensation report in 1988 which provides an equitable way to set salaries so that all employees, regardless of sex, race, disabilities, or age, are paid fairly at all levels of employment.[54]

The seminary experience still receives mixed reviews. Some seminaries have addressed long-standing theological, historical, and rhetorical biases through curricular changes. With many institutions heavily tenured with males, the number of female faculty and administrators has not kept pace with the enrollment of women. While the appointment of women in part-time and adjunct positions has had a short-range effect, it has also been described as exploitative. Recent evaluations of seminary experiences suggest that while the majority of graduates, both men and women, indicate that they were generally satisfied with the seminary, some women perceive gender bias in class and their exclusion from the total community life.[55] In response to the seminaries' efforts, some women seminarians have noted a paradoxical result from women's courses and causes that heightens their awareness of being "different."[56] A higher percentage of older students, including women, are enrolling in seminaries. Many institutions have adjusted to this, since seminaries have had diverse student bodies in the past. Nevertheless, if this percentage increases, the seminaries might find themselves considering how this student profile might affect their programmatic and curricular plans.[57]

Areas for Exploration

In other areas related to women's concerns, we raise three issues that deserve more consideration than we can give in this essay. First, there are now in Protestant churches a substantial number of "clergy couples." In producing a denominational report on clergy couples in 1976, Marney Ault Wasserman defined the term as "any two people married to each other, both of whom are ordained ministers in the United Presbyterian Church, U.S.A., and who are working (or have worked) in either shared or separate ministries."[58]

Others might use a broader description, such as one prepared for a National Council of Churches study in 1979: "Those couples who share the two covenants of marriage and ordination, now available for and practicing a variety of stimulating and creative forms of ministry."[59]

In any event, most of the mainstream denominations now are working with evolving issues concerning two ministers who are married, whether within the same denomination or in separate ones: placement, individual capabilities, the team concept or the separate choices, congregational acceptance, professional and personal consequences of combining marriage and ministry, the seminaries' responsibilities to study requirements of those students who are or intend to become clergy couples, the church's commitment to relate to this new pattern of ministry. Significant ecumenical and denominational studies, such as the two mentioned here, have appeared and will doubtless be updated throughout the rest of this century and into the next; informative articles on the subject have become common.[60]

The subject of clergy couples has recently received extensive attention on the part of the denomination itself, by the congregation as day-to-day participant in this type of ministry, and concerning the couple as professional clergy and marriage partners. Questions of authority, accountability, relationships, confidentiality, salary calculations, and style of ministry are among the many issues being discussed. As we examine personal experiences from various clergy couples, we pick up tensions based on co-pastoring (personality, style, education) and on personal conflicts (family responsibilities, diverging interests, lack of communication, pressures of the positions). In terms of the traditional expectations in many pastorates, our previous research has included historical descriptions of women as "minister's wife" and as "missionary wife," in which the spouse functioned as a co-pastor.[61] Clergy couples indicate their awareness of this factor, which might relate to how congregations view the two ministers. Will each partner be treated equally, and how is the work divided and compensated?[62] In practice, it appears that issues of gender and the nature of ministry must be considered as the church continues to follow the future of the clergy couples.

Complex issues emerge in the case of racial ethnic clergywomen and other marginalized females, such as handicapped and older women. Like the subject of clergy couples, it is not within the scope of our essay to address this topic. Briefly, however, we should point out that the Presbyterian Church (U.S.A.) recently reported that more than 95 of every 100 members of the PC(USA) are white.[63] In 1986, Presbyterian panelists were asked if they thought that Black or Hispanic women could serve effectively in non-Black or non-Hispanic churches. While a majority of the clergy and an even larger majority of specialized clergy responded positively, 57 percent of the elders and members thought that a Hispanic woman could not serve well in a non-Hispanic church and 63 percent said the same for a Black woman in a non-Black congregation.[64] A minister in Philadelphia cites what she calls "double discrimination." Her versatility has brought a variety of opportunities and calls, but she has also been rejected by both a black and a white congregation. Others have documented the issues of minority women clergy.[65] We have talked with a Hispanic clergywoman who also was caught in a double bind: she was unable to secure a pulpit in Hispanic churches despite a number of vacancies; after she accepted a call from a non-Hispanic congregation, she then was criticized by some denominational leaders for not taking a Hispanic church. In general, given the lack of enthusiasm by many to having a woman minister, the reluctance to have a racial ethnic woman is compounded.

Finally, we are aware of both individualized and generalized concerns among women clergy: sexual harassment, sexist humor, sexist language, sexual identity, loneliness, isolation, child-raising and child-care anxieties, time constraints, hostility from females in the congregation, conflict with male senior ministers or with presbyters, jealousy, competitiveness. Admittedly some of these concerns, perhaps worded differently, might be common to both males and females, but we refer here to gender-related problems.

To deal with specific incidents, women express their need for a support system of some kind—networking, denominational organizations, or conferences—to work through experiences that have no appreciable body of experiential material. This factor, and the solidification of women's units in the denominations, may tend to perpetuate the tendency toward "special purpose groups" that Robert Wuthnow has described in his book *The Restructuring of American Religion.* In reflecting on such groups, one cannot deny that women's concerns undoubtedly have influenced, polarized, even confused many in the church, although Wuthnow notes that the negative impact of feminist special-purpose groups has been less significant in "liberal" denominations such as the Presbyterian and the Episcopalian.[66] Nevertheless, the groups' viability possibly rests not only in a continuing resolve to maintain structures to support the implementation of the policy of full inclusion of women clergy in the church but also to discuss the nature of ministry and the meaning of authority. Although empowerment still is at issue, attitudinal change has assumed a great deal of importance among women in the church. As Betty Friedan has suggested in *The Second Stage,* "The second stage has to transcend the battle for equal power in institutions. [It] will restructure institutions and transform the nature of power itself."[67]

Conclusions

Beyond the present historical evidence, statistical data, denominational reports, and compilations of personal experiences, researchers are currently conducting ongoing studies and writing their findings on issues concerning women clergy that might be translated into policies and programs.[68] Along that line, there are some general questions that still need attention.

First, how flexible are methods to track whether gender plays a role in the way ministry is performed and in the way congregations perceive the minister? What kind of continuing studies can measure the extent to which the liturgical and ritualistic expressions of the church, so long dominated by male symbolism and traditions, are affected by a growing ministry of women? Will a so-called "feminization" of the clergy, with men retreating from the profession, occur if the number of male candidates continues to decline?

Practically, assuming that the trend toward more women entering seminaries continues, how will the institutions balance their programs in terms of recruitment, curriculum, continuing education, and provision of services? How is a "call" now identified? What pulpits will be available to the marginalized persons who wish to minister in this predominantly white, middle-class constituency? And, perhaps the most basic question, to what extent is a declining membership in the Presbyterian Church (U.S.A.) a factor in a declining number of candidates and what will be the impact on clergywomen?

The 1987 Study on Women's Concerns identifies a model of ministry "that reflects the wholeness of the people of God, eliminates barriers between women and men, clergy and laity, persons of racial ethnic backgrounds, and all others, and encourages solidarity among all women, both lay and clergy."[69] This ministerial model should be examined in light of a statement from *Women of the Cloth*: "Even when one argues that gender ought not, in principle, to be a relevant factor in ordained ministry, in practice it may be."[70] This needs to be further examined as more information on the impact of clergywomen on the church's theology, liturgy, and polity, on the nature of ministry, and on the denomination's receptivity and response to new forms of ministry becomes available. As contact between individual congregations and female clergy increases and women become more visible in the pulpit and in other pastoral functions, substantive data likely can be collected.

However, as Barbara Brown Zikmund wrote ten years ago, "As a seminary professor, a historian, and a clergywoman, I am too close to these trends [concerning ecclesiastical vocations] to judge their depth or lasting power."[71] We are sympathetic with this sentiment. We also feel too close to judge the implications of the past few decades.

Protestant women in the church and women clergy have seen improvements in their status in this century. But have they received full acceptance? That basic question needs further attention in the years ahead.[72]

12

Cleavage or Consensus?
A New Look
at the Clergy-Laity Gap

Keith M. Wulff and John P. Marcum

In 1969, Jeffrey K. Hadden offered an analysis of the crisis in American religion focusing on the differences between the values and worldviews of clergy and those of laity in mainstream denominations. Hadden asserted that clergy values and worldviews had become much more "liberal" than those of their parishioners.[1] The truth of this "clergy-lay split," as it came to be called, has received support in the subsequent work of other sociologists.[2] More important, in the perceptions of rank-and-file members of religious organizations, the assumption has remained that clergy are "left of center" on theological, social, and political issues. In the opinion of many, the "liberalism" of ordained clergy has caused much of the division, if not the so-called "demise," of mainline denominations in the last twenty years.

We sought to investigate the validity of this image today in the Presbyterian Church (U.S.A.). What differences do exist between Presbyterian ministers and members in the realms of values and theology? Or is the perception of division in fact a case of people trying to turn the continuities of religious and cultural life into false dichotomies?

Beyond the simple divisions between ministers and members, we also have asked two significant questions about the social level and educational background of both groups. Following the insights of Peter Berger and others, we inquired about the reality of a "new class" among members. Berger asserted that traditional class analysis—considering people as "upper," "middle," and "lower" class (and all the combinations of those terms) on the basis of socioeconomic conditions alone—failed to penetrate the nature of power differences in modern Western societies. He proposed that a "new class" had achieved hegemony, particularly in American life, a class based on the acquisition and maintenance of knowledge. More particularly, members of the "new class" derived their livelihoods from the production and distribution of symbolic knowledge. They were intellectuals, educators, media people, members of the helping professions, and a miscellany of planners and bureaucrats. By definition, ministers fit into this "new class," but did differences exist between ministers and other members of the new class to any extent?[3]

Additionally, we wondered about the worldviews of ministers and members of Presbyterian churches. We examined how other attitudes and beliefs of Presbyterian members and ministers varied on an index of "otherworldliness."[4] This index measures attitudes and values concerning the comparative worth of the present life as compared to life after death. A person who scored "high" in "otherworldliness," for example, would view this life as primarily a time of preparation for the next, would expect some final judgment from God, and would express more worry about life everlasting than about the present life. On the other hand, those scoring "low" in the scale would tend to discount preparation for another life after death, deny some final, divine judgment on a personal scale, and would be more concerned about this life than about anything hereafter. According to Dean Hoge, who developed the index, it serves as something of a proxy for theological perspective. A person holding "low otherworldliness" is generally perceived as a theological liberal today, and one holding beliefs that represent "high otherworldliness" would be considered a theological conservative.[5]

We would like to have examined differences according to gender and ethnicity as well. With such a small minority of women as ministers, however, existing data relate the opinions and experience of too few women for meaningful comparisons. Similarly, the small percentage of racial ethnic minority group members—just under 5 percent of the membership of the denomination—precludes separate analysis along this dimension.

As the major resource for this project we used the findings of the Presbyterian Panel, a panel study of constituency groups of the Presbyterian Church (U.S.A.), supported by the denomination itself. Panelists selected for the sample agree to complete questionnaires at least quarterly, and over a three-year cycle their views are solicited on matters pertinent to the church.[6] Our data came from the 1988–1990 cycle for the Panel.

All questions in our study provided for rank-order responses (for example, agree-disagree). Our analysis for each question is limited to those individuals who selected such an orderable response. Persons who did not respond to a particular question, or those who chose "Don't know" as their response, were excluded from the analysis on that question. We also limit new class/old class and otherworldly analyses to those questions in which we found at least 10 percentage-point differences between responses of ministers and members. Furthermore, we present these results only when we find differences of at least 10 percent between the old class and the new class, or between the "high," "medium," and "low" categories of worldliness. We limit our discussion to avoid making much of small, even if statistically significant, differences, and to avoid any supposed differences that in fact represent sampling errors.

We should say that the vocabulary of Hadden and the others who have studied views and beliefs of clergy and laity does not fit, strictly speaking, the situation of the Presbyterians. Historically, Presbyterians have ordained for function rather than vocation. Presbyterian churches typically termed their officers "teaching elders," "ruling elders," and "deacons." Today, according to the *Book of*

Order of the Presbyterian Church (U.S.A.), the division of "officers" and "members" continues, but with officers designated as "ministers of the Word," "elders," and (possibly also) "deacons."

Having asserted the distinctive nature of Reformed ecclesiology, however, we hasten to point to the power of the terms "clergy" and "laity." In almost every context American Presbyterians, whether as dissenters in Anglican colonial American establishments, minorities in Roman Catholic areas in the North, minorities in midwestern Lutheran, Methodist, and Disciples cultures, minorities in Southern Baptist cultures in the Southeast, or even as minorities in the generally secular, media-dominated culture of the present day, have taken up the descriptive terms of dominant bodies that do use "lay" and "clergy" for description of their constituencies. Because the terms have been commonly used by Presbyterians, and because they have descriptive power in assessing the situation of the churches, we employ them as well as the more traditional terms.

Self-Perceptions and Similarities

Many lay and clerical panelists themselves perceive some differences between the two groups.[7] Among members, 43 percent agree with the statement that "I sometimes feel my beliefs and worldview differ in important ways from the beliefs and worldview of most clergy in my denomination." Even a greater percentage of clergy (62 percent) sense a gap when asked to respond to the statement that "I sometimes feel my beliefs and worldview differ in important ways from the beliefs and worldview of most laypersons in my denomination."

Despite the perceptions of differences, and the finding of some actual differences, we did not find ministers necessarily more liberal than members in the Presbyterian Church (U.S.A.). A set of denominational questions, for example, points to specific aspects of the denomination and its current affairs. We present the results in Figure 12.1.[8]

Fig. 12.1. Presbyterian Matters

	Laity	Clergy
	Percent Agreeing	
Q1-5. Today a person who publicly opposes equal rights for women would have difficulty entering the higher policy-making levels of the Presbyterian Church (U.S.A.).*	80%	93%
Q1-6. I feel good about the directions national leaders of the Presbyterian Church (U.S.A.) are taking regarding social and political issues.*	73	62
Class		
Old	60	
New	76	
Otherworldliness		
Low	78	81
Medium	74	53
High	62	21
Q1-9. There is good communication across the various organizational levels and governing bodies of the Presbyterian Church (U.S.A.).*	57	39
Class		
Old	46	
New	61	
Q1-12. In the Presbyterian Church (U.S.A.), the policy decisions made at the national level have little impact on most local congregations.*	52	66
Q1-14. Positions taken by the Presbyterian Church (U.S.A.) on social and political issues strongly influence my personal positions on these issues.	24	40
Otherworldliness		
Low		53
Medium		35
High		12

Fig. 12.1. *cont.*

	Laity	Clergy
	Percent Agreeing	
Q1-16. I am optimistic about the long-term future of the Presbyterian Church (U.S.A.).	86	71
Otherworldliness		
Low		76
Medium		73
High		47

*On these questions the proportion responding Don't know (or giving no response) was at least 10% greater among members than among pastors.

In looking at specific aspects of the Presbyterian Church and current affairs in the denomination, pastors, for example, are much less likely to believe that good communication presently exists within the denomination, and they are more pessimistic about the future of the PC(USA) than are lay people. Pastors also are most likely than are laity to hold to the view that the denominational leadership is too concerned with social action. Note, however, that laity responded more frequently "Don't know" in most of these questions than did ministers.[9] On Q1-6, for example, concerning the positions of denominational leaders on social action, 18 percent of members but only 1 percent of pastors responded, "Don't know."

Note that those clergy with a higher degree of otherworldliness, indicating the likelihood of a conservative theological perspective, are comparatively unhappy with the directions taken by the leadership and less optimistic about the long-term survival of the church. Further, those clergy with a high degree of otherworldliness are least likely to agree that positions taken by the PC(USA) strongly influence their personal positions. In brief, among clergy, the degree of otherworldliness is inversely proportional to identification with denominational leadership.[10]

Analysis of these responses by old class/new class definitions (Fig. 12.1) does not add much to our understanding of
attitudinal differences between laity and clergy.[11] In only two
of the areas of response are the differences between old and
new class laity more than 10 percent, and in both of those
(Q1-6 and Q1-9) the clergy responses more nearly resemble
those of the old rather than the new classes among laity.

On five additional questions in this category of "Presbyterian Matters," the proportions responding in agreement
remained similar for laity and clergy, and therefore the results are not displayed. These questions concerned funding,
ecumenical relations, where power is located, and whether
national staff is "out of touch" with what is happening in
local congregations.

Again, as might be expected, a difference did appear in responses to a set of statements about denominational loyalty.
Clergy expressed greater loyalty to the PC(USA) than did
laity. The responses to these statements appear as Fig. 12.2.

Fig. 12.2. Denominational Perspectives

	Laity	Clergy
	Percent Agreeing	
Q1-1. While they may have disagreements from time to time, Christians should remain loyal to one denomination throughout their adult lives.	31%	59%
Q1-2. There are several other denominations where I could serve and be just as satisfied.	78	50
Otherworldliness		
Low		47
Medium		50
High		63
Q1-15. My denominational affiliation is an important part of my identity.	65	85
Otherworldliness		
Low		87
Medium		88
High		69

The differences between responses from old-class laity and new-class laity were less than 10 percent, and therefore we have not presented the findings separately. However, among the clergy significant differences according to their degree of otherworldliness do appear. Analysts might conclude that those with a lower degree of otherworldliness feel more at home in the PC(USA) than do those higher in the category. Alternatively, one might conclude that denominational distinctions matter less when a Christian is less concerned about life now than about eternal life.

We found considerable similarities between clergy and laity as they responded to questions about agreement on values and beliefs (Fig. 12.3). Note that members and pastors hold similar views on the priority of Christian conver-

Fig. 12.3. Agreement on Values and Beliefs

	Laity	Clergy
	Percent Agreeing	
2-2. Converting people to Christ must be the first step in creating a better society.	53%	49%
2-8. Several of my closest friends disagree with my most basic religious convictions.	39	41
2-10. One should be open to reevaluating and revising one's most central values and beliefs when new information comes along.	91	92
2-12. In life, one's relationships with family and friends are more important than what one does in one's work.	84	83
2-13. The Bible is the record of many different people's responses to God and because of this, people and churches today need to interpret for themselves the Bible's basic moral and religious teachings.	72	64
2-17. The church should include people from all types of backgrounds even if this means changing traditional doctrines and practices.	58	49

sion, the disagreement of some close friends with the values and beliefs of the respondent, the degree of perceived openness among respondents, and the importance of human relationships. Perhaps most surprising is the agreement of both groups on the need for diversity in the church, even though some cost might be involved.

Arenas of Difference

Though we found similarities in several areas among responses, we also found significant differences in perceptions on highly charged values and beliefs in American life today—including such issues as America's place in the world, economic justice, and the importance of religion for life. These results comprise Figure 12.4.

Fig. 12.4. Values and Beliefs

	Laity	Clergy
	Percent Agreeing	
Q2-1. As a nation, the United States generally treats people in the Third World unfairly.	24%	63%
Class		
Old	16	
New	27	
Otherworldliness		
Low		77
Medium		56
High		36
Q2-3. The current distribution of income in American society is unjust.	55	80
Class		
Old	40	
New	53	
Otherworldliness		
Low		88
Medium		77
High		55

Fig. 12.4. *cont.*

	Laity	Clergy
	Percent Agreeing	
Q2-4. Most poor people are poor because they fail to take steps to better themselves.	43	13
Class		
Old	49	
New	36	
Otherworldliness		
Low	32	8
Medium	47	14
High	51	28
Q2-7. It is important to me that my closest friends share my religious beliefs.	36	50
Otherworldliness		
Low	26	42
Medium	35	57
High	52	64
Q2-9. People have a responsibility to be the best they can be in their job or career, even if that means they have less time for other people.	32	19
Otherworldliness		
Low		16
Medium		18
High		35
Q2-11. Although I believe in my religion, there are other things in my life which are just as important.*	52	21
Otherworldliness		
Low	62	28
Medium	58	17
High	28	12
Q2-14. The Bible has a special place in Christian tradition, but sacred scriptures of other world religions have as much to teach us concerning faith and morals.*	49	15
Otherworldliness		
Low	65	22
Medium	48	9
High	31	7

318   *The Pluralistic Vision*

Fig. 12.4. *cont.*

	Laity	Clergy
	Percent Agreeing	

Q2-15. It would be better if public libraries removed from their shelves books that threaten Christian values.

	Laity	Clergy
	17	5
Otherworldliness		
Low	7	2
Medium	16	3
High	32	22

Q2-16. It is wrong for Christians to always refer to God as male.*

	Laity	Clergy
	30	60
Class		
Old	20	
New	37	
Otherworldliness		
Low	42	76
Medium	28	52
High	17	25

Q2-18. A person must do good for others in order to receive salvation.

	Laity	Clergy
	49	15
Otherworldliness		
Low	6	
Medium	49	
High	40	

Q2-19. In order to correct past inequities, Blacks should be given preferential treatment when applying for jobs where they are numerically underrepresented.

	Laity	Clergy
	14	47
Otherworldliness		
Low	22	59
Medium	12	39
High	10	25

Q2-20. In order to correct past unfairness, women should be given preferential treatment when applying for jobs where they are numerically underrepresented.

	Laity	Clergy
	15	45
Otherworldliness		
Low		57
Medium		38
High		17

Fig. 12.4. *cont.*

	Laity	Clergy
	Percent Agreeing	
Q2-22. The current rate of progress toward racial justice in this country is too slow.	60	83
Class		
Old	50	
New	64	
Otherworldliness		
Low		91
Medium		78
High		69
Q2-23. Denominations should set aside their differences and work together for the visible, structural reunion of the church.	83	47
Otherworldliness		
Low		51
Medium		46
High		34

*On these questions the proportion responding Don't know (or giving no response) was at least 10% greater among members than among pastors.

Questions regarding affirmative action and those addressing matters of gender language about God reveal some of the most profound differences between ministers and members. Theological educators, denominational leaders, and some ministers in the PC(USA) have been struggling with these issues for almost twenty years. Most congregations have not addressed the issues in concerted fashion, although many members have experienced similar issues in the workplace or in school.

In these issues, comparisons of clergy with new-class laity show closer affinities than with old-class members in attitudes and values. At the same time, attitudes on the part of new-class laity still bear closer resemblance to those of old-class laity than to those of clergy. The same is true, though sometimes less dramatically, for other issues and values in this table. Note, for example, that 43% of the members, but only 13% of the clergy, agree that "most poor people are poor because they fail to take steps to better themselves." The proportion of agreement among new-class laity is 36%, and among old-class laity, 49%. The 36% agreeing response pattern from new-class members is closer to the clergy's 13% than is the overall average for members, but it still remains closer to the 49% agreeing among old class. On this issue, new-class laity might be in the middle of the boat, but they list toward other laity rather than toward clergy as they balance the boat.

On questions of economics, the responses of members do not differ significantly in their otherworldliness scores. This outcome would tend to suggest the religious beliefs of members have only weak correlations with their economic views, if any at all.

For the clergy, on the other hand, religious outlook seems to be related frequently to economic reasoning. This finding might reinforce the results presented previously, showing that positions taken by the PC(USA) have greater influence on the thinking and actions of pastors than on those of members and that ministers have greater denominational loyalty than laity.

A final set of statements, concerning church priorities, further compounds the difficulty in making accurate generalizations about Presbyterian clergy and laity. Figure 12.5 shows significantly different responses to matters of evangelism, of pastors' addressing public issues, of encouraging Christian growth and autonomy, and of distance between religious and political affairs.

A majority among the laity, 61 percent, attach considerable importance to the maintenance of "distance between religious and political concerns." This result by itself may suggest that the members are not in favor of political activity on the part of clergy or religious bodies, whereas they probably are really indicating only that they put more emphasis on this matter than do the clergy. If laity were

Fig. 12.5. Church Priorities

	Laity	Clergy
	Percent Indicating Some, High, or Very High Importance	
Q4-2. Helping church members resist the temptation to experiment with new lifestyles	71%	60%
Otherworldliness		
Low	59	49
Medium	73	66
High	84	83
Q4-4. Encouraging pastors of local churches to speak out in public on social, political, and economic issues that confront American society today	72	88
Otherworldliness		
Low		91
Medium		88
High		79
Q4-5. Encouraging church members to reach their own decisions on issues of faith and morals even if this diminishes the church's ability to speak with a single voice on these issues	78	90
Otherworldliness		
Low	86	92
Medium	75	89
High	69	80
Q4-6. Providing members a comforting refuge from all the pain and suffering in this world	79	59
Q4-7. Reminding Christians of their duty to uphold and defend their country and the values it stands for	82	47
Otherworldliness		
Low	75	34
Medium	80	51
High	93	78

Fig. 12.5. *cont.*

	Laity	Clergy
	Percent Indicating Some, High, or Very High Importance	

	Laity	Clergy
Q4-8. Identifying with political movements of the poor and oppressed, even when this challenges the interests of current members	68	86
Class		
Old	58	
New	74	
Otherworldliness		
Low	76	92
Medium	64	84
High	63	73
Q4-11. Encouraging church members to make explicit declarations of their personal faith to friends, neighbors, and co-workers	72	97
Otherworldliness		
Low	56	
Medium	74	
High	88	
Q4-12. Encouraging and inspiring the church members, as individuals, to become involved in social and political issues	82	97
Class		
Old	71	
New	87	
Otherworldliness		
Low	89	
Medium	77	
High	80	
Q4-13. Maintaining an appropriate distance between religious and political concerns	61	27
Class		
Old	68	
New	55	
Otherworldliness		
Low		19
Medium		31
High		44

thoroughly opposed to religious political activity, 72 percent would not hold it a priority for ministers to speak out on public issues, nor would 82 percent see as a priority the need to encourage people to become involved in political and social issues.

These results show how difficult it is to define accurately a theological liberal or conservative. The clergy, considered by Hadden and others as more liberal than laity, are more strongly in favor of members undertaking personal evangelism than are the supposedly more conservative laity. While 72 percent of the members see as a priority the encouragement of church people to "make explicit declarations of their personal faith to friends, neighbors, and co-workers," a full 97 percent of the clergy consider that essential or desirable.

As in the previous section, most new class/old class differences in response are smaller than 10 percent, and thus excluded from the table. New class/old class differences that do make the threshold typically show new-class members closer in opinions to the clergy than are laity altogether. Yet the responses of new-class laity are generally closer to those of old-class laity than to those of clergy.

Although Figures 12.4 and 12.5 do show differences on some issues with high visibility in American culture and on some church priorities, we should note that several other statements (not displayed tabularly) in these areas yielded similar responses from clergy and laity. For example, more than 75 percent of the laity and clergy see as important priorities the establishing of new congregations, listening carefully to what the world is saying in order to understand what the church's ministry should be, and respecting a variety of views even if it is not clear that they fit in with traditional teachings of the church.

Conclusions

The results of this analysis of attitudes and beliefs among members and pastors of the PC(USA) suggest that important but complex differences distinguish these two groups.

Clergy are in general more loyal to the denomination, more knowledgeable about issues and problems facing Presbyterians, and more pessimistic about the future of the church. Clergy are also more concerned about issues of social justice in American society, such as distribution of income and affirmative action programs for women and minorities. Clergy are also less likely than laity to see patriotic duty as a legitimate activity of the church, and more likely to see the need for church to stand over against the civil government.

On the other hand, generally speaking, laity and clergy share similar views on important issues more than they disagree. Most of the time majorities coincide in reactions to statements, and many times proportions remained so similar as to indicate little significant difference at all.

Educational differences and variance in social position do explain some of the differences in opinion and worldview between clergy and laity. On most questions in which a new class/old class difference among laity can be discerned, new-class members respond in patterns closer to those of the clergy than do old-class laity. In particular, new-class laity are closer to clergy in their attitudes on racial, economic, and social justice issues. Nevertheless, even on these issues a large gap remains between the proportion of new-class laity and clergy who hold a particular attitude, and the new-class proportion is often closer to that of the old-class laity than to that of the clergy. In sum, the new class/old class distinction is not very helpful overall in explaining differences between laity and clergy. At least our division, based on the undergraduate major fields of study of laity, indicated only a mitigating of differences. Were we able to discern more exactly the job-related responsibilities of respondents, we might discover more significant correlations.

Our data also suggested some validity in the "Two-Church Hypothesis" as recently offered by Louis Weeks and William Fogelman.[12] They argue that the PC(USA) actually consists of two interdependent but distinguishable denominations, which they term the "Local Congregation Presbyterian Church" (LCPC) and the "Governing Body

Presbyterian Church" (GBPC). According to Weeks and Fogelman, denominational executives, many if not most ministers, and those elders and members heavily invested in General Assembly, synod, and presbytery matters belong to the GBPC. Most members, most elders, and many ministers belong to the LCPC. Each depends heavily on the other, and the PC(USA) is healthy not through one triumphing over the other, but in a symbiosis, or balance, between the two feeding each other.

Though our data were collected before the articulation of the thesis, we see the frequent and higher proportions of "Don't know" responses among the laity as one evidence of its validity. While patterns of responses indicate more clergy than laity identify with the GBPC in some respect, we also perceive wide differences among clergy in their patterns of responses. From our perspectives, this hypothesis certainly merits more study.

That finding—the variety of views among Presbyterian clergy themselves—also deserves greater study. We found the index of otherworldliness a useful tool, and we suggest it be refined and other pertinent measures be discerned for such study.

We also assume that a diversity of views affects Presbyterian life the most when those differences occur on the local level—between clergy and laity in a particular congregation, or for that matter among laity in the same congregation. Our samples did not provide data to address this topic, which clearly merits further study.

Overall, more agreement than disagreement between clergy and laity characterizes our findings. Still, we do find enormous diversity in views and beliefs. We wonder whether trouble lies ahead, as Jeffrey K. Hadden predicted twenty years ago, or whether a healthy diversity will bode well for the church's future.

Finally, we note the degree of optimism on the parts of both laity and clergy concerning the PC(USA) and the future of the denomination. Ministers seem more critical than laity concerning directions that the General Assembly leaders are taking, a surprising finding for us, but a major-

ity of both are optimistic about the long-term future of the
church. In the midst of much "gloom and doom" forecast-
ing about the future of the so-called "mainline denominations," we wonder if members and leaders ought rather to
take heart and focus constructively on what unites them in
mission and Christian witness.

13

The Values and Limits of Representation and Pluralism in the Church

Barbara Brown Zikmund

When sociologists and the public media look at the church in American society they see many things. They compare churches with other organizations and they assess health and well-being in categories borrowed from the secular landscape. This is only natural. Churches are voluntary associations which hold much in common with other clubs and service societies in contemporary society. Yet Christians insist that churches are different. We argue that theological and biblical values shape our common life in uncommon ways. "The church" stands apart from all other voluntary organizations. How?

Theological Assumptions

First, we insist that the church is more than its building or structures. Other organizations also do this, for when people speak about a club or a lodge they often mean more than the building. But the church's identity is always independent of its place. Physical sacred spaces, such as cathedrals and chapels, raise human awareness and remind secular society of the church, but the building is never "the church."

Second, although people sometimes speak of "my church" or "pastor Jones's church," when all is said and done the church is more than human. It is God's church. We believe that the church is ultimately accountable to and dependent on divine grace.

Third, the head of the church is Jesus Christ. Theologically we say that the church is the "body of Christ." This means that there is no human headship in the church. Protestants like this idea. They are fearful of all human leadership in the church. Yet, to affirm the headship of Christ really means that the church is not a democracy either. The church does not do what the majority of the people want (or vote)—the church has a higher loyalty to Jesus Christ. As some of the seventeenth-century Puritan writers put it, Christians are called to respect the "crown rights of the Redeemer."

And finally, fourth, we affirm the church as "the community of the faithful," or "the people of God." In ecclesiastical history this has not always been clear. Traditional ecclesiologies have sometimes identified the church with the clergy, the ruling magisterium. Since the sixteenth century, however, churches in the Reformed tradition have emphasized a theological understanding of the church as the "priesthood of all believers." And since the Second Vatican Council, Roman Catholic theology has reclaimed its understanding of the church as "the whole people of God."

The church is a community called out of the world to be faithful to the leadership of Christ, which knows itself owned by God and bigger than a building.

These four theological values are supported by different biblical texts in every era. In earlier periods of church history, ecclesiologies sometimes focused on texts to strengthen institutional power or to preserve Word and sacrament. The contemporary scene, with its renewed awareness of the "whole people," brings different concerns. Today, we live in a church where institutional power has diminished and Word and sacrament may be taken for granted. Today, even when we struggle against them, questions of representation and pluralism dominate our ecclesi-

astical agenda. What are the biblical principles that inform
our understandings of pluralism in the church? Why have
these concerns become so all-consuming among Presbyterians and other mainline Protestant denominations in the
late twentieth century? And finally, is there a way to live
faithfully with the reality of pluralism in the church?

Biblical Principles

To begin with, the vision of a unified and inclusive
church is proclaimed at many places in the Bible. Probably
the most important text referred to by contemporary Christians facing pluralism is Galatians 3:28—"There is neither
Jew nor Greek, there is neither slave nor free, there is neither male nor female; for you are all one in Christ Jesus."
Here we have specific words against the racism, classism,
and sexism of human societies. Here we have a declaration
that in spite of human divisions we are all one in Christ.

This text has had particular power in American mainline
Protestantism over the past two hundred years for several
reasons. First, American churches wish to affirm the "enlightenment democratic ideology" which created and sus-
tains our democratic political system. For democracy to
work, certain divisions have to be healed. American political struggles against slavery and women's second-class citizenship have used these biblical words about unity
repeatedly. Second, during the nineteenth and twentieth
centuries Christians have become keenly aware of the real
diversity of the world. It is increasingly impossible to ig-
nore differences or to assume that they do not matter. Biblical words about unity above and beyond such fundamental
differences as race, economic standing, and gender provide
a framework for Christian inclusiveness. If people have little experience with diversity, there is less need for such a
text, but as the realities of the world press in upon American Christians such a text speaks an important message.

Another biblical word that stretches our ecclesiologies relates to hierarchy. Liberation theologies coming from Latin
America and the experience of Blacks and women remind

us of the ways in which Jesus turned the world's values upside down. Jesus says to the disciples, "You are my friends.
. . . No longer do I call you servants, for the servant does
not know what his master is doing; but I have called you
friends" (John 15:14–15). Jesus taught that those who exalt
themselves will be humbled and those who humble themselves will be exalted (Luke 14:11). Through a story about
laborers in a vineyard, Jesus reversed the order of the
world, suggesting that through God's generosity the last
will become first and the first may find themselves last
(Matt. 20:1–16). These biblical words have always challenged human habits and assumptions about hierarchy, but
contemporary movements for justice and equality highlight
their radical message. Even though hierarchy remains one
of the classic ways human societies manage diversity, contemporary Christians living with pluralism in the church
are less accepting of hierarchy.

A third biblical word that influences contemporary ecclesiology dwells on the relationship between confession and
service. As Christians have become aware that salvation is
more than inner or individual, and that Christian social
action is corporate, biblical texts that emphasize action
have become more important. "Not every one who says to
me, 'Lord, Lord,' shall enter the kingdom of heaven, but
[the one] who does the will of my Father who is in heaven"
(Matt. 7:21). Here we are reminded that disciples are called
not simply to believe, but to put their faith into action. And
on the Day of Judgment when some may ask, "When did
we see you hungry, or thirsty . . . ?" Jesus will respond, "As
you did it to one of the least of these . . . , you did it to me"
(Matt. 25:40). Christian discipleship requires action. Not
just any action, but action especially sensitive to those in
need. In a pluralistic society it is easier to tolerate diversity
in beliefs than it is to agree on which way to go, or what to
do. In a pluralistic society it is easier to do something un-
controversial (such as confess a creed) than it is to deal with
those who are really in need. For this reason biblical texts
that call the church into action are more and more difficult
to honor in a pluralistic world.

Finally, there is the question of evangelism and mission outreach to non-Christians. As church membership figures have declined in mainline denominations, Christians remember the Great Commission. Jesus said, "Go therefore and make disciples of all nations, baptizing them in the name of the Father and of the Son and of the Holy Spirit" (Matt. 28:19). But in a pluralistic setting what does it mean to confess Jesus as Lord without putting down other religions? If we want to recognize the faithfulness of peoples of other living faiths in our pluralistic world, how can we sustain any missionary witness? Christians confronting the pluralism of world religions, as well as greater theological and cultural diversity within their churches, anguish about questions of mission and evangelism.

It is clear that the biblical principles and values that have emerged in contemporary mainline Protestant ecclesiology are both helpful and problematic. They point to the vision of a unified and inclusive church where all are one in Christ Jesus. They rebuke hierarchy by turning the values of the world upside down and challenging the church to embrace pluralism without fear or loss. They call for more than belief—insisting that Christians must *do* God's will and act with special sensitivity to those in need. And they struggle with the assumption that Christians are to make Christian disciples of all nations, while at the same time recognizing that God is at work in many religious traditions. Pluralism forces Christians to read these texts with new eyes.

Institutional Values

The most important value assumptions within the church are theological and biblical, but the church is also an organization. As an organization it participates in shared cultural and institutional values that affect all organizations. Without dwelling on them at length, it is important for us to note how issues of size, scope, and survival shape the response of the church to pluralism.

In American society, growth is an important value. We want our children to grow, we want the economy to grow. If a company or an organization is not growing, we become nervous that its stature or its health is in jeopardy. Growth is natural. And even when we agree that small may be beautiful, bigger is better.

The story of the early church in the book of Acts is a story of growth. The spread of Christianity throughout the Gentile world was a matter of some pride to the early church. Yet we know that the early church was persecuted and almost destroyed. First-century Christians saw themselves as a faithful remnant. Growth, from the biblical standpoint, was ambiguous.

At present the average congregation in mainline Protestant denominations is under two hundred members. Church membership reports and projections show steady declines in mainline church membership for the past twenty years. Most Presbyterian churches are small, and few are getting bigger. Those congregations which are growing are frequently churches serving special racial and ethnic communities.

Institutional values are also challenging some of our denominational and nationalistic habits. As America adjusts to new immigration patterns and develops global sensitivity to multinational corporations and markets, churches are caught in a dilemma. During the 1950s and 1960s, progressive mainline Protestant congregations sought to become "integrated," arguing theologically that the church must transcend racial and ethnic traditions. "In Christ there is no east or west . . . " However, as immigration patterns unfolded during the 1970s and 1980s, we discovered that the most vital and growing congregations in mainline Protestant denominations were not integrated congregations—they were very homogeneous. Church growth experts explained the situation by noting how excessive pluralism limits congregational growth. Yet church leaders also celebrated the increasing importance of the global context of the church's ministry. In these years we have seen the scope of legitimate Christian community narrow and expand in various attempts to strengthen organizational viability.

Finally, the drive for self-preservation which shapes all organizations has influenced the church. Concerns about buildings, leadership, services, and survival have pushed churches into programs and tactics that are sometimes in tension with basic theological assumptions and biblical principles. Only by confronting the ways in which institutional values borrowed from the wider culture relate to theological assumptions and biblical principles will the churches be able to move beyond this impasse.

The Factors That Have Shaped Contemporary Pluralism

Why are things this way? What are the factors that have shaped the current environment in which Presbyterian congregations and all other mainline Protestant churches exist today? It is useful to enumerate the various historical and contemporary forces that have created our present pluralistic situation. These factors are all important, but in some instances one may be dominant:

First, American history is filled with stories of immigration, migration and expansion. People came to colonial America to find religious freedom and to better themselves economically. Some took on obligations as indentured servants, and others were forced to come as slaves. In most colonies one church tradition dominated—Congregationalists in New England and Episcopalians in colonial Virginia; in other places, such as Pennsylvania, a tolerant benefactor/proprietor allowed very diverse religious communities to coexist.

As the nation grew, some of the mainline groups spread out more evenly. America was predominantly Protestant, and the Protestant ethic shaped political and social values. Protestant churches often functioned as "established churches," cultivating an "establishment mentality." Yet even within the nationally dispersed denominations (for example, Presbyterians and Methodists) distinctive regional variations developed.

Eventually, some regional patterns were formalized into separate denominations. This was especially true as groups of northern and southern churches separated over the question of slavery. By the mid-nineteenth century regional cultures were mirrored in regional churches—northern and southern Presbyterians, northern and southern Methodists, northern and southern Baptists. It was no longer enough to describe oneself as "Presbyterian," it was necessary to give it a regional explanation. During the twentieth century some of these regional splits have been healed through church mergers, but regionalism continues to contribute to the pluralism of contemporary church life.[1]

Second, Presbyterian people, along with other American Protestants, further fragmented the ecclesiastical landscape by splitting denominational structures and creating internal rivalries along theological lines. At various times Presbyterians split into new and old "sides," new and old "schools," or new and old "lights." The theological arguments were deep and bitter. They grew out of different understandings of theology and evangelism. They led to competing theological institutions and different understandings of leadership in the churches. They cultivated diverse ways of dealing with change. Some groups embraced new critical biblical scholarship with enthusiasm, others defended scriptural authority against all modern science.[2]

Theological controversies over revivalist methods, views of human nature, the work of the Holy Spirit, the theory of evolution, and biblical inerrancy have divided mainline Protestant peoples into many camps. Historians write about evangelicals versus orthodoxy, or modernists versus fundamentalists, or charismatics versus liberals, or evangelicals versus mainliners. The labels are used differently in each era, but the point is that religious pluralism generated by theological controversy is endemic to American Protestantism. In earlier eras the results of theological arguments led to heresy trials and breakaway denominations; in more recent times some of the same theological tensions create factions and divisions within major Protestant denominations.[3]

A third factor contributing to the pluralism of mainline denominations is the growing ethnic and racial diversity of this country. In the colonial period, most Presbyterians were English or Scottish. For many years the ethnic melting pot shaping mainline Protestant churches was European—blending Irish, Scottish, English, Dutch, German, French, Swiss, and many other peoples. Protestant ethnocentrism tended to be Anglo-Saxon, and it found expression in nativism, anti-Semitism, and anti-Catholic prejudice. Protestants worried that Roman Catholic loyalty to the pope would distort American liberty. Protestants agreed that Jews and Roman Catholics needed to be kept marginalized.[4]

In the twentieth century, African Americans have become an increasingly visible and vocal presence in church and society. While Blacks have strengthened the predominantly Black denominations, they have also challenged white mainline Protestants to responsible discipleship in a multiracial society. They have reminded people that America claims to be a land of equal opportunity for all. Drawing on a rich African American ecclesiastical heritage, they have expanded and strengthened many churches.[5]

Today a diverse mix of Blacks, Hispanics, Native Americans, Pacific Islanders, and Asians is stretching our pluralistic consciousness still farther.[6] The Racial Ethnic Ministry Unit of the Presbyterian Church (U.S.A.) is typical of many new agencies in mainline Protestant denominations devoted to an expanding pluralistic vision of the church. It provides a place where representatives of all these groups can give support to one another and exert leverage on the bureaucracy for a more inclusive church.

For racial and ethnic minorities in predominantly white mainline Protestant denominations, these structures have a dual purpose. On the one hand, they bring minority church members with similar concerns and problems together so that they can work within the larger church for change. Working collectively, they can more effectively call the majority into accountability. On the other hand, these structures support diverse racial and ethnic communities in their struggle to preserve unique cultural roots and traditions threatened with annihilation by a dominant ecclesiastical culture.

Many ethnic church communities, such as Koreans in the Presbyterian and Methodist denominations, function with what might be called "dual ecclesiastical citizenship." That is, they are active as minority caucuses within their respective denominations, while at the same time they participate in ecumenical networks of Korean-American churches from many denominations. Armenian churches, Chinese churches, Japanese churches, and churches of Pacific Islanders follow similar patterns. Their interdenominational activities strengthen and preserve cultural identity, and they also promote a new form of ecumenism grounded in cultural rather than theological loyalties.[7]

For a long time people assumed that Spanish-speaking immigrants were Roman Catholic. As Hispanic populations have increased, however, mainline Protestant denominations are engaged in successful ministries with Puerto Ricans, Cubans, and Mexicans. Spanish is fast becoming the second language of America. As a result, mainline Protestant churches are challenged to publish and preach in Spanish. Issues of communication and access get more and more complicated. In religious communities a common language shapes meanings and memories. Therefore, facing the fact that we may be called permanently (not just temporarily) to sustain a multilingual church is very difficult for many mainline Protestants.[8]

Finally, the racial and ethnic diversity that is invading American society brings with it unprecedented religious pluralism.[9] Immigrants from Asia often have no relationship to the Jewish and Christian legacy of Western civilization. They are Buddhists, Muslims, and Hindus. They are good citizens and neighbors, but they have no desire to become Christians. Their presence, albeit outside the church, cannot be ignored. They remind us that there are other forms of faithfulness. They challenge us to reexamine the exclusivistic claims of Christianity. They comfort us with the pluralism of the world within which the church carries out its mission.

A fourth element shaping pluralism in mainline Protestantism is found in demographic fluctuations. Throughout its early history, America was a Protestant country. The small numbers of Jews and Roman Catholics were no threat. However, when Roman Catholic immigration increased dramatically in the nineteenth century, Protestants got nervous. Defensive nativism and religious bigotry flourished. Gradually, however, Protestants relaxed. In the twentieth century Roman Catholicism has become more like Protestantism. National and regional population patterns have greatly influenced Protestant–Roman Catholic relations and attitudes toward pluralism.

Demographics and economics have also affected the ways in which churches define women's place and role. During historic periods when men outnumber women, although women are highly valued, their role is often largely limited to serving family and church as wives and mothers. However, in those eras or settings where there are more women than men (as in wartime or in communities where men are away for months at sea), women often take on roles and jobs normally carried by men. Women in American Protestantism have benefited from educational opportunities and reproductive choices available to few women in the world. And out of that freedom American Protestant women have pushed the churches to recognize their presence and to treat them as equals.[10]

A good example of how this works is found in the movement of women into ordained ministry. Women's preaching and sacramental leadership creates a different ecclesiastical environment. Some observers argue that the leadership of women clergy, especially women of color, symbolizes the radical call of the Christian church to genuine pluralism and diversity.[11] Perhaps the reason some church people fight this development so vigorously flows from their deeper fear of pluralism.

Other population patterns explain the nature of pluralism within the churches. During the post–World War II baby boom, churches focused on Christian education and youth ministries to the neglect of other things. As the average age of church populations increased, programs for children and youth declined. Likewise, with the increase in life expectancy and the fact that women are spending less time bearing and caring for children, feminist issues and the role of the elderly have become more important in the church. It is now impossible to form a committee in a mainline Protestant church without a self-conscious concern about the balance between young and old, male and female members. Our sensitivity to these things has been formed by population pressures and demographic realities.[12]

Fifth, strong pressures supporting pluralism in the Presbyterian Church, and in many mainline Protestant denominations, come from the blurring of traditional polities and the new governance documents written to serve a more pluralistic church.   Presbyterian polity is representational. Representatives are elected in local and regional bodies, and the actions taken at wider church meetings (presbyteries, synods, and General Assemblies) are binding on each local congregation. Some mainline Protestant denominations follow congregational polity. This means that each local congregation relates to denominational structures because it chooses to do so, not because it is legally obligated. When there is disagreement, the autonomy of a local church may lead it to deviate from the decisions of wider church bodies. Still other mainline Protestant denominations follow episcopal polity. These churches give certain clergy special responsibilities for the oversight of the church. Although the election of bishops follows democratic procedures, once in office the authority of a bishop is honored throughout the church.

In American history, distinctions between these three polities have become increasingly blurred. During the controversy over slavery, churches and individuals in all three polities violated ecclesiastical directives in their zeal for or against slavery. During the great expansion of missions in the nineteenth century, denominational polities were freely compromised in the name of supporting a higher calling to ecumenical missions at home and abroad. In more recent decades, the casual mobility of American church members, who join churches of different polities in different cities or neighborhoods because they are convenient, shows that mainline Protestants are quite at home with understandings of church governance.

Of course, there have also been official attempts within our denominations to live with pluralism by changing denominational polities through restructuring, ecclesiastical reunions, and ecumenical cooperation. In many cases formal structures have been created to monitor ecclesiastical bodies in an effort to ensure that they reflect the pluralistic reality and vision of the church. A case in point is the new requirement in the Presbyterian Church (U.S.A.) that each presbytery and synod and the General Assembly have a committee on representation. The major duty of this committee is to advise the governing bodies with respect to their membership and to that of their committees, boards and agencies, and other units in implementing the principles of participation and inclusiveness, to ensure fair and effective representation in the decision making of the church.[13]

> This committee acts as an advocate for persons of different age groups (youth and the elderly, for example), women, persons with disabilities, and racial ethnic group members within the structures of the governing body. The Committee on Representation is a resource for the nominating committee, suggesting persons who are willing to serve. It also seeks to insure that the hiring practices of the body are in line with what our Constitution says about inclusiveness in the church. It has no power to appoint anyone to an office or position or to require that certain quotas be filled; rather, it functions to monitor and promote inclusiveness. A majority of those on this committee are to be members of racial ethnic groups, and one does not have to be an elder to serve.[14]

Sixth, there are less distinct practices in the ways in which members and leaders are socialized to understand the nature of the church and its relationship to society. This has always been true among Protestants, but as ecclesiastical identity has focused more narrowly on clergy, matters of denominational theological education and particular understandings of ordination to ministries of Word and sacrament have become blurred. Today many seminary students do not have long experience in one confessional tradition. They may have grown up in another denomination, or have come into the church as adults. Furthermore, theological education has become more ecumenical, allowing future clergy to study in interdenominational environments and with student colleagues from many ecclesiastical traditions. Also, in an eagerness to break "old boy" staffing patterns, younger and more inclusive denominational staffs, who have not come up through a "system," are hired. These leaders have less investment in, and experience with, their denomination's understandings of church and ministry, yet they continue to be primary channels through which denominational identities are preserved.[15]

The manner in which Christians learn about their faith takes many forms. In earlier eras family, the church school, and youth programs provided a context for Christian nurture. Today television, literature, and peer influences have a much greater impact. A revival of conservative theology, greater ambiguity about values, and secular support for individualism leave many mainline Protestants confused. They surmise, therefore, that pluralism within the church is more destructive than helpful.

Worship becomes especially important under these circumstances, because hearing familiar texts and liturgies and singing well-known music is a reassuring anchor. For many people the old hymns and classic prayers are still able to give comfort and focus identity. This explains why there has been increased interest in worship resources among mainline Protestants, and it also explains why certain changes in worship generate such strong feelings.

For these and many other reasons, denominational

cultures have lost some of their distinctiveness in our pluralistic society. People move freely between mainline denominations, arguing that there is little difference between
them. Yet, each denomination continues to hang on to certain unique symbols in order to reassure laity and clergy
that they know who they are and what they believe.

*In the seventh place, the proliferation of advocacy groups
and special-interest caucuses within mainline Protestant denominations has raised the general awareness of church
members on many issues in church and society.*   The list of
special-advocacy groups in mainline Protestant denominations is legion. Alongside the obvious cluster of racial and
ethnic groups, every denomination now has recognized advocacy organizations for persons with disabilities, for gay
men and lesbians in the church, for environmentalists, for
political activists, for women, for charismatics, and for
many other constituencies. Theological conservatives organize against inclusive language, and political activists call for
boycotts. Sometimes regional or national church bodies
catch the passion of one of these groups and pass a progressive (or reactionary) resolution or overture, but most of the
time the groups count themselves successful if they are able
to keep the church informed on the issues of the day.

Advocacy groups among Protestants are nothing new.
Mission organizations, moral reform societies, abolition
associations, temperance unions, and civil rights organizations have mobilized Christians to live by their faith in the
past. What is new, however, is the increased numbers of
these groups functioning within each denomination and
the procedural leverage they exercise at all levels of church
life.[16] Instead of being a helpful prod to our ecclesiastical
conscience and a constructive resource to get things done,
today these advocacy groups seem to polarize and paralyze
the church. Some church people argue, therefore, that it is
time to limit pluralism in the church.

Summary of the pluralistic forces at work.   These are the
forces or factors at work in our churches that have created a

pluralistic ecclesiastical landscape within the Presbyterian Church (U.S.A.) and within most mainline Protestant churches: (1) regional patterns of immigration, migration, and expansion, (2) theological factions and camps, (3) ethnic and racial diversity, (4) population patterns and demographic trends, (5) the blurring of traditional polities and denominational restructuring, (6) less distinct practices in the socialization of church members and leaders, and finally, (7) the proliferation of advocacy groups within denominations.

Living with Pluralism in the Church:
Values and Limits

The Christian Church is a treasure in earthen vessels. It is God's, and it is very human. Obviously it is theologically right to insist that the church must be an inclusive and open community. On the other hand, it is becoming self-destructive for many of our churches to continue on their present course. Making sure that every constituency group or caucus is adequately represented at every level of our ecclesiastical life may express our vision of "church," but it leaves us tired and divided. What is the way out of this situation? How can we affirm the pluralism of our world and sustain the church as a community called to unity and wholeness in Christ?

One answer to this question focuses on leadership. In the past, church communities were relatively homogeneous and small. Leadership needs were simple. During the twentieth century we have moved from a society of individuals and small organizations to a society dominated by large institutions. Although mainline Protestant denominations are losing members, they remain large organizations. The problem, as one analyst sees it, is a "crisis of institutional quality." We are in trouble not so much because of the activities of "evil" people as from the sheer neglect of "good" people. And we will continue to flounder until we allow and encourage strong natural servant leaders to lead.[17]

This argument insists that all institutional change finally

comes down to the leadership of individual human beings. "What happens to our values and therefore to the quality of our civilization in the future, will be shaped by the conceptions of individuals that are born of inspiration."[18] Therefore, in its efforts to deal with pluralism, the church should not be preoccupied with procedures and representation. Instead it should focus all of its energy upon finding and following gifted leaders.

A more common response to pluralism within the Presbyterian Church (U.S.A.) and other mainline Protestant denominations is to regularize and control it through legislated patterns of representation. It may be that we are not doing this in the most advantageous way, but (the argument goes) by forcing new encounters and stretching horizons people will learn what it means to be together in Christ.

The problems with this strategy are varied. First of all, simply putting people together is not always constructive. Because no one can agree, or because everyone has to take time to "hear" everyone else, or because the group is too large, nothing happens. Taking pluralism seriously by bringing everyone in on everything often leads to paralysis.

Most mainline Protestant denominations have jokes about how many people it takes to change a light bulb in the national church—one white, one Black, one man, one woman, one youth, one senior, one Asian, one Hispanic, and so on and so on. Instead of finding energy in the mix of people who come together to "be" the church, nothing happens and the people go away frustrated.

Another difficulty with efforts to legislate representation is that it becomes very time-consuming and expensive. The church is a voluntary organization. Given its limited resources, there is increasing concern that it is not good stewardship to spend scarce time and money on excessive representative structures.

Finally, some of us who have tried to represent minority constituencies at wider church meetings are not sure that it can be done with integrity anymore. In the old days a few Blacks or several women were added to a situation controlled by a dominant group. We were there to raise consciousness and to keep people accountable. Although we were marginal, and even token, we had an impact and sometimes things happened.

Today, when representatives from our many constituencies gather, there is literally no dominant group. Everyone feels powerless. Contemporary pluralism creates a conglomerate instead of a community. Furthermore, it is more and more difficult for each "representative" to stay in touch with his or her "home" community. Theological integrity and ecclesiastical health will never be achieved by bringing together well-meaning strangers for three-day meetings at conference centers far from home.

As I reflect on this situation I see three solutions.

One response is to downplay the diversity of the church and cultivate enclaves of homogeneity. Church growth experts argue that churches should seek to attract "like" persons. Research shows that a vital sign of a healthy church is that its membership is drawn from "one homogeneous unit."[19] Therefore, if people need to be exposed to diversity, it must not be excessive. By working to nourish natural communities of faith, the argument is made, the church will slowly become more inclusive. Other people disagree. They believe that when the church refuses to face its real diversity, it becomes increasingly alienated from the world.

A second response to pluralism is to insist that the promise of the gospel demands assimilation and integration. Human differences aside, we are called to affirm our oneness in Jesus Christ and to work toward unity. The melting pot, or mosaic, imagery presses for an inclusive ecclesiastical vision. Efforts of the ecumenical movement to retrieve a common apostolic faith, or attempts by local congregations to integrate peoples from different cultural traditions, reflect this type of thinking.[20] Yet there are difficulties with this response also. By legislating togetherness and looking for unity in some past lowest common denominator, the church does not necessarily overcome its parochialism. As Christians search for shared roots, there is also a danger that the uniqueness of Christianity will be compromised and the marginal voices of the past will be forever lost.[21]

A third response to pluralism is to suggest that it is possible to cultivate a reasonable cultural-linguistic perspective that can provide an intelligible view of the world useful to modern Christians. Mainline Protestant denominations must understand themselves as post-Enlightenment communities of faith. This means that churches need to recapture their commitment to questions of religious faithfulness without forsaking post-Enlightenment intellectual and rational assumptions.

Drawing on the work of George Lindbeck, a case can be made that mainline Protestants (or postliberal Christians) do not need to choose between accommodating to modern rationalism or returning to premodern orthodoxy. We are rational beings who should draw upon modern ways to articulate a meaningful view of life. Therefore, Lindbeck argues that we must look for meaning *within* our basic texts and symbol systems.[22]

Orthodox and conservative theology locates religious meaning in transcendent reality. It has an inner logic. Post-Enlightenment theology grounds its interpretation of truth in human experience. It takes outer experience seriously. What Lindbeck calls a cultural-linguistic view of reality, however, refuses to accept this inner-outer distinction, arguing instead that religious meaning must be found in the world of religious language and metaphor. Such a postliberal theology refuses to return to a premodern naïveté, yet it recognizes how human experience is shaped, molded, and constituted by cultural and linguistic forms. Literally, no person can think, or feel, or understand what it means to be human outside of certain symbol systems.

Understood in this way, religious meaning is always grounded in the language and communal life of a community. It cannot be found in universal principles discovered by pure rationality. It cannot be authentically supported exclusively by logical arguments from a rational or cognitive mode.

Religion is analogous to a foreign language. Just as it is impossible to learn a language by memorizing objective united concepts about nouns or verbs, religions cannot be

defended or shared by showing how they explain human
experience. People seldom learn to speak or read a foreign
language by studying its grammar; rather they live with it
and learn to think in the idioms and symbols of its "conversation." People do not embrace a religious worldview by
accepting certain logical explanations of life's mysteries.
For this reason, when rationalists try to defend religious
faith in the language of science, philosophy, and psychology they are bound to fail.

Protestant rationalism remains useful, however, because
it reminds us of the commonality of human experience. But
rationalism is never sufficient because of its preoccupation
with the individual quest for personally meaningful symbols of transcendence. According to Lindbeck, the viability
of authentic religiosity will "depend upon communal enclaves that socialize their members into highly particular
outlooks supportive of concern for others rather than for
individual rights and entitlements, and of a sense of responsibility for the wider society rather than for personal
fulfillment."[23]

Here is a theological framework for dealing with pluralism in contemporary mainline Protestant denominations.
At its core, Christianity is driven by the paradox that those
who lose their lives for others will find fulfillment and redemption. Faithfulness requires living in very particular
ways to serve others and the wider society. For this reason
liberal Protestantism refuses to retreat to a worldview exclusively dependent on transcendent reality. However, it is
time, according to Lindbeck, to cultivate a postliberal Protestantism that retains a post-Enlightenment appreciation
for reason, but tempers it with the recognition that religious
life and meaning can never be completely grounded in rational principles or in an individualistic quest. Faithfulness
is always found in communities. Such a postliberal Protestantism will find that within various "communal enclaves"
and "highly particular outlooks" Christians can discover
again how to cultivate "supportive concern for others" and
"a sense of responsibility for the wider society."

This theological stance invites the Presbyterian Church

(U.S.A.) and other mainline Protestant denominations not to be embarrassed about cultivating particular religious cultures and subcultures. It reminds us that we have a linguistic faith heritage which needs to be nurtured. And it argues that only by living together with our shared symbols and biblical faith, resisting every temptation to translate, transpose, or reduce these common insights into rational explanations, will we be able to deal creatively with pluralism. Our success will depend not on our ability to redescribe our faith in new concepts, nor on our skill in expressing foundational concepts that unify our diversity. We will flourish only when we teach the language and practices of Christianity as a common resource and framework for living in a pluralistic world.

Two analogies reinforce this argument. We could say that the various caucuses and special-interest groups within our pluralistic denominations must be nurtured ecologically. This means that the survival of any particular group is not necessarily the goal. Environmentalists have learned that natural forest fires are needed to keep a forest healthy. In nature, some things die in order that other parts of the forest can live. Burning reduces the brush that fuels destructive "superfires," and the heat of small fires enables new trees to germinate. In the ecology of the church, diversity does not need to fear the fire of controversy.

Second, mainline Protestants need to embrace a third-generation approach to Christianity. In the history of immigration the first generation speaks the language of the old country and enough of a new language to survive. The second generation usually rejects the language of home and parents and embraces the new language and culture uncritically. This is what many liberal Christians have done in their rejection of orthodoxy. By the third generation, however, there is a renewed appreciation for the old language and culture. Third-generation immigrants reclaim the old language not simply to "translate" better into a new language and culture, they rediscover the values of the "old country" and want to preserve and cherish that heritage. They find that being bilingual is more satisfying.

Living in a pluralistic church follows a similar pattern. Some Christians refuse to move into the modern world. They retain a premodern worldview and "get by" with enough rationalism to survive. Other Christians, especially those of us in mainline Protestant denominations, have embraced the language of rationalism completely. We explain our faith in that universal tongue, but we discover that it does not always make religious sense. Our liberal experiential-expressive rhetoric fails to communicate through the differences we encounter in the church. The time has come for us, like third-generation immigrants, to honestly face the limits of rationalism and to rediscover the cultural-linguistic world of the Bible. By cultivating vital biblical communities of faith we will be able to provide a framework for people to live creatively with diverse meaning systems. And we will also uncover ways whereby we can respect the integrity of other Christians who live with that same biblical faith quite differently.

Finally, the question of religious pluralism must reach out beyond the question of diversity and pluralism *within* various Protestant denominations, or even among all Christians, to address the encounter of Jesus with other living religions.[24] As we learn how to nurture vital cultural-religious communities within our particular denominations, we will also gain greater capacity to enter into genuine dialogue with persons of other faith traditions. Vital interreligious conversation does not limit opportunities for Christian witness. But living in a religiously pluralistic world demands that Christians be open to the possibility that Christianity and the church and their faith might be changed in such encounters. The values and limits of representation and pluralism in the church are encountered first in local experiences and frustrations, but the question of pluralism has global ramifications.

Notes

Series Foreword

1. Arthur M. Schlesinger, Sr., "A Critical Period in American Religion, 1875–1900," first appeared in the *Massachusetts Historical Society Proceedings* 64 (1930–32) and is reprinted in John M. Mulder and John F. Wilson, eds., *Religion in American History: Interpretive Essays* (Englewood Cliffs, N.J.: Prentice-Hall, 1978), pp. 302–317.

2. Robert T. Handy, "The American Religious Depression, 1925–1935," *Church History* 29 (1960): 3–16, reprinted in Mulder and Wilson, *Religion in American History,* pp. 431–444; Handy, *A Christian America: Protestant Hopes and Historical Realities,* 2nd ed. (New York: Oxford University Press, 1984), pp. 159–184.

3. Sydney E. Ahlstrom, "The Radical Turn in Theology and Ethics: Why It Occurred in the 1960s," *Annals of the American Academy of Political and Social Science* 387 (1970): 1–13, reprinted in Mulder and Wilson, *Religion in American History,* pp. 445–456; Ahlstrom, "The Traumatic Years: American Religion and Culture in the 1960s and 1970s," *Theology Today* 26 (1980): 504–522; Ahlstrom, *A Religious History of the American People* (New Haven, Conn.: Yale University Press, 1972), pp. 1079–1096.

4. Wade Clark Roof and William McKinney, *American Main-*

line Religion: Its Changing Shape and Future (New Brunswick, N.J.: Rutgers University Press, 1987); Robert Wuthnow, *The Restructuring of American Religion: Society and Faith Since World War II* (Princeton, N.J.: Princeton University Press, 1988).

5. John V. Taylor, *The Primal Vision: Christian Presence Amid African Religion* (Philadelphia: Fortress Press, 1964), chapter 13, "The Practice of Presence," pp. 196–205.

Introduction

1. Leonard J. Trinterud, *The Forming of an American Tradition* (Philadelphia: Westminster Press, 1949).

2. Louis B. Weeks, "Presbyterianism," in *Encyclopedia of the American Religious Experience,* ed. Charles H. Lippy and Peter W. Williams (New York: Charles Scribner's Sons: 1988), vol. 1, pp. 499–510.

3. Ben M. Barrus, Milton L. Baughn, Thomas H. Campbell, *A People Called Cumberland Presbyterians* (Memphis: Frontier Press, 1972), pp. 50–104.

4. George M. Marsden, *Fundamentalism and American Culture: The Shaping of Twentieth Century Evangelicalism, 1870–1925* (New York: Oxford University Press, 1980), pp. 172–193.

5. *The Plan for Reunion of the Presbyterian Church in the United States and the United Presbyterian Church in the United States of America to form the Presbyterian Church (U.S.A.).* (Stated Clerk of the General Assembly of the Presbyterian Church in the United States, 1981), 3.2 (p. 16).

1: The Predicament of Pluralism

1. Worthington Chauncey Ford, ed., *The Letters of Henry Adams (1892–1918)* (Boston and New York, 1938), vol. 2, pp. 279–280; cited in Robert S. Michaelsen, "The Protestant Ministry in America: 1850–1950," in *The Ministry in Historical Perspectives* rev. ed., ed. H. Richard Niebuhr and Daniel D. Williams (San Francisco: Harper & Row, 1983), p. 250.

2. Arthur M. Schlesinger, Sr., "A Critical Period in American Religion, 1875–1900," in *Religion in American History,* ed. John M. Mulder and John F. Wilson (Englewood Cliffs, N.J.: Prentice-Hall, 1978), pp. 302–317; Paul A. Carter, *The Spiritual Crisis of*

the Gilded Age (DeKalb, Ill.: Northern Illinois University Press, 1971).

3. Lefferts A. Loetscher, *The Broadening Church: A Study of Theological Issues in the Presbyterian Church Since 1869* (Philadelphia: University of Pennsylvania Press, 1954), p. 75.

4. *Union Theological Seminary in Virginia Catalogue* (1926–1927), p. 52.

5. Loetscher, *Broadening Church,* p. 25.

6. James O. Farmer, Jr., *The Metaphysical Confederacy: James Henley Thornwell and the Synthesis of Southern Values* (Macon, Ga.: Mercer University Press, 1986); John B. Adger, ed., *The Collected Writings of James Henley Thornwell,* 4 vols. (Richmond: Presbyterian Committee of Publication, 1871–1873); Benjamin M. Palmer, *The Life and Letters of Robert Lewis Dabney* (Richmond: Whittet and Shepperson, 1875; reprint, New York: Arno Press, 1969); Robert Lewis Dabney, *Lectures in Systematic Theology* (reprint, Grand Rapids: Baker Book House, 1985). For introductions to southern Presbyterian theology, Thornwell, and Dabney, see David F. Wells, ed., *Reformed Theology in America* (Grand Rapids: Wm. B. Eerdmans Publishing Co., 1985), pp. 189–243.

7. Loetscher, *Broadening Church,* pp. 69–71, 74–89; Robert T. Handy, *A History of Union Theological Seminary in New York City* (New York: Columbia University Press, 1987), pp. 136–137, 198–199.

8. This study is based primarily on the catalogs of the ten Presbyterian seminaries affiliated with the Presbyterian Church (U.S.A.). In the case of Pittsburgh Theological Seminary, the catalogs of Pittsburgh/Xenia and Western seminaries were analyzed prior to the union of the two institutions in 1959. The catalogs for Johnson C. Smith were analyzed from 1925 to 1969 when it affiliated with the Interdenominational Theological Center in Atlanta. In focusing on the Presbyterian seminaries, we did not analyze developments at the Presbyterian School for Christian Education.

We have supplemented the research with institutional histories, course syllabi, and informal interviews with faculty and graduates. We are aware that our dependence on catalogs will not provide a complete picture of the content of a curriculum; one person has wryly described seminary catalogs as works of institutional fiction. And yet, they are documents that reveal, however imperfectly, a seminary's identity and goals, and over the fairly long period of time covered in this essay they provide a means of tracking theological and curricular changes. Finally, this essay studies primarily the curriculum in theology from the 1920s to the 1980s, with occasional glimpses at changes in biblical studies. During that time, the so-called practical fields exploded in size and significance, and a full account of the history of the entire curricula of Presbyterian theological seminaries remains to be written.

9. Lawrence Veysey, *The Emergence of the American University* (Chicago: University of Chicago Press, 1965); Clyde W. Barrow, *Universities and the Capitalist State: Corporate Liberalism and the Reconstruction of American Higher Education, 1894–1928* (Madison, Wis.: University of Wisconsin Press, 1990); Christopher Jencks and David Riesman, *The Academic Revolution* (Garden City, N.Y.: Doubleday & Co., 1968).

10. John F. Wilson, "Introduction: The Background and Present Context of the Study of Religion in Colleges and Universities," in *The Study of Religion in Colleges and Universities*, ed. Paul Ramsey and John F. Wilson (Princeton, N.J.: Princeton University Press, 1970), pp. 3–21; R. Laurence Moore, "Secularization: Religion and the Social Sciences," in *Between the Times: The Travail of the Protestant Establishment in America, 1900–1960*, ed. William R. Hutchison (New York: Cambridge University Press, 1989), pp. 233–252.

11. *Association of Theological Schools Bulletin* 38, 1989, Part I, p. 1.

12. Charles Hodge, *Systematic Theology*, 3 vols. (New York: Charles Scribner's Sons, 1871–1873). For studies of the Princeton theology, see Loetscher, *Broadening Church*, and *Facing the Enlightenment and Pietism: Archibald Alexander and the Founding of Princeton Theological Seminary* (Westport, Conn.: Greenwood Press, 1983); Theodore Dwight Bozeman, *Protestants in an Age of Science: The Baconian Ideal and Ante-Bellum American Religious Thought* (Chapel Hill, N.C.: University of North Carolina Press, 1977); Jack C. Rogers, *The Authority and Interpretation of the Bible: An Historical Approach* (San Francisco: Harper & Row, 1979), pp. 263–379; Brooks Holifield, *The Gentlemen Theologians: American Theology in Southern Culture, 1795–1860* (Durham, N.C.: Duke University Press, 1978); George M. Marsden, *Fundamentalism and American Culture: The Shaping of Twentieth-Century Evangelicalism: 1870–1925* (New York: Oxford University Press, 1980); and *Reforming Fundamentalism: Fuller Seminary and the New Evangelicalism* (Grand Rapids: Wm. B. Eerdmans Publishing Co., 1987); Ernest R. Sandeen, *The Roots of Fundamentalism: British and American Millenarianism, 1800–1930*

(Chicago: University of Chicago Press, 1970); Wells, ed., *Reformed Theology in America*, pp. 15–86. For works by and about others in this school of thought, see Augustus H. Strong, *Systematic Theology* (Rochester, N.Y.: Press of E. R. Andrews, 1886); Grant Wacker, *Augustus H. Strong and the Dilemma of Historical Consciousness* (Macon, Ga.: Mercer University Press, 1985); W. G. T. Shedd, *Dogmatic Theology*, 3 vols. (New York: Scribner, 1888–1894).

The seminaries using Hodge as a primary text in 1925 were Louisville, Columbia, Princeton, and Western. Strong was used at San Francisco and McCormick, while Dabney was used at Austin and in conjunction with Hodge at Union and Columbia. Loetscher comments that Hodge's "masterly three-volume *Systematic Theology* (1871–1873) along with the systematic theologies of Augustus H. Strong (1886), the Baptist, and William G. T. Shedd (1888–94), the Presbyterian, constituted a late-autumn harvest of American Calvinism" (*Broadening Church*, p. 23).

13. Ernest Trice Thompson, *Presbyterians in the South*, Vol. 3: *1890–1972* (Richmond: John Knox Press, 1973), pp. 302–339; John W. Hart, "Princeton Theological Seminary: The Reorganization of 1929," *Journal of Presbyterian History* 58 (1960): 124–140; Loetscher, *Broadening Church*, pp. 136–147; Marsden, *Fundamentalism and American Culture*, pp. 109–118 and passim, and *Reforming Fundamentalism*, pp. 31–52; Bradley Longfield, *The Presbyterian Controversy: Fundamentalists, Modernists, and Moderates* (New York: Oxford University Press, 1991).

14. Sydney E. Ahlstrom, *A Religious History of the American People* (New Haven, Conn.: Yale University Press, 1972), p. 934. The phrase is Karl Adam's.

15. For a study of the rise of the fourfold pattern in theological education, see Edward A. Farley, *Theologia: The Fragmentation and Unity of Theological Education* (Philadelphia: Fortress Press, 1983), and for an overview of the history of theological education in the United States, see Glenn Miller and Robert W. Lynn, "Christian Theological Education," in *Encyclopedia of the American Religious Experience*, ed. Charles H. Lippy and Peter W. Williams (New York: Charles Scribner's Sons, 1988), pp. 1627–1652.

16. *Columbia Theological Seminary Catalog, 1933–1934*, p. 22; *Louisville Presbyterian Theological Seminary Catalog, 1932–1933*, p. 26.

17. Robert L. Kelly, *Theological Education in America* (New York: George H. Doran Co., 1924); William Adams Brown, *The*

Education of American Ministers, Vol. 1: *Ministerial Education in America* (New York: Institute of Social and Religious Research, 1934); Mark A. May, *The Education of American Ministers,* vol. 3: *The Institutions That Train Ministers* (New York: Institute of Social and Religious Research, 1934).

18. Longfield, *The Presbyterian Controversy,* ch. 7.

19. The impact of neo-orthodoxy and Barth was by no means uniform. The continuing influence of conservative Calvinism can be seen in the lectures by Cornelius Van Til (1935–1936) and Clarence Macartney (1936–1937) at Columbia and by Macartney on "Inspiration" (1930) at Pittsburgh/Xenia.

20. See the disclaimer in the *Western Theological Seminary Catalog* on its English Bible offerings starting in 1930–1931: "All these courses are based on the English version as revised by modern criticism and interpreted by scientific exegesis" (p. 43); *Columbia Catalog,* 1937–1938, pp. 34, 35; *Dubuque Catalog,* 1933–1934, p. 82; *Johnson C. Smith Catalog,* 1937–1940, pp. 95–97; *Pittsburgh/Xenia Catalog,* 1937–1938, p. 21.

21. E. G. Homrighausen, "Calm After Storm," *Christian Century* 56 (April 12, 1939): 478.

22. G. J. Slosser, *Christian Unity* (New York: E. P. Dutton & Co., 1929); Peter Ainslie, *The Scandal of Christianity* (Chicago: Willett, Clark, & Colby, 1929); H. Richard Niebuhr, *The Social Sources of Denominationalism* (New York: Henry Holt and Co., 1929); Robert T. Handy, "The American Religious Depression, 1925–1935," in Mulder and Wilson, eds., *Religion in American History,* pp. 431–444; *A Christian America: Protestant Hopes and Historical Realities,* rev. ed. (New York: Oxford University Press, 1984), pp. 159–184.

23. *University of Dubuque Catalog,* 1937–1938, p. 39; see also *San Francisco Theological Seminary Catalog,* 1938–1939, p. 25, or *McCormick Theological Seminary Catalog,* 1937–1938, p. 41, for descriptions that strike a similar accent.

24. John A. Mackay, "Our Aims," *Theology Today* I (1944): 3–4.

25. Ibid., p. 5. A related development for the biblical theology movement was the founding of *Interpretation,* "A Journal of Bible and Theology," at Union Seminary in Virginia in 1947.

26. "Neo-orthodoxy" was less a well-defined school than a perspective or a movement with differing emphases. Indeed, some theologians associated with neo-orthodox points of view disclaimed their adherence to this perspective. See Jack Rogers,

"Biblical Authority and Confessional Change," *Journal of Presbyterian History* 59 (1981): 135; Dennis Voskuil, "Neo-Orthodoxy," in Lippy and Williams, eds., *Encyclopedia of the American Religious Experience,* pp. 1147–1157; Wells, ed., *Reformed Theology in America,* pp. 247–298.

27. *McCormick Theological Seminary Catalog,* 1942–1943, p. 29.

28. James C. Goodloe II, "Kenneth J. Foreman, Sr.—A Candle on the Glacier," *Journal of Presbyterian History* 57 (1979): 467–484.

29. H. Richard Niebuhr, *Christ and Culture* (New York: Harper & Brothers, 1951).

30. *Pittsburgh/Xenia Theological Seminary Annual Catalog,* 1941–1942, p. 29; Rogers, "Biblical Authority and Confessional Change," p. 137.

31. William Temple, *The Church Looks Forward* (New York: Macmillan & Co., 1944), p. 2.

32. "A Conversation with Edward A. Dowey," *Princeton Theological Seminary Bulletin* 9 (1988): 90; *Union Theological Seminary Catalog,* 1947–1948, p. 29; *Austin Presbyterian Theological Seminary Bulletin,* 1946–1947, p. 40; *Pittsburgh/Xenia Theological Seminary Catalog,* 1948–1949, p. 33; *Johnson C. Smith Catalog,* 1940–1941, p. 108; 1942–1944, p. 110.

33. E. T. Thompson, *The Spirituality of the Church* (Richmond: John Knox Press, 1961); Rick Nutt, "The Tie That No Longer Binds: The Origins of the Presbyterian Church in America," in *The Confessional Mosaic: Presbyterians and Twentieth-Century Theology* ed. Milton J Coalter, John M. Mulder, and Louis B. Weeks (Louisville: Westminster/John Knox Press, 1990).

34. Marsden, *Reforming Fundamentalism.*

35. Sydney E. Ahlstrom, "The Ministry from the Placid Decade to the Present: 1950–1980," in *The Ministry in Historical Perspectives,* ed. H. Richard Niebuhr and Daniel D. Williams, rev. ed. (San Francisco: Harper & Row, 1983), pp. 290, 291.

36. Robert Wuthnow, *The Restructuring of American Religion: Society and Faith Since World War II* (Princeton, N.J.: Princeton University Press, 1988), pp. 35–53.

37. James H. Moorhead, "Theological Interpretations and Critiques of American Society and Culture," and Deane William Ferm, "Religious Thought Since World War II," in Lippy and Williams, eds., *Encyclopedia of the American Religious Experience,* pp. 101–115, 1159–1172; James H. Gustafson, "Christian

Ethics," in *Religion,* ed. Paul Ramsey (Englewood Cliffs, N.J.: Prentice-Hall, 1965), pp. 285–354.

38. *San Francisco Theological Seminary Catalog,* 1950–1951, p. 44; *Union Theological Seminary Catalog,* 1953–1954, p. 35, 1954–1955, p. 32; *Princeton Theological Seminary Bulletin,* 1954, p. 71; A. B. Rhodes, ed., *The Church Against the Isms* (Nashville: Abingdon Press, 1958); Ben Johnson, "From Old to New Agendas: Presbyterians and Social Issues in the Twentieth Century," in Coalter, Mulder, and Weeks, eds., *Confessional Mosaic.*

39. *McCormick Theological Seminary Catalog,* 1956–1957, pp. 6–7, 36; another interesting example is the syllabus for the course "The Doctrine of the Church and the Christian Life," taught by George S. Hendry at Princeton during the 1956–1957 academic year. The reading included Oscar Cullman (scripture and biblical theology), Brunner and Reinhold Niebuhr (neo-orthodoxy), Calvin's *Institutes* and the Westminster Confession (historical theology), and the 1954 World Council of Churches' report, *Christ the Hope of the World* (the ecumenical movement).

40. *The Theological Seminary at the University of Dubuque Catalog,* 1950–1952, pp. 52–53; *Columbia Theological Seminary Catalogue,* 1955–1956, p. 64; 1956–1957, p. 66. W. C. Robinson was the professor, and in this shift Barth was transformed from the enemy of orthodoxy to a strong proponent of the Reformation doctrine of justification by grace alone.

41. *Princeton Theological Seminary Bulletin,* 1951–1952, p. 45. See also the description of the "Old Testament and the Modern World" offering at Louisville, beginning in 1953–1954 with A. B. Rhodes; *Louisville Presbyterian Theological Seminary Catalog,* 1953–1954, p. 26. *Columbia Theologial Seminary Catalog,* 1956–1957, p. 43.

42. See, for example, George Hendry's course on "The Doctrine of Providence" at Princeton during the 1950s and other courses on the theology of history at Princeton, Austin, Columbia, and Western during the decade.

43. For examples of the influence of existentialism, see catalogs from Princeton and Western. Arthur Cochrane at Dubuque was influenced by the movement, and it informed his teaching. He published *The Existentialists and God* (Philadelphia: Westminster Press, 1956). For the influence of Tillich, see the catalogs of Columbia (1959–1960), Union (1959–1960), McCormick (1952–1953, 1957–1958), Dubuque (1954), Western (1957–1958), and Austin (1950–1951).

44. *Johnson C. Smith Theological Seminary Catalog,* 1956–1957; see also *McCormick Theological Seminary Catalog,* 1955–1956; *Princeton Theological Seminary Bulletin,* 1956–1957, 1957–1958, 1958–1959.

45. E. Brooks Holifield, "Pastoral Care and Counseling," in Lippy and Williams, eds., *Encyclopedia of the American Religious Experience,* pp. 1590–1591; *A History of Pastoral Care in America: From Salvation to Self-Realization* (Nashville: Abingdon Press, 1983), pp. 210–356.

46. Miller and Lynn, "Christian Theological Education," in Lippy and Williams, eds., *Encyclopedia of the American Religious Experience,* pp. 1627–1652.

47. Claude Welch, "Theology," in *Religion,* ed. Paul Ramsey, pp. 219–284; Sydney E. Ahlstrom, *Theology in America* (Indianapolis: Bobbs-Merrill Co., 1967); see also Ahlstrom's essay "Theology in America: A Historical Survey," in *The Shaping of American Religion,* ed. James Ward Smith and A. Leland Jamison (Princeton: Princeton University Press, 1961), pp. 232–321.

The classic studies of theological education in the 1950s also reveal a theological consensus that differs sharply with the contemporary situation. See H. Richard Niebuhr, Daniel Day Williams, and James M. Gustafson, *The Advancement of Theological Education* (New York: Harper & Brothers, 1957), and Niebuhr, *The Purpose of the Church and Its Ministry* (New York: Harper & Brothers, 1956).

48. Sydney E. Ahlstrom, "The Radical Turn in Theology and Ethics: Why It Occurred in the 1960's," reprinted in Mulder and Wilson, eds., *Religion in American History,* p. 446; and Ahlstrom, *A Religious History of the American People,* pp. 1079–1099.

49. Ahlstrom, *A Religious History of the American People,* pp. 947–948.

50. Will Herberg, *Protestant, Catholic, Jew* (Garden City, N.Y.: Doubleday & Co., 1955); Peter L. Berger, *The Noise of Solemn Assemblies: Christian Commitment and the Religious Establishment in America* (Garden City, N.Y.: Doubleday & Co., 1961); Gibson Winter, *The Suburban Captivity of the Churches* (Garden City, N.Y.: Doubleday & Co., 1961); Martin E. Marty, *The New Shape of American Religion* (New York: Harper & Brothers, 1959).

51. William McGuire King, "The Reform Establishment and the Ambiguities of Influence," in Hutchison, ed., *Between the Times,* pp. 122–140.

52. "Time for a Critical Theology," *Theology Today* 20 (1964); 461–466, reprinted in *Our Life in God's Light: Essays by Hugh T. Kerr,* ed. John M. Mulder (Philadelphia: Westminster Press, 1979), pp. 57–63. Emphasis Kerr's.

53. Todd Gitlin, *The Sixties: Years of Hope, Days of Rage* (New York: Bantam Books, 1987), p. 7.

54. See Brevard Child, *Biblical Theology in Crisis* (Philadelphia: Westminster Press, 1970). It should be noted that some of the new courses in this area moved on to deal with the "new quest" and the "new hermeneutic" of the post-Bultmannians. This does not, however, represent a break but rather a continuing refinement of Bultmann's fundamental lines of thought.

55. Ahlstrom, *A Religious History,* pp. 1009–1018, 1085; see also the fiftieth-anniversary articles in *Theological Studies* 50 (1989), which survey the changes in twentieth-century Catholic biblical scholarship, and Gerald P. Fogarty, S.J., "American Catholic Biblical Scholarship," in *Altered Landscapes: Christianity in America, 1935–1985,* ed. David W. Lotz, Donald W. Shriver, Jr., and John F. Wilson (Grand Rapids: Wm. B. Eerdmans Publishing Co., 1989), pp. 226–245.

56. See Wuthnow, *Restructuring;* Roof and McKinney, *American Mainline Religion;* Leonard I. Sweet, "The 1960s: The Crises of Liberal Christianity and the Public Emergence of Evangelicalism," in *Evangelicalism and Modern America,* ed. George Marsden (Grand Rapids: Wm. B. Eerdmans Publishing Co., 1984), pp. 29–45; Ahlstrom, "The Radical Turn," and *A Religious History of the American People,* pp. 1079–1096.

57. Harvey Cox, *The Secular City: Secularization and Urbanization in Theological Perspective* (New York: Macmillan Co., 1965); Dietrich Bonhoeffer, *Letters and Papers from Prison* (New York: Macmillan Co., 1967).

58. *Austin Presbyterian Theological Seminary Catalog, 1958–1959; Columbia Theological Seminary Catalog, 1964–1965; University of Dubuque Theological Seminary Catalog, 1966–1968;* for courses featuring critiques and critics of the church and Christianity, see, for example, representative catalogs of the 1960s from Princeton, Dubuque, Pittsburgh, Louisville, and McCormick.

59. James H. Cone, "Black Religious Thought," in Lippy and Williams, eds., *Encyclopedia of the American Religious Experience,* pp. 1173–1187; King's writings were widely read: see *Stride Toward Freedom* (New York: Harper & Brothers, 1958); *Strength to Love* (New York: Harper & Row, 1963); *Letter from Birming-*

ham City Jail (Philadelphia: American Friends Service Committee, 1963); *Where Do We Go from Here: Chaos or Community* (New York: Harper & Row, 1967). The best introduction to Black theology of the 1960s and 1970s is Gayraud S. Wilmore and James H. Cone, *Black Theology: A Documentary History, 1966–1979* (Maryknoll, N.Y.: Orbis Books, 1979).

60. *Johnson C. Smith Catalog,* 1964, p. 122. San Francisco established a Department of Christianity and Culture in 1960–1961, and Robert Lee, a new professor, launched an Institute of Ethics and Society two years later. A similar move was made in 1962 by Louisville Seminary with the creation of a church and society program and the appointment of Hal Warheim to the faculty. *San Francisco Theological Seminary Catalog,* 1960–1961; 1962–1963, p. 23; *Louisville Presbyterian Theological Seminary Catalog,* 1962. The impact of the 1960s is evident in the memoirs of Jesse H. Ziegler, who served as the executive director of the Association of Theological Schools during the 1960s and 1970s. He wrote, "A large part of 1960–1980 was characterized by social struggle and unrest. If not revolution, there was at least marked dissatisfaction with the status quo which resulted either in organized or inchoate efforts to bring about change." *ATS Through Two Decades: Reflections on Theological Education, 1960–1980* (Vandalia, Ohio: n.p., 1984). See also Howard Miller, "Seminary and Society: A Case Study of Their Interrelationship. David Leander Stitt and Austin Presbyterian Theological Seminary, 1945–1971," a report submitted to the Lilly Endowment, June 9, 1987.

61. Arnold B. Come, "The Occasion and Contribution of the Confession of 1967," *Journal of Presbyterian History* 61 (1983): 24.

62. *Princeton Theological Seminary Bulletin,* 1961–1962; *San Francisco Theological Seminary Catalog,* 1969–1970; *Pittsburgh Theological Seminary Catalog,* 1969–1970; *Louisville Presbyterian Theological Seminary Catalog,* 1967–1968; *McCormick Theological Seminary Bulletin,* 1967–1968, pp. 4–17; *Pittsburgh Theological Seminary Catalog,* 1968–1969, p. 51. For a study of the curricular debates at Pittsburgh, see Robert Ousley Brown, "Curricular Change at the Pittsburgh Theological Seminary: A Critical Analysis of Challenge and Change" (Ph.D. diss., University of Pittsburgh, 1980).

63. James I. McCord, "Whither American Protestantism?" *Theology Today* 24 (1967): 270. See also Glenn T. Miller, "Professionals and Pedagogues: A Survey of Theological Education," and

Gabriel Fackre, "Theology: Ephemeral, Conjunctural, and Perennial," in *Altered Landscapes,* ed. Lotz, Shriver, and Wilson, pp. 189–208, 246–267.

64. Ahlstrom, "The Ministry from the Placid Decade to the Present, 1950–1980," pp. 303–304. Indicative of the near shell-shock experience of the 1960s was the significant decline in scholarly publications by the faculties of Presbyterian seminaries during the 1970s, a pattern that was matched at other mainstream Protestant seminaries during the decade.

65. In the late 1970s, Presbyterian seminary deans gathered to discuss the development of a common Doctor of Ministry program based on the Reformed tradition. The consultation broke down when agreement could not be reached about what constituted the Reformed tradition. (Conversation with C. Ellis Nelson, June 1, 1989.) Nelson had initiated the idea of the consultation as president of Louisville Seminary.

66. For attempts to reconceive the unity of theological education, see Max L. Stackhouse, *Apologia: Contextualization, Globalization, and Mission in Theological Education* (Grand Rapids: Wm. B. Eerdmans Publishing Co., 1988); Joseph C. Hough and John B. Cobb, *Christian Identity and Theological Education* (Chico, Calif.: Scholars Press, 1985); Charles M. Wood, *Vision and Discernment: An Orientation to Theology Study* (Atlanta: Scholars Press, 1985); Joseph C. Hough and Barbara G. Wheeler, eds., *Beyond Clericalism: The Congregation as a Focus for Theological Education* (Atlanta: Scholars Press, 1988). For a survey of the discussion, see Merle D. Strege, "Chasing Schleiermacher's Ghost: The Reform of Theological Education in the 1980s," *This World* 26 (1989): 102–115.

67. *McCormick Theological Seminary Catalog,* 1978–1979, p. 25.

68. See the *University of Dubuque Theological Seminary Catalog,* 1978–1979, p. 47. Note as well Austin's "trimodal" structuring of its program in 1974, which featured "academic study, supervised practice of ministry, and evaluation-reflection." *Austin Presbyterian Theological Seminary Bulletin: Curriculum Edition* (June 1974), p. 1. This emphasis is particularly clear in the curricular restructurings at Austin and Dubuque and in the Urban Training Clinic begun at Columbia in 1972–1973.

69. Association of Theological Schools, *Fact Book on Theological Education,* 1976–1977, 1981–1982, 1986–1987, table E-3.

70. For a typology of the development of feminist theology, see

Barbara Brown Zikmund, "Theological Education as Advocate," *Theological Education* 25 (1988): 44–61. See also Katie G. Cannon, et al. (The Mud Flower Collective), *God's Fierce Whimsy: Christian Feminism and Theological Education* (New York: Pilgrim Press, 1985); The Cornwall Collective, *Your Daughters Shall Prophesy: Feminist Alternatives in Theological Education* (New York: Pilgrim Press, 1980); Rosemary Radford Ruether, "The Feminist Critique in Religious Studies," *Soundings* 64 (1981): 388–402, and "The Future of Feminist Theology in the Academy," *Journal of the American Academy of Religion* 53 (1985): 703–713.

71. Columbia's establishment of an ethics and society department in 1974–1975 was a somewhat belated example of this powerful trend. As had been the case earlier, ethics courses in the seminaries tended to focus on issues. In the 1980s, "justice" became a common theological construct for conceiving of ethics generally, and peacemaking was the most widely discussed issue. As examples, see the catalogs from McCormick, 1984–1986; Pittsburgh, 1980–1981; Columbia, 1987–1988; Union, 1983–1984; Dubuque, 1983–1984; San Francisco, 1982–1984.

72. Examples of the attempt to integrate sociological methods with biblical studies are Norman K. Gottwald, *The Tribes of Yahweh: A Sociology of the Religion of Liberated Israel, 1250–1050 B.C.E.* (Maryknoll, N.Y.: Orbis Books, 1979), and Wayne A. Meeks, *The First Urban Christians: The Social World of the Apostle Paul* (New Haven, Conn.: Yale University Press, 1983).

73. See George Kehm's course, "Hermeneutical Theology" at Pittsburgh (1983–1984); David Willis taught a course, "The Novelist as Theologian," at San Francisco and Princeton during the 1970s and 1980s; Edler Hawkins probed the "Black theater" for theological themes (Princeton, 1971–1979); Burton Cooper taught "Theology and Literature" at Louisville, 1975–1979; for examples of the influence of narrative theology, see courses offered by David Jobling at Louisville during the 1970s, George Stroup at Princeton, Austin, and Columbia during the 1970s and 1980s, Sang Lee at Princeton during the 1980s, and Roy Fairchild at San Francisco during the 1980s.

74. See James Overbeck's course at Columbia, "Spirituality and Social Responsibility," 1983–1984; "Spirituality Disciplines for Ministry Today," Union, 1981–1982; Dan and Jen Wessler, "Life Springs: Developing Faith for Ministry," Louisville, 1982–1983. During the decade, Princeton added the post of chaplain, a

development many would have considered unheard-of two decades earlier. For an overview of the changing understanding of spirituality in theological seminaries, see Steve Hancock, "Nurseries of Piety? Spiritual Formation at Four Presbyterian Seminaries," ch. 2 in this book, and the articles on "Theological Education as the Formation of Character," *Theological Education* 24 (Supplement, 1988).

75. Loetscher, *Broadening Church*, p. 135.

76. James H. Moorhead, "Redefining Confessionalism: American Presbyterians in the Twentieth Century," *The Confessional Mosaic*, ed. Coalter et al.; David B. McCarthy, "The Emerging Importance of Presbyterian Polity," *The Organizational Revolution: Presbyterians and American Denominationalism*, ed. Coalter, Mulder, and Weeks (Louisville, Ky.: Westminster/John Knox Press, 1991).

77. This point emerges from George Marsden's excellent survey of strains within the fundamentalist and evangelical movements in *Reforming Fundamentalism*.

78. Ronald F. Thiemann, "Making Theology Central in Theological Education," *Christian Century* 104 (Feb. 4–11, 1987): 106; John B. Cobb, "Claiming the Center," *Criterion* 25 (1986): 3; James I. McCord, "Foreword" to Dean R. Hoge, *Division in the Protestant House* (Philadelphia: Westminster Press, 1976), pp. 7–9, and "The Seminary Enterprise: An Appraisal," *Theological Education* 17 (1980): 53–58; Diogenes Allen, "What's the Big Idea?" *Theology Today* 30 (1974): 333–334; Fackre, "Theology: Ephemeral, Conjunctural, and Perennial," *Altered Landscapes*, pp. 246–267.

79. Roof and McKinney, *American Mainline Religion*, p. 242, emphasis theirs; for further information on the disaffiliation of people from mainstream Protestant churches, see Wuthnow, *Restructuring American Religion*, pp. 71–99, and "The Restructuring of American Presbyterianism: Turmoil in One Denomination," *The Presbyterian Predicament: Six Perspectives*, ed. Milton J Coalter, John M. Mulder, and Louis B. Weeks (Louisville, Ky.: Westminster/John Knox Press, 1990), pp. 27–48; Dean Hoge and David Roozen, *Understanding Church Growth and Decline, 1950–1978* (New York: Pilgrim Press, 1979); and C. Kirk Hadaway, "Denominational Defection: Recent Research on Religious Disaffiliation in America," *The Mainstream Protestant "Decline": The Presbyterian Pattern*, ed. Milton J Coalter, John M. Mulder, and Louis B. Weeks (Louisville, Ky.: Westminster/John Knox Press, 1990).

80. Roof and McKinney, *American Mainline Religion,* p. 241.

81. Robert Wuthnow, *The Struggle for America's Soul: Evangelicals, Liberals, and Secularism* (Grand Rapids: Wm. B. Eerdmans Publishing Co., 1989).

The authors wish to thank the librarians and archivists of the Presbyterian seminaries for lending copies of their catalogs, a small platoon of Louisville Seminary students who helped analyze the catalogs in a seminar on American Presbyterianism, and more than a score of colleagues who offered helpful criticism of earlier drafts of this essay.

2: Nurseries of Piety?

1. For a discussion of the importance of what the authors call "ministry from a personal commitment of faith," see David S. Schuller, Merton P. Strommer, and Milo L. Brekke, eds., *Ministry in America* (San Francisco: Harper & Row, 1980), pp. 37–39.

2. See Elwyn Allen Smith, *The Presbyterian Ministry in American Culture* (Philadelphia: Westminster Press, 1962), pp. 143–150, for a discussion of the concern for "eminent piety" in the Princeton Seminary Plan; see also Lefferts A. Loetscher, *Facing the Enlightenment and Pietism: Archibald Alexander and the Founding of Princeton Theological Seminary* (Westport, Conn.: Greenwood Press, 1983).

3. *San Francisco Theological Seminary Catalog,* 1948, p. 12.

4. *The Register* (Catalog Issue), Louisville Presbyterian Theological Seminary, Spring 1967, p. 3.

5. Columbia Theological Seminary *Vantage,* 1977–1978 Issue, p. 4.

6. The *Princeton Theological Seminary Bulletin,* 1988, p. 26.

7. See Richard P. McBrien, *Ministry* (San Francisco: Harper & Row, 1986), p. 43.

8. See the Vatican II document "Optatam Totius Ecclesia Decree on Training for the Priesthood," October 28, 1965, as cited in *Official Catholic Teachings: Clergy and Laity* (Wilmington, N.C.: McGrath Publishing Co., 1978), pp. 203–217.

9. Peter C. Bower, "Editorial Introduction," *Reformed Liturgy and Music* vol. XX, no. 2 (Spring 1986): 54.

10. Howard G. Hageman, "Reformed Spirituality," *Protestant Spiritual Traditions,* ed. Frank Senn (Mahwah, N.J.: Paulist Press, 1986), p. 66.

11. See "Growth and Transformation in Christian Life and Faith," a paper presented to the Theology and Worship Ministry Unit of the Presbyterian Church (U.S.A.) by the Task Force on the Life of Faith. Draft copy dated September 21, 1988, p. 53.

12. Shirley C. Guthrie, Jr., *Christian Doctrine* (Atlanta: John Knox Press, 1968), quote taken from pages 229–230. See also pp. 307ff. and 323ff.

13. See the following issues of *Theological Education:* vol. VIII, no. 3 (Spring 1972); vol. XVII, no. 1 (Autumn 1980); vol. XXIV, no. 1 (Autumn 1987); vol. XXIV, Supplement 1, 1988.

14. See *Christian Century,* vol. 101, no. 5 (Feb. 6–13, 1985).

15. Forster Freeman, *Readiness for Ministry Through Spiritual Direction* (Washington, D.C.: The Alban Institute, 1986).

16. *Spiritual Formation in Theological Education* (Geneva: World Council of Churches Publications, 1987).

17. An example of the concern about spiritual formation was an overture from Lake Michigan Presbytery to the 1985 General Assembly. It asked the Assembly to tell the seminaries that they were responsible for "the full preparation of their students for ministry, spiritually as well as intellectually" and that "spiritual development" should be "a fully sanctioned part of seminary life." This overture was referred to the Church Vocations Ministry Unit for response.

18. Frank Senn, *Protestant Spiritual Traditions* (Mahwah, N.J.: Paulist Press, 1986), p. 2.

19. In an article by Tilden H. Edwards, Jr., entitled "Spiritual Formation in Theological Schools: Ferment and Challenge," in *Theological Education* vol. XVII, no. 1 (Autumn 1980), "spiritual formation" is defined on page 10 as "involving all the intentional provisions we may have for nourishing our faith life as members of the body of Christ." For this study, we are using this definition, but leaving out the word "intentional." This is because we are interested not only in intent but also result; that is, what effect did the variety of intentional *and* unintentional influences have on seminary students' spiritual growth and development?

20. These four seminaries were chosen simply on the basis of geographic diversity.

21. Those interested in seeing a copy of the questionnaire may write the author for a copy.

22. There are some obvious limitations to this research design. One is that graduates from six of the PCUSA seminaries are not involved in the study at all. It is quite possible that their experi-

ences were very different from the graduates who were questioned. Also, it is possible that the other schools had self-understandings that differed significantly from the schools that were involved in the study. A second problem is that the perceptions of graduates of non-PCUSA seminaries are not part of the study. A third limitation is that while approximately half of the candidates now pursuing ordination in the PCUSA are women, less than 20 percent of the respondents to the questionnaires are women. That is because the enrollment of women in seminaries in large numbers is still a relatively recent phenomenon, and this study is intended more as a historical sketch than as a contemporary survey. That does not, however, mitigate the fact that, once again, experiences of women are underrepresented. A fourth drawback is that almost half the responses were from Princeton graduates. Princeton is the largest PCUSA seminary, but its graduates do not dominate (at least in number!) the ministry of the PCUSA to the extent they do our sample.

Thanks go to Grayson Tucker, retired professor of church administration and evangelism at Louisville Presbyterian Theological Seminary for his help in designing the questionnaire and analyzing the data, and to Dean Hoge, professor of sociology at the Catholic University of America, for his suggestions regarding the presentation of the data.

23. Ellis Larsen and James Shopshire, "Seminarians: Older and Wiser? (A Profile of Contemporary Seminarians)" (Vandalia, Ohio: Association of Theological Schools, 1988), p. 9.

24. *The Register* (Catalog Issue), Louisville Presbyterian Theological Seminary, March 1948, pp. 7–8.

25. From the Introduction by Henri Nouwen to Kenneth Leech's *Soul Friend* (San Francisco: Harper & Row, 1980), p. vi.

26. *Annual Catalog of San Francisco Theological Seminary,* 1948, p. 47.

27. Ibid., p. 38.

28. *Catalogue of Princeton Theological Seminary,* 1947–1948, p. 54.

29. *The Princeton Seminary Bulletin* (Catalogue Issue), July 1977, p. 106.

30. *Louisville Presbyterian Theological Seminary Catalog,* 1977–1978, p. 51.

31. *Columbia Seminary Catalog,* 1986–1987, p. 55.

32. For example, the Louisville catalog of 1948 stated on page 5 that chapel services "afford students a spiritual setting for student

growth. . . . Chapel attendance is not required; it is taken for granted." The Columbia catalog of 1948 says that chapel services (especially observance of the sacraments) "rightly hold the place of preeminence in the devotional and spiritual life of the campus" (p. 58). And the 1988 catalog of San Francisco says, "Worship claims its place as the primary force binding all together with thrice weekly chapel as well as services for every special observance."

33. Jane I. Smith has raised these and other questions in her article "Spiritual Awareness and the Formation of Character," *Theological Education* vol. XXIV, 1988, Supplement, p. 82.

34. For a fascinating essay on the embrace of the social sciences by liberal Protestantism, see R. Laurence Moore, "Secularization: Religion and the Social Sciences," in *Between the Times: The Travail of the Protestant Establishment in America, 1900–1960* ed. William Hutchison (New York: Cambridge University Press, 1989), pp. 233–252.

3: Presbyterian Colleges in Twentieth-Century America

1. Donald G. Tewksbury, *The Founding of American Colleges and Universities Before the Civil War* (New York: Teachers College, Columbia University, 1932; reprint, New York: Arno Press & The New York Times, 1969), p. 69; John M. Mulder, "Presbyterians and Higher Education: The Demise of a Tradition?" unpublished address delivered to the meeting of the presidents of the Association of Presbyterian Colleges and Universities, March 1990, pp. 1–2. We are indebted to John Mulder for his helpful comments in this paper and elsewhere.

2. In this essay, "Presbyterian colleges" refers to those schools related to the churches that now comprise the Presbyterian Church (U.S.A.). These churches include the Presbyterian Church in the U.S.A., the Cumberland Presbyterian Church, the Presbyterian Church in the U.S., the United Presbyterian Church of North America, and the United Presbyterian Church in the U.S.A. It is, of course, impossible to deal with all the colleges now or formerly affiliated with the Presbyterian Church (U.S.A.) in a paper of this scope, but the sample of schools examined here appears to be representative of the majority of Presbyterian colleges. For a geographic distribution of Presbyterian colleges and universities, see map included in this essay (fig. 3.1).

3. "A Statement of the Association of Presbyterian Colleges and Universities," March 25, 1990, p. 6.

4. Mulder, "Presbyterians and Higher Education," p. 7; Robert G. Hutcheson, Jr., "Are Church-Related Colleges Also Christian Colleges?" *Christian Century,* Sept. 28, 1988, 839–840. See also the perceptive essay by Robert W. Lynn, " 'The Survival of Recognizably Protestant Colleges: Reflections on Old-Line Protestantism, 1950–1990," in *The Secularization of the Academy,* George M. Marsden and Bradley J. Longfield, eds. (New York: Oxford University Press, 1992).

5. See Mark A. Noll, *Princeton and the Republic, 1768–1822: The Search for a Christian Enlightenment in the Era of Samuel Stanhope Smith* (Princeton, N.J.: Princeton University Press, 1989).

6. The question of whether changing church support of its colleges aided their secularization is a particularly difficult one due to the varied, and scattered, sources of church support (General Assembly, synods, presbyteries, individual congregations, and individual members) and the changing value of the dollar over the period under examination. In the United Presbyterian Church in the U.S.A., General Assembly allocations to the colleges peaked in the mid to late 1960s and plummeted in the 1970s. The colleges, however, were moving away from explicitly Christian commitments even while church funding was relatively high in the 1960s. Nevertheless, the church's declining support obviously did nothing to inspire greater loyalty from its colleges. (See *Minutes of the General Assembly of the Presbyterian Church in the United States of America* [Philadelphia: Office of the Stated Clerk, 1900–1957] and *Minutes of the General Assembly of The United Presbyterian Church in the U.S.A.* [Philadelphia: Office of the General Assembly, 1958–1982], hereafter cited as G.A., PCUSA, and, after 1957, G.A., UPCUSA).

7. Tewksbury, *American Colleges,* p. 69; Paul M. Limbert, *Denominational Policies in the Support and Supervision of Higher Education* (New York: Teachers College, Columbia University, 1929), p. 64.

8. G.A., PCUSA, 1883, p. 582.

9. Ibid., p. 585.

10. *The University of Wooster Catalogue, 1910–11* (Wooster, Ohio: University of Wooster, 1910), p. 13.

11. See Alfred O. Gray, *Not by Might: The Story of Whitworth College, 1890–1965* (Spokane, Wash.: Whitworth College, 1965),

368 Notes for Longfield and Marsden

p. 58; George L. Landolt, *Search for the Summit, Austin College Through XII Decades, 1849–1970* (Sherman, Tex.: Austin College Alumni Association, 1970), p. 187; William E. Parrish, *Westminster College: An Informal History, 1851–1969* (Fulton, Mo.: Westminster College, 1971), p. 66; and Cornelia R. Shaw, *Davidson College* (New York: Fleming H. Revell Co., 1923), p. 45.

12. C. Harve Geiger, *The Program of Higher Education of the Presbyterian Church in the United States of America: An Historical Analysis of Its Growth in the United States* (Cedar Rapids, Iowa: Laurence Press, 1940), p. 87.

13. Carl R. Kelly, "The History of Religious Instruction in United Presbyterian Colleges" (Ph.D. diss., University of Pittsburgh, 1952), pp. 7–8; James F. Gordon, Jr., *A History of Belhaven College, 1894–1981,* ed. Linda M. Hill (Jackson, Miss.: Belhaven College, 1983), p. 18; Ben H. Hammet, *The Spirit of PC: A Centennial History of Presbyterian College* (Clinton, S.C.: Jacobs Press, 1982), p. 21; *Seventh Annual Report of the Executive Committee of Christian Education and Ministerial Relief . . . Presented to the General Assembly of the Presbyterian Church in the United States* (Louisville, Ky.: n.p., 1917) p. 65; Ernest T. Thompson, *Presbyterians in the South,* 3 vols. (Richmond: John Knox Press, 1963–1973), 1: 499, 2: 357–359, 3: 455.

14. *The Davidson College Bulletin,* February 1910 (Charlotte, N.C.: Queen City Printing Co., 1910), pp. 47, 50.

15. See, e.g., *Fifteenth Annual Report of the Executive Committee of Christian Education and Ministerial Relief . . . Presented to the General Assembly of the Presbyterian Church in the United States* (n.p., 1925), p. 20.

16. Ralph W. Lloyd, *Maryville College: A History of One Hundred Fifty Years, 1819–1969* (Maryville, Tenn.: Maryville College Press, 1969), p. 193; Parrish, *Westminster College,* p. 116; Frank E. Weyer, *Hastings College: Seventy-five Years in Retrospect, 1882–1957* (Hastings, Neb.: Hastings College Anniversary Committee, 1957), p. 62.

17. Kelly, "United Presbyterian Colleges," p. 92.

18. *Muskingum College Bulletin,* March 1906, p. 24, quoted in ibid., p. 69. In 1909 the Board of Education of the PCUSA said of its colleges, "This [the Bible] is systematically taught, with reverence and sincere love for the Word. It is not a book of historic literature but God's Book. The critical examination of the text is the basis for seeking the meaning of the inspired writer who penned the words" (G.A., PCUSA, 1909, Part I, p. 72).

19. David M. Dayton, *'Mid the Pines: An Historical Study of Grove City College* (Grove City, Pa.: Grove City College Alumni Association, 1971), p. 126; *Twenty-eighth Annual Catalogue . . . 1896–1897,* pp. 12–13, quoted in Donald E. Everett with Eugenia DeB. Reiwald, Blanche M. Mason, and Ann H. Prassel, *Trinity University: A Record of One Hundred Years* (San Antonio, Tex.: Trinity University Press, 1968), p. 28.

20. Everett, *Trinity University,* p. 27; Lloyd, *Maryville College,* p. 195.

21. Quoted in Joseph T. Fuhrmann, *The Life and Times of Tusculum College* (Greenville, Tenn.: Tusculum College, 1986), p. 139.

22. *The University of Wooster Catalogue, 1910–11* (Wooster, Ohio: University of Wooster, 1910), p. 15.

23. See Lefferts Loetscher, *The Broadening Church: A Study of Theological Issues in the Presbyterian Church Since 1869* (Philadelphia: University of Pennsylvania Press, 1954), pp. 108–156, and Bradley J. Longfield, *The Presbyterian Controversy: Fundamentalists, Modernists, and Moderates* (New York: Oxford University Press, 1991), for a discussion of the controversy surrounding these developments.

24. "Second Annual Report of the Board of Christian Education," G.A., PCUSA, Part II, 1925, pp. 7–8.

25. Quoted in William L. Fisk, *A History of Muskingum College* (New Concord, Ohio: Muskingum College, 1978), p. 149.

26. Kelly, "United Presbyterian Colleges," pp. 112–114.

27. Fisk, *Muskingum College,* pp. 149, 164.

28. *Seventh Annual Report of the Executive Committee of Christian Education and Ministerial Relief,* pp. 65–66.

29. Quoted in Robert L. Kelly, "Davidson College: A Diagnosis and a Prescription," *Christian Education* 9 (May 1926): 342.

30. Landolt, *Austin College,* p. 187.

31. Kenneth J. Foreman to Walter W. Lingle, May 1, 1934, pp. 4–5. File: Foreman, K.J. (1), Davidson College Library Archives, Davidson College, Davidson, N.C. (hereafter "Davidson College Library Archives").

32. Quoted in Daniel D. Rhodes, "Fragments from Davidson's Religious Heritage," *Davidson Journal* 2 (Fall/Winter 1987): 8.

33. George A. Works, director, *Report of a Survey of the Colleges and Theological Seminaries of the Presbyterian Church in the United States* (Louisville: n.p., 1942), pp. 145, 121–131, 135.

34. Gordon, *Belhaven College,* p. 64; William H. Dusenberry,

The Waynesburg College Story, 1849–1974 (n.p.: Kent State University Press, 1975), p. 235.

35. Thomas R. Ross, *Davis and Elkins College: The Diamond Jubilee History* (n.p.: Davis and Elkins College, 1980), p. 67.

36. Lucy L. Notestein, *Wooster of the Middle West,* vol. 2: *1911–1944* (n.p.: Kent State University Press, n.d.), p. 252.

37. Merrimon Cuninggim, *The College Seeks Religion* (New Haven, Conn.: Yale University Press, 1947), p. 58.

38. *Monmouth College Catalogue,* 1945, p. 71, quoted in Kelly, "United Presbyterian Colleges," p. 128; Woodbridge O. Johnson, "Cure for a Blind Spot in American Education," *Christian Education* 35 (March 1952): 60.

39. G.A., PCUSA, 1943, Part I., p. 189.

40. *Annual Report of the Executive Committee of Christian Education and Ministerial Relief . . . Presented to the General Assembly of the Presbyterian Church in the United States* (n.p., 1947), pp. 19–20; *Minutes of the Eighty-Seventh General Assembly of the Presbyterian Church in the United States* (Richmond: Presbyterian Committee of Publication, 1947), pp. 69–70.

41. J. Arthur Heck, "The Distinctive Opportunities of the Church-related College as a Christian Institution," *Christian Education* 24 (June 1941): 286; Charles P. Proudfit, "Channeling 'The Four Freedoms,' Through Christian Education," *Christian Education* 27 (March 1944): 146.

42. Kenneth I. Brown, "Six Responsibilities of the Christian College in 1942," *Christian Education* 25 (March 1942): 133–134.

43. See Christopher Jencks and David Riesman, *The Academic Revolution* (Chicago: University of Chicago Press, 1969) for an account of the values of the modern university and contemporary academia in general. Chapter 8 specifically examines church-related colleges.

44. Quoted in *Wooster, Adventure in Education* (Wooster, Ohio: The College of Wooster, 1948), p. 26.

45. Howard Lowry, *The Mind's Adventure: Religion and Higher Education* (Philadelphia: Westminster Press, 1950). See also Lynn, "Survival of Recognizably Protestant Colleges," in *Secularization of the Academy,* eds. Marsden and Longfield.

46. See Will Herberg, *Protestant, Catholic, Jew: An Essay in American Religious Sociology* (Garden City, N.Y.: Doubleday & Co., 1955), who documents this impulse.

47. "Blue Book," 164th General Assembly, the Presbyterian

Church in the United States of America, New York, N.Y., May 22–28, 1952, p. 166.

48. John Dillenberger, "A Symposium: II: Christianity Not the Only Option," *Christian Scholar* 37 (March 1954): 19.

49. Ibid., 20–21.

50. Robert McAfee Brown, "The Reformed Tradition and Higher Education," *Christian Scholar* 41 (March 1958): 23.

51. Ibid., 31–32.

52. See, e.g., Parrish, *Westminster College*, p. 222; Dusenberry, *Waynesburg College*, p. 329; *Wooster Voice*, Dec. 6, 1957.

53. See, e.g., Fuhrmann, *Tusculum College*, pp. 306–309, 321–322, 340; Ross, *Davis and Elkins College*, p. 255; William Urban with Mary Crow, Charles Speel, and Samuel Thompson, *A History of Monmouth College Through Its Fifth Quarter Century* (n.p.: Monmouth College, 1979), p. 130; *Wooster Voice*, Jan. 14, 1965, Oct. 24, 1974; *Davidsonian*, Oct. 11, 1968.

54. *Davidsonian*, Feb. 14, 1969; Paul Gamble, *History of Westminster College, 1852–1977* (n.p.: Westminster College, 1977), p. 91; Charles E. Frank, *Pioneers Progress: Illinois College, 1829–1979* (n.p.: Southern Illinois University Press, 1979), p. 312.

55. *Wooster Voice*, Oct. 2, 1970; Frank, *Illinois College*, p. 313; Lloyd, *Maryville College*, 27; Gamble, *Westminster College*, p. 91; *Davidsonian*, Feb. 16, 1979; James E. Roper, *Southwestern at Memphis, 1948–1975* (Memphis: Southwestern at Memphis, 1975), pp. 73–74; Emil Nyman, "A Short History of Westminster College, Salt Lake City: The First Century, 1875–1975" (n.p., n.d.), p. 57, mimeographed. See also Arthur S. Graff, "Religious Life in the Cocurriculum: An Argument Described with the United Presbyterian Colleges" (Ed.D. diss., Teachers College, Columbia University, 1981), p. 158.

56. Leonard I. Sweet, "The 1960s: The Crises of Liberal Christianity and the Public Emergence of Evangelicalism," in *Evangelicalism and Modern America*, ed. George M. Marsden (Grand Rapids: Wm. B. Eerdmans Publishing Co., 1984), p. 33.

57. See "The Church and Higher Education," G.A., UPCUSA,1961, Part I, pp. 149–182.

58. G.A., UPCUSA, 1963, Part I, pp. 136–137.

59. The southern church apparently did not officially abandon its requirement concerning Christian faculty until 1982, but southern Presbyterian colleges began ignoring this stipulation by the late 1960s. See *Presbyterian Outlook* 150 (Nov. 4, 1968): 14; *Presbyterian Survey* 59 (April 1969): 4; and below.

60. *Davidsonian,* Feb. 21, 1964, May 6, 1977.

61. *Davidsonian,* May 15, 1964, May 6, 1977.

62. *Davidsonian,* May 6, 1977.

63. Quoted in "To: The Faculty of Davidson College" from "Committee on Professional Affairs," April 29, 1977, File: Faculty Christian Commitment, Davidson College Library Archives.

64. *Davidsonian,* Feb. 6, 1975.

65. Samuel R. Spencer to Ronald H. Linden, Feb. 9, 1977; Ronald H. Linden to Samuel R. Spencer, March 24, 1977, Items no. 4 and no. 5 in "A narrative of events in the Linden Case as reported by the Davidson College Chapter of the American Association of University Professors," File: Faculty Christian Commitment, Davidson College Library Archives.

66. "Davidson Profs Describe Anguish," unidentified newspaper clipping, File: Faculty Christian Commitment, Davidson College Library Archives.

67. *New York Times,* May 1, 1977; *Washington Post,* April 28, 1977.

68. *Charlotte Observer,* May 7, 1977.

69. Ibid.

70. *An Act to Incorporate the Biddle Memorial Institute,* Sept. 23, 1867. State Archives, Raleigh, N.C., p. 1, quoted in Arthur A. George, "A History of Johnson C. Smith University, 1867 to the Present" (Ed.D. diss., New York University, 1954), p. 20.

71. *Thirty-first Annual Session of Biddle University, 1899–1900* (n.p., n.d.), pp. 15–18.

72. *Johnson C. Smith University Catalogue, 1983–1985,* (n.p., n.d.), pp. 14, 66; *Johnson C. Smith University Catalogue, 1988–1990,* (n.p., n.d.), pp. 59, 73–74. See also Inez M. Parker, *The Biddle-Johnson C. Smith University Story,* ed. Helen V. Callison (Charlotte, N.C.: Charlotte Publishing, 1975), p. 38. For more on the history of predominantly Black colleges related to the Presbyterian Church (U.S.A.), see Carrie Washington, "The Roles of the Presbyterian Church, U.S.A., the Presbyterian Church in the U.S., and the United Presbyterian Church of North America in the Establishment and Support of Five Black Colleges" (Ph.D. diss., North Texas State University, 1986).

73. G.A., UPCUSA, 1968, Part I, pp. 163–164; *Presbyterian Life,* July 1, 1968: 8.

74. G.A., UPCUSA, 1973, Part I, pp. 582–583.

75. *The Church's Mission in Higher Education: A Report and Recommendations,* United Presbyterian Church in the U.S.A.,

193rd General Assembly (1981), pp. 21–22; G.A., UPCUSA, 1981, Part I, p. 383.

76. *Faith, Knowledge, and the Future: Presbyterian Mission in the 1980s* (Atlanta: Office of Higher Education, 1982), p. 33.

77. Booze, Allen, and Hamilton, "Summary of Existing College-Church Relationships" and "Considerations for Future College-Church Relationships," a study of the Association of Episcopal Colleges, mimeographed, 1969, p. 7, quoted in Robert R. Parsonage, "An Overview of Current Denominational Policies and Studies in Higher Education," in *Church Related Higher Education: Perceptions and Perspectives,* ed. Robert R. Parsonage (Valley Forge, Pa.: Judson Press, 1978), p. 206.

78. Parsonage, "Overview," in *Church Related Higher Education,* pp. 203, 261.

79. See Noll, *Princeton.*

80. On Woodrow Wilson, see John M. Mulder, *Woodrow Wilson: The Years of Preparation* (Princeton, N.J.: Princeton University Press, 1978).

81. See Herberg, *Protestant, Catholic, Jew;* and Douglas Sloan, "The American Theological Renaissance and 'The Crisis in the University,' 1949–1969: A Case Study in the Faith-Knowledge Relationship," unpublished paper, 1989, where Sloan shows that during the 1950s the popular neo-orthodox critique of modernist accommodation of Christianity to modern thought was rarely applied to education itself.

82. H. Richard Niebuhr, *The Church Against the World,* from excerpt in *Theology in America: The Major Protestant Voices from Puritanism to Neo-Orthodoxy,* ed. Sydney E. Ahlstrom (Indianapolis: Bobbs-Merrill Co., 1967), p. 616.

83. See, e.g., Hutcheson, "Are Church-Related Colleges Also Christian Colleges?"; and "A Statement of the Association of Presbyterian Colleges and Universities," March 25, 1990.

4: Presbyterian Campus Ministries

1. Jerry Van Marter, "Recapturing the Campuses," *Presbyterian Survey* (September 1989): 16. One needs to be careful with all statistics of this kind. Presbyterians participated increasingly in ecumenical campus ministries in these years, so that it is not always easy to designate who is Presbyterian. At the same time ministries have been combined. For example, at Princeton University the Wesley-Westminster Foundation was staffed for many years

by a Methodist who represented Presbyterian campus ministry, and today is staffed by a Presbyterian.

2. I am indebted to a number of campus ministers for their insights. The individuals have all invested decades of their lives in ministry in both church and university. I am especially grateful to Charles W. Doak, Presbyterian university pastor at U.C.L.A. for sharing with me his insight and his private library. His study "History of the Association of Presbyterian University Pastors, 1930–1965: A Study of a Specialized Clergy Organization with Interpretations for the Future" (unpublished D.Min. diss., San Francisco Theological Seminary, 1985), is foundational for any study of Presbyterian campus ministry. In the course of preparing this essay I interviewed A. Myrvin DeLapp, who served as a national leader in the United Presbyterian Church in the U.S.A., and learned much from a conversation with Clyde Robinson, longtime leader in the Presbyterian Church U.S. who presently divides his time as Associate for Higher Education Ministries in the Presbyterian Church (U.S.A.) and Administrative Coordinator of the ecumenical organization Ministries in Higher Education.

My empathy for the possibilities and problems of campus ministry comes from having served as a minister to college students in a college-related church, as chaplain of a Presbyterian college, as chaplain of a private college with no church affiliation, as assistant to the dean of the chapel at a private university, and as board member of a Wesley-Westminster Foundation.

As part of my research I want to thank the men and women who accepted me as an eavesdropper and fellow campus minister at the annual gathering of the Presbyterian Ministers in Higher Education meeting at the University of San Diego in 1988.

3. Donald G. Tewksbury, *The Founding of American Colleges and Universities Before the Civil War* (New York: Teachers College, Columbia University, 1932), pp. 55, 90, cited in Kenneth Underwood *The Church, the University, and Social Policy,* Vol. 1, (Middletown, Conn: 1969), p. 51. To suggest church sponsorship has often been misunderstood to mean that these were all denominational colleges. The College of New Jersey was founded in 1746 in the ferment of the Great Awakening. For two hundred years most of the presidents of what became Princeton in 1896 were Presbyterian ministers or the sons of Presbyterian ministers. But it was never a denominational college. It is correct to credit the churches with part of the impetus for the majority of the early colleges, but there were many patterns of church involvement.

4. William C. Ringenberg, *The Christian College: A History of Protestant Higher Education in America* (Grand Rapids: Christian University Press, 1984), p. 57.

5. Seymour A. Smith, *The American College Chaplaincy* (New York: Association Press, 1954), pp. 23–25.

6. Clarence Prouty Shedd, *Two Centuries of Student Christian Movements* (New York: Association Press, 1934), p. xiii.

7. Luther D. Wishard, "The Beginning of the Students Era in Christian History" (New York: typescript, YMCA Historical Library, 1917); Charles K. Ober, "The Beginnings of the American Student Movement," *Student World* VI (January 1913): 10–18. See also C. Howard Hopkins, *History of the Y.M.C.A. in North America* (New York: Association Press, 1951), pp. 271–308; and Ruth Rouse, *The World's Student Christian Federation: A History of the First Thirty Years* (London: SCM Press, 1948), pp. 23–29.

8. For an excellent biography of Mott, see C. Howard Hopkins, *John R. Mott, 1865–1955* (Grand Rapids: 1979).

9. I am aware of some significant ministries by college-related churches, but not cognizant of any study of these ministries.

10. Smith, *American College Chaplaincy*, pp. 14, 16, 18.

11. Edward Danforth Eddy, Jr., *Colleges for Our Land and Time: The Land-Grant Idea in American Education* (New York: 1957).

12. Lawrence Veysey, *The Emergence of the American University* (Chicago: 1965), p. 2.

13. Edna Cumming French and James Leslie French, *The Pioneer Years of the University Pastorate, with Particular Reference to the Presbyterian Student Work at the University of Michigan* (Ann Arbor: 1956), pp. 20–21.

14. Shedd, *The Church Follows Its Students* (New Haven, 1938), 14–16; Doak, "Presbyterian University Pastors," pp. 30–34.

15. Ernest Trice Thompson, *Presbyterians in the South,* vol. 3, *1890–1972* (Richmond: John Knox Press, 1973), p. 190.

16. Shedd, *The Church Follows Its Students,* pp. 93–96; James H. Smylie, "Hope, History, and Higher Education," in *The Church's Ministry in Higher Education,* ed. John H. Westerhoff (New York: 1978), pp. 8–9.

17. Doak, "Presbyterian University Pastors," p. 47.

18. Ibid., p. 48.

19. Hugh A. Moran, "The University Pastor," in *Religion in Higher Education,* ed. Milton Carsley Towner (Chicago: University of Chicago Press, 1931), pp. 185–186.

20. Association of Presbyterian University Pastors, 1940, *Minutes,* p. 33.

21. Thompson, *Presbyterians in the South,* vol. 3, p. 459. For an exploration of the religious attitudes among students from 1914 to 1969, see Dean R. Hoge, *Commitment on Campus* (Philadelphia: Westminster Press, 1974).

22. Phillip E. Hammond, *The Campus Clergyman* (New York: 1966), p. 64. Used by permission.

23. This impression of the lone ranger is my own. In 1985 I was asked to address contemporary problems of campus ministry in the keynote address to the New Jersey Campus Ministry Association and made this metaphor central to my analysis of the contemporary situation. Both at this conference and at the Presbyterian Ministers in Higher Education Meeting in San Diego in 1988 I found a willingness to accept this critique and a desire to recover a more holistic ministry.

24. I am grateful to Myrvin DeLapp for this information and insight (interview, March 31, 1988).

25. D. Keith Naylor, "Liberal Protestant Campus Ministry: The Dilemma of Modernity" (Ph.D. diss., University of California at Santa Barbara, 1987), p. 137, footnote 1.

26. Shedd, *The Church Follows Its Students,* pp. 69–72; Doak, "Presbyterian University Pastors," pp. 34–37.

27. Doak, "Presbyterian University Pastors," p. 124.

28. For a study of UMHE, see Darrel W. Yeaney, "The United Ministries in Higher Education: A Historical and Critical Approach" (unpublished Ph.D. diss., Boston University, 1975); Doak, "Presbyterian University Pastors," p. 140.

29. Robert Rankin, ed., *Recovery of Spirit in Higher Education: Jewish and Christian Ministries in Campus Life* (New York: Seabury Press, 1980), p. 11–13.

30. Doak, "Presbyterian University Pastors," pp. 155–159.

31. Phillip E. Hammond has a very suggestive essay, "The Extravasation of the Sacred and the Crisis in Liberal Protestantism," in Robert S. Michaelsen and Wade Clark Roof, *Liberal Protestantism: Realities and Possibilities* (New York: Pilgrim Press, 1986), pp. 51–64. Naylor applies this to campus ministry, "Dilemma of Modernity," pp. 120–121.

32. Some of the information in the following discussion comes from conversations at the 1988 annual meeting of the Presbyterian Ministers in Higher Education at the University of San Diego.

33. Allison Stokes, "Denominational Ministry on University Campuses," pp. 1, 8–17.

34. Naylor, p. 134.

35. Lewis Wilkins, "Commitment of the Presbyterian Church to Higher Education Ministry in the Twentieth Century: Summary of Data and Reflections," Lilly Foundation study: American Presbyterianism in the Twentieth Century," p. 18, footnote 15.

36. Neil W. Brown, "Why Not Try Doing What We Say We Believe: A Modest Proposal for the Church's Ministry in Higher Education," unpublished paper, 1987.

37. John N. Brittain, "Revitalizing College Ministry: The 'Church-on-Campus' Model," *The Christian Century* (July 20–27, 1988): 673–675.

38. See Hubert C. Noble, "Campus Ministry: A Two-Way Street," *Connexion* (Fall, 1980).

39. Clyde Robinson, "Ministries in Higher Education and the Current Ecumenical Scene," paper delivered at the PMHE meeting, San Diego, 1988.

5: Presbyterians and Their Publishing Houses

1. M. W. Armstrong, L. A. Loetscher, and C. A. Anderson, eds., *The Presbyterian Enterprise* (Philadelphia: Westminster Press, 1956), p. 183. See also W. L. Jenkins, *Propagating the Faith* (Philadelphia: Board of Christian Education, UPCUSA, 1963), p. 3.

2. Robert E. Thompson, *A History of the Presbyterian Church in the United States* (New York: Charles Scribner's Sons, 1902), p. 81.

3. Elizabeth Young, "Juvenile Biographies of the Presbyterian Board of Publication: 1838–1887," *Journal of the Department of History* 33:3 (September 1955): 181; Jenkins, *Propagating the Faith*, p. 3.

4. Jenkins, *Propagating the Faith*, pp. 4–6.

5. Young, "Juvenile Biographies," p. 186; Armstrong et al., *Presbyterian Enterprise*, p. 186. According to Joseph M. Wilson, editor, *The Presbyterian Almanac* (Philadelphia: 1860), there were 263 such colporteurs at work in 1858 (p. 50).

6. Young, "Juvenile Biographies," p. 190.

7. Wilson, *Presbyterian Almanac*, pp. 52–62.

8. Anna Jane Moyer, *The Making of Many Books: A History of the Publishing House of the Presbyterian Church in the United States of America, 1838–1957* (Philadelphia: The Drexel Institute of Technology, 1958). Many of the titles and the general direction

of this portion of the essay came from the research and its representation in this work.

9. Ibid., p. 55. Also see *Publishers Weekly* (1897), p. 665.

10. After the Civil War broke out, the Board of Publication reported that many of its colporteurs were caught behind the Confederate lines, and approximately $17,000 worth of books had been lost with them. The whole lot was eventually written off as a loss, or perhaps as an evangelistic enterprise, since most of the books were distributed among Confederate soldiers. By 1864, William E. Schenck had replaced Engles as editor. Wilson, *Presbyterian Almanac,* pp. 64–76.

11. Wilson.

12. *Publishers Weekly* (1915), pp. 1189, 1244.

13. Edward L. Sheppard, "Religious Book and Bible Publishing," *Library Trends* 7 (1958–1959): 154.

14. Jenkins, *Propagating the Faith,* p. 7.

15. *Publishers Weekly* (1925–1942).

16. *Publishers Weekly* (1936), pp. 971ff.

17. *Publishers Weekly* (1941), p. 1023.

18. Notice, for example, that Mulder and Wyatt (see ch. 1 of this volume) find the neo-orthodox movement important in seminaries by that time. First-rate critical scholarship accompanied the revisiting of traditional, Reformed emphases.

19. *Publishers Weekly* (1942), pp. 2300, 1280, 1281, 1518, 1519.

20. Ibid.

21. *Publishers Weekly* (1944), Supplement 57.

22. *Publishers Weekly* (1948), pp. 320, 1185; (1949) p. 1994.

23. *Publishers Weekly.*

24. Sheppard, "Religious Book and Bible Publishing," p. 156.

25. Many of these works are still in print.

26. Charles Coleman III, "We Have Been Asked," *Alert* (August 1979): 34.

27. Ernest Trice Thompson, *Presbyterians in the South,* vol. 1 (Richmond: John Knox Press, 1963), p. 19. Thompson provides a thorough and dependable account of the history of the John Knox Press. This whole section depends heavily on his work.

28. *Minutes,* PCCSA (1861–1865).

29. Thompson, *Presbyterians in the South,* vol. 3, p. 333.

30. Ibid., pp. 333–335.

31. Ibid., pp. 141–142. See also 1948 Report of the Executive

Committee on Religious Education and Publication to the General Assembly.

32. Ibid., p. 444.

33. Grant M. Stoltzfus, *Survey of the History and Present Publishing Program of the Presbyterian Church in the United States* (Richmond: Union Theological Seminary, 1955), p. 40.

34. Thompson, *Presbyterians in the South,* vol. 3, p. 502.

35. John Knox Press, *Report,* 1961, p. 28.

36. Published at Auburn Seminary, 1988.

6: A Brief History of a Genre Problem

1. See Dwayne Huebner, "The Tasks of the Curricular Theorist," in *Curriculum Theorizing,* ed. William Pinar (Berkeley, Calif.: McCutchan Publishing Corp., 1975), pp. 260–262.

2. There are many studies of the Sunday school movement as a whole and some histories of the educational enterprises of particular denominations and even of the emergence of various curriculum series, but none that we know of that trace the shifting genres.

3. See George Herbert Betts, *The Curriculum of Religious Education* (New York: n.p., 1924), pp. 55ff.; also, Frank Glenn Lankard, *A History of the American Sunday School Curriculum* (New York: n.p., 1927), pp. 21ff.

4. Robert W. Lynn and Elliott Wright, *The Big Little School: 200 Years of the Sunday School,* 2nd ed. (Birmingham, Ala.: Religious Education Press, 1980), p. 36.

5. See Anne M. Boylan, *Sunday School: The Formation of an American Institution, 1790–1880* (New Haven, Conn.: Yale University Press, 1988), pp. 40–45.

6. Lynn and Wright, *Big Little School,* p. 57. See also Boylan, *Sunday School,* pp. 48–52.

7. American Sunday School Union, *Sixth Annual Report* (1830), p. 3, quoted in Lynn and Wright, *Big Little School,* p. 41.

8. See Lynn and Wright, *Big Little School,* p. 56.

9. See Boylan, *Sunday School,* pp. 126–131.

10. Willard M. Rice, *History of the Presbyterian Board of Publication and Sabbath-School Work* (Philadelphia: Presbyterian Board of Publication and Sabbath School Work, 1888), pp. 8–9.

11. Ibid., pp. 27–38.

12. Boylan, *Sunday School,* p. 126.

13. Ibid., p. 127

14. See ibid., p. 104.

15. *Descriptive Catalogue of the Publications of the Presbyterian Board of Publication, with Priced Alphabetical Index* (Philadelphia: Presbyterian Board of Publication and Sabbath School Work, 1871), pp. 8–9.

16. The choice of the Bible as the basis of the system was itself a source of considerable debate. Other options included Christian doctrine, "Christian duties," and the ecclesiastical year. See Edwin W. Rice, *A Short History of the International Lesson System* (Philadelphia: n.p., 1902), p. 11.

17. Among these leaders were John Wanamaker, H. J. Heinz, William Reynolds, and Dwight L. Moody, "Chicago salesman turned full-time evangelist." See Lynn and Wright, *Big Little School,* pp. 90–91, for the beginning of this story, and the whole of their ch. 5, for an excellent rendition of the major events and spirit of this period.

18. Ibid., p. 92.

19. See Boylan, *Sunday School,* pp. 150–151.

20. For example, Orange Judd's *Lessons for Every Sunday in the Year* (1864). See Boylan, *Sunday School,* pp. 149–150.

21. Rice, *History of the Presbyterian Board,* p. 122.

22. Ibid., p. 121.

23. Ibid.

24. "The Ninth Annual Report of the Board of Christian Education of the Presbyterian Church in the U.S.A.," *Minutes of the 144th General Assembly of the Presbyterian Church in the U.S.A.* (Philadelphia: Office of the General Assembly, 1932), p. 10.

25. *Journal of Presbyterian History* 58:4 (Winter 1980): 326–370. This article is based on Kennedy's 1957 Ph.D. dissertation (Yale University), "The Genesis and Development of the Christian Faith and Life Series."

26. On the impact of neo-orthodox theology on the curriculum and the effectiveness of the *Christian Faith and Life* series to communicate it in the church, see William A. Silva's recent dissertation, *The Expression of Neo-Orthodoxy in American Protestantism, 1939–1960* (Ann Arbor, Mich.: University Microfilms, 1988), especially ch. 5.

27. "The Twenty-fifth Annual Report of the Board of Christian Education of the Presbyterian Church in the U.S.A.," *Minutes of the 160th General Assembly of the Presbyterian Church in the U.S.A.* (Philadelphia: Office of the General Assembly, 1948), 72.

28. "The Twenty-fourth Annual Report of the Board of Christian Education of the Presbyterian Church in the U.S.A.," *Min-*

utes of the 159th General Assembly of the Presbyterian Church in the U.S.A. (Philadelphia: Office of the General Assembly, 1947), p. 92. A little over a decade later, the United Church of Christ, like the PCUS, decided to follow the same course. Roger Shinn, one of the continuing consultants for their curriculum, in *The Educational Mission of Our Church* (Boston: United Church Press, 1962), explained the choice for books this way:

> Christian education in America has scarcely done justice to the possibilities in books.
>
> Often church schools have relied on "lesson leaflets," which were studied on Sunday mornings, then thrown away. Those who were absent on Sunday missed the material for that week. The "quarterly" was an improvement. It bound together several lessons in more durable form and provided more information.
>
> But the use of real books brings new opportunities. A book allows more space for interpretation of Scripture, more materials for discussion. It develops a consistent idea over a period of months. The best of church school books have displayed a lively style, penetrating biblical and theological insight, and real relevance to the lives of people in the world of today.
>
> Until recently, however, such books were obviously textbooks, divided into weekly lessons. They looked very different from books one might get from the library or bookstore simply to read at home. No one was expected to sit down and read the lesson book straight through—and no one did.
>
> Actually there is no reason why people should read about Christian faith in a series of lessons. The Bible itself is not a lesson book. Educators and publishers can produce books that are more inviting to readers and more provocative of thought than conventional textbooks. This fact led to a decision about the nature of students' books in the United Church Curriculum.

29. William B. Kennedy, "Neo-Orthodoxy Goes to Sunday School," *Journal of Presbyterian History* 58:4 (Winter 1980): 356.

30. "The Eighth Annual Report of the Board of Christian Education of the United Presbyterian Church in the U.S.A.," *Minutes of the 178th General Assembly of The United Presbyterian Church in the U.S.A.* (Philadelphia: Office of the General Assembly, 1966), p. 35.

31. *Teacher's Guide, Grades 5–6, Year I,* ed. Carol Rose Ikeler (Philadelphia: The Geneva Press, 1971), p. 8.
32. Ibid.
33. Ibid., p. 43.

7: The Use of the Bible in Presbyterian Curricula

1. See Robert W. Lynn and Elliott Wright, *The Big Little School: 200 Years of the Sunday School,* 2nd ed. (Birmingham, Ala.: Religious Education Press, 1980), pp. 98–102. Craig Dykstra and Bradley Wigger provide an excellent description of the Uniform Lessons as the first true curriculum and detail Presbyterian participation in its development in ch. 6 of this volume in the essay, "A Brief History of a Genre Problem: Presbyterian Educational Resource Materials."

2. Helm Bruce, *A Savior: Christ the Lord* (Louisville, Ky.: J. P. Morton, 1931), pp. 5ff.; quoted in Louis B. Weeks, *Kentucky Presbyterians* (Atlanta: John Knox Press, 1983), p. 113.

3. See Jack B. Rogers and Donald K. McKim, *The Authority and Interpretation of the Bible* (San Francisco: Harper & Row, 1979), pp. 360–367.

4. Quoted in ibid., p. 365.

5. Ibid., p. 366.

6. "Report of the Board of Christian Education," *Minutes of the General Assembly of the Presbyterian Church in the U.S.A.* (hereafter cited as GA, PCUSA), 1929, Part II, p. 7.

7. Ibid., p. 14.

8. Ibid., p. 8.

9. Ibid.

10. Ibid.

11. Ibid.

12. BCE Report, GA, PCUSA, 1936, II:18.

13. BCE Report, GA, PCUSA, 1928, II:111.

14. Paul H. Vieth, *Objectives in Religious Education* (New York: Harper & Brothers, 1930), p. 155.

15. Ibid., p. 142.

16. Ibid., p. 116.

17. Ibid., p. 147.

18. BCE Report, GA, PCUSA, 1929, II:6.

19. Ibid., p. 7.

20. Vieth, *Objectives,* p. 256.

21. For the complete text of the overture, see GA, PCUSA, 1932, I:28.

22. Ibid., p. 80.

23. William B. Kennedy, "Neo-Orthodoxy Goes to Sunday School: The Christian Faith and Life Curriculum," *Journal of Presbyterian History* 58:4 (Winter 1980): 326–370. On the innovative character of the curriculum structure, see the essay by Craig Dykstra and J. Bradley Wigger, ch. 6 of this volume.

24. BCE Report, GA, PCUSA, 1941, I:114–115.

25. Kennedy, "Neo-Orthodoxy," pp. 334–335.

26. BCE Report, GA, PCUSA, 1947, II:91. This report was published in a revised and expanded form in a series of books designed to introduce each of the year-long themes, "Jesus Christ," "The Bible," and "The Church." For issues under consideration here, see *The Bible in Christian Faith and Life,* 3rd. ed. (Philadelphia: Westminster Press, 1952).

27. Ibid.

28. Ibid.

29. Ibid.

30. Ibid.

31. Ibid., p. 83.

32. Ibid.

33. Ibid., p. 82.

34. Ibid., p. 77. The image here is sharply reminiscent of H. Richard Niebuhr's *The Meaning of Revelation* (New York: Macmillan Co., 1946).

35. Brevard S. Childs, *Biblical Theology in Crisis* (Philadelphia: Westminster Press, 1970), p. 21.

36. Robert Wuthnow, *The Restructuring of American Religion: Society and Faith Since World War II* (Princeton, N.J.: Princeton University Press, 1988), p. 53.

37. Ibid., pp. 67–68.

38. Ibid., p. 140.

39. On the history of Covenant Life, see the very helpful study of Byron Jackson, "Covenant Life Curriculum Within Its Historical Setting," diss. for Teachers College, Columbia University, 1980.

40. See Lewis J. Sherrill, *Lift Up Your Eyes: A Report to the Churches on the Religious Education Re-Study* (Richmond: John Knox Press, 1949).

41. Randolph Graham, Jr., and William Ramsay, *Covenant Life Core Guide* (Atlanta: John Knox Press, n.d.), p. 2.

42. *Education for Covenant Living* (Richmond: Board of Christian Education of the Presbyterian Church in the United States, 1962), p. 21.

43. William B. Kennedy, *Into Covenant Life* (Richmond: Covenant Life Curriculum Press, 1963), p. 173.

44. *Education for Covenant Living,* p. 27.

45. Kennedy, *Into Covenant Life,* pp. 305–309.

46. BCE Report, *Minutes of the General Assembly of The United Presbyterian Church U.S.A.,* (hereafter cited as GA, UPCUSA), 1964, Part II, p. 20.

47. Nelson's address is reprinted in *Christian Faith and Action: Designs for an Educational System: A New Venture in Church Education* (Philadelphia: The Board of Christian Education, UPCUSA, 1967), pp. 26–32.

48. Ibid., p. 10.

49. Stephen Szikszai, *Covenant in Faith and History* (Philadelphia: Geneva Press, 1968), p. 30.

50. *Christian Faith and Action: Designs,* p. 10.

51. Ibid., p. 11.

52. GA, UPCUSA, 1978, I:393.

53. For a full text of Overture 168–84, see *Minutes of the General Assembly of the Presbyterian Church (U.S.A.)* (hereafter cited as GA, PC(USA)), 1984, Part I, p. 699.

54. Overture 134–84, GA, PC(USA), 1984, I:686.

55. GA, PC(USA), 1985, I:450.

56. *Educational Ministry of the Presbyterian Church (U.S.A.): A Paper for Reflection and Discussion,* PC(USA), 1984, p. 16.

57. Ibid., p. 8.

58. Ibid., p. 9.

59. David R. Cartlidge, "Listening for the Word of God: Essays on Interpreting Scripture," in *An Invitation to Learning,* ed. Lindell Sawyers (Atlanta: Presbyterian Publishing House, 1988), p. 45.

60. Ibid., p. 49.

61. C. Ellis Nelson, *How Faith Matures* (Louisville, Ky.: Westminster/John Knox Press, 1989), pp. 203–230.

62. I am indebted throughout this paper to the painstaking and thorough research contributed by my assistant, Julie Hager-Love.

8: Changing Leadership Patterns

1. Sydney E. Ahlstrom, *A Religious History of the American People* (New Haven, Conn.: Yale University Press, 1972), p. 726.

2. Biographical data were collected from a number of sources, including the biographical files of the Department of History at Philadelphia and Montreat; E. D. Witherspoon, Jr.'s *Ministerial Directory of the Presbyterian Church in the U.S., 1861–1967;* biographical catalogs of Princeton Theological Seminary, Auburn Theological Seminary, Presbyterian Theological Seminary (Chicago), Union Theological Seminary (N.Y.), Union Theological Seminary (Va.), Yale Divinity School, Pittsburgh Theological Seminary, Western Theological Seminary; *Who's Who in America, Who's Who in Religion;* memorial minutes in General Assembly *Minutes;* and *New York Times* obituaries. In addition, the following persons were interviewed: John F. Anderson, Jr., James E. Andrews, Lawrence W. Bottoms, G. Thompson Brown, William J. Fogleman, George L. Hunt, Patricia McClurg, James I. McCord, Sara Bernice Moseley, and Robert C. Worley.

3. Ernest Trice Thompson, *Presbyterians in the South,* 3 vols. (Richmond: John Knox Press, 1963–1973), vol. 1, pp. 510–516; David W. A. Taylor, "A History of PCUS Program Structures," unpublished paper, May 6, 1981.

4. Thompson, *Presbyterians in the South,* vol. 3, pp. 136, 253; Samuel Hall Chester, *Memories of Four-Score Years: An Autobiography* (Richmond: Presbyterian Committee of Publication, 1934).

5. *Minutes of the General Assembly of the Presbyterian Church in the United States* (hereafter cited as GA, PCUS), 1927, pp. 134–139; Taylor, "PCUS Program Structures," p. 8; Thompson, *Presbyterians in the South,* vol. 3, pp. 374–375. It is plausible, of course, that the Depression may have had more to do with the decline in giving than unhappiness with centralization in the church.

6. Hallie Paxson Winsborough, *Yesteryears* (Atlanta: Assembly Committee on Women's Work, PCUS, 1937).

7. Taylor, "PCUS Program Structures," p. 4.

8. GA, PCUS, 1944, p. 60; 1965, p. 61; 1968, pp. 25, 58.

9. Interview with G. Thompson Brown, Atlanta, Georgia, August 1, 1988.

10. Thompson, *Presbyterians in the South,* vol. 3, p. 444.

11. GA, PCUS, 1949, pp. 130–171.

12. Ernest Trice Thompson, *The Spirituality of the Church: A Distinctive Doctrine of the Presbyterian Church in the United States* (Richmond: John Knox Press, 1961); Thompson, *Presbyterians in the South,* vol. 3, pp. 486–589.

13. Interview with Lawrence Bottoms, Atlanta, Georgia, August 1, 1988.

14. Interview with G. Thompson Brown, Atlanta, Georgia, August 1, 1988.

15. William Fogleman, phone interview, August 15, 1988; John F. Anderson, Jr., telephone interview, August 17, 1988; Lawrence W. Bottoms, "The Church, Black Presbyterians, and Personhood," *Journal of Presbyterian History* 56:1 (Spring 1978): 47–61.

16. Louise H. Farrior, *Journey Toward the Future: A History of the Women of the Church, Presbyterian Church, U.S., for a Quarter of a Century 1958–1983* (n.p., n.d.), pp. 1–14; interviews with Anderson, Fogleman.

17. GA, PCUS, 1972, pp. 85–120.

18. Interview with Fogleman.

19. GA, PCUS, 1972, p. 94; 1973, p. 164; interview with James E. Andrews, telephone, March 4, 1990.

20. Lillian McCulloch Taylor, "On the Crest of the Present: Women's Story in the PCUS," in *Our Rightful Place: The Story of Presbyterian Women 1970–1983,* ed. Elizabeth Howell Verdesi and Lillian McCulloch Taylor (New York and Atlanta: The Council on Women and the Church, the General Assembly Mission Board and the Program Agency, (Presbyterian Church (U.S.A.) 1985), pp. 57–91.

21. Interviews with Sara Bernice Moseley, telephone, September 13, 1988; Brown, Fogleman.

22. GA, PCUS, 1976, pp. 110–150; interviews with Patricia McClurg, telephone, September 7, 1988; and with Moseley.

23. Richard G. Hutcheson, Jr., *Wheel Within the Wheel: Confronting the Management Crisis of the Pluralistic Church* (Atlanta: John Knox Press, 1979), passim.

24. Interview with Fogleman.

25. Dorothy C. Bass, "Teaching with Authority? The Changing Place of Mainstream Protestantism in American Culture," in *Mainstream Protestantism in the Twentieth Century: Its Problems and Prospects.* Papers presented to the 1986 annual meeting of the Council on Theological Education, Presbyterian Church (U.S.A.).

9: Transformations in Administrative Leadership

1. See, for example, William H. Willimon and Robert L. Wilson, *Rekindling the Flame: Strategies for a Vital United Methodism* (Nashville: Abingdon Press, 1987), pp. 58–69; Richard G. Hutche-

son, Jr., *Wheel Within the Wheel: Confronting the Management Crisis of the Pluralistic Church* (Atlanta: John Knox Press, 1979); and Richard G. Hutcheson, Jr., *Mainline Churches and the Evangelicals: A Challenging Crisis* (Atlanta: John Knox Press, 1981), pp. 154–164.

2. There are numerous treatments of this phenomenon. H. Richard Niebuhr's *Christ and Culture* (New York: Harper & Brothers, 1951) sets forth a basic typology. David Little, *Religion, Order, and Law: A Study in Prerevolutionary England* (New York: Harper & Row, 1969) demonstrates how important the third use of the law became in the Calvinists' transformative perspective. See also Douglas F. Ottati's analysis of the Presbyterian debt to *Christ and Culture* and the transformative paradigm in *American Presbyterians* 66:4 (Winter 1988): 320–325.

3. Lawrence Stone, "Prosopography," *Daedalus* 100 (Winter 1971): 1146–1179.

4. The following persons were interviewed in preparation for this article: Donald Black, James R. Gailey, Frank Heinze, George L. Hunt, Earl Larson, G. Daniel Little, Oscar McCloud, James I. McCord, Kenneth Neigh, Robert Rodisch, William C. Schram, S. David Stoner, Theophilus M. Taylor, Margaret J. Thomas, William P. Thompson, Hamlin Tobey, and Robert C. Worley.

5. Richard W. Reifsnyder, "The Reorganizational Impulse in American Protestantism: The Presbyterian Church (U.S.A.) as a case study, 1788–1983" (Ph.D. thesis, Princeton Theological Seminary, 1984), pp. 291–297.

6. Biographical data were collected from a number of sources, including the biographical files of the Department of History at Philadelphia and Montreat; E. D. Witherspoon, Jr., *Ministerial Directory of the Presbyterian Church in the U.S., 1861–1967;* biographical catalogs of Princeton Theological Seminary, Auburn Theological Seminary, Presbyterian Theological Seminary (Chicago), Union Theological Seminary (N.Y.), Union Theological Seminary (Va.), Yale Divinity School, Pittsburgh Theological Seminary, Western Theological Seminary; *Who's Who in America, Who's Who in Religion;* memorial minutes in General Assembly *Minutes;* and *New York Times* obituaries.

7. Reifsnyder, "Reorganizational Impulse," pp. 291–297; William Reginald Wheeler, *A Man Sent from God: A Biography of Robert E. Speer* (Westwood, N.J.: Fleming H. Revell Co., 1956).

8. Sydney E. Ahlstrom, *A Religious History of the American*

People (New Haven, Conn.: Yale University Press, 1972), pp. 1079–1096.

9. "William Barrow Pugh, 1889–1950: An Appreciation," *Journal of Presbyterian History* 29 (1951): 65–74.

10. Interview with Donald Black, New York, August 5, 1988; Donald Black, *Merging Mission and Unity* (Philadelphia: Geneva Press, 1984), pp. 121–174.

11. William B. Kennedy, "Neo-Orthodoxy Goes to Sunday School: The Christian Faith and Life Curriculum," *Journal of Presbyterian History* 58:4 (Winter 1980): 326–370.

12. R. Douglas Brackenridge, *Eugene Carson Blake: Prophet with Portfolio* (New York: Seabury Press, 1978), pp. 51–55; telephone interviews with James R. Gailey, August 13, 1988; interviews with George L. Hunt, Richmond, Va., July 25, 1988; Earl Larson, Huntington, N.Y., December 4, 1987; Hamlin Tobey, Lakeville, Conn., December 30, 1987.

13. Interview with Kenneth Neigh, Princeton, N.J., July 8, 1988.

14. Interview with Kenneth Neigh, Princeton, N.J., July 8, 1988; John Coventry Smith, *From Colonialism to World Community: The Church's Pilgrimage* (Philadelphia: Geneva Press, 1982), p. 195.

15. Philadelphia, Presbyterian Historical Society, taped interview with Max E. Browning, conducted by Charles E. Quirk, August 12, 1981.

16. Interview with Neigh. This story is told by the participants with varying details, but with the same basic thrust.

17. Interviews with Neigh, Black, and telephone interviews with G. Daniel Little, August 12, 1988. Philadelphia, Presbyterian Historical Society, taped interview with John Coventry Smith, conducted by Gerald W. Gillette, October 5, 1978.

18. Brackenridge, *Eugene Carson Blake,* pp. 56–61, 92–102, 128–146.

19. Brackenridge, *Eugene Carson Blake,* pp. 186–187; James H. Smylie, "Stated Clerks and Social Policy: American Presbyterians and Transforming American Culture," *American Presbyterians* 67:3 (Fall 1989): 189–197.

20. Reifsnyder, "Reorganizational Impulse," pp. 364–431; Black, *Merging Mission,* pp. 144–174.

21. Neigh is perhaps the strongest proponent of this view, but nearly all observers agree that the desire to inhibit the rise of strong, semiautonomous leaders was a significant factor in the re-

organization. See also the controversial analysis of John R. Fry, *The Trivialization of the United Presbyterian Church* (New York: Harper & Row, 1975).

22. Telephone interviews with Theophilus Taylor, August 17, 1988; interviews with William P. Thompson, New York, N.Y., July 22, 1988; Frank Heinze, Fort Washington, Pa., August 3, 1988.

23. Telephone interviews with G. Daniel Little, August 12, 1988; Oscar McCloud, New York, September 21, 1988. Fanniel, realizing he was in a job for which he was ill suited, resigned in 1975 in a gracious speech described by Little as a "model of statesmanship."

24. Interviews with Little; Margaret Thomas, telephone, September 10, 1988.

25. Dennis E. Shoemaker, "Ecclesiastical Future Shock," *Christian Century* 90 (1973): 312–315.

26. Interview with Heinze.

27. Interviews with McCloud, Larson.

28. Interviews with Black, McCloud.

29. Interview with Black.

30. Interview with Heinze.

31. Interviews with Black, Heinze, Little, McCloud, and Robert Rodisch, November 14, 1988.

32. G. Daniel Little, "Ten Years of GAMC." Unpublished paper, March 18, 1983.

33. Interviews with Hunt, Little, Heinze, McCloud, Thomas.

34. Richard G. Hutcheson, Jr., *Wheel Within the Wheel,* passim.

35. Interview with Black.

36. Interview with Neigh.

37. Interviews with Little, McCord, Larson, Browning.

38. Dorothy C. Bass, "Teaching with Authority? The Changing Place of Mainstream Protestantism in American Culture," in *Mainstream Protestantism in the Twentieth Century: Its Problems and Prospects.* Papers presented to the 1986 annual meeting of the Council on Theological Education, Presbyterian Church (U.S.A.).

10: Looking for Leadership

1. *The Plan for Reunion of the Presbyterian Church in the United States and The United Presbyterian Church in the United States of America to Form the Presbyterian Church (U.S.A.)* (New

York and Atlanta: Joint Committee on Presbyterian Union, 1981).

2. *Minutes of the General Assembly of the Presbyterian Church (U.S.A.)* (hereafter GA, PC(USA), 1986, pp. 364–418.

3. George L. Hunt, "Consistent Choices," *Presbyterian Outlook* (April 6, 1987): 14–15; interviews with George L. Hunt, Richmond, July 25, 1988; Oscar McCloud, New York, September 21, 1988; and S. David Stoner, telephone, September 14, 1988. Stoner finished his term in 1991 and chose not to run again.

4. Interviews with Donald Black, New York, August 5, 1988; Frank Heinze, Fort Washington, Pa., August 3, 1988; telephone interviews: William Fogleman, August 15, 1988; Sara Bernice Moseley, September 13, 1988; and James E. Andrews, March 4, 1990.

5. Biographical information was collected from data provided by the office of the General Assembly Council as well as denominational and seminary directories, General Assembly *Minutes,* and articles in denominational publications.

6. George L. Hunt, "Who Runs the Church?" *Presbyterian Outlook* (May 4, 1987): 10.

7. *Presbyterian Outlook* (Nov. 21, 1988): 5.

8. In February 1990 the Rev. Donald L. Brown was elected director for the Education and Congregational Nurture Ministry Unit.

9. In February 1990, the Rev. Andrea Pfaff was elected director for the Evangelism and Church Development Ministry Unit. She is the first clergywoman to serve as a ministry unit director.

10. George L. Hunt, "Consistent Choices," pp. 14–15.

11. GA, PC(USA), 1989, p. 305. The remainder of the budget is for related bodies, mission partnership funds, and common administrative expenses.

12. Interviews with John F. Anderson, Jr., telephone, August 17, 1988; Fogleman; McCloud; and Kenneth Neigh, Princeton, N.J., July 8, 1988.

13. GA, PC(USA), 1984, pp. 151–161; *Presbyterian Outlook,* May 28, 1984; June 18, 1984; June 25, 1984; telephone interviews with Hunt and Patricia McClurg, September 7, 1988. McClurg does not believe the women's issues played a major part in this episode.

14. GA, PC(USA), 1989, pp. 74, 275–276; *Presbyterian Survey* (July/August 1988): 27–28; *Presbyterian Outlook,* April 24, 1989;

May 4, 1989; May 15, 1989; June 26, 1989; 8; interview with James E. Andrews, telephone, March 4, 1990.

15. GA, PC(USA), 1989, pp. 74, 274–275.

16. Interview with Robert Worley, telephone, November 29, 1988.

11: Presbyterian Women Ministers

1. Constant H. Jacquet, Jr., *Women Ministers in 1986 and 1977: A Ten-Year View* (National Council of Churches publication, 1988). Table 2 in this thirteen-page document gives the year in which reporting groups authorized ordaining women. The United Methodist Church shares the 1956 date when Presbyterians agreed to ordain women as ministers. Among others, the United Church of Christ lists 1853, the Lutherans 1970, Brethren 1948, Mennonites 1973, Disciples 1888, Nazarenes 1908, and American Baptists ca. 1893.

2. In this essay we refer to the Presbyterian Church in the United States of America (PCUSA), which became the United Presbyterian Church in the United States of America (UPCUSA) in 1958, the Presbyterian Church in the United States (PCUS), and the recently united Presbyterian Church (U.S.A.) (PC(USA)). Materials in the prefatory paragraphs are based on a study of General Assembly *Minutes* of the denominations. See also R. Douglas Brackenridge and Lois A. Boyd, "United Presbyterian Policy on Women and the Church—An Historical Overview," *Journal of Presbyterian History* 59:3 (Fall 1981): 383–407, and a comprehensive listing of all references to women in General Assembly *Minutes* for the period 1969–1979 in typescript form, compiled by Brackenridge and filed at the Presbyterian Historical Society, Philadelphia.

3. See Tables 1 and 2 in Jacquet, *Women Ministers in 1986 and 1977.* Presbyterians report a 310 percent increase in the number of women clergy from 1977 to 1986. Table 2 lists 289 heads of pastoral staffs, 383 associates or assistants, and 151 serving in "other roles." The largest figure, however, is 571 serving outside the congregation. See also the booklet *Statistical Comparisons 1989,* published by the Presbyterian Church (U.S.A.).

4. In 1977, "the Pentecostal family of churches accounted for 32.2% of the female clergy; 30.4% were found in denominations such as the Salvation Army, Volunteers of America, and American Rescue Workers; and 17.7% of women clergy were found in

ten major denominations. The bulk of the increase over the decade 1977–1986 has been accounted for by significant increases in the Assemblies of God (+ 2,146) and ten denominations related to the National Council of Churches (+ 5,686)." (Quoted from Jacquet, *Women Ministers in 1986 and 1977,* p. 3.)

5. For further reference, see such readings as Lynn N. Rhodes, *Co-Creating: A Feminist Vision of Ministry* (Philadelphia: Westminster Press, 1987), p. 14; Suzanne R. Hiatt, "Do We Have an Advocate?" *Christian Century* (Feb. 7–14, 1979): 124–125; Robert Wuthnow, *The Restructuring of American Religion* (Princeton, N.J.: Princeton University Press, 1988), pp. 225–235; Letty M. Russell, "Clerical Ministry as a Female Profession," *Christian Century* (Feb. 7–14, 1979): 125–126; Barbara Brown Zikmund, "Women in Ministry Face the '80s," *Christian Century* (Feb. 3–10, 1982): 113–115. For confirming statistics, see Table 2 in Jacquet, *Women Ministers in 1986 and 1977.*

6. Jacquet, *Women Ministers in 1986 and 1977,* pp. 12–13. Cited are "Women Priests in the Episcopal Church in the U.S.A." (Women in Ministry, Episcopal Church Center) and "Women Clergy Still Experiencing Discrimination, UCC Survey Finds" (Office of Communication, United Church of Christ, December 18, 1986) as well as a study by the American Baptists. Our informal conversations with women in other denominations confirm this statement.

7. Questions about denominational support for women clergy prompted the denomination to undertake a study of practices in the church that limit or deny vocational opportunities for female ministers. *Minutes of the General Assembly of the Presbyterian Church (U.S.A.)* (hereafter referred to as GA PC(USA)), 1987, Part I, pp. 457–461. (*Minutes* are hereafter referred to as GA, with the denominational abbreviation.)

8. The following is based in large part on materials in Lois A. Boyd and R. Douglas Brackenridge, *Presbyterian Women in America: Two Centuries of a Quest for Status* (Westport, Conn.: Greenwood Press, 1983). Other important sources include Elizabeth Verdesi, *In but Still Out* (Philadelphia: Westminster Press, 1973); Barbara Brown Zikmund, "Winning Ordination in Mainstream Protestantism 1900–1965," in *Women and Religion in America,* ed. Rosemary Radford Ruether and Rosemary Skinner Keller, vol. 3 (San Francisco: Harper & Row, 1985), and Zikmund's article, "Presbyterian Women in American Life," *Austin Seminary Bulletin, Faculty Edition* 104:4 (October 1988): 25–33.

9. See especially pp. ix–x and chs. 1 and 6 in Boyd and Brackenridge, *Presbyterian Women in America.*

10. See especially part 2 in Boyd and Brackenridge, *Presbyterian Women in America.*

11. Boyd and Brackenridge, *Presbyterian Women in America,* pp. 109–112; GA, PCUSA, 1892; pp. 169–170; *The Presbyterian Journal* (April 16, 1891): 242–243; Joseph F. Jennison, *Deaconesses in the Primitive and Later Church* (Baltimore: 1891), pp. 16–17.

12. Boyd and Brackenridge, *Presbyterian Women in America,* p. 226; GA, UPCUSA, 1969, I:314–342.

13. GA, PCUSA, 1956, I:105, and GA, PCUS, 1964, I:110.

14. Boyd and Brackenridge, *Presbyterian Women in America,* p. 154. See also R. Douglas Brackenridge, *Eugene Carson Blake: Prophet with Portfolio* (New York: Seabury Press, 1978), p. 74. This is also described in letters from Blake to women administrators and in an interview conducted with Blake by Brackenridge and Boyd, February 28, 1977.

15. According to Betty Friedan in *The Second Stage* (New York: Summit Books, 1981), p. 293, after the winning of the vote for women a leading female suffragist and philosopher did not see the vote as the end of the struggle for equal rights, in her case speaking of the situation of housewives. The churchwomen undoubtedly viewed the situation in the church in the light of discussions of "women's role" in popular and scholarly periodicals and of their own experiences in the home and society.

16. GA, UPCUSA, 1969, I:319.

17. Ibid., pp. 319–320.

18. Boyd and Brackenridge, *Presbyterian Women in America,* p. 226. For the full report, see GA, UPCUSA, 1969, I:314–342.

19. For a summary of these activities, see the typescript mentioned in note 2. An interesting discussion of the ideological differences engendered by such denominationally supported activities is in Wuthnow, *Restructuring of American Religion,* pp. 225–235.

20. Boyd and Brackenridge, *Presbyterian Women in America,* chs. 13 and 14; *Concern* (February 1977): 23–24; *Presbyterian Survey* (May 1980): 21–23; Lillian McCulloch Taylor, "On the Crest of the Present: Women's Story in the Presbyterian Church, U.S." (prepared at the request of the Office of Review and Evaluation, Presbyterian Church (U.S.A.), on behalf of the Joint Committee on Women, April 1985).

21. Specific information on the activities of these groups can be found in the General Assembly *Minutes* as well as in various typescript histories. See especially Lillian Taylor, "On the Crest of the Present" and Elizabeth Verdesi, "Survival, Change & Promise: Women in the UPCUSA 1971–1983" (April 1985).

22. Penelope Morgan Colman and Ann DuBois, "A Review: Vocation Agency Major Mission Fund Women in Ministry Project." Typescript, n.d.

23. Edward C. Lehman, Jr., "Research on Lay Church Members' Attitudes Toward Women Clergy: An Assessment," *Review of Religious Research* 28:4 (June 1987): 319–329. See also, Edward C. Lehman, Jr., "What Do Laypersons Think About Women Clergy?" *Concern* (January 1988): 6–7.

24. Ann DuBois, "From Research to Policy and Program," *Review of Religious Research* (June 1987): 383–384 and GA, PC (USA), 1987, I:458–459. See also Rhodes, *Co-Creating,* pp. 14–15; Jacquet, *Women Ministers in 1986 and 1977,* pp. 12–13.

25. GA, PC (USA), 1987, I:458.

26. This applies to other denominations as well. See Jacquet, *Women Ministers in 1986 and 1977.* Also, Jean Caffey Lyles, "UMC's Women Clergy: Sisterhood and Survival," *Christian Century* (Feb. 7–14, 1979): 117–119, for example.

27. GA, PC(USA), 1986, I:383–385.

28. GA, PC(USA), 1988: I:791 and *Sharing: Information by Women Clergy/Seminarians* (December 1987): 1.

29. *Statistical Comparisons 1989.* See also Vocation Agency Statistics on Women, December 1987. Typescript. Jacquet's *Women Ministers in 1986 and 1977* lists comparative figures as follows: in 1986, heads pastoral staff, 389; assoc./asst. pastor, 383; serving in other role, 151; number serving outside congregation, 571; number retired, 25.

30. Marianne O. Rhebergen, *Varieties of Gifts: A Study of the Placement of Clergywomen, Racial and Ethnic Minority Ministers, Clergycouples, Part-time and Older Pastors in Churches of the Synod of the Northeast, United Presbyterian Church* (an Alban Institute Publication, 1983). Also, conversations with Ann DuBois, October 1988 and January 1989.

31. GA, UPCUSA, 1972, I:281–282. Information gathered at that time also indicated that very few women were employed on seminary faculties and none had attained full professor status.

32. Joy Charlton, "Women in Seminary: A Review of Current

Social Science Research," *Review of Religious Research* 28:4 (June 1987): 305–318.

33. See current seminary catalogs for examples.

34. GA, PC(USA), 1988, I:413–417.

35. *Presbyterian Panel* (September 1986), published by the Research Unit, Support Agency of the Presbyterian Church (U.S.A.), pp. i–iii. The "panel" consists of 3,700 randomly selected Presbyterians including church members, elders, pastors, and specialized clergy. See interpretation of this panel in *Sharing: Information by Women Clergy/Seminarians* (October 1987): 1–2. We also examined similar Panel studies from 1976 and 1980.

36. Lehman, "Research on Lay Church Members' Attitudes," p. 324.

37. Edward C. Lehman, Jr., *Women Clergy: Breaking Through Gender Barriers* (New Brunswick, N.J.: Transaction Books, 1985), p. 188.

38. Boyd and Brackenridge, *Presbyterian Women in America,* p. 235. Conversation with Ann DuBois concerning Suwanee Presbytery. Mention in interview with Diane Tennis in *Presbyterian Survey* (May 1988): 17.

39. Oral history interviews, Women Clergy, Office of History, Presbyterian Historical Association, Philadelphia. This collection contains some sixty tapes of interviews or self-interviews with Presbyterian clergywomen conducted in the late 1980s; some are transcribed and some have summaries on file. Some are restricted.

40. Private conversations at national AAR/SBL (American Academy of Religion/Society of Biblical Literature) meeting (1988).

41. *Statistical Comparisons 1989.*

42. Ibid.; *Presbyterian Panel* (1986).

43. Lehman, *Women Clergy,* p. 284.

44. Jacquet, *Women Ministers in 1986 and 1977,* p. 6. "Positions held by Clergywomen," typescript, December 31, 1988.

45. See Edward Lehman, "Research on Lay Church Members' Attitudes," p. 322, and Carole Carlson, "Clergywomen and Senior Pastorates," *Christian Century* (Jan. 6–13, 1988): 15–17. Unquestionably the stereotypical image of women as having poor management and budgetary skills plays a part in the reluctance to consider a woman for a minister of many congregations.

46. Oral history interview no. 1623, Clergywomen, Presbyte-

rian Historical Society. Susan R. Andrews, March 10, 1987. Used with her permission.

47. Maxine Walaskay, "Gender and Preaching," *Sharing: Information by Women Clergy/Seminarians* (October 1982). See also Patricia A. Yeaman, "Prophetic Voices: Differences Between Men and Women," *Review of Religious Research* (June 1988): 367–382, and Zikmund, "Women in Ministry Face the '80s," pp. 113–114.

48. Various clergywomen also have described successful experiences in the pulpit. Many factors are involved in how congregations respond to a sermon but gender would appear to be one. See also Martha Long Ice, *Clergy Women and Their Worldviews: Calling for a New Age* (New York: Praeger Publishers, 1987), pp. 48, 65, 112, and chs. 6 and 8.

49. Male clergy share this difficulty. A recent publication states that some 3,700 Presbyterian ministers are actively seeking another call and that it is not unusual for a congregation of more than 200 members to receive 100 to 200 dossiers. Moreover, there are approximately 250 candidates (seminary graduates) from recent years still seeking a first position. See Kurtis C. Hess, "The Crisis in the Placement System," *As I See It Today: Union Theological Seminary in Virginia* (December 1988): 1–2.

50. Lehman, *Women Clergy,* p. 325.

51. Jackson W. Carroll, Barbara Hargrove, Adair T. Lummis, *Women of the Cloth: A New Opportunity for the Churches* (San Francisco: Harper & Row, 1983), p. xx. Also, L. Ronald Brushwyler, *Sharing: Information by Women Clergy/Seminarians* (March 1984): 1–2. Jacquet's *Women Ministers in 1986 and 1977* lists 571 as "serving outside of congregation." We did an unscientific and informal survey of the number of women who transferred to other denominations (19) and those who were removed from office (23) since 1982. This indicates to us that not a high percentage are demitting.

52. Constant H. Jacquet, Jr., *Clergy Salaries and Income in 1982 in Eleven U.S. Denominations* (National Council of Churches publication, 1983), pp. 1–5.

53. Ann DuBois, "Is There Justice in the Church?" *Church and Society* LXXIX (November/December 1988): 32. See also Jacquet, *Women Ministers in 1986 and 1977,* p. 12.

54. GA, PC(USA), 1988, I:795–800.

55. Charlton, "Women in Seminary," pp. 309–310. See also Jackson W. Carroll, Barbara Hargrove, Adair T. Lummis, *Women*

of the Cloth: A New Opportunity for Churches (San Francisco: Harper & Row, 1983), p. 107. A woman student at a seminary of another denomination described to us field work assignments and placements for women as applied "nonaggressively." Although nonsexist policies are clearly in place, the administrators accede to the congregations' wishes, she claims.

56. Charlton, "Women in Seminary," p. 311.

57. Evelyn Claxton, "There's More Gray Hair Now in Seminaries," *Presbyterian Survey* (April 1988): 32–35.

58. Marney Ault Wasserman, "Clergy Couple Research Project" (Office of Women in Ministry, the Vocation Agency, May 1976), p. 1.

59. Nancy Jo von Lackum and John P. von Lackum III, "A Report on Clergy Couples and the Ecumenical Clergy Couple Consultation" (prepared for Professional Church Leadership, National Council of Churches, March 15, 1979), p. 1.

60. Eva Stimson, "The Road Is Uphill," *Presbyterian Survey* (May 1988): 15–16; Penelope Morgan Colman, "Couples in Ministry," *A.D.* (November 1978): 28–31.

61. Boyd and Brackenridge, *Presbyterian Women in America,* ch. 12; Lois A. Boyd, "Presbyterian Ministers' Wives—A Nineteenth-Century Portrait," *Journal of Presbyterian History* 59 (Spring 1981): 3–17.

62. Stimson, "The Road Is Uphill," p. 16.

63. *Statistical Comparisons 1989.*

64. *Presbyterian Panel* (1986). Stimson, "The Road Is Uphill," p. 14. A report from a recent conference on racial ethnic women in ministry indicates a high level of commitment by racial ethnic women in ministry "to question, identify, and analyze the possible 'seeds of negation' at the 'get-go' so that they can have the opportunity in their ministries to bear witness effectively to God's redeeming work in Jesus Christ." Katie G. Cannon, "Racial/Ethnic Women in Ministry Conference: An Overview." Typescript.

65. Stimson, "The Road Is Uphill," p. 14. See also Hiatt, "Do We Have an Advocate?" pp. 124–125.

66. Wuthnow, *Restructuring of American Religion,* p. 229. See also Wade Clark Roof and William McKinney, *American Mainline Religion: Its Changing Shape and Future* (New Brunswick, N.J.: Rutgers University Press, 1987), pp. 204–209. We might point out a decidedly negative response among Presbyterians to women's claim to the right of ordination evident in the formation

of new conservative Presbyterian groups, such as the Presbyterian Church in America.

67. Friedan, *The Second Stage,* p. 30.

68. The entire issue of the *Review of Religious Research* 28 (June 1987), entitled "Special Issue Dealing with 'Blindspots and Breakthroughs' in Women-in-Ministry Research," contains excellent articles summarizing research on women in ministry, reactions to the research, and an overview by Barbara Hargrove, "On Digging, Dialogue, and Decision-Making."

69. GA, PC(USA), 1987, I:460–461.

70. Carroll et al., *Women of the Cloth,* p. 11. Martha Long Ice, in her book *Clergy Women and Their Worldviews,* p. 191, writes, "In admitting women to official religious influence, groups already indicate some redefinition of reality, in that it signals both a changed outlook among existing authorities and the incorporation of new authorities with a different perspective."

71. Barbara Brown Zikmund, "Upsetting the Assumption," *Christian Century* (Feb. 7–14, 1979): 128.

72. We appreciate the assistance of many persons as we have gathered information for this essay. We especially wish to thank the Women's Unit, Louisville; the Presbyterian Historical Society, Philadelphia; and the individual clergy who talked with us. We wish to acknowledge the assistance of Christopher Nolan of the Maddux Library, Trinity University, San Antonio, who conducted a computer resource search for us.

12: Cleavage or Consensus?

1. Jeffrey K. Hadden, *The Gathering Storm in the Churches* (Garden City, N.Y.: Doubleday & Co., 1969). See also Dean R. Hoge, *Division in the Protestant House: The Basic Reasons Behind Intra-Church Conflicts* (Philadelphia: Westminster Press, 1976); Dean R. Hoge, Everett L. Perry, and Gerald L. Klever, "Theology as a Source of Disagreement About Protestant Church Goals and Priorities," *Review of Religious Research* (Winter 1978): 116–138; Donald A. Luidens, "After the Storm: Closing the Clergy-Laity Gap," *Review of Religious Research* (December 1989): 183–195.

2. "The Class Struggle in American Religion," *Christian Century* (February 25, 1981): 194–199. See also Peter L. Berger, "Different Gospels: The Social Sources of Apostasy," in *American Apostasy: The Triumph of "Other" Gospels* ed. Richard John Neu-

haus (Grand Rapids: Wm. B. Eerdmans Publishing Co., 1989), pp. 1–14.

3. See also Wade Clark Roof and William McKinney, *American Mainline Religion: Its Changing Shape and Future* (New Brunswick, N.J.: Rutgers University Press, 1987): pp. 115–117; James Davison Hunter, "The New Class and the Young Evangelicals," *Review of Religious Research* 22 (December 1980): 155–169.

4. See Hoge, *Division*, p. 149. We also examined lay-clerical attitudinal differences by responses to two other theological belief indexes: one measuring relativism (belief that one's religion is or is not the only true religion), and one measuring individualism (one's views on the authority of institutions to interpret religious doctrine). In general, the results for these two indexes parallel those for the otherworldliness index, so to conserve space we present only the results for the last index.

5. See Hoge, *Division*, pp. 77–78.

6. The data analyzed in this paper come from two waves of the 1988–1990 cycle of the Panel. This cycle consists of approximately 3,900 Presbyterians in four national probability samples (members, elders, pastors, and clergy in specialized, or nonpastoral, ministries). Panelists were sampled in the fall of 1987, and the Wave 1 questionnaire was completed at that time. Wave 8 was mailed to panelists in March 1989, with returns accepted through May 1989. The current analysis is restricted to the member and pastor samples and to those panelists who completed both the Wave 1 and Wave 8 questionnaires. The number of cases is 597 in the member sample, and 869 in the pastor sample.

For an overall discussion of the Panel and the Wave 1 results, including the complete list of questions asked and responses for all four samples, see Keith M. Wulff, *Background Report for the 1988–1990 Presbyterian Panel* (Louisville, Ky.: Research Services, Presbyterian Church (U.S.A.), 1989). For details on the Wave 8 questionnaires, see Keith M. Wulff, *Denominational Perspectives, Individual Beliefs, and Church Priorities* (March 1989 *Panel Report*) (Louisville, Ky.: Research Services, Presbyterian Church (U.S.A.), 1989).

7. These data come from the Wave 8 questionnaire. The questions used in Wave 8 of the Panel were adapted from a questionnaire developed by William McKinney of Hartford Seminary, and we gratefully acknowledge his permission to use these questions.

8. To save space, we present only the proportion agreeing (i.e.,

the combined responses of "tend to agree," "agree," and "strongly agree")—the percentage disagreeing is simply the difference between the proportion agreeing and 100 percent.

9. On some questions the proportion responding "Don't know," or simply leaving the question blank, is very large, particularly among members (over 60 percent of members responded "Don't know" to one question). Hence, in some comparisons the proportion of all returned questionnaires that provide substantive responses differs greatly between members and pastors. To indicate where this differential pattern of substantive vs. don't know/ no response occurs, we place an asterisk (*) beside those questions for which proportion of don't know/no response is *at least 10 percent greater for the laity than for the clergy.*

10. The three statements (from the Wave 1 questionnaire) are:

The primary purpose of men and women in this life is preparation for the next life.

I believe in a divine judgment after death where some shall be rewarded and others punished.

It is not as important to worry about life after death as about what one can do in this life.

Panelists were given five choices for each statement: "strongly agree," "agree," "uncertain," "disagree," and "strongly disagree." On the first two of these statements, codes were assigned from 5 (strongly agree) to 1 (strongly disagree). On the last statement, strongly disagree was coded 5 and strongly agree, 1. The responses were summed and divided by 3, for a theoretical range of 5 (high otherworldliness) to 1 (low otherworldliness).

11. Data for old class/new class come from the Wave 1 questionnaire. All panelists without any college experience were excluded from the new class/old class analyses, as well as those who did not give a major or otherwise did not respond to this question.

12. Louis Weeks and William J. Fogelman, "A 'Two Church' Hypothesis," *Presbyterian Outlook* (March 26, 1990): 8–10.

13: Representation and Pluralism in the Church

1. See Edwin Scott Gaustad, *Historical Atlas of Religion in America,* rev. ed. (New York: Harper & Row, 1976).

2. See Lefferts A. Loetscher, *A Brief History of the Presbyterians,* 3rd ed. (Philadelphia: Westminster Press, 1976).

3. A recent examination of some of the theological tensions *within* major Protestant denominations is found in Ronald H.

Nash, ed., *Evangelical Renewal in the Mainline Churches* (Westchester, Ill.: Crossway Books, 1987).

4. See John Higham, *Stranger in the Land: Patterns of American Nativism, 1860–1925* (New York: Atheneum Publishers, 1975).

5. See Hart M. Nelsen, Raytha L. Yokely, and Anne K. Nelsen, eds., *The Black Church in America* (New York: Basic Books, 1971).

6. A helpful article which places the Black experience in the context of new immigration laws and trends is James H. Hargett, "Black Church Ministry in a World-Inclusive U.S.A., 2000 A.D.," *Bulletin of the Martin Luther King Fellows* (New York: n.d.).

7. See chapters on minority churches with "dual citizenship" who relate to the United Church of Christ (Armenian, Chinese, and Japanese) in Barbara Brown Zikmund, *Hidden Histories in the United Church of Christ,* vols. 1 and 2 (New York: United Church Press, 1984 and 1987).

8. See James Mencarelli and Steve Severin, *Protest: Red, Black, Brown Experience in America* (Grand Rapids: Wm. B. Eerdmans Publishing Co., 1975).

9. For an interesting examination of the ways in which pluralism has influenced mainline Protestants throughout American history, see Dorothy C. Bass, "Faith and Pluralism in the United States," *On the Way: Occasional Papers of the Wisconsin Conference of the United Church of Christ,* III (Summer 1985).

10. See Lois W. Banner, *Women in Modern America: A Brief History* (New York: Harcourt Brace Jovanovich, 1974).

11. See my chapters on "Women and the Churches" in *Altered Landscapes: Christianity in America, 1935–1985,* ed. David W. Lotz, Donald W. Shriver, Jr., and John F. Wilson (Grand Rapids: Wm. B. Eerdmans Publishing Co., 1989), pp. 125–139, and "Ministry of Word and Sacrament: Women and Changing Understandings of Ordination," in *The Presbyterian Predicament: Six Perspectives,* ed. Milton J Coalter, John M. Mulder, and Louis B. Weeks (Louisville, Ky.: Westminster/John Knox Press, 1990), pp. 134–158. Also Lynn N. Rhodes, *Co-Creating: A Feminist Vision of Ministry* (Philadelphia: Westminster Press, 1987).

12. See Wade Clark Roof and William McKinney, *American Mainline Religion: Its Changing Shape and Future* (New Brunswick, N.J.: Rutgers University Press, 1987).

13. *The Constitution of the Presbyterian Church (U.S.A.),* Part II: *Book of Order* (1983), G-9.0105.

14. Joan S. Gray and Joyce C. Tucker, *Presbyterian Polity for Church Officers* (Atlanta: John Knox Press, 1987), pp. 120–121.

15. See Jackson Carroll and Wade Clark Roof, eds., *Beyond Establishment: Protestant Identity in a Post Protestant Age.* A forthcoming study of the ways in which denominational cultures are sustained and weakened.

16. See Robert Wuthnow, *The Restructuring of American Religion: Society and Faith Since World War II* (Princeton, N.J.: Princeton University Press, 1988).

17. The idea of seeking natural servant leaders whom diverse people are willing to follow is developed in Robert Greenleaf, *Servant Leadership* (New York: Paulist Press, 1977). See especially ch. 1, "The Servant as Leader," pp. 44–45.

18. Greenleaf, *Servant Leadership,* pp. 14–15.

19. See C. Peter Wagner, *Your Church Can Grow* (Glendale, Calif.: Regal Books, 1976) and *Our Kind of People* (Atlanta: John Knox Press, 1979).

20. The classic call for an inclusive church is now thirty years old. See Gibson Winter, *The Suburban Captivity of the Churches* (Garden City, N.Y.: Doubleday & Co., 1961).

21. One effort to look at the ways in which pluralism, diversity, and change can strengthen ecclesiology is found in Letty M. Russell, ed., *Changing Contexts of Our Faith* (Philadelphia: Fortress Press, 1985).

22. George Lindbeck, *The Nature of Doctrine: Religion and Theology in a Postliberal Age* (Philadelphia: Westminster Press, 1984).

23. Lindbeck, *Nature of Doctrine,* p. 127.

24. A helpful book among a growing body of literature on interreligious dialogue is Donald G. Dawe and John B. Carman, eds., *Christian Faith in a Religiously Plural World* (Maryknoll, N.Y.: Orbis Books, 1978).

Index

United Presbyterian Church
in the U.S.A. (UPCUSA):
Agency boards, 268; church
colleges, 27; colleges,
119–120; Curriculum
Appraisal Project, 199;
decision-making style, 277;
gender equality and,
293–294; General Assembly
Mission Council, 270, 271;
leadership patterns, 31–32,
260–275; merger with
PCUS, 29, 148;
participatory leadership
model, 265–271; 1970s
restructuring, 265–266,
268–269; 1960s leadership,
260–265; Westminster
Press, 157–160

United Presbyterian Church
of North America
(UPCNA), 29, 41;
leadership trends, 31–32,
255, 258, 259; merger with
PCUSA, 51, 157, 260

university campus ministry,
131–140; beginnings,
131–134; goals, 134–135;
local congregations and,
136–139; ministry to
structures, 139–140; social
issues and, 136–138;
twentieth-century growth,
134–136. *See also* campus
ministry

University Christian
Movement (UCM),
141–142

University of Michigan at
Ann Arbor, 132

UPCNA. *See* United
Presbyterian Church of
North America

UPCUSA. *See* United
Presbyterian Church in the
U.S.A.

value assumptions, 66–67,
327–333; biblical, 329–331;
institutional, 331–333;
theological, 327–329
values and beliefs of clergy
and laity, 315–320
Veysey, Lawrence, 132
Viehman, Hal, 136, 144
Vieth, Paul, 212
voluntary societies, 149

Walaskay, Maxine, 300
Walters-Bugbee, Christopher,
175, 176
Ward, Edgar W., 282
Wasserman, Marney Ault, 302
Weeks, Louis, 324–325
Western cultural values,
122–123
Westminster Departmental
Graded Materials, 31,
209–213, 215–216
Westminster Houses, 28, 135
Westminster/John Knox Press,
29, 172–174; publication
and financial policies,
176–177
Westminster Press, 149,
151–160; books for youth,
195–197; early
denominational emphasis,
151–154; ecumenical
emphasis, 156–160;
emergence as significant
publisher, 154–156;
financial issues, 160;